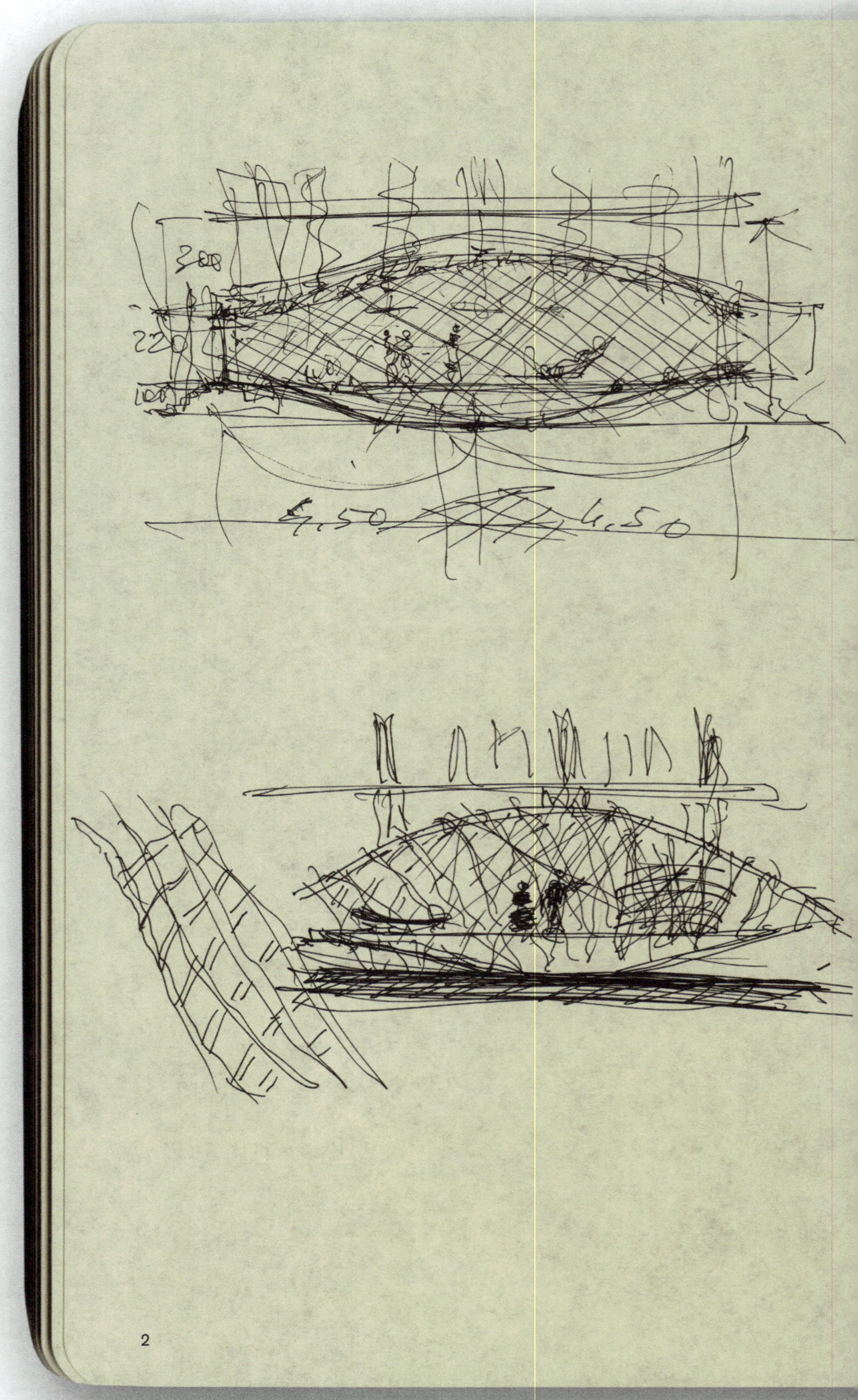

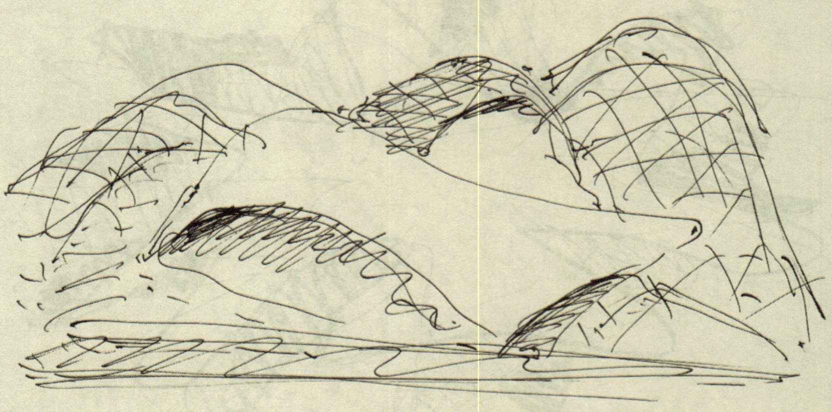

DALL'ALTO / *FROM THE TOP:*
• UNA SPIAGGIA / *A BEACH* • PESCA CON LE NASSE / *TRAP FISHING* • "MAMUTHONES", TRADIZIONALE FIGURA DELLA FESTA DI CARNEVALE CHE SI SVOLGE A MAMOIADA (NUORO) / *"MAMUTHONES", A TRADITIONAL CARNIVAL FIGURE AT MAMOIADA (PROVINCE OF NUORO)* • ORGOSOLO, IL PAESE DEI / *THE TOWN OF* MURALES

Questo è l'ambiente in cui si esercita la faticata vita contadina e la dura, arcaica vita pastorale. Nonostante lo sviluppo dell'industria e del terziario, è ancora la pastorizia a dare l'impronta di fondo al paesaggio, anzi all'immagine generale della sua popolazione e della sua economia. Il mondo dei pastori resiste quasi intatto nelle sue strutture tradizionali, ancora capace di produrre un reddito senza il quale l'economia isolana conoscerebbe drammi anche più profondi. In Sardegna ci sono quattro milioni di pecore, più di un quarto dell'intero patrimonio ovino nazionale. Sul loro latte e sul loro formaggio vive non solo un'economia robusta, ma una vera e propria civiltà con le sue regole e i suoi comportamenti.

LA CULTURA POPOLARE. I luoghi dove più si esprime la profonda cultura tradizionale sono le feste: quelle religiose dei santuari popolari, quelle pagane del Carnevale, sagre importanti, perché migliaia di sardi di tutti i paesi vestono l'antico costume di gala, ricco di colori, di ricami, di ori e di gioielli, un tempo usato nelle occasioni solenni, soprattutto nelle feste e nei matrimoni. Ogni paese ha il

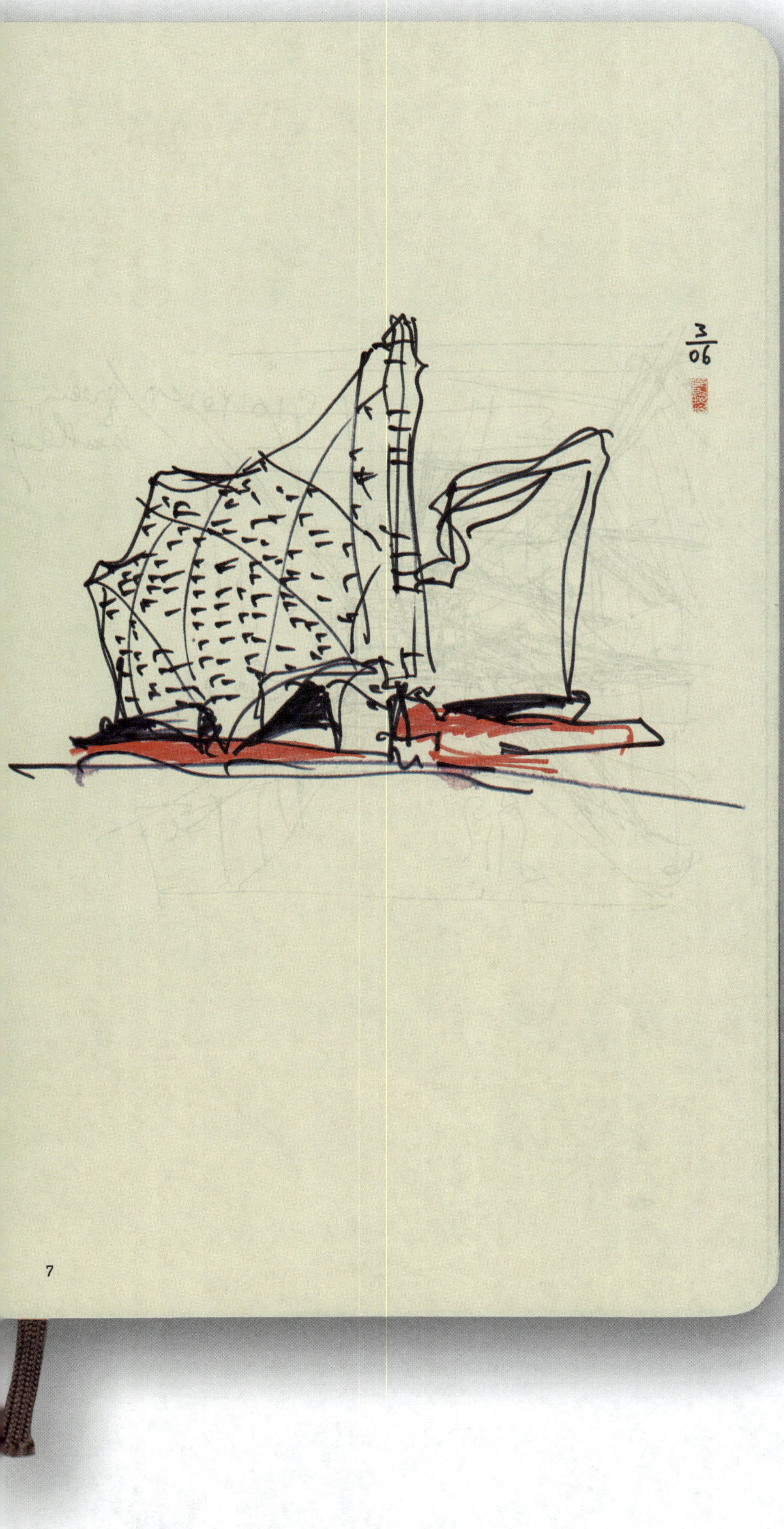
3/06

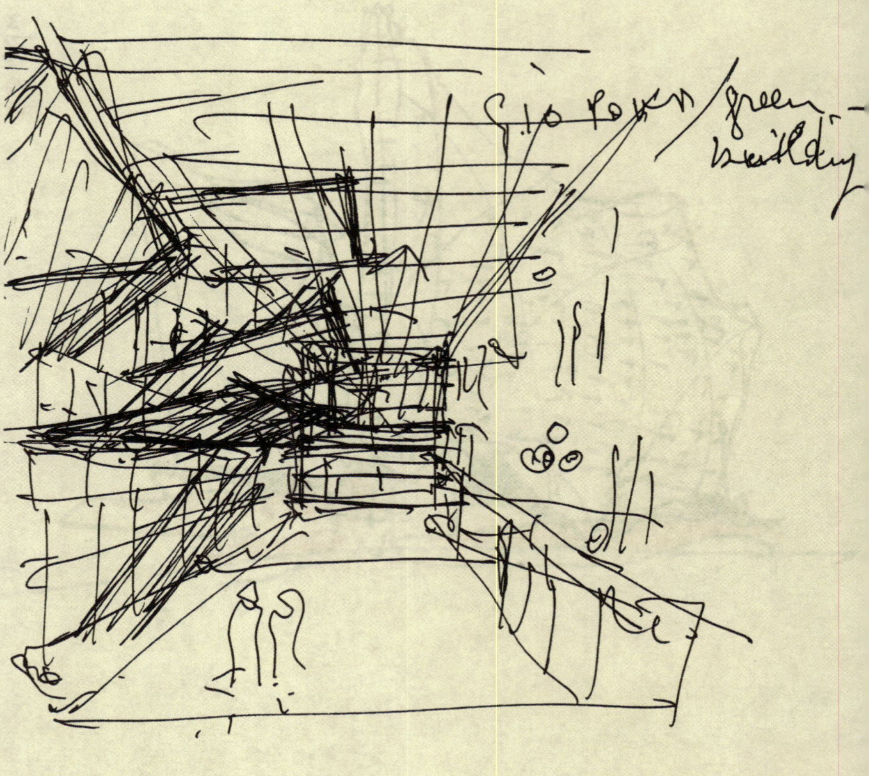
green-
building

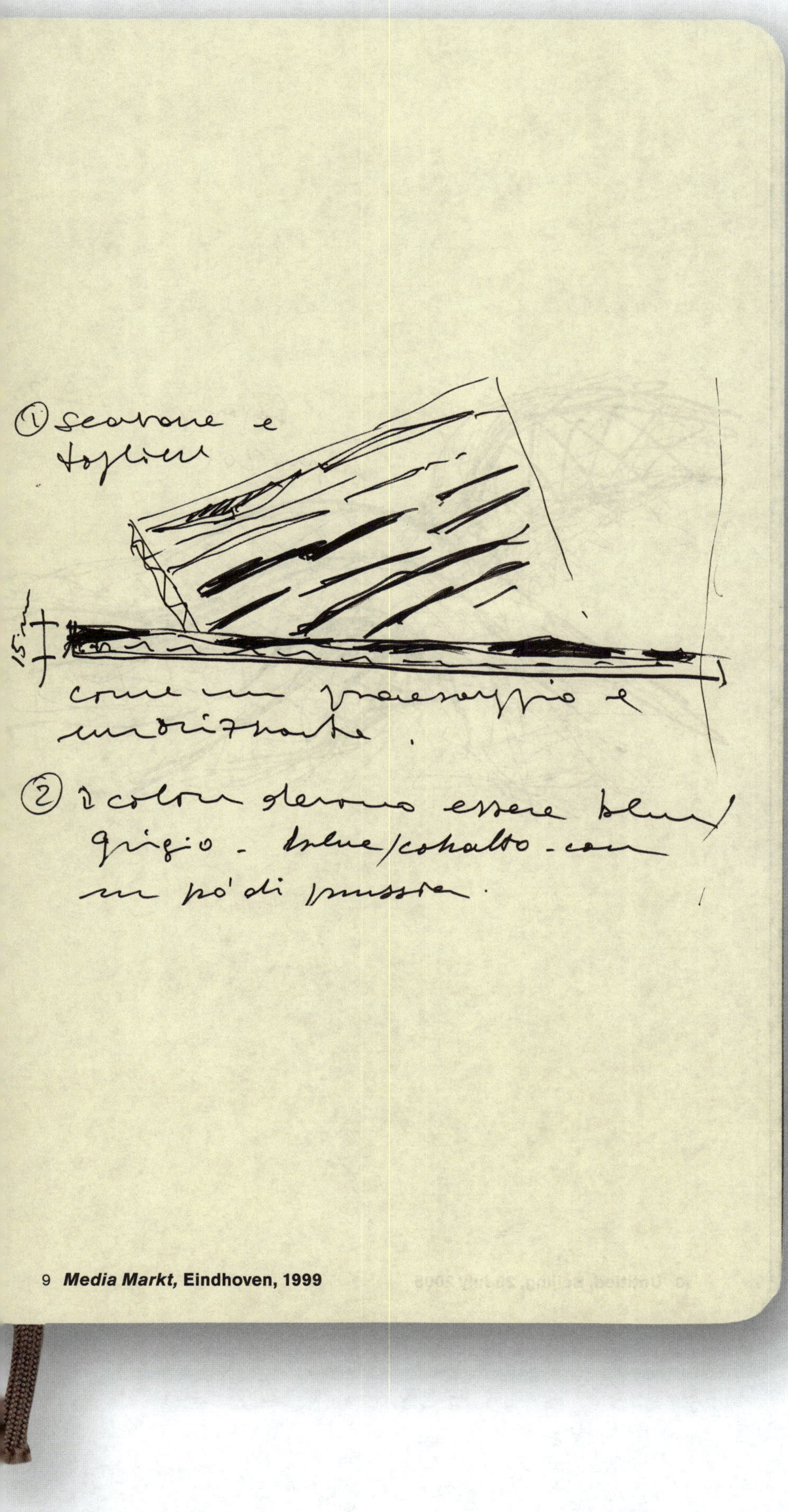

9 *Media Markt,* Eindhoven, 1999

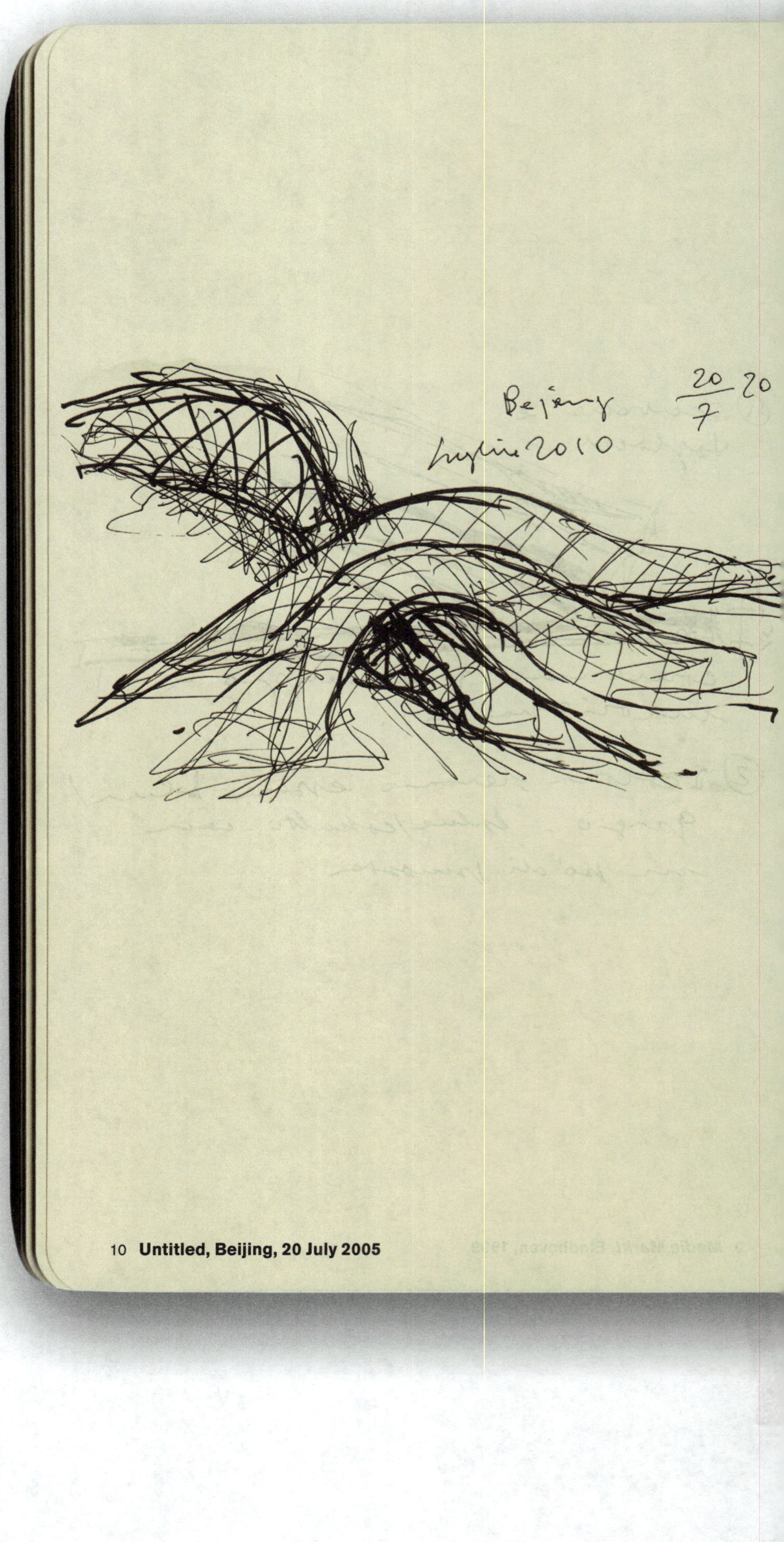

10 **Untitled, Beijing, 20 July 2005**

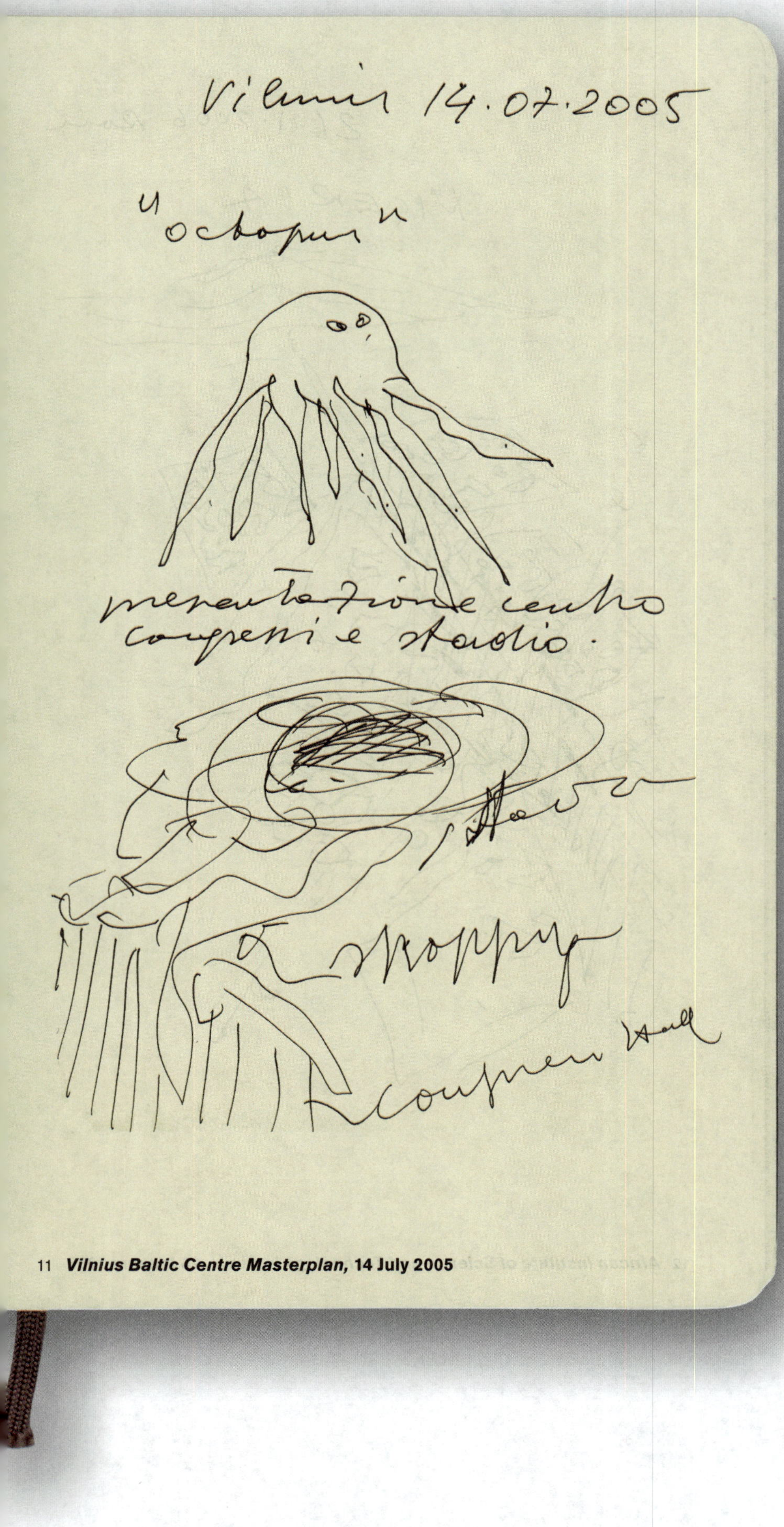

11 ***Vilnius Baltic Centre Masterplan*, 14 July 2005**

12 ***African Institute of Science and Technology in Abuja*, 26 January 2006**

13 ***Phare Tower, La Défense*, Paris, 2006**

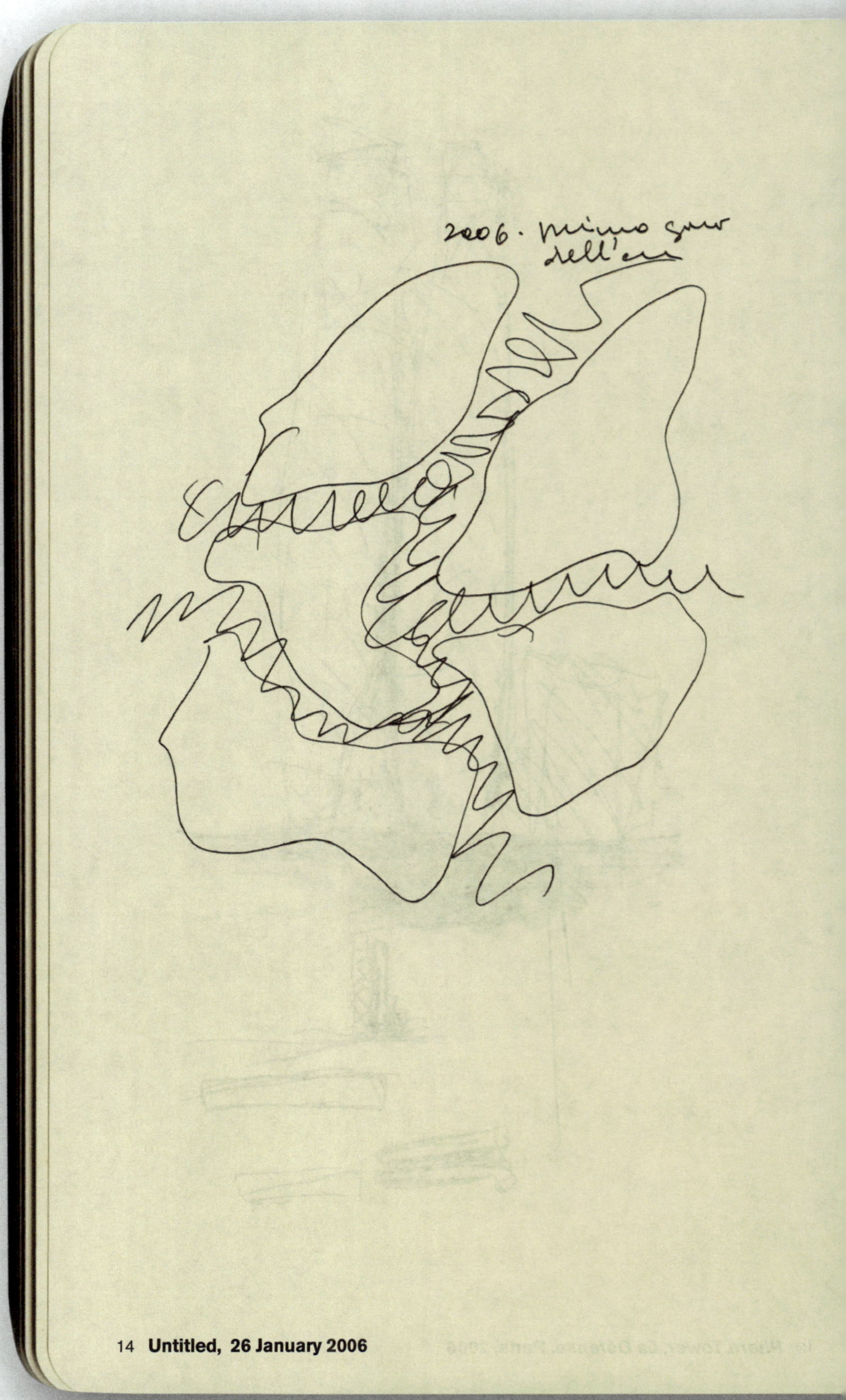

14 **Untitled, 26 January 2006**

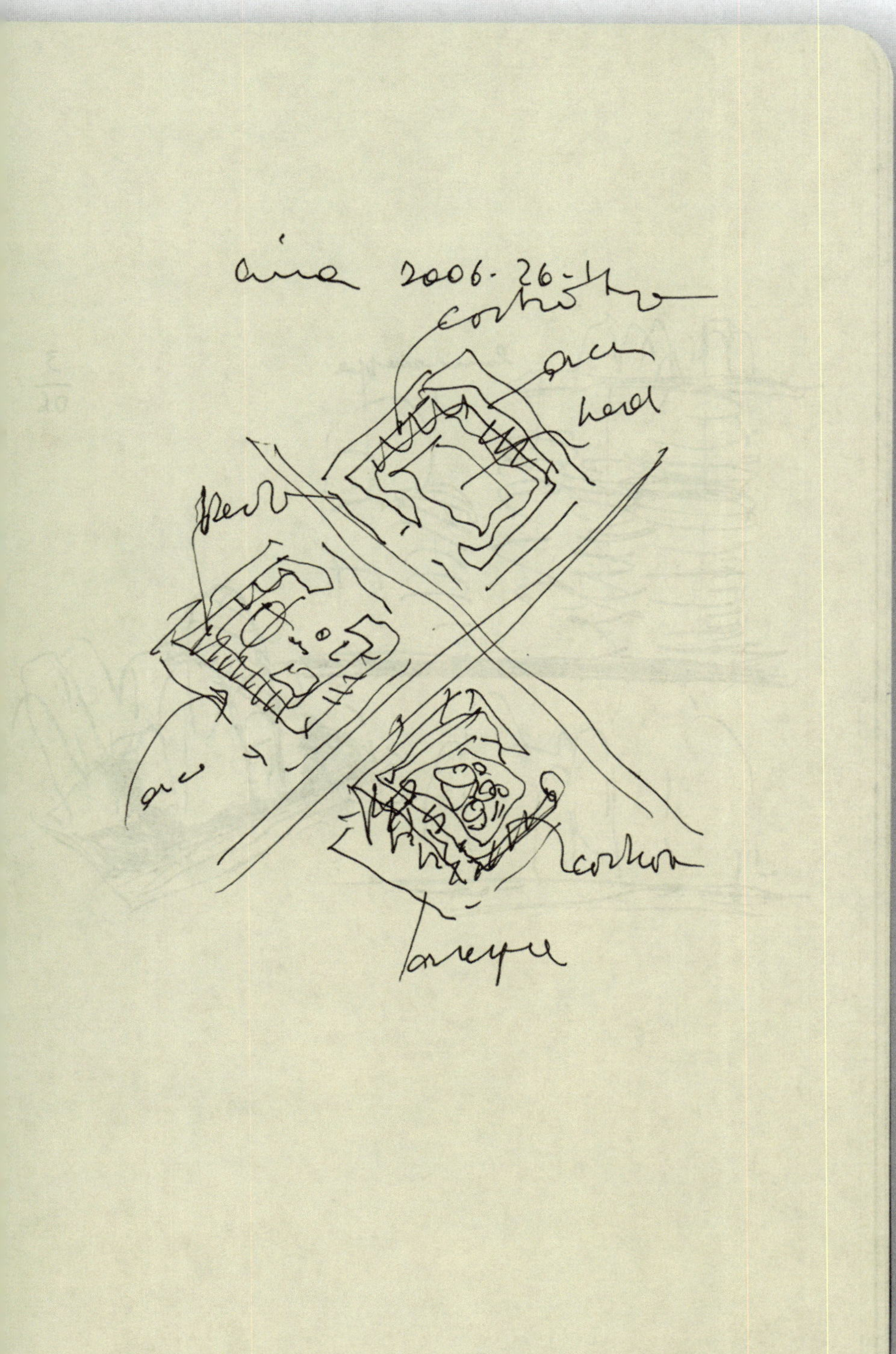

15 ***University's Foreign Affairs Exstention*, Sha-He, *2006***

16 ***Morgans Hotel,*** **Las Vegas, March, 2006**

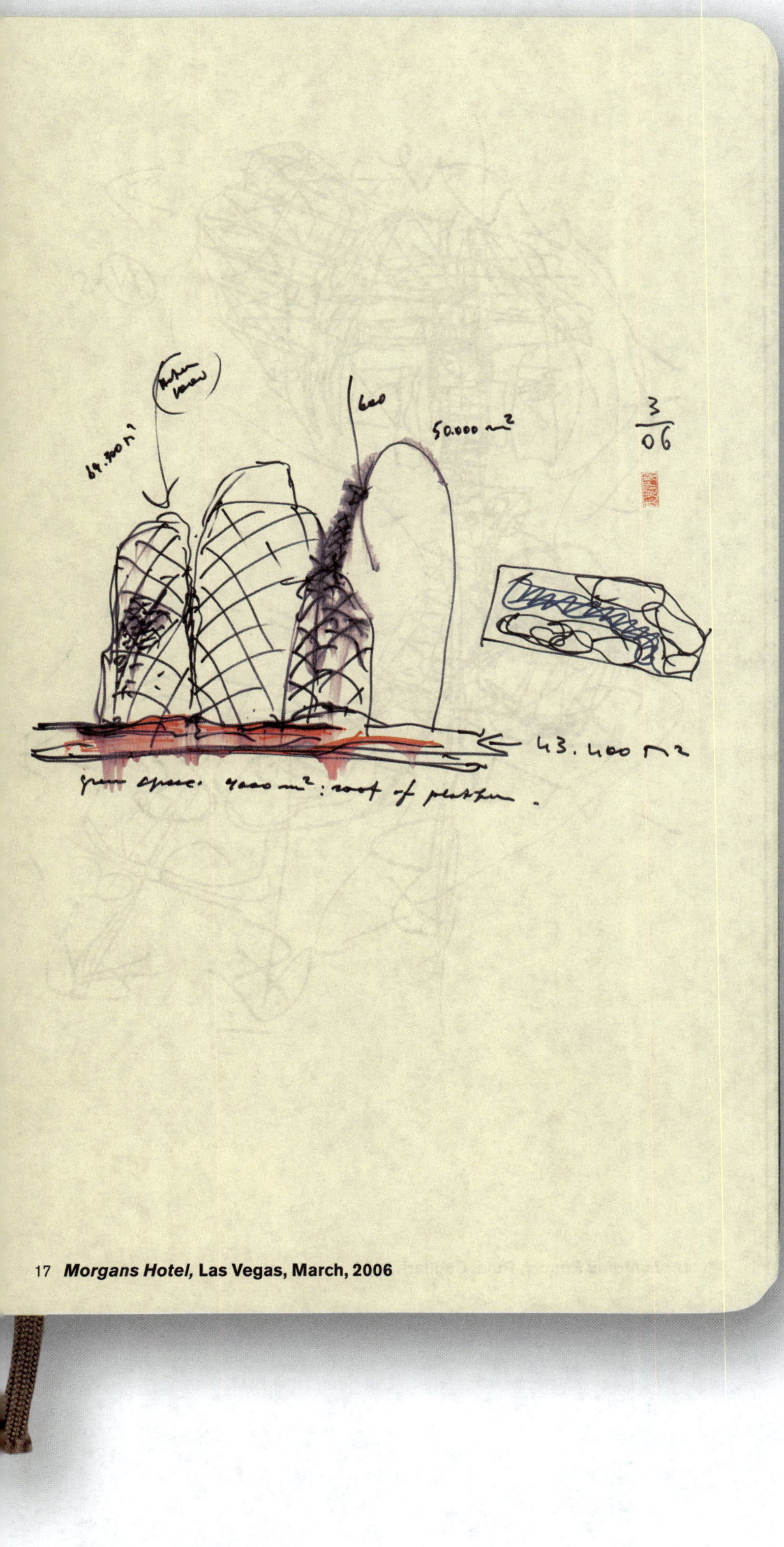

17 ***Morgans Hotel,*** **Las Vegas, March, 2006**

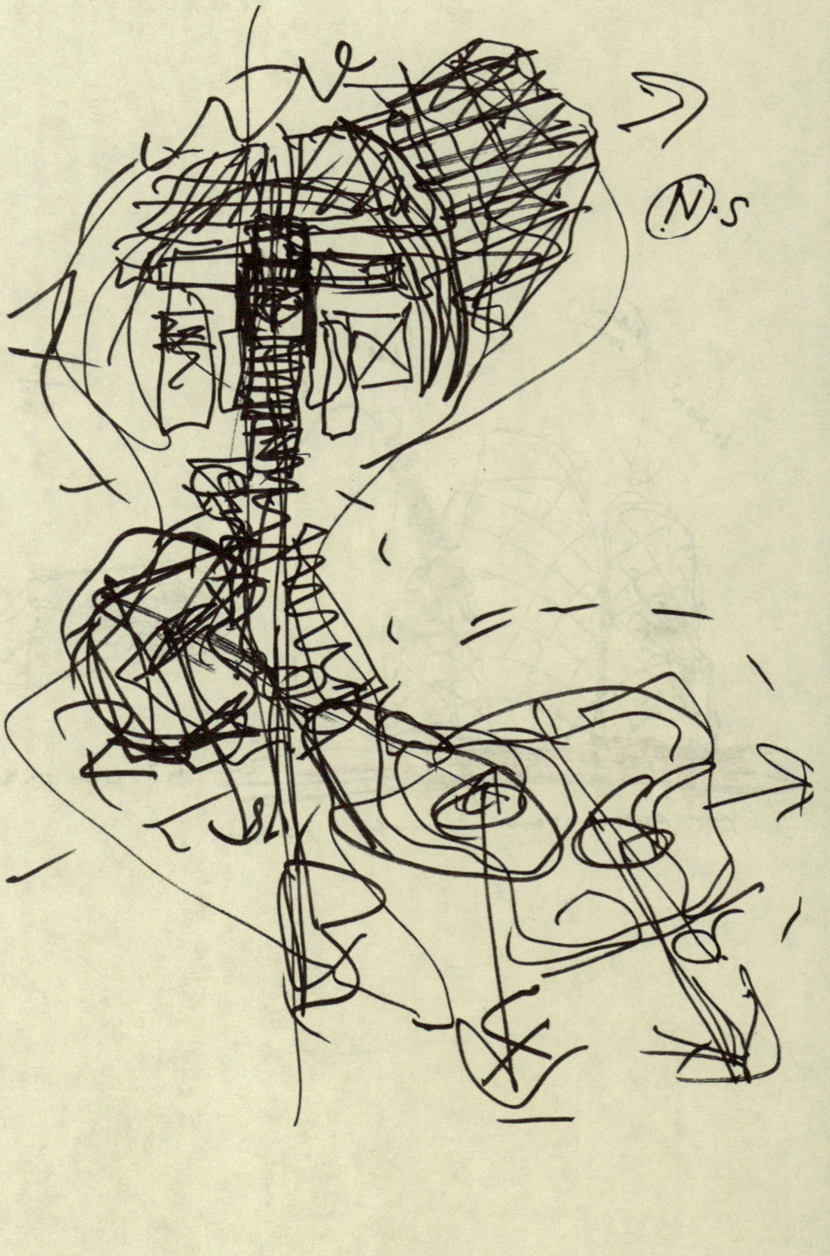

18 ***Is Molas Resort,*** **Pula, Cagliari, 2006**

19 ***Beijing Wangjing Design Competition*, 2009**

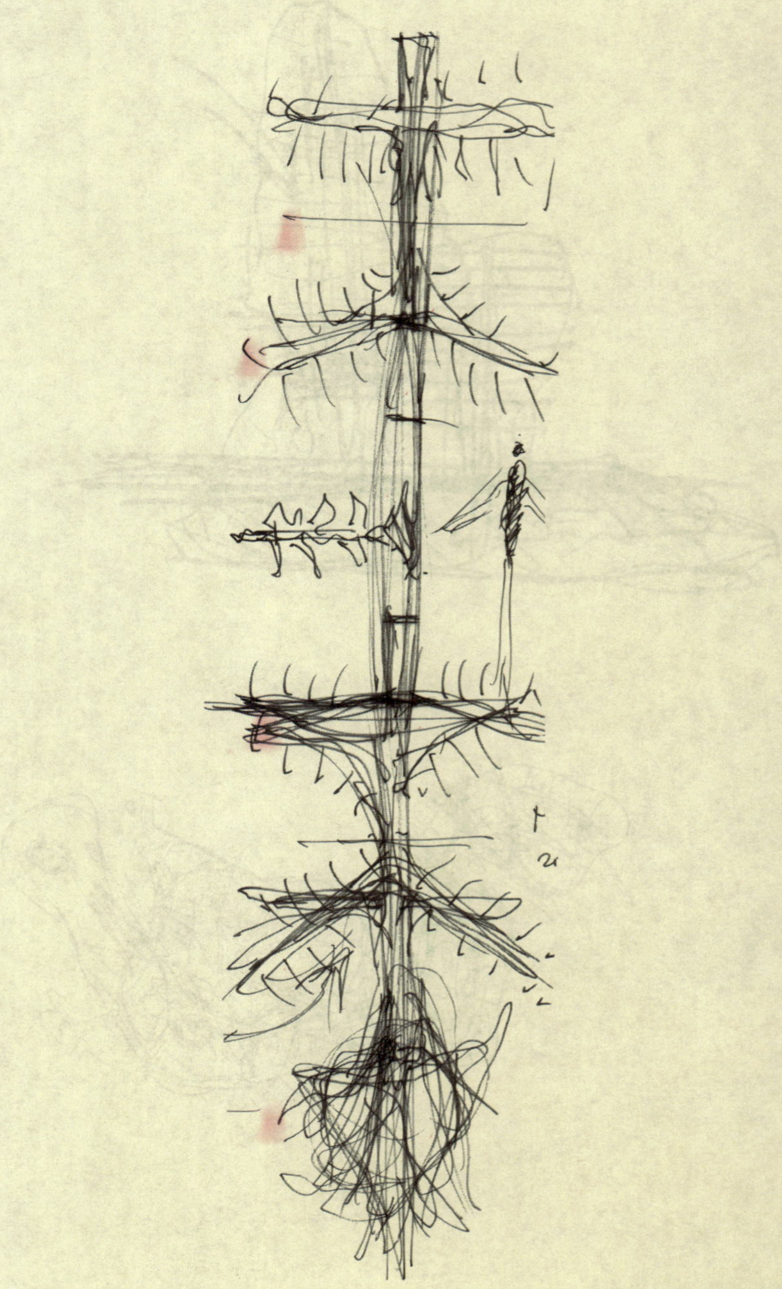

20 ***Chongqing Airport in Beijing, 2009***

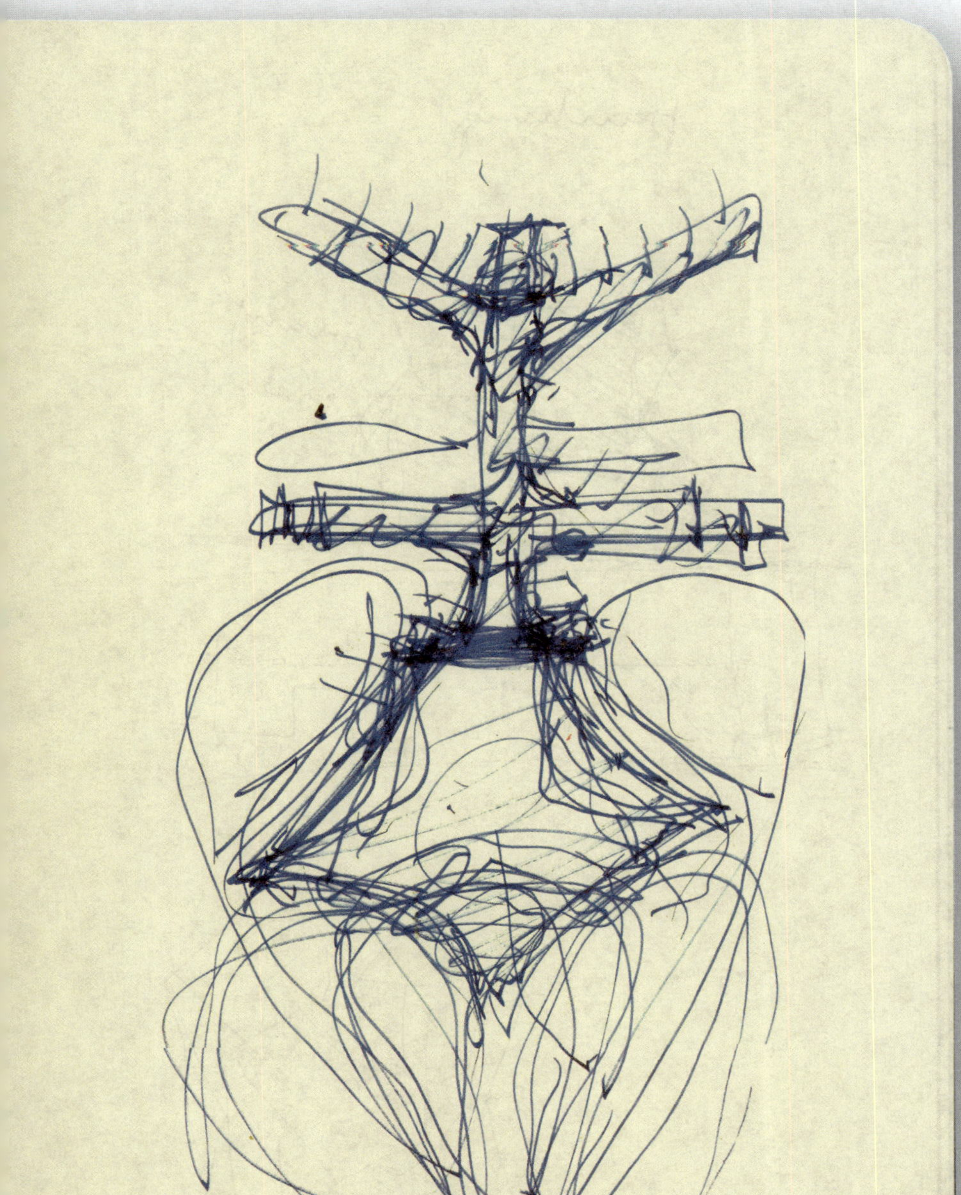

21 ***Chongqing Airport in Beijing, 2009***

Mainz
22 Power Station in Mainz, 2009

23 ***Power Station in Mainz*, 17 July 2010**

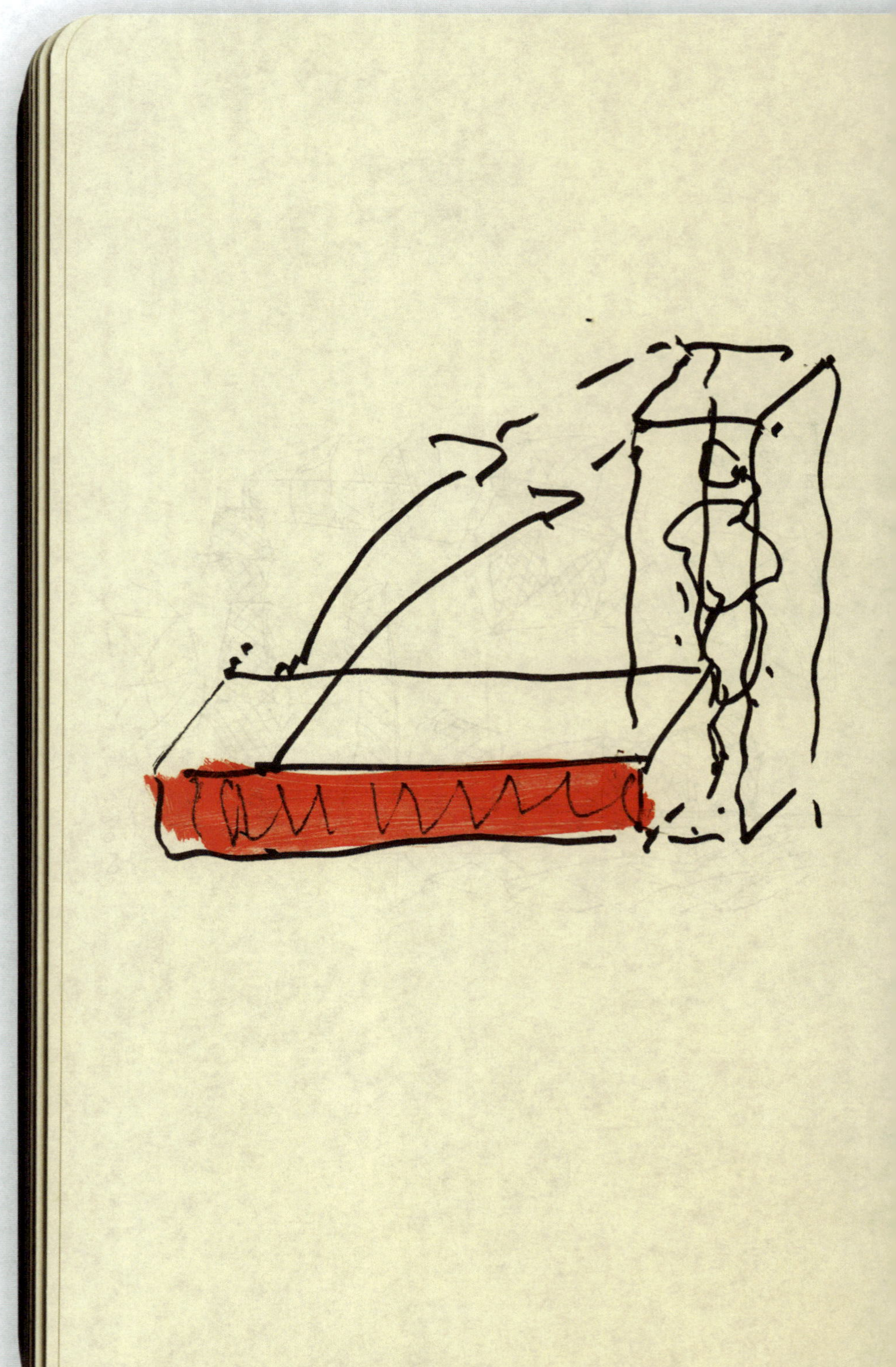

24 ***Container Sculpture*, June 2010**

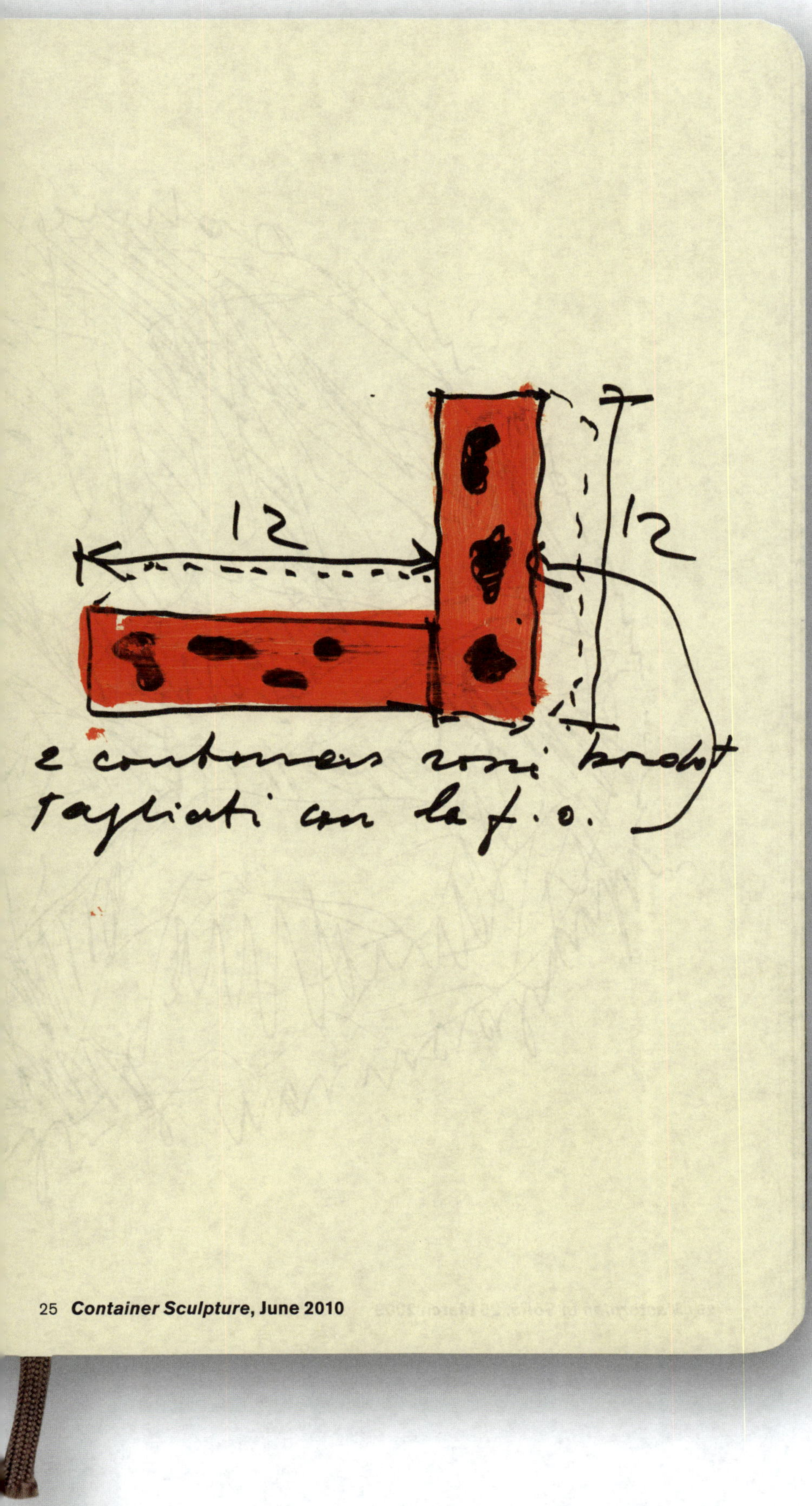

25 ***Container Sculpture*, June 2010**

26 ***Masterplan in Sofia*, 25 March 2009**

Roma 2009
Marzo 25
nel

 ***Masterplan in Sofia,* 2010**

29 **Untitled, Rome, 18 January 2010**

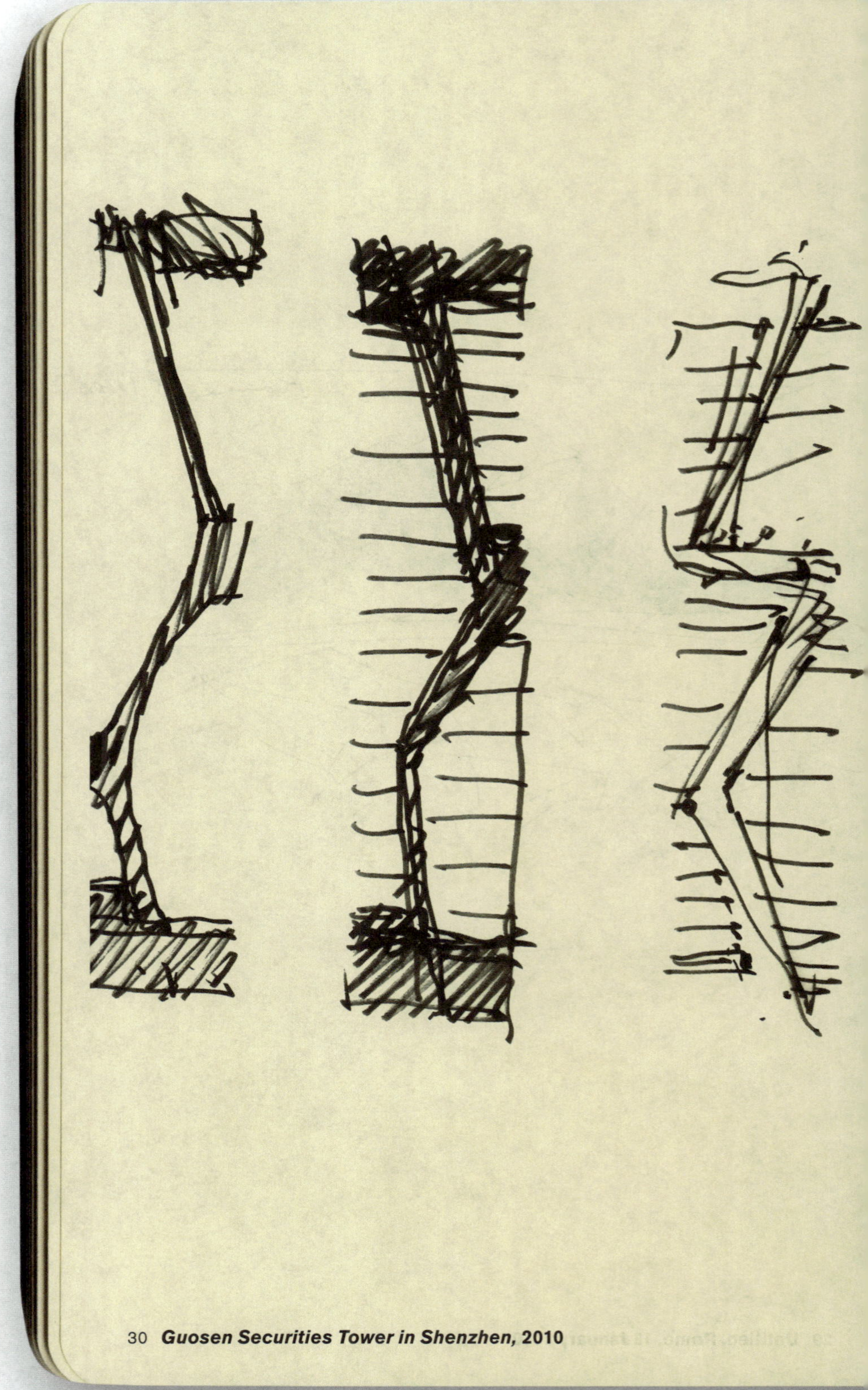

30 ***Guosen Securities Tower in Shenzhen*, 2010**

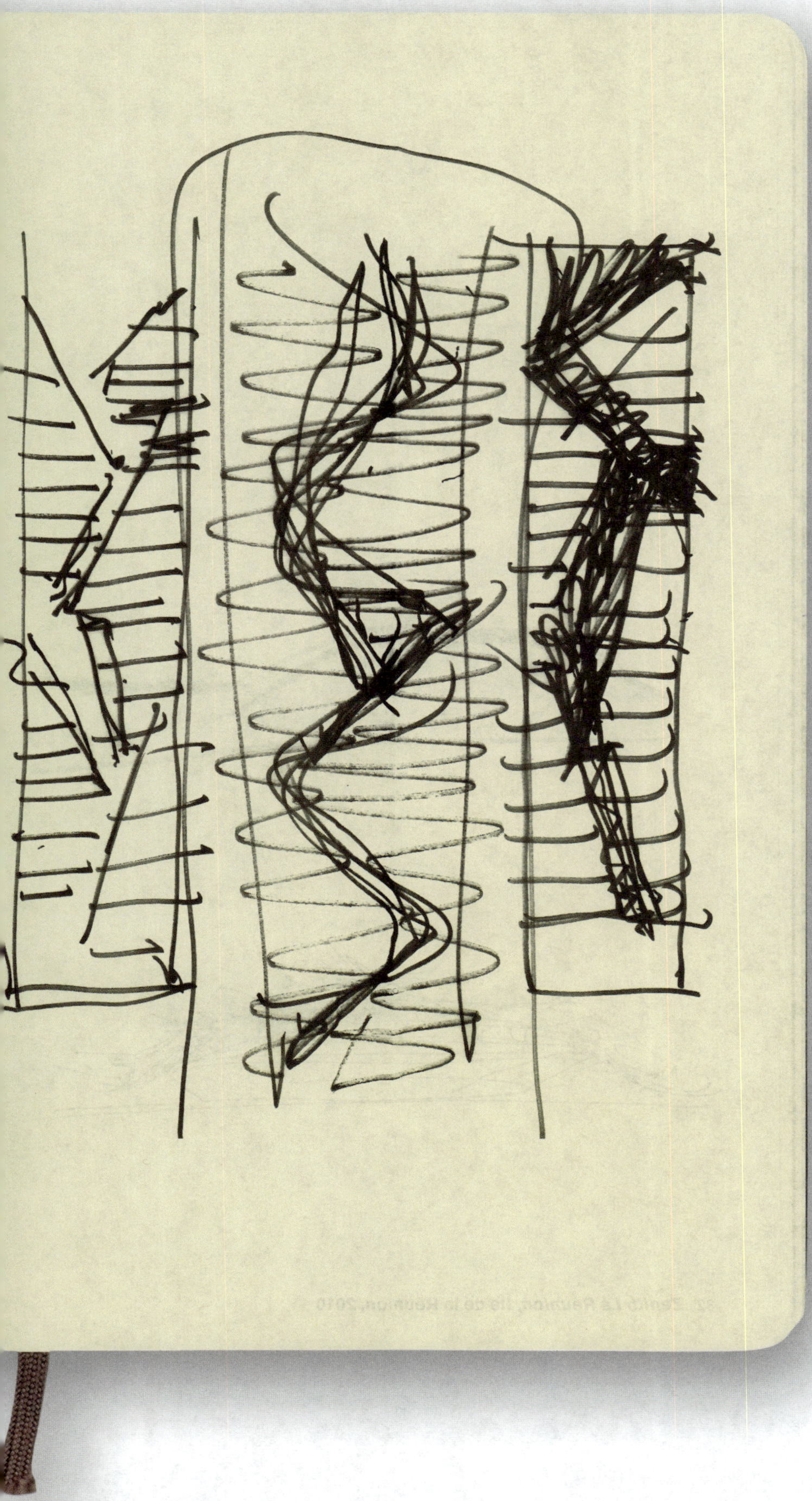

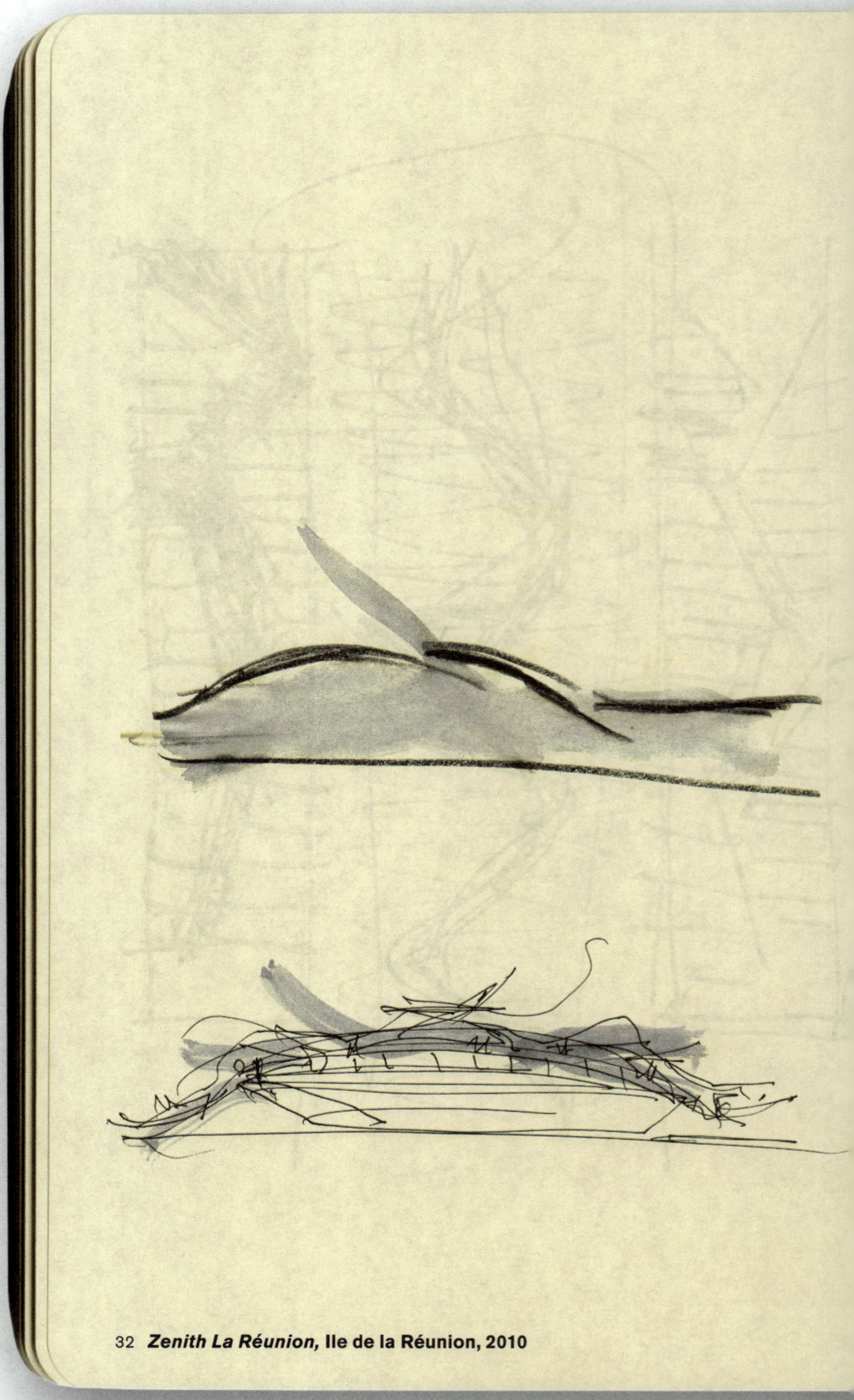

32 *Zenith La Réunion,* Ile de la Réunion, 2010

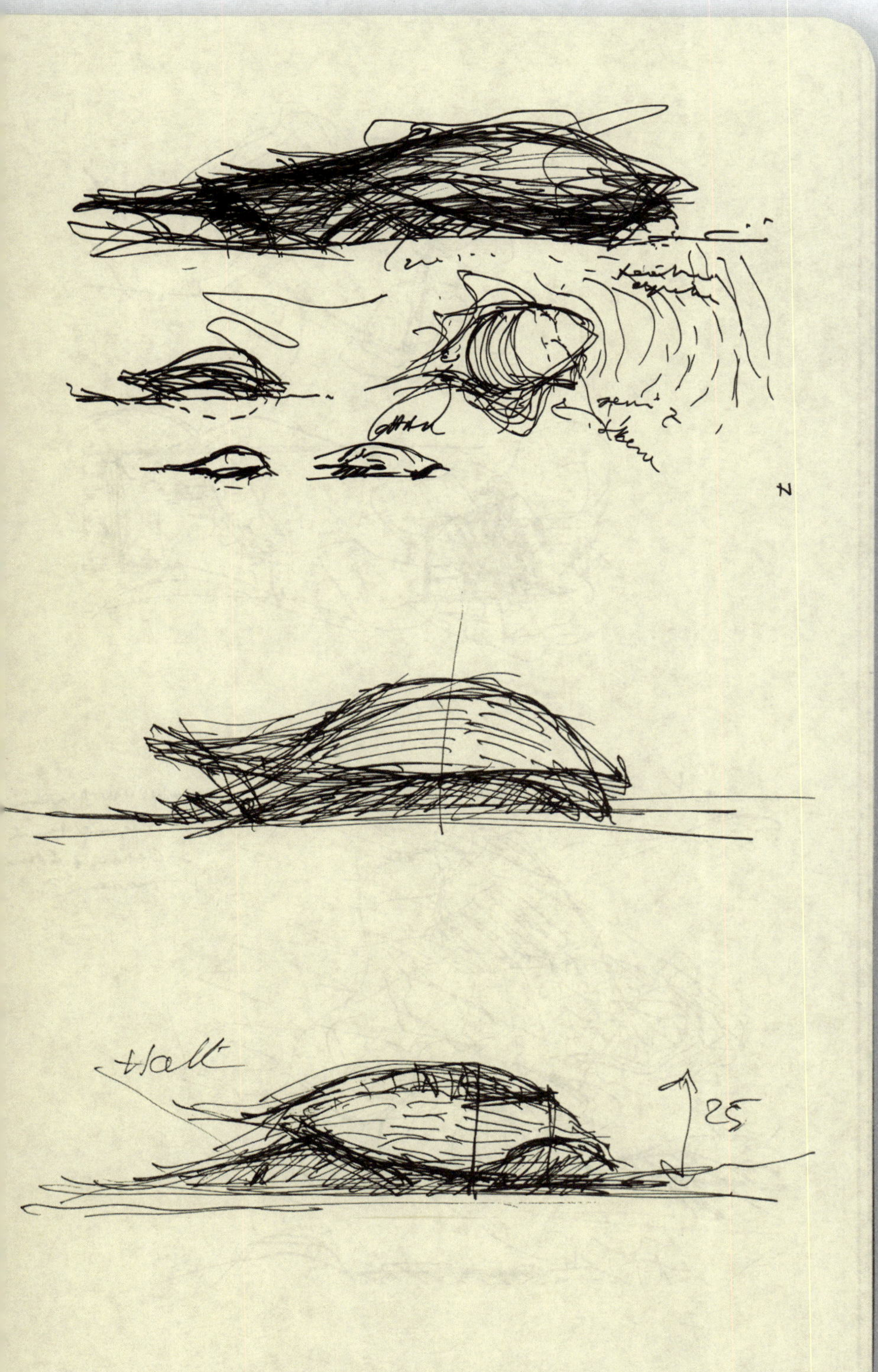

33 ***Zenith La Réunion,*** **Ile de la Réunion, 2010**

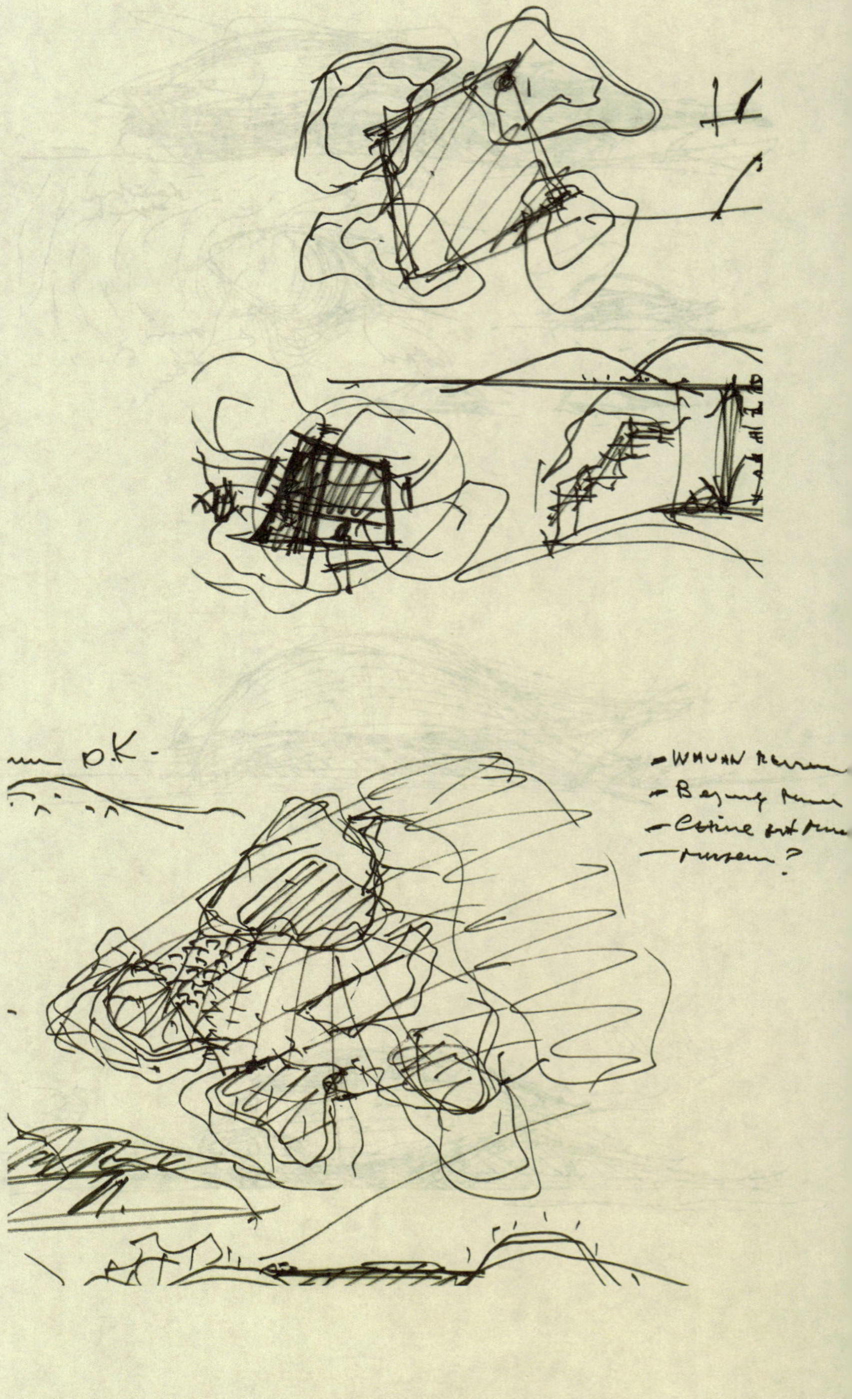

34 ***Garden Museum in Beijing*, 2010**

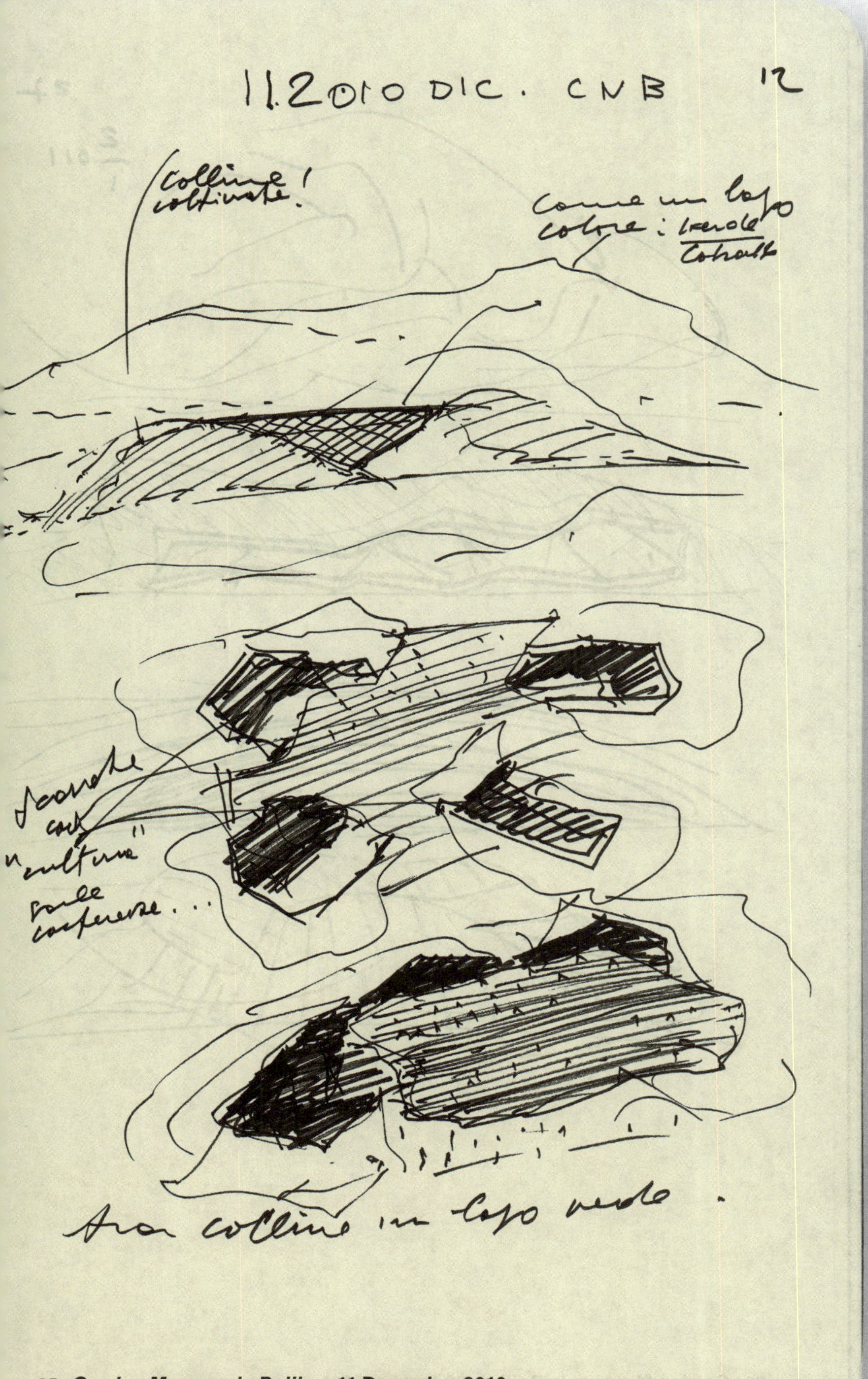

35 *Garden Museum in Beijing*, 11 December 2010

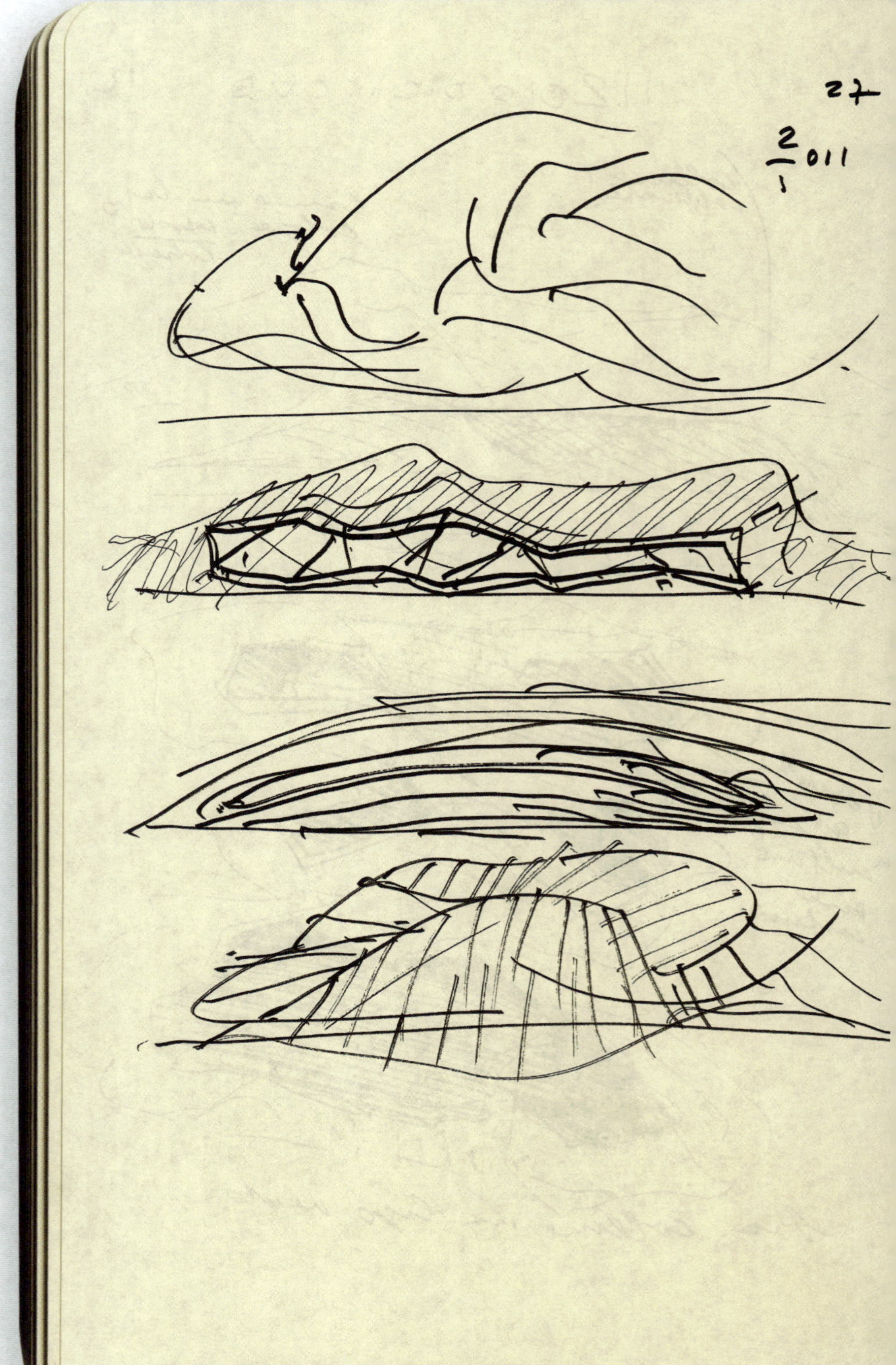

36 ***Garden Museum in Beijing*, 02 January 2011**

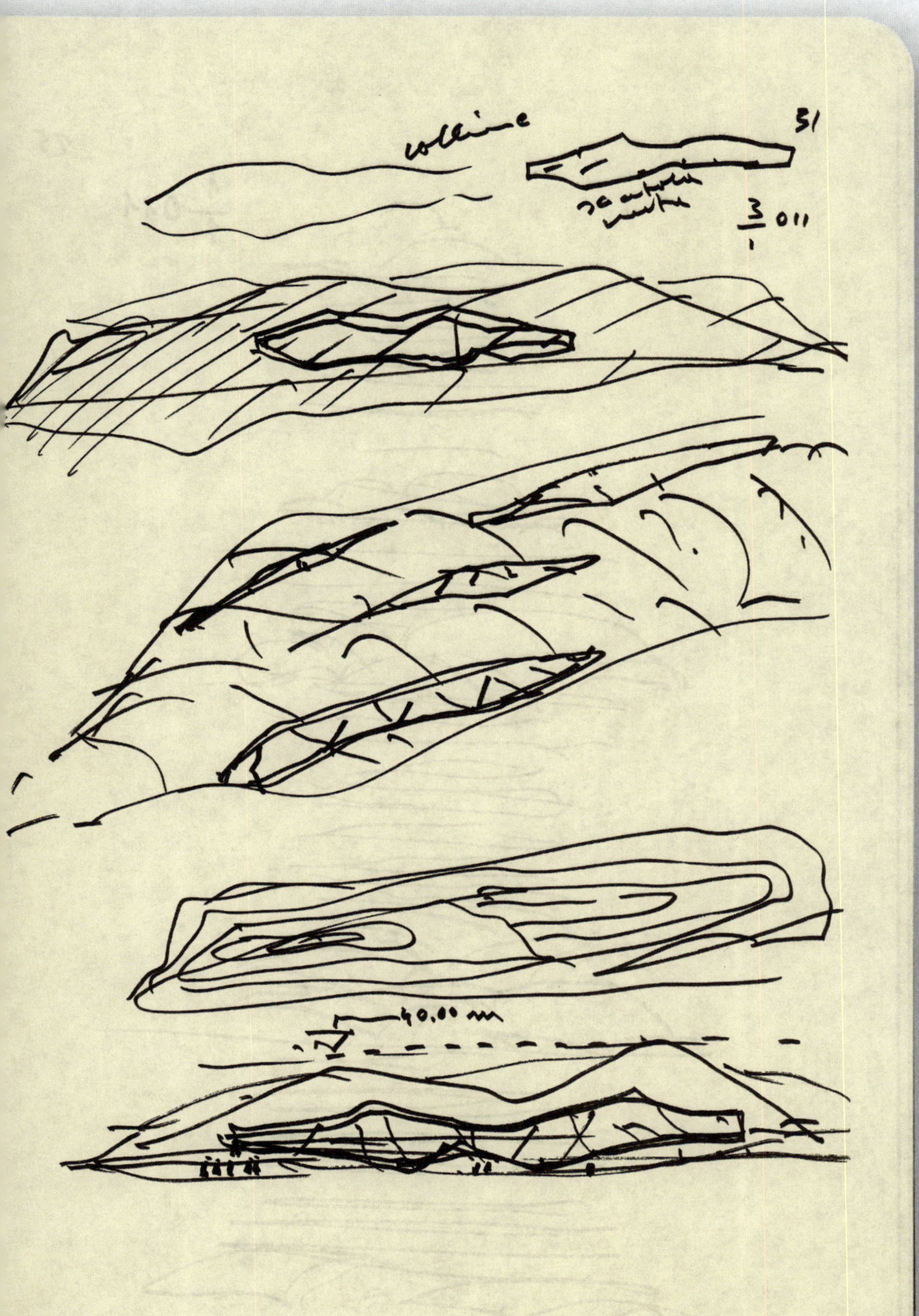

37 ***Garden Museum in Beijing*, 03 January 2011**

 Untitled, 01 January 2011

39 **Untitled, 03 January 2011**

Painting

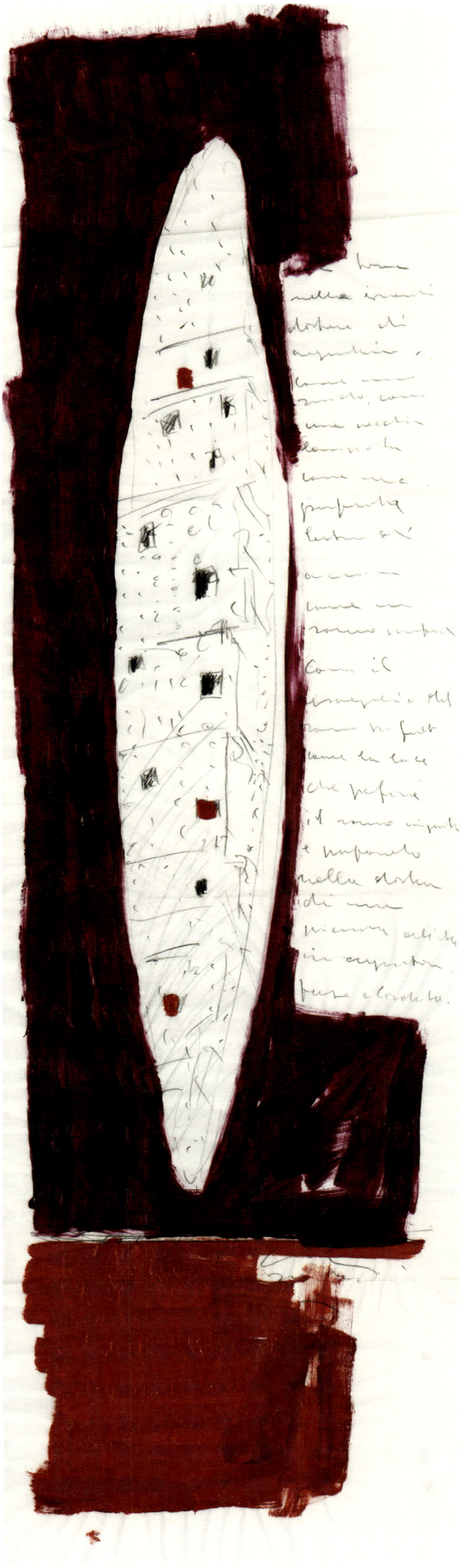

46 ***European tower*****, Herouville St. Claire, 1987**

47 *European tower,* Herouville St. Claire, 1987

48 ***European tower,* Herouville St. Claire, 1987**

49 ***European tower*, Herouville St. Claire, 1987**

 ***Ritornando a casa: a Doriana*, 20 June 1987**

 Untitled, Rome, 17 July 1987

53 *Una torre di sfondo*, **1987**

 ***Un'estate al mare*, Herouville St. Claire, 17 May 1988**

55 **Untitled, 1988**

 ***Maison de la communication*, St. Quentin en Yvelines, 1991**

 ***EUR New Congress Centre in Rome*, 02 April 1999**

59 ***EUR New Congress Centre in Rome*****, 1999**

 ***EUR New Congress Centre in Rome*, 2000**

***ASI_Italian Space Agency*, Rome, 2000** (at the left)
 ***EUR New Congress Centre in Rome*, 1999** (at the right)

 ***University Michel Montaigne - Maison des Arts*, Bordeaux, 1999**

 Untitled, January, 2000

 ***Europark*, Salzburg, September, 2001**

 ***New Trade Fair in Milan*, 2002**

 ***New Trade Fair in Milan*, 2007**

67 ***New Trade Fair in Milan*, 2007**

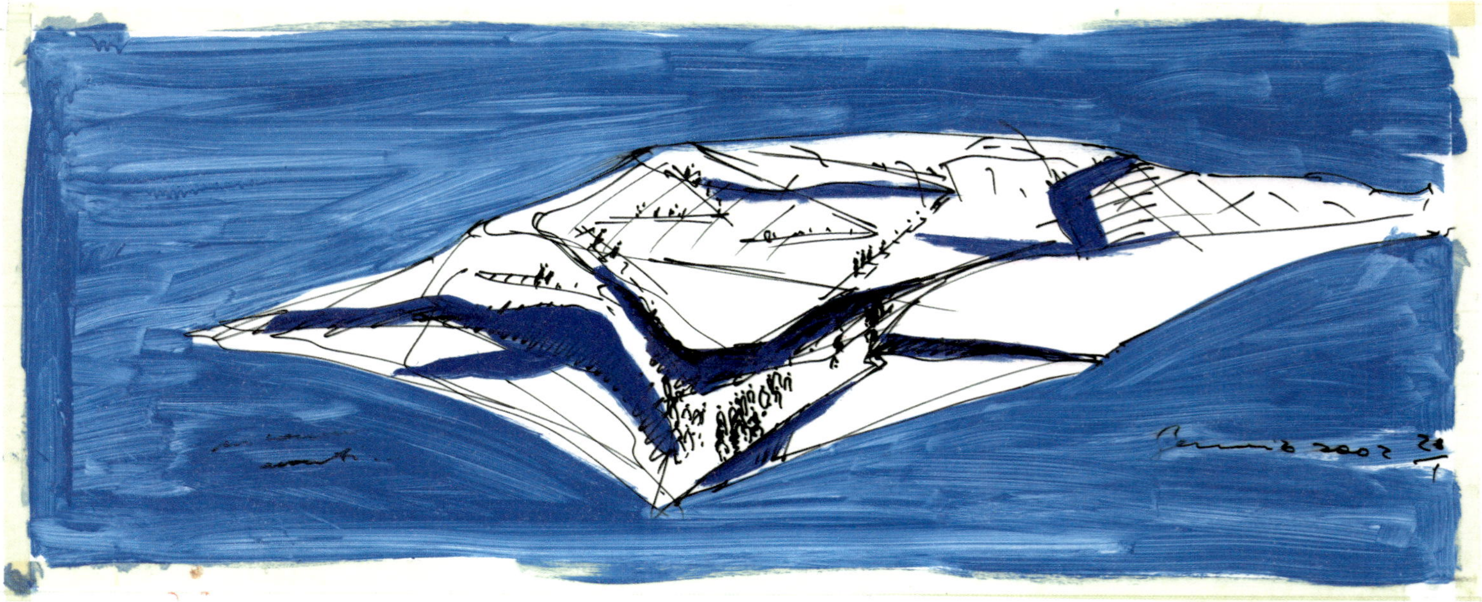

 Untitled, 2002

69 ***St. Paolo Church in Foligno*, December 2003**

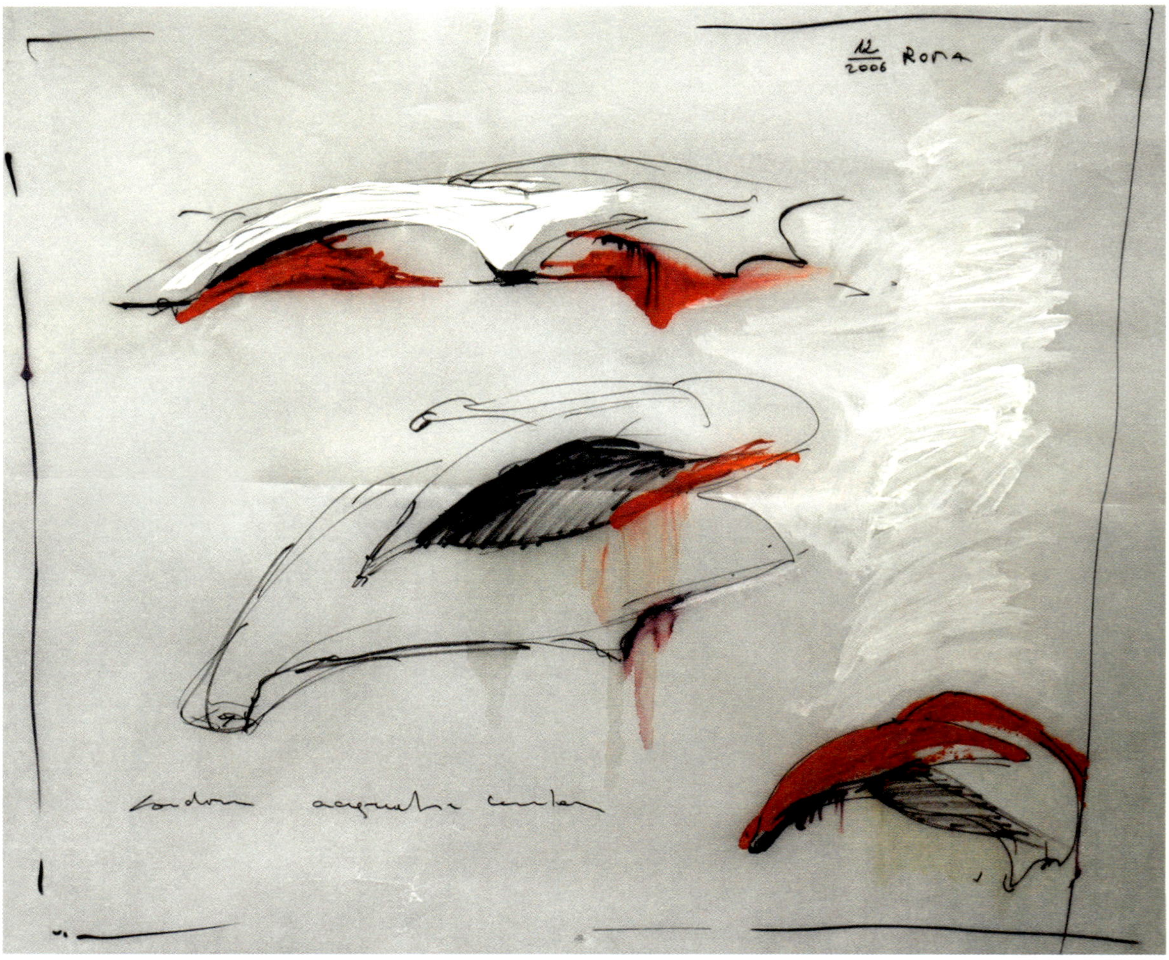
12
2006
ROMA

71 ***Gazprom Tower*, Saint Petersburg, 2006**

 ***Phare Tower, La Défense in Paris*, September/October 2006**

Untitled, 07 October 2006

 ***Zenith Music Hall in Strasbourg*, 2007**

75 ***Article 25, Charity Auction*, Rome, 2009**

 ***Some flowers, someday,* Rome, 2011**

 ***Promenade, dans les bois*, Rome, March 2011**

Word

All texts by Massimiliano Fuksas

It's not enough

I've often asked myself what the alchemy is that makes all human beings so different. Some say psychoanalysis, others the enlightenment that the encounter with an artwork or a famous building brings. Artists usually try to reconstruct their own history, but architects hardly ever do. I still don't understand what makes my architect's profession so unique. I only know that I didn't want to be one.

I became an architect because my mother was afraid I'd become an artist and, to her way of thinking, artists were people who never had any money. Anyway, I've never met God, or a psychoanalyst for that matter. I prefer other things. What I can say is that I decided to enroll in the architecture faculty in order to make my mother happy, but architecture didn't interest me in the least, it really didn't excite me at all. My mother has always been very pragmatic. She was a philosophy teacher and always a communist. so she was convinced that her son had to get a good degree. I didn't really agree with her, I never have. I left home at the age of sixteen and went to school as usual, but painting was everything to me, it was the only thing that I really loved. So even though it may seem paradoxical, I started university with no desire whatsoever to become an architect. Only as time went by did I start to fall in love with this discipline. Anyway, when I went to university I didn't know anything about architecture, and that was terrible. Italy has no architecture high schools, only university faculties. A law dating from the Fascist period established the creation of a Faculty of Architecture, somewhere between Engineering and Fine Arts. The sum of the two disciplines resulted in a course that was ferociously difficult. There were 39 exams, 19 of which had to be passed in the first two years, otherwise the student was not admitted to the third year. Again, to keep my mother happy, I took all the exams, which was crazy. Despite all this I knew nothing, which shows that one can do anything without knowing anything. There are hundreds of useless exams. I finished them all, before the scheduled time too, so I spent six months in Denmark. I visited Jorn Utzon's studio where I went back to work the fo-llowing summer and, at the same time, began to look very carefully at contemporary buildings. On the whole, I didn't think they were that bad. When I came back I wasn't so in love with architecture anymore, but I began to do some work on the subject. I read books, copied plans and cross sections. I was simply trying to understand. The only subject I was really interested in was the History of Architecture. Contemporary art, on the other hand, was my life, my real love. I've always refused to revere any master, but there have been some people in my life that I'm thankful to and to whom I could dedicate many of my projects. The first is Jurgis Baltrusa•tis, an art historian known mainly for his studies of anamorphosis and the fantasy world of the Middle Ages. Like me he was Lithuanian, so when I lived in Paris we used to meet frequently. I really liked seeing him as he reminded me of my roots and I could speak to him using the few words of Lithuanian that I still remember.

The other person I'd like to mention is Giorgio Caproni, one of the most important Italian contemporary poets and one of the greatest translators of Celine. His works have been translated all over the world. He was my primary school teacher and I often went to his house in the afternoon when school had finished. We've always been very close. He played the violin and adored electric trains, which we often assembled together. We built landscapes while I read him my poems, which were clearly those of a ten-year-old child. I was mad about poetry and his world.

Another person I owe a lot to is Giorgio Castelfranco, who I've known since I was a child. I met many artists through Castelfranco, including Giorgio de Chirico who I worked with for a while in his studio in Piazza di Spagna. At the time I didn't feel alive if I didn't paint every day.

Anyway, I'm sure all my projects show that my mental frame of reference certainly hasn't come from architecture. My interests as well as my training have always been closer to art. I love Burri, Fontana, Fluxus, Gordon Matta Clark, Beuys, Arte Povera and Land Art, the world of violence and poetry, the world of Krzysztof Wodiczko and Pierpaolo Pasolini. In other words, I'm interested in becoming part of a process that is different from the architecture we experience every day.

My real obsession is landscapes, like Ayers Rock, now renamed Uluru, the red mountain in Australia, the atolls of Polynesia, the enormous dunes that form and dissolve in the deserts, icebergs, islands. I've always been fascinated by the beauty of formlessness, the imperfection of beauty. I've always wondered how it might possible to create a shapeless form of architecture with no dimensional geometry or complexity. This is why I believe that artists, even the worst ones, are better than architects, because artists always start from a vision, whereas architects never speak about it. They always speak about a project.

My dream, on the other hand, is that everyone can have ideas, passions and feelings. What's the point in struggling to earn more and more, to gain more power? In my opinion, capitalism and power are concepts that belong to the field of metaphysics. They are only myths that exist to maintain their own myth. The human situation is much less metaphysical. All of us try to deal with it as best we can. All of us try to find solutions to the innumerable problems of everyday life. We obviously can't dedicate all our daily energies to politics or what is wrong with the system, as we all have difficult lives. We leave home in the morning and come back at night. What can architecture do to help us live better? It can say NO. Obviously, this is not particularly revolutionary, but it does mean making certain choices instead of others. Some time ago, a big investor asked me to design a vast plan for 25.000 inhabitants next to the Appia Antica, the great archaeological park.

I refused, but someone else, who is said to be left wing, accepted and the project was immediately approved.

TO REFUSE IS AT LEAST SOMETHING,
AND EVERY TIME WE SAY NO IS IMPORTANT.

We must always ask ourselves the same question: do we want to give people what they ask for, that is to say, a world that often has no taste or culture, or do we want to take the risk of trying to create a better quality of life?

A man that I have always admired very much for the stands he has taken and the courage of his choices, is Bruno Zevi, my teacher at university. This is despite the fact that we have always disagreed ever since I was a student. After years of ups and downs, Zevi finally wrote an article where he admitted that I at least had some merits. I called him up and, as usual, he asked me to go to visit him, immediately! It was April 1995. He was living in Via Nomentana. I found him in good shape in his dusty studio, surrounded as always by the most up to date books. I tried to give him a hug, though he tried to stop me with his usual "I only hug women" (we did it anyway) and then he fired a question straight at me, point-blank. What are you going to do over the next ten years, apart from architecture? I must say that it took me several weeks to recover. Put this way, the question doesn't have any great answers, unless I start questioning much of what I have done and thought over the years.

This attempt at savage psychoanalysis made me think a lot.

Frames, Barcelona: Actar 2003

Sustainable architecture

In 1979, not uncoincidentally a major crisis year for energy in the aftermath of the Iranian revolution, Edward Lorenz gave a talk to the American Association for the Advancement of Science whose title asked *Does the flap of a butterfly's wings in Brazil set off a tornado in Texas?*

Edward Lorenz (1917-2008), the great meteorologist, mathematician and father of Chaos Theory, used an aphorism to describe the problematic complexity of the infinitesimal, of things so small that we normally think can be overlooked.
What has Lorenz's title to do with the ecological emergency we read about in the newspapers and experience first-hand every day; with global warming, air-conditioning in May and "sustainable" glass skyscrapers in Dubai; with the energy crisis and the urgent need to find a way of keeping the world turning and safeguarding our own and our children's lives, even when the oil has run out?

Can his title not be seen as a kind of prediction, a way of imagining our future (though obviously one whose existence can't be proved), a reality that can be described only using complex, non-linear equations that can be made linear only under local conditions? Architecture alone is capable of doing something about this, of finding ways to turn a negative trend into a positive scenario, of doing something for the good.
The truth is that our Earth is weary of us, of our disrespect and greed. We have robbed, pillaged and disfigured our planet.

But now we have to do more than complain. Bemoaning the loss of the Golden Age certainly won't help any of us to live better, always assuming there really was a time when everything worked as it should, honey flowed from trees and grapes were always ripe. It's time to be proactive, to think things through.
Jeremy Rifkin's concept of buildings as power plants is technologically, economically and philosophically advanced.

In his view, every building, every object resting on the ground should first of all be energy self-sufficient, and then capable of generating surplus energy for distribution on a power grid similar to the Internet that enables it to be shared like information.

One example of this was the decision by Frito-Lay, the potato chips and snack-foods giant, to make its Casa Grande facility in Arizona totally independent of the power grid by 2010 using renewable energy and recycled water. Fine, but don't forget that its fatty, dietetically non-essential products will produce generations of obese adults with heart conditions and children addicted to TV snacks. Which raises the question of entropy.

Returning to Rifkin's challenge to architects, contractors, financiers and developers, the most difficult thing seems to be how to manage the Internet-style power grid he envisages.

The problem isn't so much how to make a building energy self-sufficient – we already know how to use solar panels, wind power, tides, recycled waste and so on – as how to manage this new resource on what must necessarily be a global scale.

The world Rifkin envisages looks like a laboratory in which everyone is prepared to work on the same experiment. A total sharing of intentions, desires and aims. But we all know that, at least until now, the reality has been the opposite of this.

The fight for supremacy seems permanently written in our DNA. Architects can make a real contribution – and I don't mean through design and aesthetics – only when this problem has been solved.

In the meantime, we mustn't forget that the building industry is Europe's largest employer, even though it produces 30-40% of its carbon dioxide and the consumes the same percentage of its energy.

We neither can nor want to make excuses. We just want to make things better. For now, we can do this by changing our construction methods, tailoring them to the needs of building users, construction workers themselves, and contemporary architecture.

It's a question of using our common sense, at least until we have a world without petroleum and perhaps without wars.

L'Espresso, May 2008

Innovation

Having devoted years of our lives to designing and building structures on every possible scale, we architects are beginning to realise (too late, of course) that the most important thing isn't what we build but the environment we live in, the air we breathe, the lives we live, the fact that geography needs to be seen as context rather than landscape.

Looking back at the Sixties, one realises that, abundant as it was, most of the theorising, research and utopian speculation that came to a head in 1968 simply vanished from sight over the next twenty years. Only in 1989, when the Berlin Wall fell, did we start thinking again, step by step, crisis and difficulty notwithstanding, about issues that had been almost completely forgotten, such as environment, people, cities, economics, politics, work, information, control. We started creating visions of the future again, and began to realise that what architects want most of all is not just to be a witness, but also to play an active role in the process, to create ideas and programmes.

Intellectually speaking, we are moving from critical, even aristocratic detachment from the world's seething mass of relationships and influences, towards an unknown "discipline" full of energy and contradictions whose so far minimal achievements are also ours because we are responsible for making them happen.

The choice is always the same: to be part of the process, or to remain onlookers permanently resigned to what is going on around us. Architects need to reassert their creative credentials instead of being "cynically" content with what they already have, passively or submissively acquiescing to the ongoing destruction of life and the mushrooming development of our cities (greater Calcutta, 50 million inhabitants; greater Mexico City, 22 million).

I think we need to harness circumstances and resources that have never been tapped before. To start resolving today's contradictions and conflicts, these resources must be used carefully and energy must be concentrated in the right places.

For most of the 20th century, our cities were tragic stages on which society played out its contradictions and conflicts. Despite the intensity and complexity of urban relationships, the city has lost the centrality it once enjoyed within the wider context of Western culture. The sheer ferocity of the unholy war between the old and new economies has dispelled the dream of restoring our failed cities to their previous glory. They will never be as they once were, places where the exercise of economic power and control was plain for all to see. Europe's historical cities are now a memory of how we used to live: densely populated centres, abundant space for the new middle classes, and virtually unlimited room for expansion.

The conflicts in our society and cities need to be faced and we have to work with the materials available to us, without forgetting, in meanwhile, to look at nature, the sky, the wind and the stars. In all our projects we try to draw trajectories instead of restricting ourselves to a given context. Like city areas, our buildings are made to be walked through, not just looked at. They are meant to arouse emotional reactions, and there is no precise standpoint or preferred direction from which to view them. They are cinematographic rather than photogenic.

We also try to choose classic materials which, though common enough, become unconventional when "rediscovered" and put to new uses. One such material is tuff, an ancient volcanic stone discovered by the Etruscans which we used without mortar for cemetery in Orvieto, Italy. Another is the pre-varnished black zinc we used for the Media Library in Rezé, and the naturally-coloured zinc roofing of the large "wave" of housing in Candie Saint-Bernard, a stone's throw from the Bastille. There's also the pre-oxidised copper we used for the Arts Centre in Bordeaux, and the Corten steel of the large wings of the strange prehistoric animal at the entrance to the Musée des Graffiti in Niaux. As with Land Art, such buildings cannot be classified as either architecture or sculpture because they are both. In one of our early projects, the sports centre in Anagni, Italy, you can see the marks left by the formwork of the concrete, but these imperfections make it almost a precious material.

Generous use of colour is another essential feature of our projects at a time when the façades of European buildings are exclusively white, black or shades of grey.

In conclusion, we always strive to create unclassifiable architecture that is charged with tension from roof to foundations, constantly exploring and refining our initial ideas using the best resources and the latest software, not for innovation's sake but to arrive at optimum solutions that exceed our clients' expectations.

Speech given by Massimiliano Fuksas on the occasion of the recognition of the Honorary Fellowship of AIA (2002)

Excerpts from: Massimiliano Fuksas, Paolo Conti. *Caos Sublime*, Milan: Rizzoli 2009

Materials

Cinema, literature, geography

Geography

When I have to get to get down to work on a new project, and I might be feeling a bit down because I still haven't worked out a basic idea that seems plausible enough to fly with, the first thing I do is buy a copy of *National Geographic* and let myself be hypnotised by the woven bamboo of some remote Asian building. I always start by observing nature. A spectacular dawn, the undersea world, drifting clouds or erupting volcanoes might do the trick, to say nothing of a stream flowing through a rock desert where it merges with the blue of the sky and looks deeper or shallower depending on the light (my inspiration for the MyZeil building in Frankfurt). I've always painted and always will. A lot of my ideas about materials come from painting. I say painting, which is very different from drawing buildings. Even now, when universities ask me to give student lectures, I instinctively start painting.

At first there's only what I've done on canvas or paper. Then comes the next stage, which is the creation of a model. For example, if the starting-point is a parallelepiped, I might try splitting and puncturing it to produce empty space inside and out, and then see how what remains relates to what has been removed. I invariably subtract, rarely add. With the advent of computers and new technology, these two stages have grown to three. The use of virtual reality in architectural design is a revolution comparable to the discovery of perspective in painting. It's indispensable if you want to work on interiors even before the actual building has taken shape because it speeds everything up and gives you greater control over the operation as whole, leaving you more time to think.

Working on the Cloud section of the Congress Centre in the EUR district of Rome, we wore ourselves out trying to make a physical model for what we were doing. In the meantime, we went ahead with the inside of the Cloud on our computer screens. In situations like these, CAD is superior to physical material, i.e. models. However, the Cloud became increasingly virtual, while the virtual image increasingly became our model, and therefore reality. In the end, the project as a whole was a matter of superimposing virtuality on reality and vice versa. At a certain point I took hold of the model and made a hole in it with my hand, without realising that the programme was simultaneously telling is that we should create an opening exactly where I had just removed some material. And so, virtual reality and my own hands gave me the result I was looking for: a building that would breathe life into the city.

Reflections in water, cranes in the sky

Construction sites are both useful and beautiful

From project and construction site to construction site and end result. The dynamics of change. A glimpse of sky can be important.

A real project demands a construction site ready and willing to run with the changes that constantly need to be made. At least a third of the changes to an original design take place once the project becomes a construction site. Changes that can't be predicted or designed for are identified and dealt with straightaway. The whole idea of what a future building is changes when you compare the en result with the expected result.

As it develops and grows, a construction site bodies forth the "incompleteness" inherent in every human creation, architecture included.

"Incompleteness" keeps things fresh and alive, whereas "completeness" kills the ability to move on, project yourself into the future. The "completion" of a city spells the death of an urban agglomeration.

On a construction site you rediscover a project's raison d'être, the forces that brought it into existence. Sometimes, putting a roof on may be enough to cause a rethink of the project during the construction phase. At others it might be rusted iron, or rediscovery of the sky, or of open space before partition walls have been installed. A rainy day might leave puddles whose reflections suggest a new way of seeing of the building. A construction site is a splendid thing when something new happens every day. It's beastly, stale, repetitive when things just drag on, when nothing clicks, when the music fails to resonate. A piece of music may be wonderful in the mind of a musician but the notes have to be heard, they have to leave the instrument and resonate, body forth the music. A construction site, the place where projects are realised, is like a concert hall except that the rehearsals are always held in the same place where the performance, the realisation of the project, takes place. Construction is the most agreeable, most gratifying part of what we do. The construction site is the magic of building, and of a building.

Watching cranes at work as an antidote to tiredness and depression. The architect's presence. Being with site workers.

Without construction sites, any form of architecture or urban planning is, in effect, an incomplete statement, an act of deferral, a non-functional entity. A construction site can often be therapeutic and invigorating. When I'm worried about something, perhaps nothing to do with my work, when I just can't keep up with the pace and demands of life, when I get involved in arguments, I spend a couple of days on site because it restores my sense of reality. Moodiness turns into positive energy, which makes you feel you want to do things. It's like being purified, taking a swim in the Ganges.

Seeing cranes reminds me of the *power* of building. I forget everything: all the petty daily annoyances, the bureaucratic hassles, the misunderstandings with clients and the general public. The construction site brings you back what the project is really all about. I feel can express myself again, relish the joy of hard work.

When it's good, a building is always a kind of synthesis that sends you back to some notion of a utopia. It's a cultural synthesis in the broadest sense of something that enriches and enhances the meaning of "culture". Utopia can also mean that, a hundred years from now, someone will see your work and say what he would say when looking at a painting or watching a film: this was what that period was all about, this was their culture, this is what people dreamt of before our time.

Through architecture you can show, explain what things were like to the people who come after you. It may well be that your contemporaries, people rooted in your time, will understand less of your architecture than those who look at it in the future. This is a calculated risk you have to take.

Architecture always looks to the future, rarely to the present, never to the past. Examining, revisiting, reworking the past is sheer madness.
In a world of comforting certainties I live with uncertainties, which is why I hate "discipline".

A construction site is a place where the unexpected can happen.

Unexpectedness also applies to economics. Economists will tell you that today's global crisis was "unpredictable". Yet look where we are now. I recently quoted Edward Lorenz to Giulio Tremonti during a lecture at the Aspen Institute. I sent him a note saying that the current global economic crisis was as unpredictable as bad weather.

New materials we dream of before they exist

Architects don't know what the materials of the future will be. Our desires are younger than we are. It's like cars: our technological ideas are highly advance yet we use tons of scrap metal to move just one human being. The car is an antiquated, cumbersome, polluting means of transport. Positively ancient, in fact. So there's a contradiction: on the one hand, the new architecture we're all imagining, mainly thanks to virtual reality; on the other, "postulated" materials that aren't available yet for the simple reason that they don't exist.

Many of my projects postulate the use of an aqueous, liquid material. On a computer screen the Cloud looks like a jelly-fish. Today's best material – soft, liquid, translucent, almost transparent – is used in space research to test new forms of habitation and cohabitation, new kinds of clothing, new ways of doing things. All this shows that there's a vast number of materials that still haven't become a part of our lives now, but certainly will in the future.

Many tastes have grown obsolete. Opaque walls, masonry, are on the way out. Today we all want to bring as much light as possible into enclosed spaces, regardless of latitude, and this is giving rise to a contradiction. To save energy, especially in heating and air-conditioning, we need highly efficient insulation. But what does an ordinary person basically want from a house? Lots of space, and lots of windows to see the world through and capture more light. This poses major problems in climates that are too hot or too cold.

As well as stone, other materials are having a hard time of it at the moment, at least in architecture. Steel, as we have understood and used for many years, and even brick, except that now it's "reused", "readapted", reorganised". We use it as we use stone: if stone is visible at all it's no longer the oppressive mass it once was, but a subtle way to set off a glass wall.

The inexorable growth of cities

Megalopolis, metropolis, countryside

Tokyo, a city that hasn't devoured itself

The great urban planner Kazuo Shinohara showed in the 1970s that Tokyo is a form of progressive anarchy. Anarchy not as chaos but as a kind of "sublime order".

In today's Tokyo young managers spend the whole day working in skyscrapers then return in the evening to their roots, the grids of streets and alleyways in the old quarters, where they go to ground in rooms tucked away in low-rise, often derelict buildings. Washing lines festoon the streets, thick bundles of overhead electric cables obscure the sky. Such disorder, contradiction, lack of geometry can't be obliterated at a stroke, not unless you adopt the kind of authoritarian solution you see in Beijing and other big Chinese cities, where a centuries-old architectural culture has been bulldozed away. Tokyo is chaos, and that chaos is sublime because it's the natural way to lay out buildings. There's no plan, no project.

Tokyo is more interesting than New York, which until now most people have unconsciously thought of as the prototype of the modern city. The truth is that New York is now a historical city where modernity is an accepted part of the scene.

Tokyo has instinctively given itself two structures. On the one hand, there are skyscrapers and office buildings, an often multipurpose verticality in the sense that on one floor there might be offices, on another a museum, and on another a handful of apartments. On the other, there is tradition, low-rise housing, the kind of tumbledown dwellings you might see in a southern Italian town after an earthquake. Some areas look very like the Magliana district of Rome.

Far from bursting at the seams after opting for the vertical-horizontal planning model, Tokyo has actually improved. Tokyo-dwellers seem to have rediscovered the pleasures of neighbourhood life in their attachment to their sushi bars, nightspots and theatres. The complexity of a megalopolis has been sorted out without summoning the help of one of those presumptuous "healers" who fly in, take a look around and decide to adopt a plan, invent rules, fix the unfixable.

In Tokyo as in many other cities, no-one is interested in the quality of the architecture. Nearly all the skyscrapers and tower blocks are ugly, but the visual stratification and conflict doesn't make people unhappy. On the contrary, Tokyo works as a city because people are happy there, unlike so many of the designer cities created by one or other of today's urban-planning geniuses. With its soaring, often ugly skyscrapers, Tokyo is the clearest demonstration that people can live happily without the likes of *auteur* architects, genius architects or demiurge architects, as we have romantically dubbed them up to now.

This horizontal-vertical model was the inspiration for my twin-towers project in Vienna. I went 30 metres underground then came back up, situating car parks, cinemas, restaurants, shops and offices along the way. We tried to bring together in a single place the things that most people's public and private lives are made of. Personally I'd also have included private housing, especially on the upper floors, but people haven't got round to that way of thinking yet. Le Corbusier is at the bottom of it all: save as much space as you can, make as much use as you can of a single area.

To impose is to destroy

Against imposed solutions and the mythology of the horrible term “archistar” (and whoever invented it)

Ugliness and beauty are difficult to define and difficult to tell apart.

Who decides what’s ugly and what’s beautiful? Who can “objectively” tell them apart? Paul Virilio (who summoned me to the École Spéciale d’Architecture in Paris, where we taught together) used to ask his students to do a beautiful school project. Then he would say: “Now do me an ugly one.” Finally he would ask: “Which is really more beautiful, this one or that one?”

What is beauty? Whatever interests or intrigues you. Beauty in the classical sense has now been internalised and to an extent eliminated. So we need to abandon that approach and concern ourselves with something different .

We need to abandon “beauty” and style” and think instead about the future. However, there’s no guarantee that things will turn out the right way, no certainty that the outcome will be great architecture. But the outcome is no less uncertain for today’s opportunists. Today is already too late to be thinking about the future. The journey is much more important than the destination. As Kavafis says in *Journey to Ithaca*, Ulysses’ journey home is much more important than actually arriving there.

Patron fare thee well

The problem with clients

A personal call and a rare personal commission

One day Giuseppe Nardini called me up with a personal commission. He was seventy-eight at the time.

I don't go looking for work from private clients, it's they who call me and if the project looks interesting I do it.

Nardini said he had no brief, no specific request to make, not even a definite budget to work with. "My family has worked at the distillery here in Bassano del Grappa for two hundred years and we'd like to treat ourselves to one of your projects, something architectural, something that bears your mark."

It all seemed ridiculous. We ate out in Rome. He showed me photos of the place. It was full of trees, a wonderful forest of American oaks planted by the great landscape architect Pietro Porcinai. I drew something with a felt-pen on a restaurant plate: two bubbles floating among the trees, a lift leading down into the earth, a water pool at ground level, a theatre. The result was a piece of architecture that helped Bassano del Grappa to find its modern identity.

Visitors go there now for the arts events and ballet performances in the two glass bubbles. Not a single tree was cut down. A dream come true for the townspeople thanks to a bold, intelligent, freethinking client.

Conclusions

(that aren't)

Live for your work

I love what I do, I couldn't live any other way. Sometimes I'm even amazed that people pay me to do what I love doing.
There's no lack of stimuli at the present moment. The whole world, at its best and worst, is your oyster

Some quick suggestions for students and young people (architects or otherwise)

Young architects often write to me. Lots of them, in fact. Reading their letters I see courage, frustration, denial of opportunity.
There are no does and don'ts. It's more a question of alchemy.

Choose the path of most resistance. Don't think about the past, except to study and forget about it. We can't carry the burden of history around with us, and we can't assume it would be good for us even if we did.

Think briefly about the present and then devote all your energy to the future
Keep reality constantly in your sights, Stay alert, use your eyes and intelligence, be curious.

Make what is happening outside architecture your main concern. Be ready to seize on ideas and steal them, but never, never copy: theft is allowed in fields other than architecture. It's morally acceptable to steal a vibration, a reflection of light, a way things are grouped. In such cases, an architect would define stealing as being able to see something not through your own eyes but through those of people who don't do your job.
So design something not as it is in itself, but as you interpret it.

Always remember that beyond your projects, your obsession with getting things right, there's a whole world of disasters and conflict where life is harder and realer.
A true architect, a true urban-planner can't remain aloof from the turmoil of life.
You have to take the plunge.

Building

PALATINO CENTRE
TURIN, ITALY
1998–2011

Client
City of Turin

Architects
Massimiliano and Doriana Fuksas

Area
Built surface: 13.000 m²

Contractor
Imp. La Sorgente

Lighting
Lamp "Lavinia" - iGuzzini
(design by Doriana &
Massimiliano Fuksas)

Facade
Focchi Group S.p.A. – Rimini
Façade elements: 60,000 glass
elements and 150,000 kg of steel;
Façade surfaces: around 2000 m²

Engineering
AI ENGINEERING s.r.l. - Turin

Artistic intervention
Mimmo Paladino

The Palatino Centre is in the Porta Palazzo district of Turin, one of the city's oldest areas. Studio Fuksas won the 1998 open international competition for a shopping mall on the site of the now-demolished covered clothing market, as part of a plan to revitalise the entire Porta Palazzo district.

The new five-storey building has two underground levels, one for parking, the other for technological plant, and three upper levels, two for retail and the third entirely for catering venues.

The 4700 sq.m car park accommodates 110 vehicles on three levels. A wall separates the parking area from the archaeological site where two underground ice-houses are being excavated.

The main entrance is at ground level on the south-east side of the building near the crossroads between Via Giulio Cesare and Via Regina Margherita.
Retail is located around the perimeter of the building so as to create a central court above the two 18th-century ice-houses.

The usable ground-floor area has been trimmed to fit the outline of archaeological site below, which can be viewed from above thanks to the wall separating them from the rest of the parking level. The central court is syntaxed by 11 multi-level prismatic pillars, each 13 m high, fitted with embedded metal brackets to support the three metal bridges that connect the various floors.

The first floor has the same layout as the ground floor with perimeter retail areas – shops, bars and a retailers' service facility in the south-west corner – accessible by a circular balcony and a system of ramps that crisscross the central void, connecting the various floors as far as the roof.

The top floor is occupied by the restaurant with a viewing terrace overlooking part of the old city centre and, in the distance, landmark buildings like the Mole Antonelliana and Guarini Chapel.

The zinc-clad metal roof reproduces the cut-out design of the ground-floor plaza and circulation, allowing natural light into the interior through vertical and horizontal glazing.

The double external façade consists of horizontal glass modules, each with a different strip pattern, supported by pairs of C-section steel uprights. In the basement areas the glass layers are gradually replaced by steel ones. The cavity space between the glass double façade and the masonry wall accommodates the emergency stairs. At night the illuminated cavity space makes the centre shine like an Aladdin's lamp.

SUPER
IMMOBILIARE
Gastone
GENZIA

AGENZIA
VIAGGI

LYON CONFLUENCE
LYON, FRANCE
2005–2010

Client
Bouwfonds Marignan Immobilier

Architects
Massimiliano and Doriana Fuksas

Masterplan
Massimiliano Fuksas
HTVS
Clement Vergely
Enzo Amantea

Contractors
Inox facades: Raimond
Aluminium facades: Acem
Reinforced concrete: Lamy, Eab
Frames: Mbe, PrincepsRaimond

Structures
MARTIN
CETIS
ARCADIS

Engineering
BERGA
PRELEM

HQE
Terao

Area
Residences: 28,955 sq. m.
Commerce: 1,807 sq. m.

Quite apart from the major infrastructures planned for the site, the Lyon Confluence is first and foremost a place of great intrinsic appeal in a beautiful natural setting, with the green hill of Sainte-Foy behind, the Rhône and Saône on either side, and the old centre of Lyon, steeped in history, a short distance away.

The project began with a feasibility study for the construction of a residential complex around two large, interconnecting empty spaces – the park and the old river port area – which form the backbone of the project. In deciding where to position the buildings, priority was given to longitudinal flow through the park to the dock. A secondary configuration of empty spaces between the buildings forms the heart of the complex. The central area was left open on the west side facing the hill, and since the empty spaces between the buildings are never aligned, they generate multiple lines of sight towards the park and port. All the buildings occupy interstices where light from the empty spaces picks out the solids and voids. In the constant play of light on the buildings' shimmering surfaces, rotations and distortions of volume create blocks of material resembling habitable sculptures.

The buildings in the old port are literal and poetical renderings of dockside cranes and containers, a reminder that the area was once a fully operational river port. The result is piece of city whose colours and materials are mirrored in the water, creating a multitude of reflections and vibrations.
The volumes of the building that closes off the park in the direction of Rue Denuzière open like a chest-of-drawers towards the warm western sun and the green hill of Sainte-Foy.
Everything plays a part the bustling life of the ever-changing city, responsive to the shimmering light that hides, highlights and changes the aspect of the different buildings.

bouwfonds marignan

A LOUER
04 72 75 40 40

ADMIRANT ENTRANCE BUILDING
EINDHOVEN, THE NETHERLANDS
2003–2010

Client
Rond de Admirant CV

Architects
Massimiliano and Doriana Fuksas

Contractor
Heijmans Bouw

Area
3,000 sq.m

Engineering
Realization of the covering:
Waagner Biro Stahlbau AG, Wien

Structures:
Knippers-Helbig Beratende Ingenieure, Stuttgart

Studio Fuksas has developed four of the projects envisaged in the 1998 masterplan (1998) for the centre of Eindhoven in the Netherlands:

— 18-Septemberplein, a 7000 sq.m city square with a 2300 sq.m underground parking lot for 1700 bicycles
— The Piazza Shopping Mall of approximately 20,000 sq.m with 6000 sq.m of office space;
— The Media Markt electrical goods and electronics store
— The **Admirant Entrance Building**.

The focal point of the masterplan is the 18-Septemberplein and its surrounding buildings, which form Eindhoven's commercial hub.
Taken together, the four projects have proved highly successful in revitalising the city centre.

The **Admirant Entrance Building** is part of a shopping district built by Heijmans Real Estate, a prominent Dutch property developer. It straddles the border between the new precinct and the 18-Septemberplein, forming the main gateway to the new commercial hub. Such prominent positioning called for an iconic building, and the Admirant Entrance Building is exactly that. It attracts the eye like a precious jewel, drawing passers-by into the heart of the new district.

The design process was a long quest to find exactly the right form, and the outcome was an "unexpected" building in which conventional design rules lose their meaning.
Compared with its the immediate surroundings, at first glance the new building looks like some amorphous organic object. Silhouetted between the façades of the other buildings, it resembles an unidentified celestial body that has plummeted to earth, where it has remained frozen in the ground.

On closer inspection, however, it seems full of movement, as if sliding away in different directions at different speeds. Its contrasting façade materials – crystalline navy-blue glass and matt white panels – also help to create this impression. Alternating transparent and opaque surfaces flow smoothly into and around each other.

The building has two components: a 5-storey concrete structure and a glass and steel envelope. Shops are located on the ground and first levels, with offices on levels three and four, and technical plant on the extra fifth level.
The façade geometry, a mixture of vertical surfaces and amorphous shapes, generates the internal dynamics of the building. The floors, whose shapes are also determined by the shape of the façade, taper from 950 sq.m at ground level to 250 sq.m. on level four. Apart from the stairwell, there are no vertical barriers to sightlines inside the building.
Due to its non-orthogonal shape, the Admirant is also a non-directional building, a dynamic flow of smooth, rounded curves with no front or back. The glass and steel envelope reveals itself in a continuous process of discovery. Seen from a certain distance, the building appears to rotate. Like some marine mammal rising to the surface, it shows itself for a brief moment before sinking into the depths again.

DE ADMIRANT

TE HUIR KANTOOR
V&D
heijmans
BUS

PHILIPS
USINE
USINE
Alle richtingen

USINE

Grolsch
McDonalds
SISSY-BOY

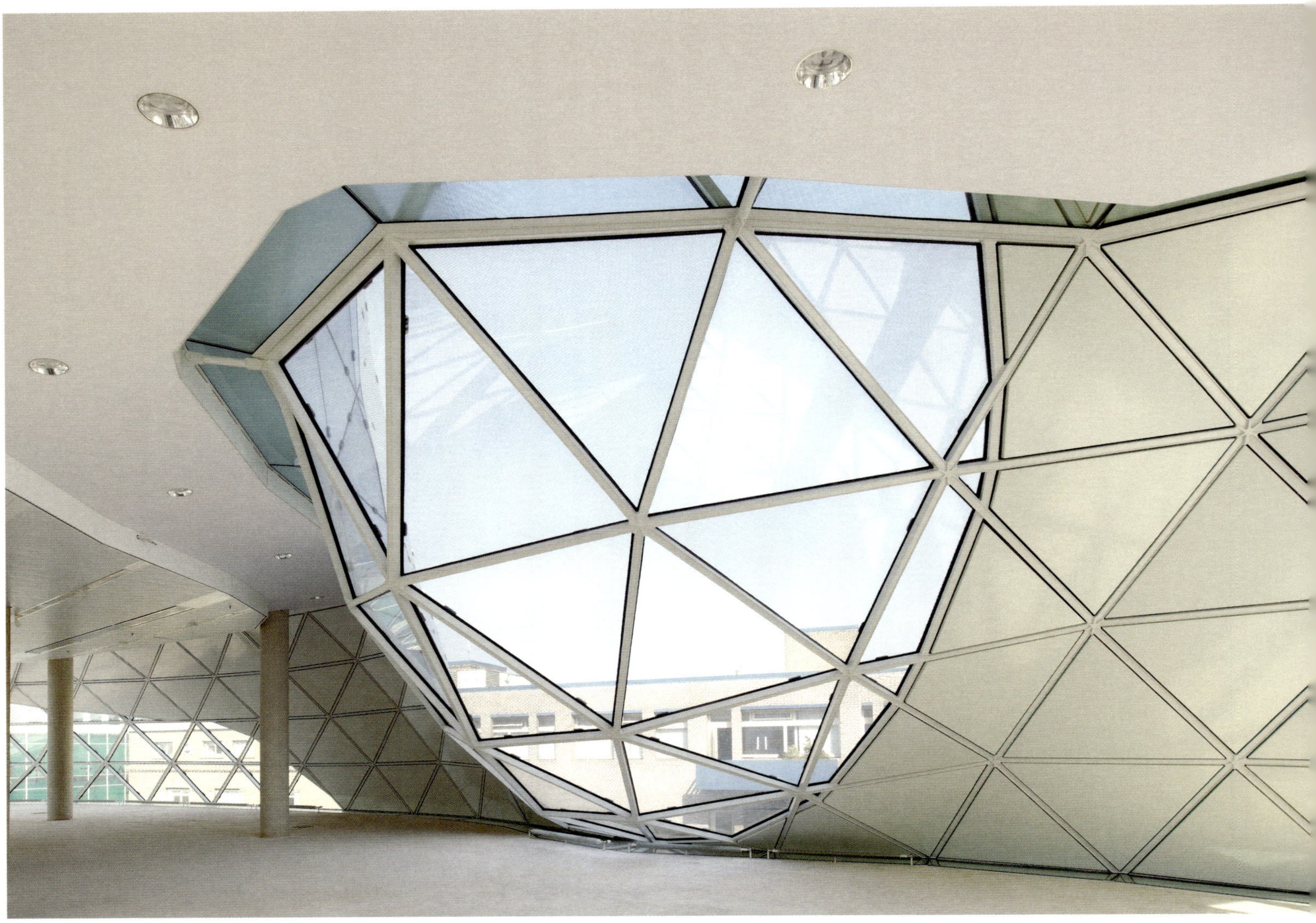

PIAZZA
PIAZZA
PIAZZA
Emmasingel

PERES PEACE HOUSE
JAFFA, TEL AVIV, ISRAEL
1999–2009

Client
Peres Center For Peace

Architects
Massimiliano and Doriana Fuksas

Local Architect
Yoav Messer Architects Ltd

Landscape
TeMA, Tel Aviv

Interior Design
Fuksas Design

Engineering
Rokach-Ashkenazi - Engineer, Consultant Ltd

Structures contractor
Kal-Binian Ltd

Engineering contractor
Rom Geves Ltd

Area
7,000 Sq. m

Total Floor Area
2,500 Sq. m

A home port for all sailors and a haven for the shipwrecked.

To imagine a place that is not virtual but real, a place dedicated to peace, is a difficult undertaking of profound ethical significance.

Peace is a spiritual state, an aspiration, yearning and utopia. The projection of will into the future is also the hope that our children, generations to come, will live in a better world.
Being a universal value, peace doesn't come ready-packaged. It is the longing for fullness and peace of mind that a place or a building can communicate.

I thought of stratification, a structure that might represent time and patience in strata of alternating materials representing places that have suffered heavily. A stone base to raise the building above the meeting place also seemed necessary. From the slightly sunken plaza, two long ramps lead to a place of rest, a sunlit well whose size and height help us to forget the troubles of the world, instilling in us the positive attitude that meeting other human beings requires. The façade forms sedimented layers of translucent glass and green concrete composed of alternating, superimposed mixtures of sand and aggregate. The glass filters light through to the inside during the day and sends it back outside at night, a magical image conveying the spiritual and worldly message the site is intended to evoke.
If it is to work, a building must offer us aid and succour as we come to grips with the world's problems. This building seeks to be a place for meeting and dialogue.

בית פרס לשלום
بيت بيرس السلام

ST. PAOLO CHURCH
FOLIGNO, ITALY
2001–2009

Client
Conferenza Episcopale Italiana – Diocesi di Foligno

Architects
Massimiliano and Doriana Fuksas

Interior Design
Fuksas Design for iGuzzini

Contractor
Ediltecnica SpA, Foligno

Area
1,300 sq.m

Intervention Area
20,690 sq.m

Structures and engineering
AI Engineering s.r.l.,Torino;
Engineer Gilberto Sarti, Rimini

Artistic interventions
Enzo Cucchi
Mimmo Paladino

"One volume suspended inside another. Sky visible through concrete from the outside, on the inside and on the outside."
Massimiliano Fuksas

This project, which dates from 2001, won the national competition organised by the Italian Episcopal Conference to attract designs for new churches and parish centres. In its deliberation, the jury panel described it as "a bold, original statement that incorporates the latest findings of anti-seismic research worldwide, making it a symbol of the town's post-earthquake renascence."

The complex has two main buildings, both of which perform key religious functions. The first, the church proper, is a perfect double monolith, a cube within a cube, measuring 30 x 22.5 x h25 m on the outside. The second is a long two-storey parallelepiped that houses the vestry, parish facilities and offices, and the rectory. The two main buildings are both joined and separated by a bridge-like glass corridor that also serves as a weekday chapel. Inside the church, spirituality and quiet prayer become one as natural light streams sideways and from above to illuminate the altar, ambo and baptismal font.

The massive church building standing 1.5 m above grade level is reached by crossing the parvis, a long walkway leading to the entrance where it forms a clean horizontal cut, a strip of light that interacts with the outside to offset the otherwise windowless front elevation.
The interior furnishings and fittings, custom-made by local craftsmen, alter perceptions of the religious artwork. Outside, Enzo Cucchi's monumental *Stele-Croce* (Stele-Cross) sculpture made of concrete and white Carrara marble stands 13.5 metres tall and is an architectural feature in its own right.

Artist Mimmo Paladino created the 14 stations of the Via Crucis.

MYZEIL
FRANKFURT AM MAIN, GERMANY
2002–2009

Client
PalaisQuartier GmBH & CO., UK

Architects
Massimiliano and Doriana Fuksas

Interior Design
Fuksas Design

Surface
Built surface: 77,000 sq.m.
Façade: 8,500 sq.m.
Cover: 13,000 sq.m.

Engineering
Realization of the façade and covering:
Waagner Biro Stahlbau AG, Wien

Structures:
Knippers-Helbig Beratende Ingenieure, Stuttgart; Krebs und Kiefer Beratende Ingenieure für das Bauwesen GmbH, Darmstadt

The MyZeil building is located halfway along Haupteinkaufsstrasse, Frankfurt's main shopping street. The brief envisaged the construction on a 105,000 sq.m. site of a building containing a shopping mall, a film theatre, a fitness centre and a hotel, plus meeting rooms, offices and parking. Its many functions affect not just the main features of the design but also the logistics, opening hours and subdivisions of the building. The complexity of the structure meant that one access level wouldn't be enough, so we provided another on the fourth floor.

The retail area is located between these two levels, while the film theatre, sports centre and restaurants are on the fourth floor, making it the reference point for all the entertainment facilities and the main level of the building. The structure is a fluid form connecting the Zeil, an important shopping street, to the Thurn und Taxis Palais (a Baroque palace destroyed in the war and subsequently rebuilt). People never stay on the ground floor: upon entering the building, they find fluid pathways that ease circulation. A sequence of voids between the six floors lets natural light into the interior, creating a pleasant ambience.

All this means that MyZeil can function 24 hours-a-day, not only for shopping (even though there are more than 100 shops) but also for leisure activities, meeting friends, watching a movie, etc. It's a nice place to be in, especially when it's cold and snowing outside. The building's two sections, one along the Zeil, the other facing the Thurn und Taxis Palais, are characterised in different ways. The Zeil façade conveys a sense of leisure, entertainment and relaxation. The other façade is where the entrances to the hotel and offices are located. The hotel lobby is near the art gallery and the big-brand shops in the mall, and the hotel rooms are accessed by lifts. The conference centre and sports facilities are on the third and fourth floors.

The main entrance to the offices (27.5 m high) on Neue Eisenheimerstrasse has lifts to the upper floors. The fourth floor also plays a key role as the hub leading to the offices. There are also reception points leading to roof areas open to the general public. Considering the vast number of people working here, they form another attractive public area. A glass-and-steel translucent skin envelops and shapes the entire building.

possible

MyZeil
RENO

comma

ARMANI FIFTH AVENUE
NYC, USA
2007–2009

Client
Gruppo Giorgio Armani

Architects
Doriana and Massimiliano Fuksas

Address
5th Avenue - 56th Street, NYC

Interior design
Fuksas Design

Contractor
Americon Construction Inc.

Area
2,800 sq. m.

Lighting
Speirs & Major Associates

Engineering
Engineer Gilberto Sarti

Armani/Fifth Avenue in New York completes the trilogy of Armani concept stores designed by Doriana and Massimiliano Fuksas. The other two are Armani/Chater House in Hong Kong, and Armani/Ginza Tower in Tokyo.

Situated in midtown Manhattan in one of the world's best-known streets, the store occupies the first three floors of two buildings on 5th Avenue and 56th Street.

The four-level showroom (there is also a basement level) is a single, fluid, intercommunicating space held together by the impact of the staircase, the heart of the building, which connects the first (ground), second and third levels. Made of rolled calendar steel coated in plastic to enhance its sculptural effect, it is totally free-standing structure that defies any simple geometrical description, a swirling vortex of bands that barely touch each floor as they glide over the vertical surface of the interior, thwarting any attempt to define their geometry and statics.

The general layout of each floor is an ever-changing pattern of curved surfaces that add visual interest to the light, putty-coloured walls.
Nothing remains unaffected by this interior movement, not even the external façade. Though aligned with the rigid Manhattan grid, it simulates the building's internal movement in images and colours projected onto a LED curtain. As well as being an external projection of internal space, the façade pays a special tribute to New York City, the yardstick of modernity and dynamism that all architects have to reckon with.

The internal space is made fluid by continuous wall bands faced with monochrome lacquered wood panels. The different radii of each wall curve create bends and twists where products can be displayed. In some places they accommodate fitting-rooms and VIP lounges; in others, staff areas, cash desks and special product locations such as Armani Dolci. Special attention has been paid to the lighting, which defines and emphasises the curvature of the walls and spaces, and locates functions within the general layout.

The movement of the staircase is evident in every aspect of the interior design, from floor and wall display units to desks and armchairs, which mirrors, enhances and becomes part of the same vortex. The layout and circulation implied by the staircase are equally fluid. Glossy walls and furnishings are offset by black ceilings and black marble floors.

Similarly, the apparent simplicity of the interior is offset by the otherworldliness of the Armani/Ristorante heralded by the elevator entrance's curved bronze panels whose colours and reflections are foretaste of things to come. Sunken floor lights draw attention to the sensual curvature of the wall leading to restaurant, where colours and the materials, though the same as in the rest of the store, are put to different use to create a more relaxed, recreational ambience. The restaurant has stunning views of 5th Avenue and Central Park beyond, filtered through an amber haze.

ARMANI/5th AVENUE

ARMANI JEANS
GIORGIO ARMANI
DON'T BLOCK THE BOX
EMPORIO ARMANI

DON'T BLOCK THE BOX
FINE +2 POINTS
ONE WAY
OMEGA

EXIT

MECHANIC

EXIT

MAINZ MARKTHÄUSER 11-13
MAINZ, GERMANY
2003–2008

Client
Wohnbau Mainz GmbH

Architects
Massimiliano and Doriana Fuksas

CONSULTING
Competition
Structures: Knippers Helbig beratende Ingenieure
Plans: HL-Technik, Hr. Daniels
Engineering: HHP-Berlin, Hr. Foth

Project
Façade structures: Knippers Helbig beratende Ingenieure
Structures: Baucon beratende Ingenieure
Plans: HL-PP Consult
Engineering: IBB Lorenz
Electrical Services: b.i.g. Bechtold Ing.

Area
9,000 sq.m

The building is located in the centre of Mainz. Its new façade overlooks the traffic-free Rebstockplatz market square and the existing one the landmark Mainzer Dom (Mainz Cathedral) dating from the 10th century. Alongside there is a shopping centre built in 1970.
Like many other European city centres, this important location was compromised by hasty post-war reconstruction in the mid 20th century. Nothing is authentic – even the historical buildings are almost all reconstructions. However, many feel that everything should remain as it "was", an eclectic mix that has become synonymous with the beauty of the city centre.

"The most important issue for me," says Fuksas, "was to create a building with a sense of history, but with no rhetoric. I didn't want to design a new old building."

Though, as requested, Fuksas used the pitched roof design typical of the region to restore the façade overlooking the market square, he also added a surprising new feature, an external cladding layer. This white laminated ceramic skin, with its irregular pattern of windows and openings, envelops almost the entire structure but leaves the part of the old front façade where the cafeteria is located open to view, providing an attractive solution at the rear where the offices are located.
The dazzling translucence of the polished glazed surface, and the gap between the external layer and the building underneath, makes this a cutting-edge contemporary building. Fuksas compares the light at different times of day and as the weather changes to "musical composition", where surprise plays a fundamental role.

Inside the Mainz building there is a soaring vertical space. On entering, visitors find themselves in a full-height five-storey atrium, a small vertical plaza connecting the various functions.
Tall white columns draw the eye upwards, creating visual linkage between the different levels.
This open space helps to relate the site to the surrounding pedestrian area of small, interconnected squares leading to the Rhine.
The top-floor apartments all have balconies and terraces overlooking the city and the Cathedral.

The "Piazzetta"
The existing "historical" facade and the new Rebstockplatz façade carry over to the walls of an inner courtyard open to the sky though protected from the elements, a semi-open space extending from the basement to the third level, with terraces and access levels to offices and apartments along the way.
The Piazzetta provides core linkage between the building's individual functions, a role emphasised by the soaring, sculpture-like white columns that carry the eye upwards through the various levels.
All the ground-floor areas, including retail and services, are accessible to pedestrians from the market square and the two side streets. An escalator in the atrium leads to the shops in the basement.

ZENITH MUSIC HALL (6.000–8.000 SEATS) AMIENS, FRANCE 2003–2008

Client
Communauté d'Agglomération Amiens Métropole

Architects
Massimiliano and Doriana Fuksas

Interior Design
Fuksas Design

Structures and engineering
Betom

Scenography
Jacques Moyal

Acoustics
Altia

Area
11.100 sq.m

The building is single, autonomous sculpture that groups all the functions specified in the brief under one roof.

Here the Zenith concept of jaunty, cutting-edge entertainment venues has generated a massive structure whose concrete and steel frame contrasts with the lightness of a red PVC membrane stretched across giant elliptical rings.

The roof beneath the entertainment hall is a set of perforated hemispheres that provide heat and sound insulation.

The entire building is wrapped in polyester fabric coated with PVC on both sides which bathes the hall and public spaces in soft red light.

The 6000-seat hall also has standing room for up to 2000 people, bringing its total capacity to 8000. Special care was taken when designing the transitional spaces where young concert-goers experience the building for the first time. The lighting was also designed to create constantly-changing moods and atmosphere.

The Amiens Zenith is the first of two Zeniths designed by Studio Fuksas. The Strasbourg Zenith develops on the original Amiens concept.

ZENITH MUSIC HALL
(10.000–12.000 SEATS) STRASBOURG, FRANCE 2003–2008

Client
Communauté Urbaine
de Strasbourg

Architects
Massimiliano and Doriana Fuksas

General contractor
Pertury Construction

Area
14,000 sq.m

Consulting
Structures and engineering: Betom
Scenography: Architecture
et Technique
Acoustics: Altia
Illuminating engineering: Pixelum

Reinforced concrete and
metallic structures of the foyer:
Simon & Christiansen
Metallic structures of the hall:
Zwahlen & Mayr SA
Textile structure: Form TL
Wrapping and laying of the toile:
Canobbio

Making of the ATEX 5000 TRIAL toile
and façade wrapping: Interglas

Located outside Strasbourg in a sparsely-built area between the suburbs and city centre, Zenith Strasbourg is a concert hall for what sophisticates would call "uncultured" music. With its 10-12,000 capacity, it is a shrine for hip-hop music and other events tailored to the tastes of people who live outside the city centre. Or, to put it another way, the aim was to create a home-from-home for new suburban cultures and multi-ethnic languages. Zenith Strasbourg throbs with the languages and dialects of Strasbourg's outsiders and outcasts, but it also belongs to the concert-going multitudes who follow top bands and entertainment events across Europe. Its semi-circular space brings people together, imbuing entertainment-hungry audiences with a single body and soul.
Zenith Strasbourg is the biggest concert venue in France, and the Zenith concert-hall concept has now spawned the Zenith recording label.

This strange orange object come to earth in a flat landscape looks more like a sculpture (or signal) than a music and entertainment venue. Moving out from the centre, beyond the tiers concrete, you come to an interstitial space proclaiming that the outside world lies beyond. The orange fabric coated on both sides with fibreglass and silicon is both a transitional space and a filter between the 20 m high, steel-framed foyer and the exterior. The opaque sculpture with its eye-catching ellipsoidal folds becomes almost transparent at night, a jack-o'-lantern shining bright as darkness descends on the non-places all around. Let the party begin.

The building's geometry was achieved by layering and rotating the ellipsoidal façade structure to product a dynamic shape with multiple viewpoints.
Endless things could be said about the exterior because it can be perceived in endless ways.
The edge of the spectacular roof descends in an asymmetrical oval movement. The foyer, where people gather before joining in the rituals of light, sound and noise on stage, also hosts meetings and events. Zenith Strasbourg has impressive stage machinery, as can be seen from the roof structure of trusses 4-6 m in height and up to 110 m in length, radiating from a bouquet-like central hub, which facilitate the technological functioning of the stage apparatus.

23
porte
21

DE CECCO OPERATIONAL HEADQUARTERS
PESCARA, ITALY
2001–2008

Client
De Cecco S.p.a.

Architects
Massimiliano and Doriana Fuksas

Area
6,300 sq. m.

Built area
Operational Headquarters:
11.000 sq.m.
Underground parking: 200 spaces
Building height: 39,94 m

Consulting
General coordination and safety, engineering and space planning:
Progetto CMR, Milan
Structures: Studio Engineer Toniolo, Sirmione (BS)

The De Cecco headquarters building is an architectural landmark in a heavily built-up area. Effectively two buildings in one, its visually distinct lower and upper sections are connected by staircases and lifts. Full-height glazing on each level of the cube-shaped lower section hollows out the façades, reducing the sense of weight and bulk. In complete contrast with the horizontal lines of its counterpart below, the circular upper section, where the management offices are located, has an unusual squashed-ring shape that makes it a landmark on the city skyline.

The two-fold nature of the composition is reflected in differences of structure, technology and functions. The lower load-bearing structure is a framework of steel-clad concrete pillars and columns, while the upper structure is supported by tubular steel tripods, and geometry and structure are enhanced by a double-shell façade of reflecting triangles. One interesting technological detail is that the glass panes are fitted on the inside of the steel lattice.

The gap between the two buildings, above the sixth storey of the lower section, gives a strong sense of physical separation. A water pool traversed by wooden footbridges is let into the floor, which has large circular apertures serving as skylights, a motif repeated on lower floors so that natural light penetrates right through the interior. The layout creates upward, downward and crossways sightlines at differing heights, which greatly contributes to workplace well-being. Outside walks and terraces provide a variety of recreational areas.

Being modular in design, the internal layout is flexible and easy to change round. Partitions mark out the space between load-bearing walls, while the bathrooms, lifts, stairs and light-wells are all concentrated in a central nucleus. The two sections are connected by this vertical circulation shaft: while the lower building's horizontal communication runs parallel to the central nucleus, the rooms in the upper building fan off a corridor that forms an inner circle concentric to the perimeter.

NEW TRADE FAIR
RHO-PERO, MILAN, ITALY
2002–2005

Client
Fondazione Fiera Milano

Architects
Massimiliano Fuksas

Designer and Art Director
Doriana O. Mandrelli

Lighting
Lampada Lavinia - iGuzzini, (design by Doriana & Massimiliano Fuksas)

General Contractor
Astaldi SpA, Vianini SpA, Pizzarotti SpA

Area
2,000,000 sq. m.

Built area
1.000.000 sqm

Steel structure
Icom Engineering, Ask Romein, Carpentieri d'Italia

Roof
Bemo Systems

Curtain walls
Permasteelisa SpA

Parkings
Visitors: 20,050
Lorries: 7,000
Exhibitors: 4,320

Length of central axis
1.500 m

Number of pavilions
8

Exhibition area
Over 400,000 sq. m.

Outdoor exhibition area
60,000 sq. m.

Conference center
47,000 sq. m.

Conference rooms
80

Central axis veil
Structural design: Mero GmbH & Co.
Structural consulting: Schlaich Bergermann und Partner

Logo service centre
Structural design: Schlaich Bergermann und Partner

With its 5 km perimeter and approximately 1 million sq.m of built area on a site of 2 million sq.m, Fiera Milano's new out-of-town exhibition centre is certainly an impressive affair. Its eight single- and two-storey halls provide gross indoor exhibition area of approximately 345,000 sq.m, plus 60,000 sq.m outdoors.

A covered concourse extending along the axis joining the main east and west entrances groups all the site's internal entrances and exits. Set among water pools, trees and stretches of epoxy resin flooring, the buildings along the concourse include a multiservice service centre, bars, cafés and restaurants, offices, hotels, a shopping arcade, smaller exhibition areas and reception facilities for the main halls. The imposing glass and polished stainless steel façades of the halls form an appropriately theatrical backdrop.

The entire concourse lies beneath a billowing glass roof ("The Sail") whose constantly changing levels form what appear to be craters, waves, dunes, hills and other natural features mirroring the nearby Alps. 1500 m long and 32 m wide with a covered area of 47,000 sq.m, this breath-taking spinal column is the landmark feature of the project.
However, this is more than just architecture designed to do business in. The exhibition centre finds its natural extension as a communication hub and forum for ideas in a purpose-built conference centre with ten halls totalling 2600 seats, and an adjacent multiservice centre at the mid-point of the sail roof.

Finally, the northwest halls stand in 9 hectares of parkland with a green corridor running across the site to another park to the south, forming a recreational area of approximately 180,000 sq.m.

7 G

7E
7D

Piano Floor
3
Vip Club
Sale Riunioni
Piano Floor
2
Self Service
Sale Riunioni
Meeting Rooms
Piano Floor
1
Area Relax
Relax Area
Caffè

28
VESTIAIRE
29

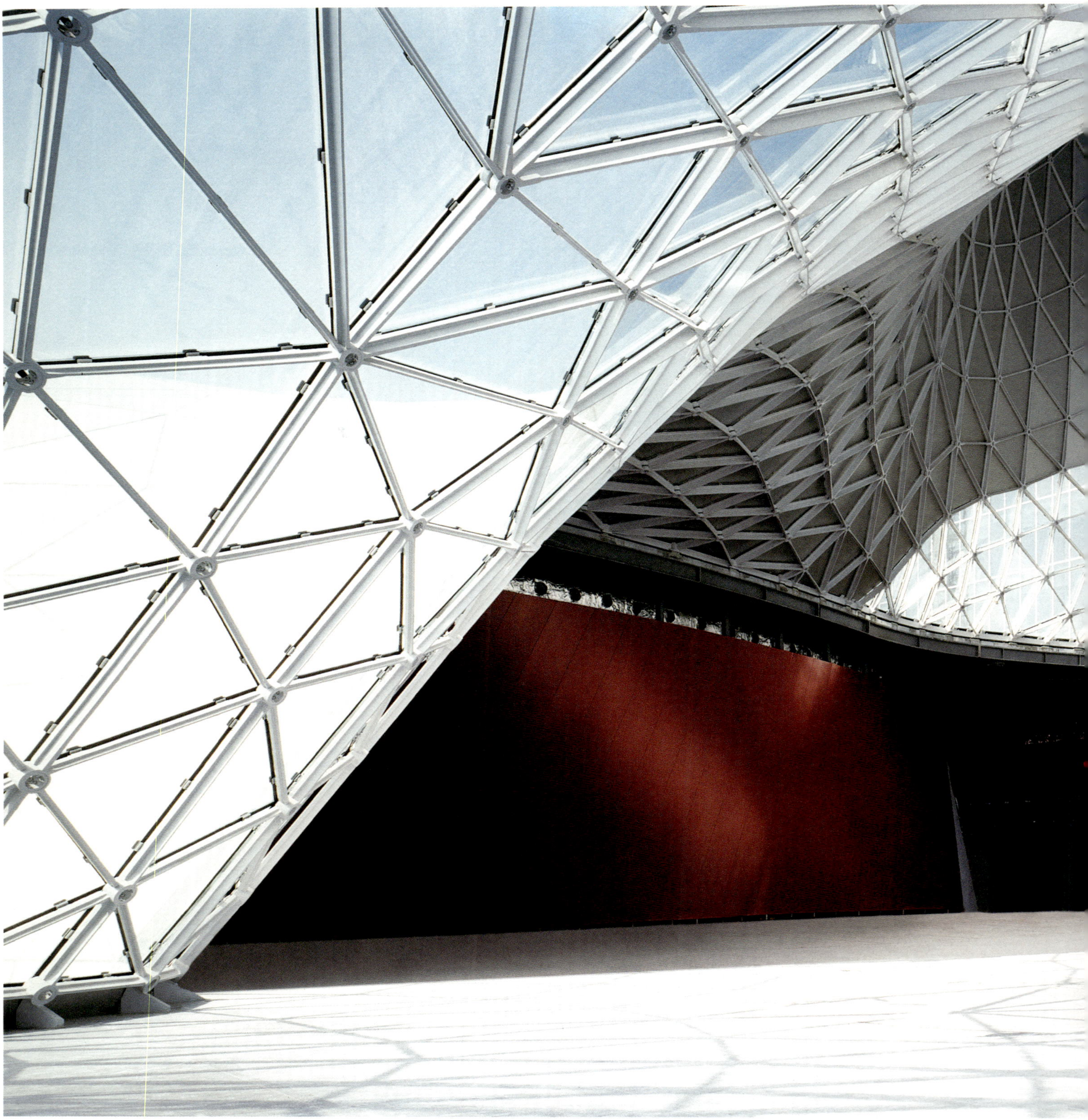

ASTALDI S.p.A

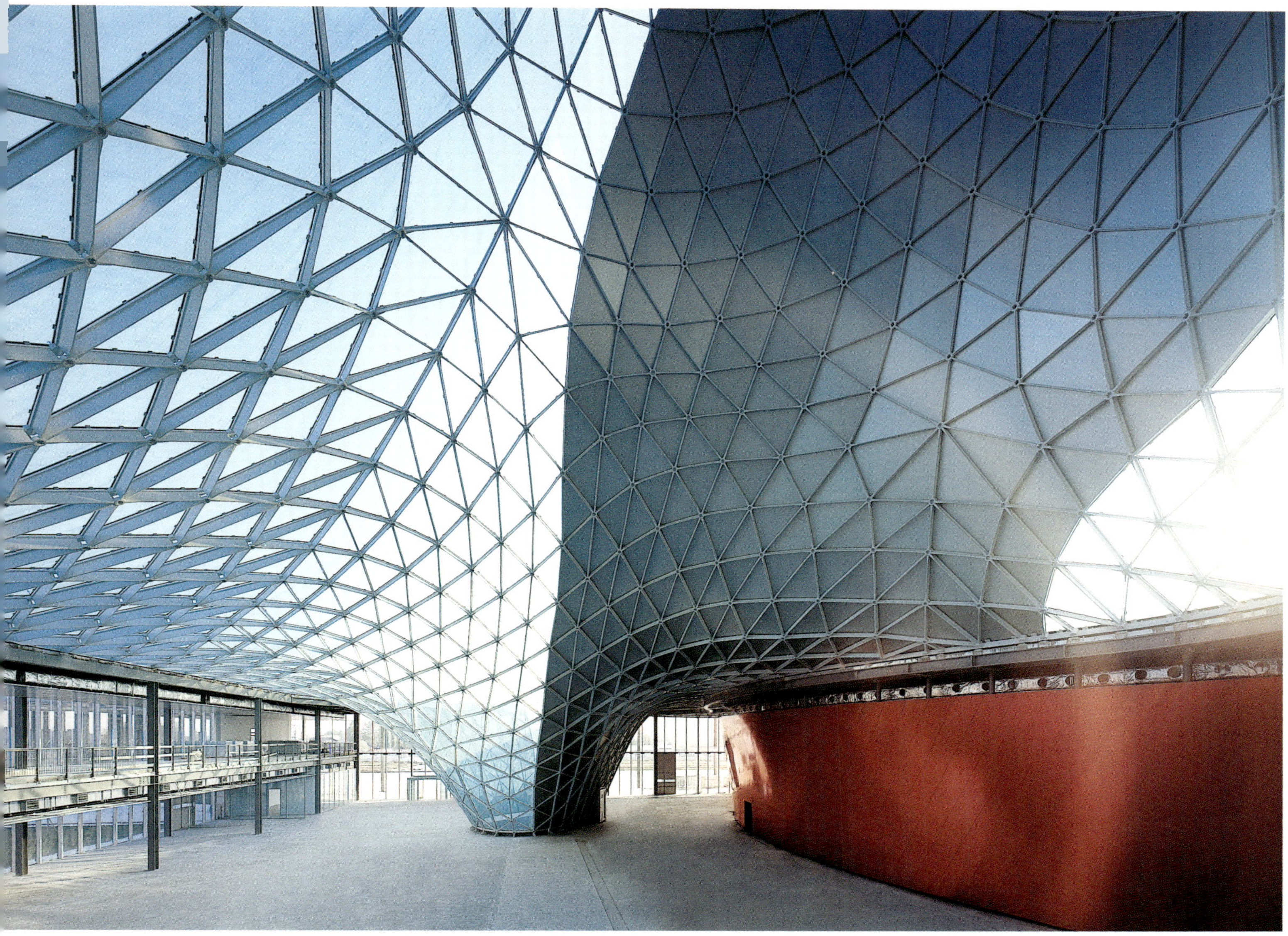

NARDINI RESEARCH CENTRE AND AUDITORIUM
BASSANO DEL GRAPPA, VICENZA, ITALY
2002–2004

Client
Giuseppe and Cristina Nardini –
Ditta Bortolo Nardini SpA

Architects
Massimiliano and Doriana Fuksas

Interior Design
Fuksas Design

Contractor
Impresa Paolin, Bassano del Grappa

Consultants
Engineering: Engineer Gilberto Sarti, Rimini
Services: AI Studio, Torino

A giant "still" dedicated to the famous Nardini distillery.

There are two worlds here. One, formed by two transparent ellipsoidal bubbles containing the research laboratories, seems to float in the air. The other, a sunken space cut into the ground like a natural canyon, accommodates a 100-seat auditorium. The ramp leading down to the auditorium generates the canyon space and also serves as an outdoor stage. These contrasting stages form single, seamless arena in which to host events. Seated spectators find themselves in a landscape generated by an irregular flow of sloping walls.

At ground level, a mirror pool creates a reverberation and shimmer in the entrance area between the two floating bubbles. Its underwater skylights let water-softened light into the underground space during the day. At night they provide lighting. The slender columns lean in different directions, in dynamic opposition to the oblique lift shaft.

What visitors see is a sequence of constantly changing vistas generated by the carefully-gauged asymmetry of the various architectural components: the two staggered, overlapping ellipsoids, the sloping lift shaft contrasting with the line of aerial stairway, and the curve of the entrance ramp. The bubbles have a totally transparent double skin permitting all-round views of Montegrappa's mountain landscape.

So there are two styles here. One is elegant, sophisticated, technological and intangible.
The other is brutal, in which material – reinforced concrete – reveals form.

A container and its contents, a constant tension between positive and negative connected by the oblique lift structure, though also steeped in an energy of opposition that thrusts the glass laboratory bubbles upwards and the weighty auditorium downwards into the ground.
The columns supporting the building seem to anchor the structure to the ground. Shimmering water creates a mirror-like surface, a geometry of nonsensical correspondences where space vibrates and dilates.

The water, in reality just 5 cm deep, suddenly acquires a depth of several metres.
Walking across the footbridge is a thrilling experience.

FERRARI OPERATIONAL HEADQUARTERS AND RESEARCH CENTRE

MARANELLO, MODENA, ITALY
2001–2004

Client
Ferrari S.P.A

Architects
Massimiliano and Doriana Fuksas

Interior Design
Fuksas Design

Ceneral contractor
Cogei Costruzioni SpA, Bologna

Area
17,000 Sq. m

Structures
Ing. Gilberto Sarti, Rimini

Engineering
AI Engineering, Torino

The area lies at the heart of Ferrari the industrial complex in Maranello.

Located between the wind tunnel and the engineering building, the Management and Research Centre is the company's flagship asset housing both its research facilities and technical management division.

The aim was to bring nature environment inside the high-tech complex so as to create a comfortable place to work in. Light, water and bamboo plants are deployed to make the building a landscape in its own right.

The ensemble is dominated by an overhanging volume that extends 7 m across the entrance area. Separate from the rest of the building, it hangs over the pool on the roof of the volume below, giving the building its iconic status.

Footbridges across the pool form an interconnected network between the two meeting-rooms, one red, the other yellow.

Water and reflections are key design features. Reflections modify spatial and temporal perceptions of water, effectively eliminating space and time.

Here, water alters architecture by creating new spaces with the reflections and glare of light from slits in the suspended upper volume. When sunlight strikes it, the shallow pool, seems filled with some precious liquid metal, a crucible of industrial manufacturing. Down below there is a bamboo garden, an orderly rectangle of nature that dissects the light, scattering it in a thousand directions.

Construction

FRENCH NATIONAL ARCHIVES
PIERREFITTE SUR SEINE-SAINT DENIS, PARIS, FRANCE
2005–ongoing

Client
Ministry of Culture and Communication

Developer
OPPIC

Architects
Massimiliano and Doriana Fuksas

Interior design
Fuksas Design

General contractor
Bouygues

Area
800.000 sq.m

Engineering
Betom – Bet Tce

Consultants
ALTIA – BET acoustics
Florence MERCIER landscape

Artistic intervention
Antony Gormley
Susanna Fritscher
Groupe Convert

The design draws inspiration from its context. The city is seen as a world of perpetual movement where nothing stops changing, a duality of chaos and order that is also reflected in the two worlds of the building, one "suspended, light, transparent, vital", the other "imposing, shiny, rooted in the ground".

The first contains administrative facilities and offices, a conference room and the reception area, the second the archives themselves and a spacious reading-room.

Like a polished casket, the Archives block is clad in shiny aluminium that reflects its surroundings, including the "suspended, transparent" administration block.

The aluminium cladding of the Archives block and in the glass façades of the six "satellite" blocks share the same lozenge-shaped geometrical design. The two worlds are also reflected in the water surrounding the complex, and are linked by footbridges. Water and aluminium both play a part in the architectural transformation as they create new spaces by reflecting natural light.

Rather than just a building, this is a new concept of landscape, a new geography. Water, trees, superior materials and technical concept are there to make a place that people will be happy to live and work in.

JCB

10

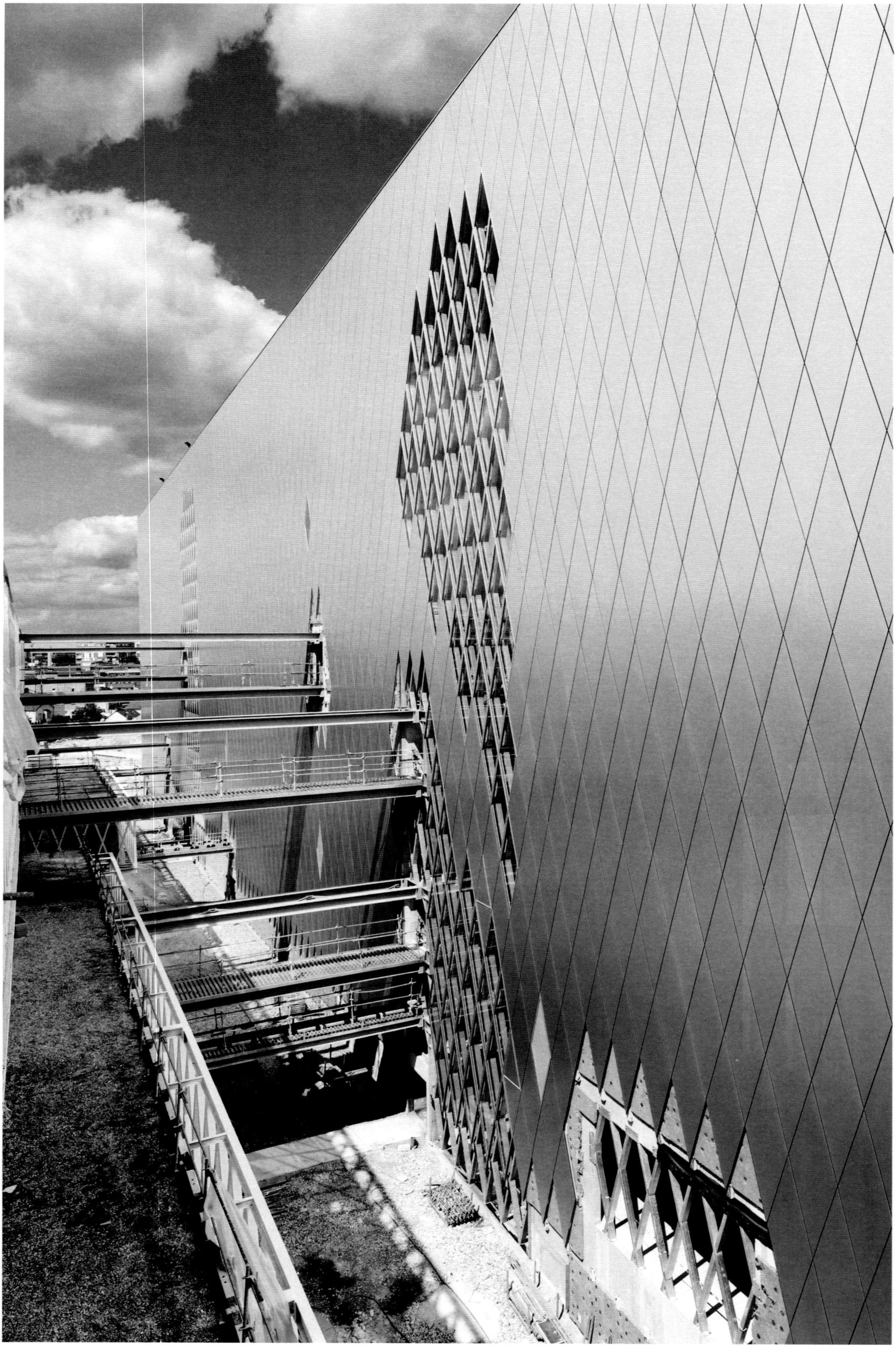

ACCES
JLG

LYCÉE HÔTELIER GEORGES–FRÊCHE
MONTPELLIER, FRANCE
2006–ongoing

Client
Région Languedoc-Roussillon

Developer
Languedoc-Roussillon Aménagement

Architects
Massimiliano and Doriana Fuksas

Interior design
Fuksas Design

Contractors
GFC – structure
SMAC – façades
BARSALOU – frames

Area
Net surface: 23,600 sq.m.
Gross surface: 25,736.80 sq.m.
Area surface:16,500 sq.m.

Consultants
ALTIA – Acoustics
NEVEUX-ROUYER –
Landscape Architects
ALMA Consulting – Kitchen design

Engineering
IOSIS

Artistic Interventions
Matali Crasset

The project specifications and the smallness of the site generated a combination of solidity and fluidity, expressive sculptural masses flowing smoothly and effortlessly into one another.
The set of five solid-looking yet oddly unassertive buildings blends well with urban fabric, like a single entity encompassing a variety of individual shapes.

The school's two main buildings form the sculptural mass around which the gym, students' residence and administrative offices gravitate. The best place from which to view the complex is the Place Odysseum, where its full extent can best be appreciated. The buildings face Rue Le Titien and are set back from Avenue du Mondial with an outdoor track sandwiched between, accentuating the separation.

The entrances are on Rue Le Titien; the school itself has a main students' and a smaller teachers' entrance set back in the façade.

The only vehicle entrance is between the gym and the students' residence. Traffic is restricted on site to make more room for pedestrian and recreational areas.

The two school buildings are connected by footbridges. The first building facing Rue Le Titien houses the multipurpose hall, administrative offices, classrooms, and a cafeteria overlooking the recreational areas outside. The second, housing student functions, contains a cafeteria overlooking the internal courtyard, kitchen and hotel resources, and, on the upper floors, the registry and information centre. The gourmet restaurant, brasserie and 4-star hotel, all visible from Rue Le Titien and Avenue del Mondiale, show off the students' professional expertise and are major assets to the school.

The complexity of the volumes is also evident inside the various buildings, where all the rooms and spaces are uniquely different. A curved concrete inner shell makes the complex an extremely efficient passive structure that stores solar heat in winter and rejects solar heat in the summer.

The 17,000 sq.m external façade exactly fits the structural curves of the volumes, giving the complex a sleek, unbroken appearance. Its triangular, lacquered, anodised-aluminium panels and triangular window frames and openings create the alternations of solids and voids, light and shadow, that are a hallmark feature of the design.

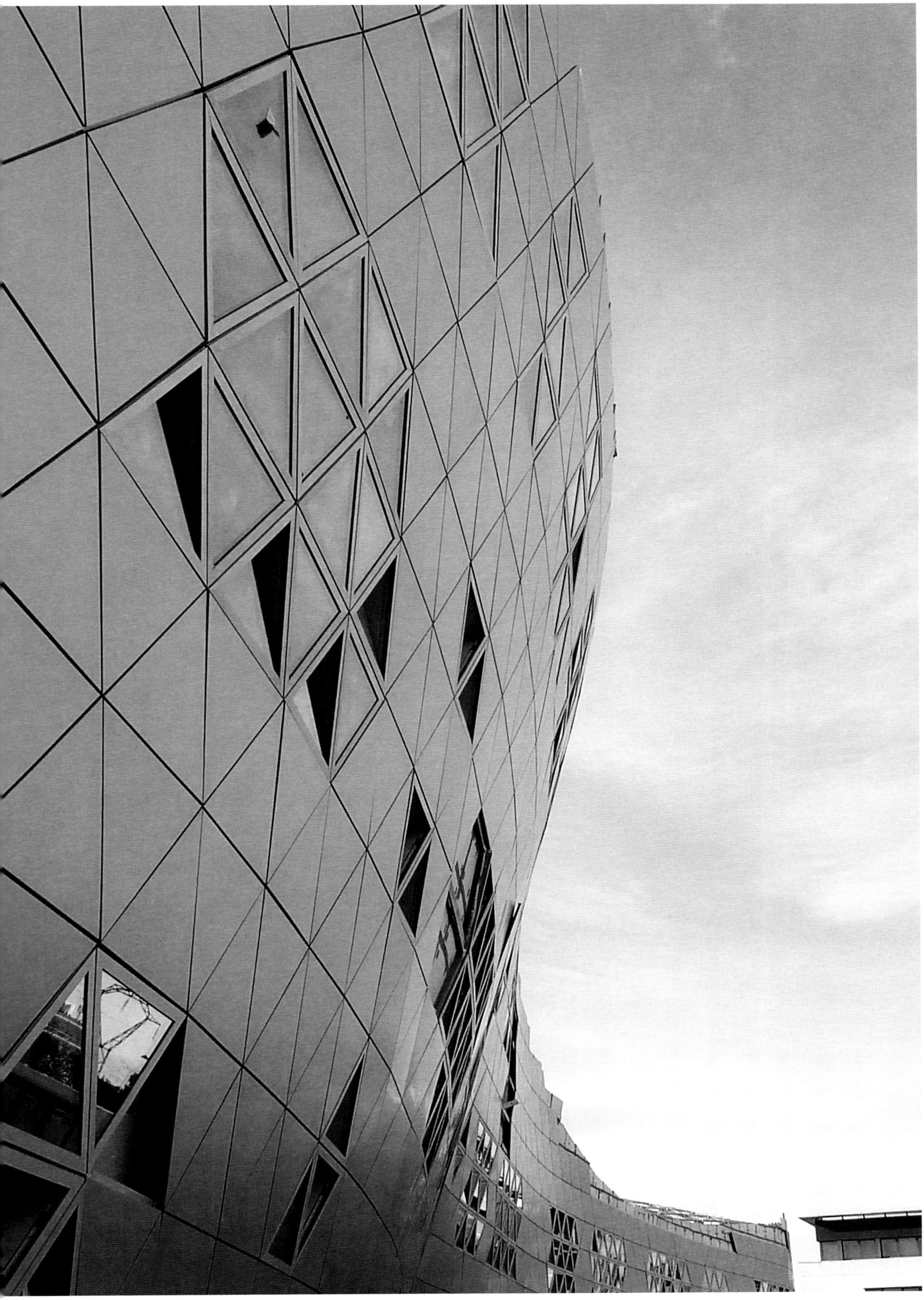

Construction du Lycée Georges

1000 élèves
Construction du Lycée

SHENZHEN BAO'AN INTERNATIONAL AIRPORT, TERMINAL 3

SHENZHEN, CHINA
2008–ongoing

Client
Shenzhen Airport (Group) Co., Ltd.

Developer
Shenzhen Planning Bureau;
Shenzhen Airport (Group) Co., Ltd.

Architects
Massimiliano and Doriana Fuksas

Interior design
Fuksas Design

General contractor
China State Construction Engineering Corporation, Beijing

Area
400.000 sqm in Phase 3

Structures, facade, parametric design
Knippers Helbig Engineering, Stuttgart, NY

Architect of record
BIAD (Beijing Institute of Architectural Design), Beijing

Lighting consulting
Speirs & Major Associates, Edinburgh, London

Shenzhen is one of China's most important industrial areas, as well as a very popular tourist destination. The fast developing city is located in the south of the Guangdong Province near the Pearl River delta and Hong Kong. Shenzhen Bao'an International Airport is China's fourth largest airport after Beijing, Shanghai, and Guangzhou. Massimiliano and Doriana Fuksas won the 2008 international competition for a new terminal (Terminal 3) to enlarge Shenzhen Bao'an International Airport. The sculptural, organically-shaped structure has a steel space-frame with a honeycomb skin inside and outside, and a concrete sub-frame.

The 300,000 sq.m façade consists of partially opening metal and glass panels of various sizes. The roof reaches a height of 80 m.

The double skin lets in daylight through and creates dappled light effects. When they think of an airport, most passengers think of the terminal building and concourse. Here the concourse, a key airport areas, has three separate levels for departures, arrivals and services. The ground-level plaza provides access to departures and arrivals, as well as to cafés, restaurants, offices and business-meeting facilities.

The arrival level outside the airport is 14.4 m above the ground. The fluid interior conceptually combines the ideas of movement and pause, time. The honeycomb skin carries over into the building on a variety of scales. The retail units repeat it on a larger scale, and most of the public areas have 3D honeycomb ceiling and wall cladding.

中建钢构
中建钢构

EUR NEW CONGRESS CENTRE
ROME, ITALY
1998–ongoing

Client
E.U.R. S.p.A.

Architects
Massimiliano and Doriana Fuksas

Interior design
Fuksas Design

General Contractor
Società Italiana per
Condotte d'Acqua SpA

Built Surface
55,000 sq. m.

Engineering
Plans: A. I. Engineering, Torino
Structures: Studio Majowiecki;
Studio Sarti
Safety: Studio Sarti

Acoustics
XU – Acoustique, Paris

Strategically sited in Rome's Fascist-built EUR residential and business district, the convention centre will have a built area of 55,000 sq.m.

Essentially, the design concept centres on three images: the Display Case and the Cloud that form the convention centre, and the "blade" of the adjacent hotel. The steel-framed Display Case with a glass double-façade contains the Cloud, the heart of the project. Its imprisonment within the box-like Display Case underlines the contrast between amorphous space and geometrically defined shape.

The Cloud contains a 1850-seat auditorium, catering venues and support services for the auditorium. The Cloud is, without doubt, the hallmark feature of the project, an amazing-looking steel-ribbed structure covered in 15,000 sq.m of transparent sheeting. The underground parking level will accommodate 600 cars. The adjacent 441-room hotel (the "blade") is a free-standing autonomous structure.

With its ground-breaking logistics and high-tech materials, the new Congress Centre will make a major architectural statement as well as being a highly flexible structure able to host congress and exhibition events for almost 9000 people at any one time, spread between the 1850-seat Cloud auditorium and the large conference rooms totalling 6500 seats.

The centre is designed to be as energy-efficient as possible. VRF air-conditioning will provide high efficiency and low running costs by adjusting temperature and air-flow to the number of people actually present in the auditorium and individual rooms. Solar panels on the roof will supply renewable energy and protect the building from overheating by reducing solar radiation, as well as significantly reducing energy consumption compared with standard air-conditioning throughout the entire building.

JLG ULTRA BOOM
JLG ULTRA BOOM
JLG

JOST

GROVE

ULTRA BOOM
H43TPX
Haulotte

CH 891WF

Project

EUR New Congress Centre

ROME, ITALY
1998—ONGOING

Tower for Regione Piemonte New Headquarters
TURIN, ITALY
2001

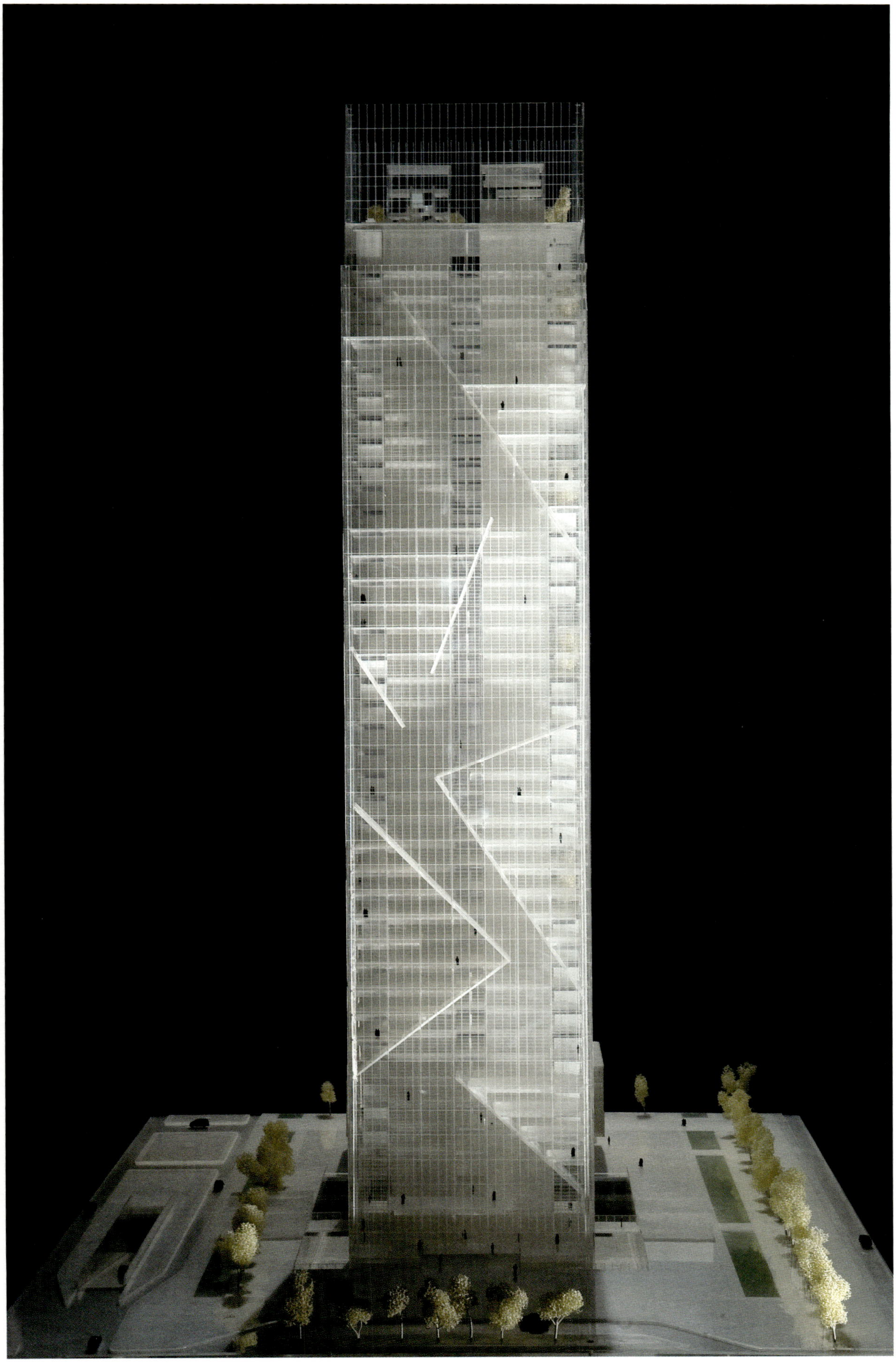

Bern-Mall and entertainment Center
BERN, SWITZERLAND
2000

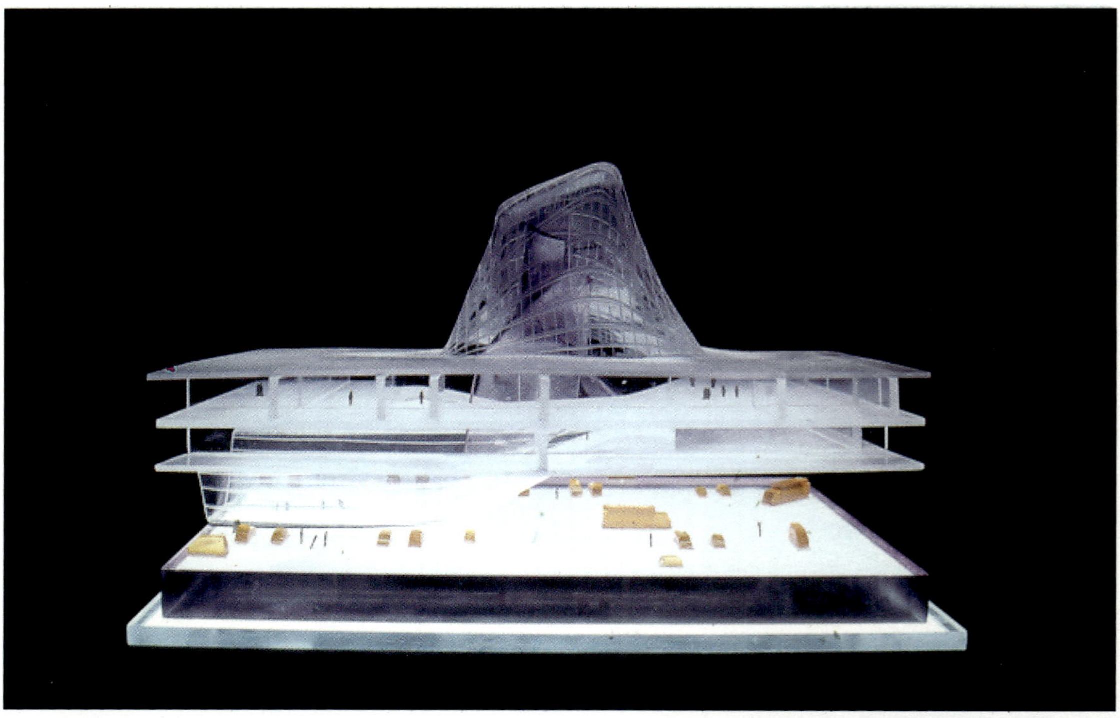

London Aquatics Center
LONDON, UNITED KINGDOM
2004

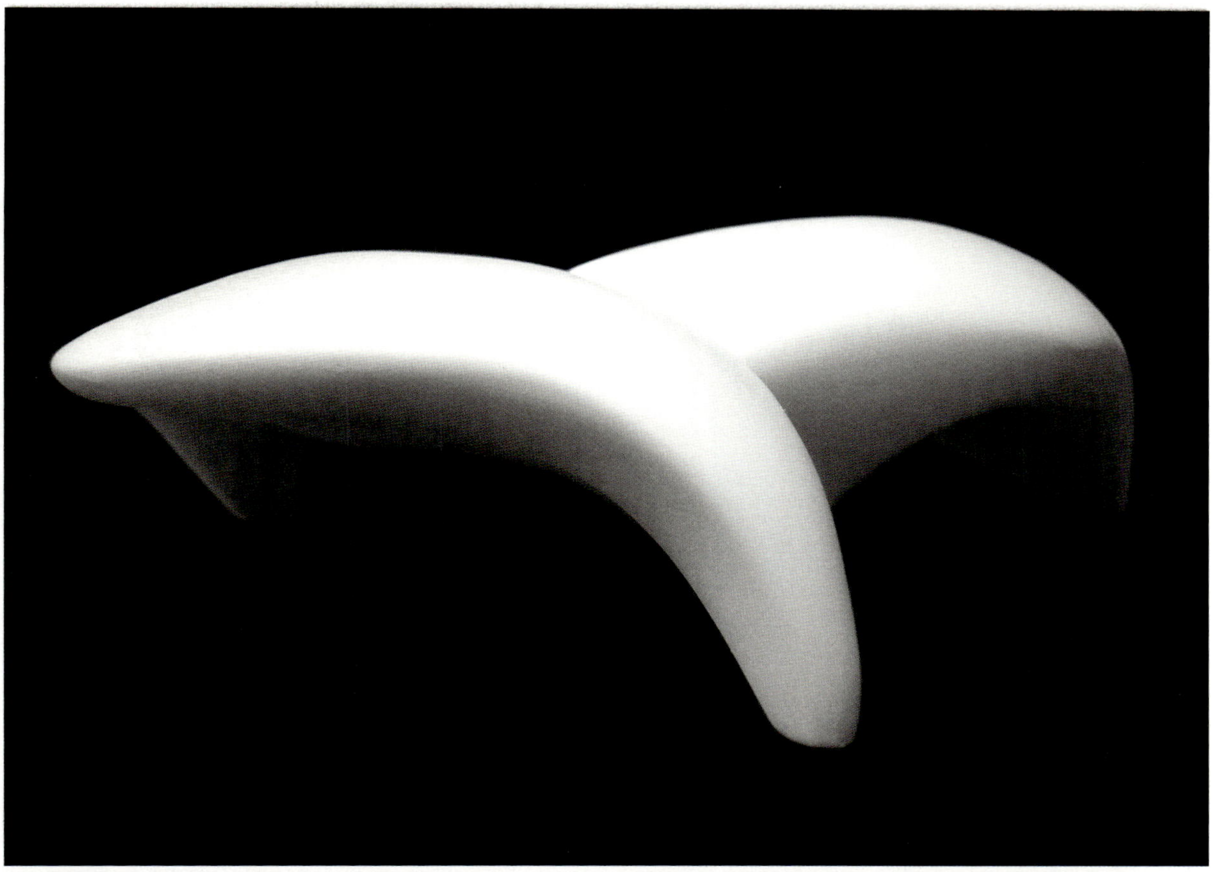

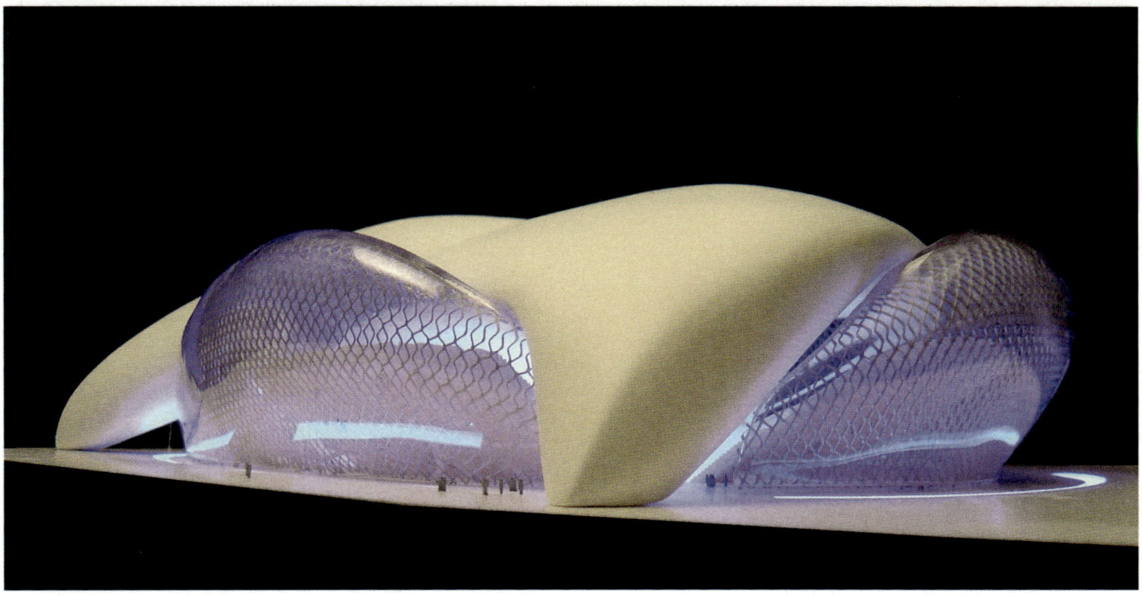

French National Archives

PIERREFITTE SUR SEINE-SAINT DENIS, PARIS, FRANCE
2005—ONGOING

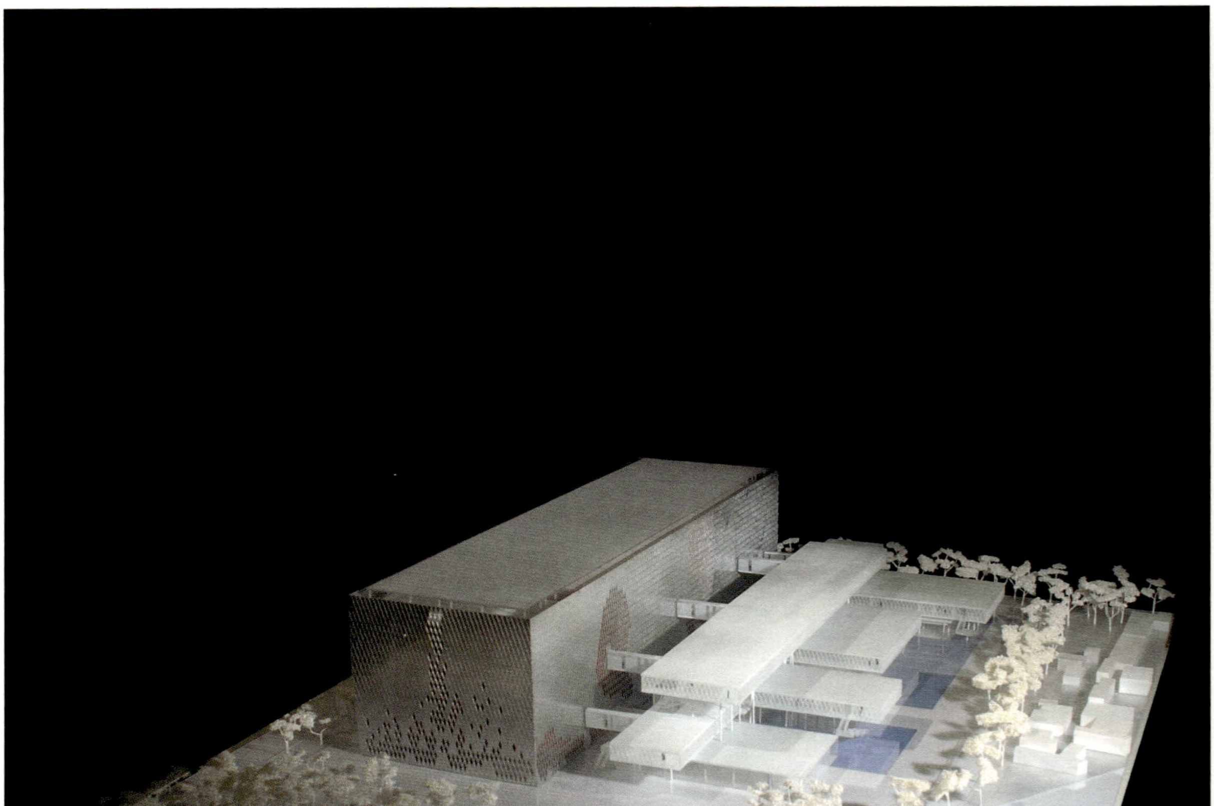

FUKSAS

Piaggio New Historical Museum
PONTEDERA, PISA, ITALY
2006

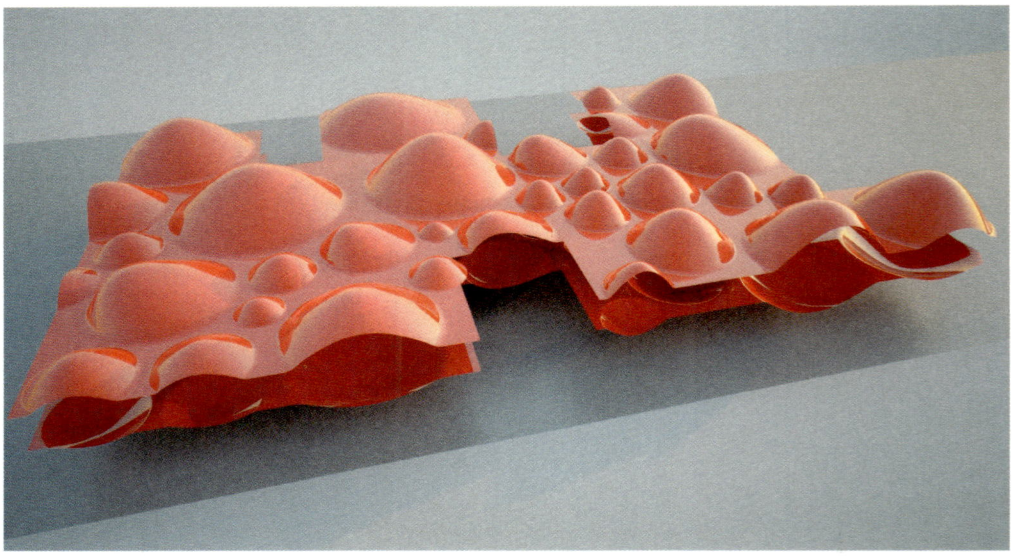

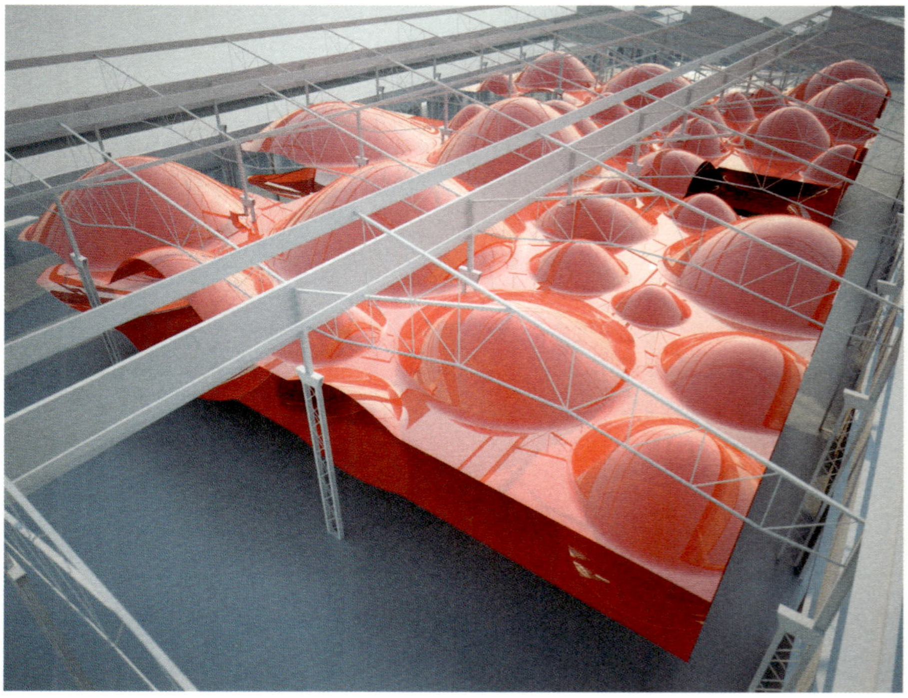

Phare Tower
LA DÉFENSE, PARIS, FRANCE
2006

Shenzhen Bao'an International Airport, T3
SHENZEN, CHINA
2008—ONGOING

Chongqing Airport
CHONGQING, CHINA
2009

Formule One Racing Circuit for the Gran Prix
FLINS-SUR-SEINE, FRANCE
2009

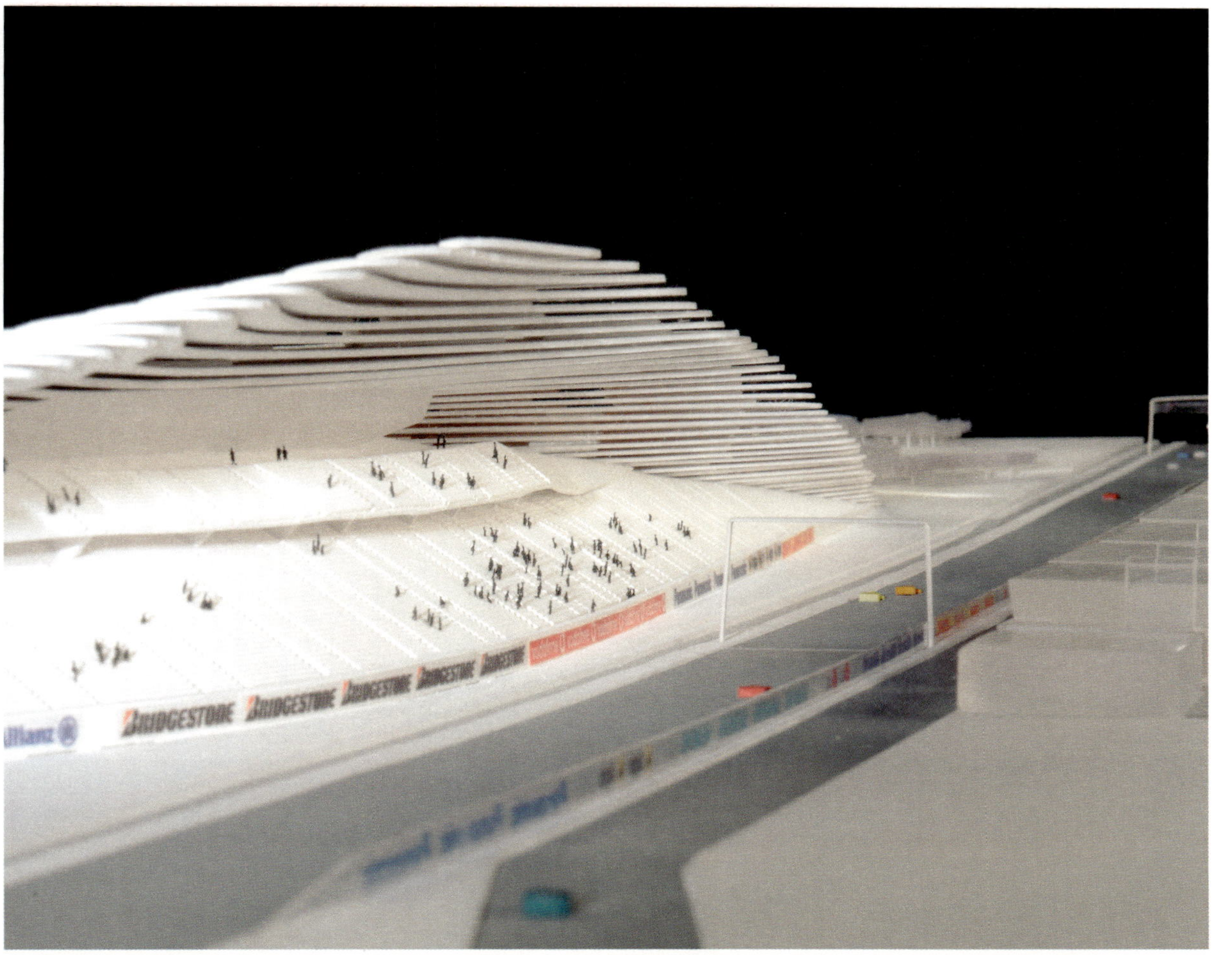
BRIDGESTONE

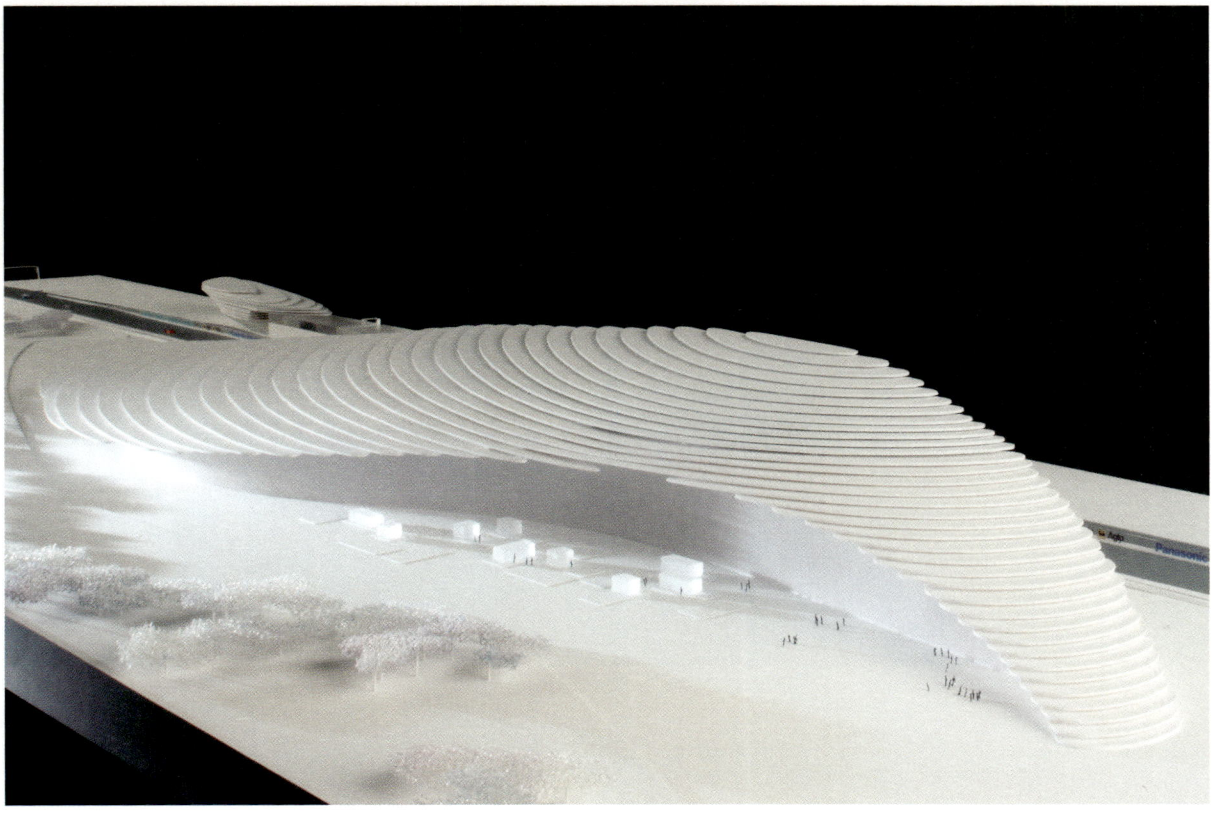
Panasonic

Judicial Complex
MAKKAH, SAUDI ARABIA
2009

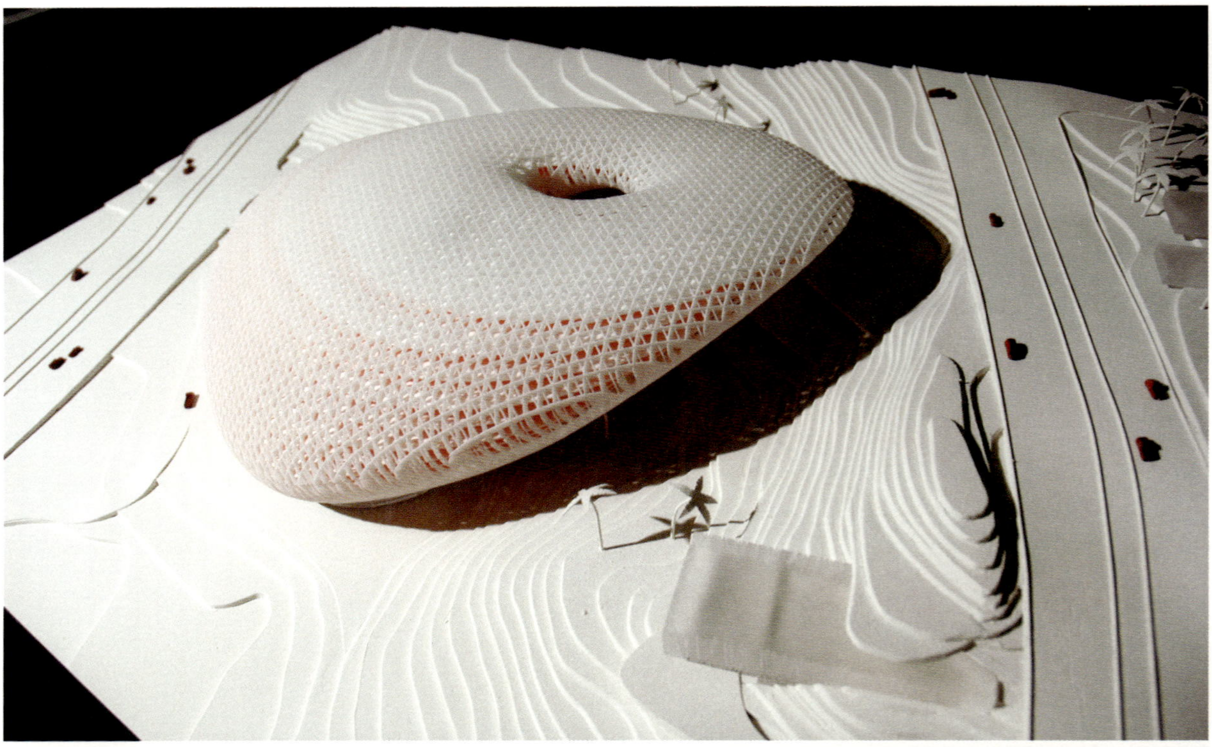

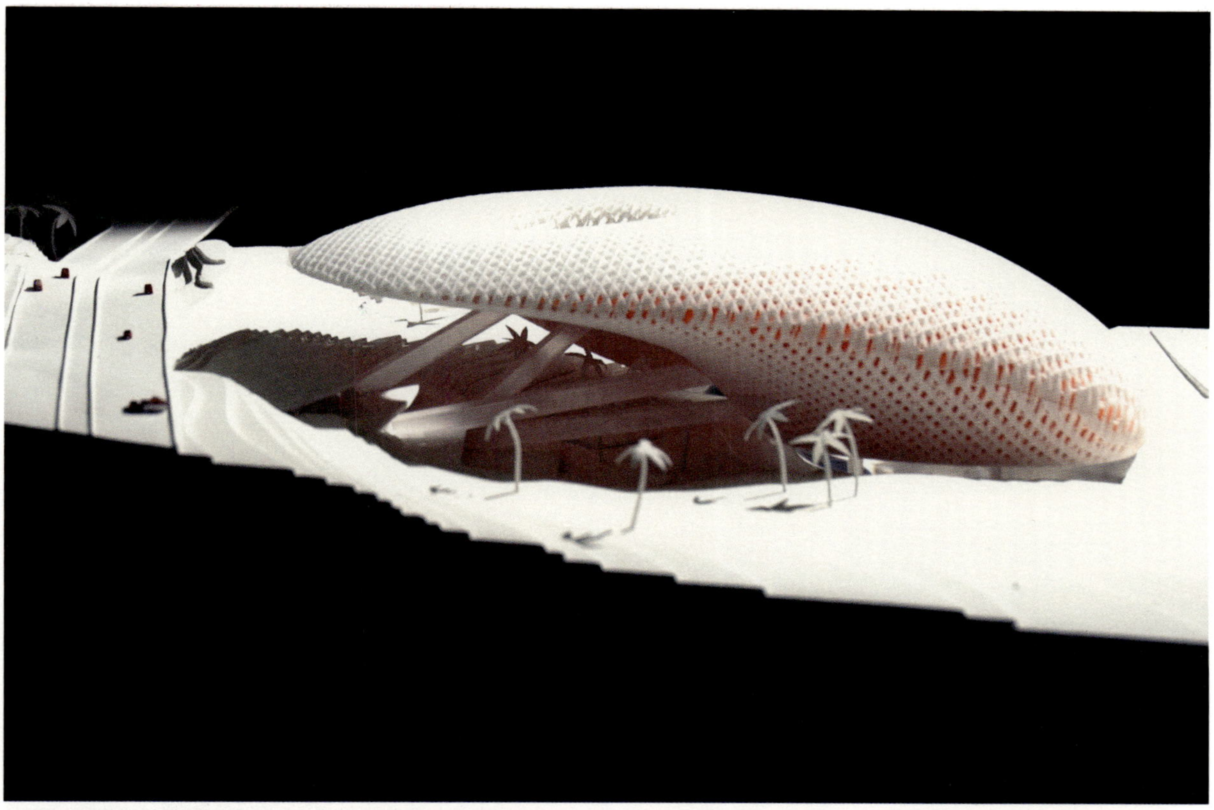

Wangijing Competition

BEIJING, CHINA
2009

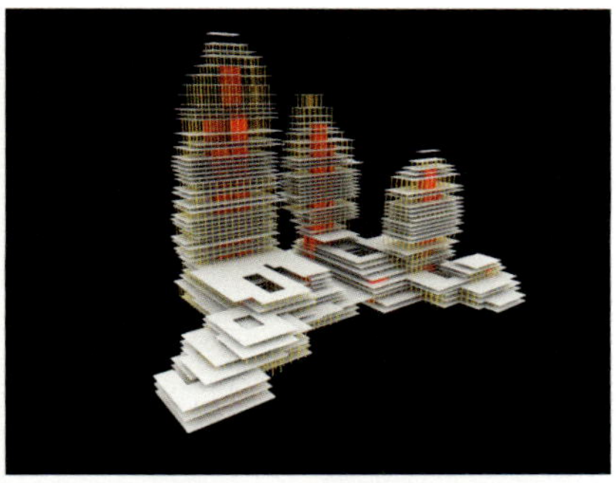
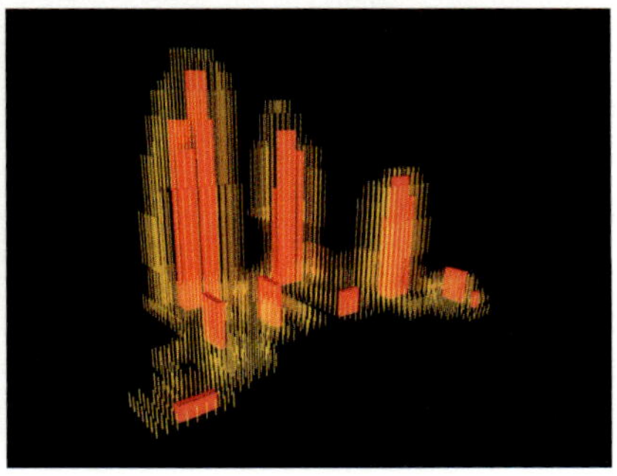

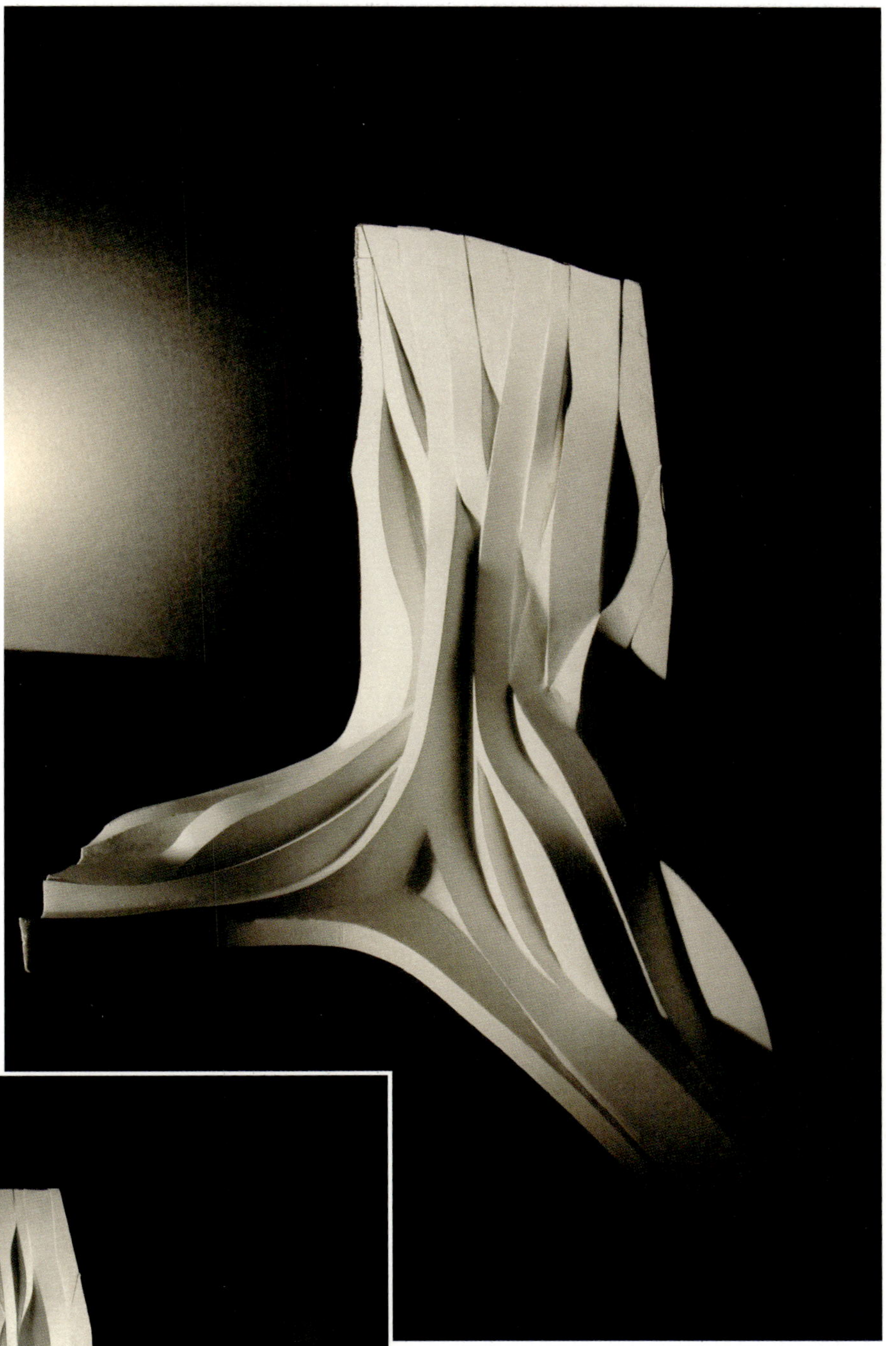

Twin Towers
SHENZHEN, CHINA
2009

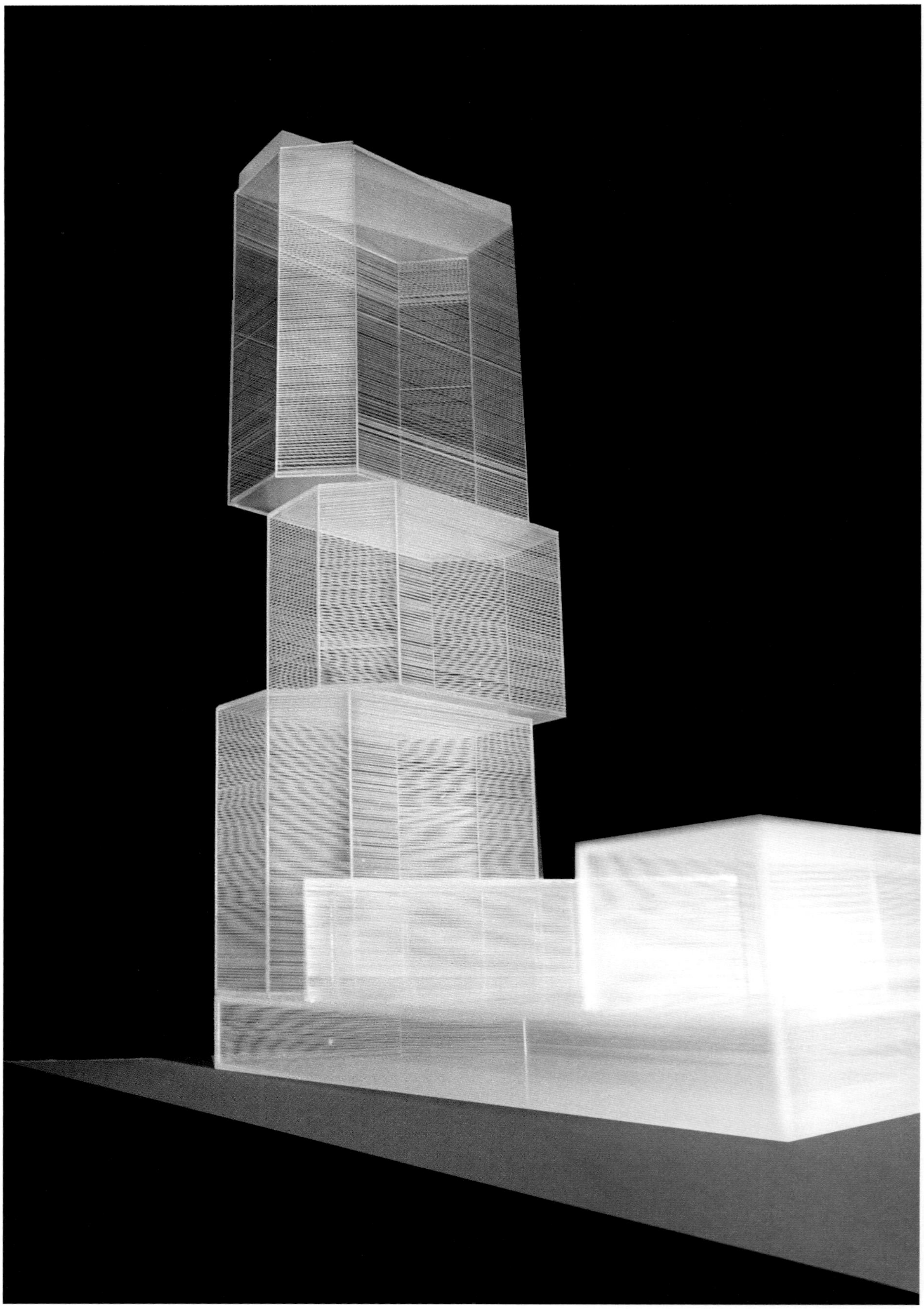

Extension de l'Esplanade dévoilé
LOUVAIN-LA-NEUVE, BELGIUM
2010

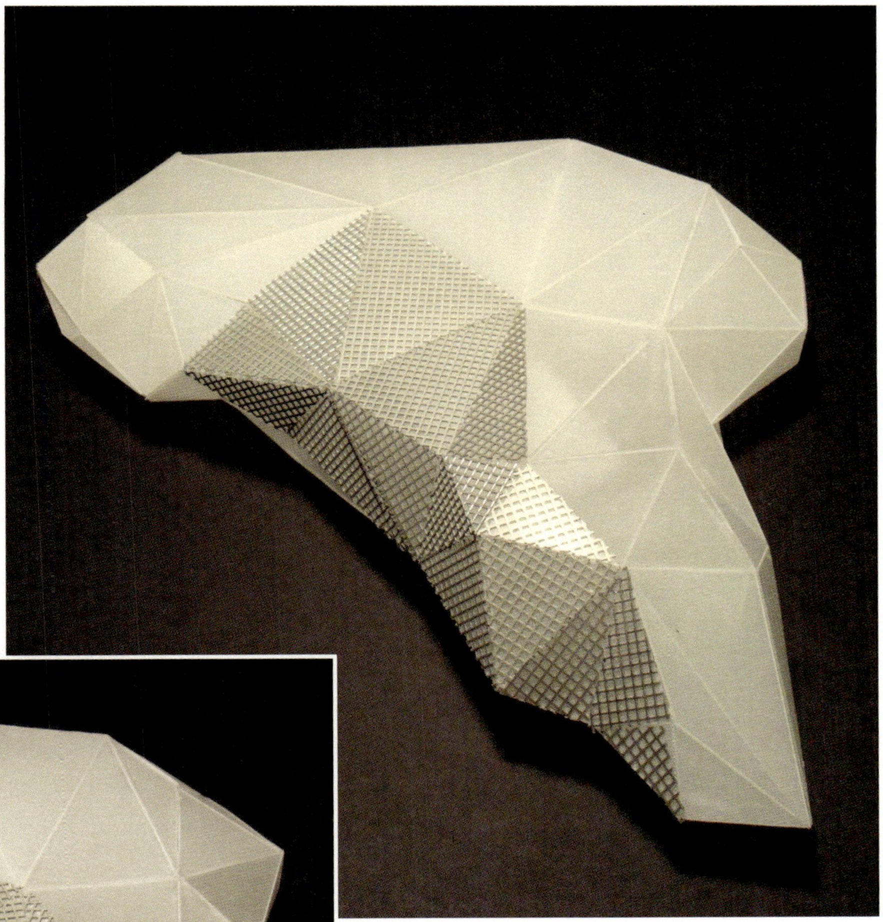

Guosen Securities Tower
SHENZHEN, CHINA
2010

Rhike Park
TBILISI, GEORGIA
2010

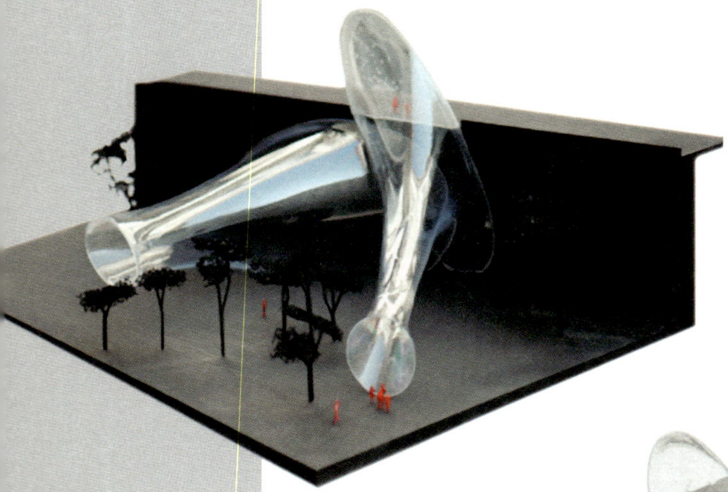

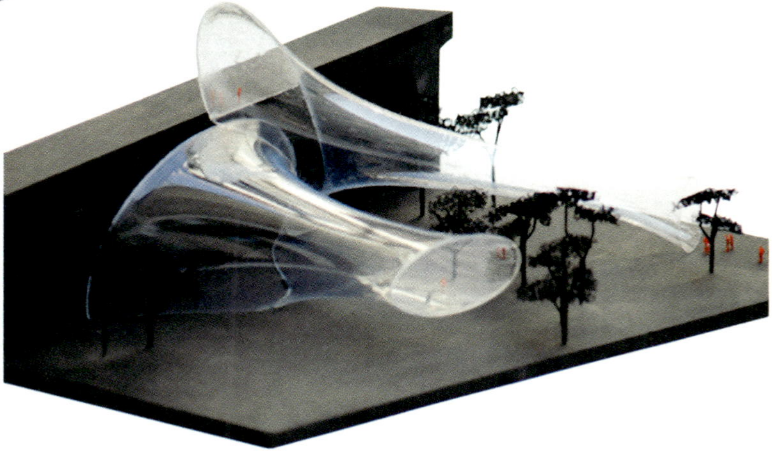

House of Justice
TBILISI, GEORGIA
2010

Drawing and Detail

PALATINO CENTRE
TURIN, ITALY
1998–2011

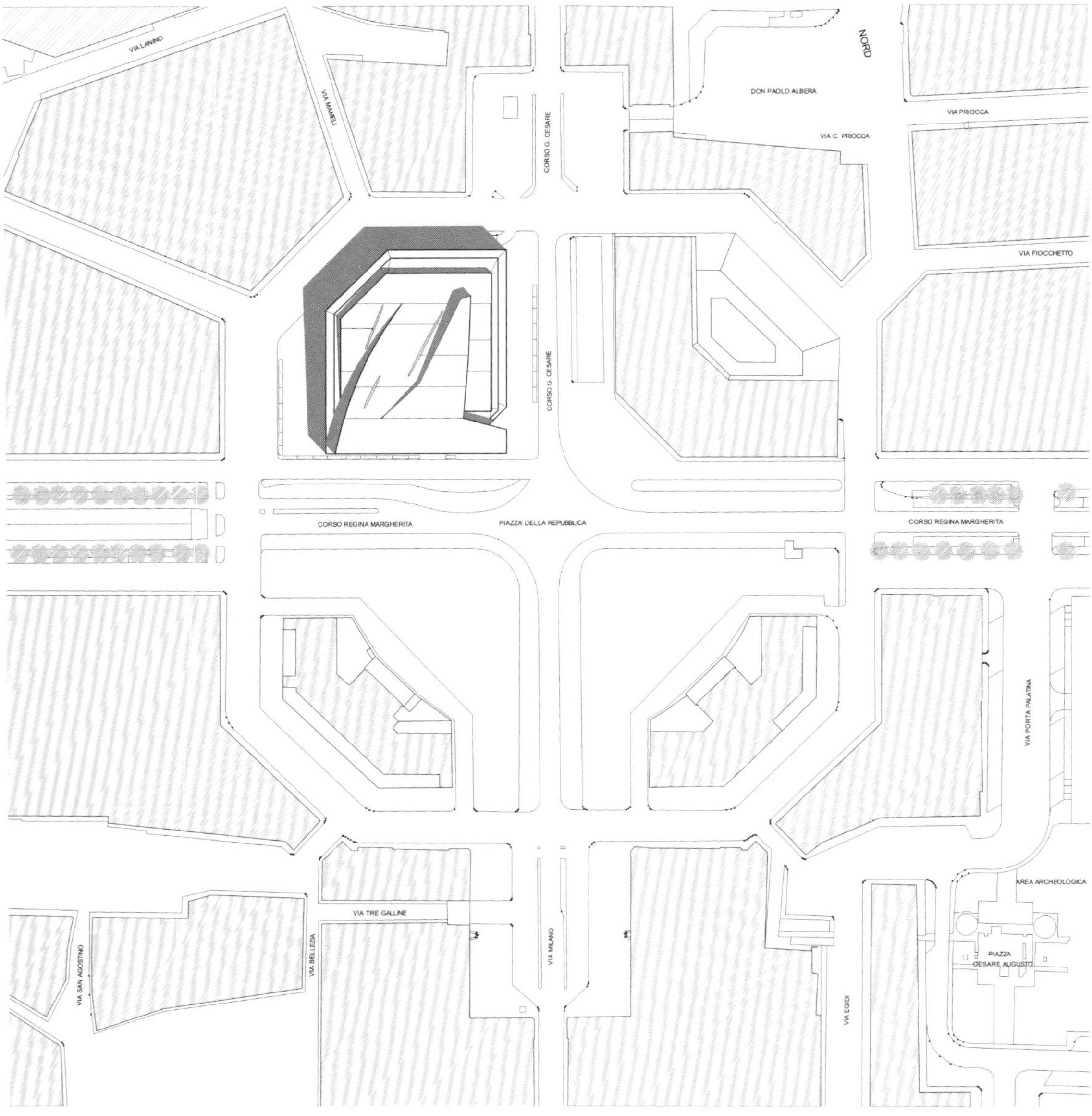

General plan

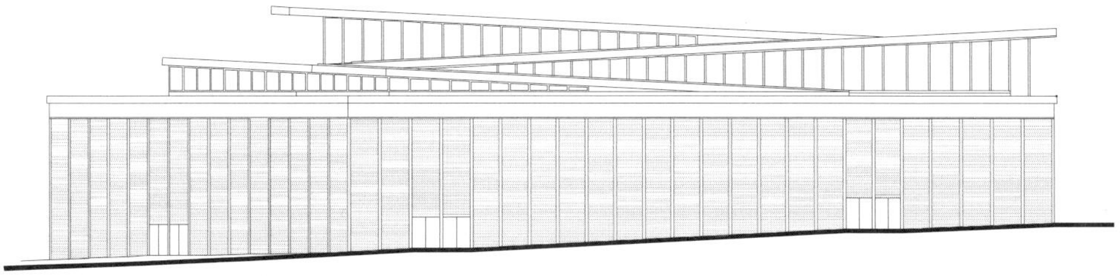

Elevation East

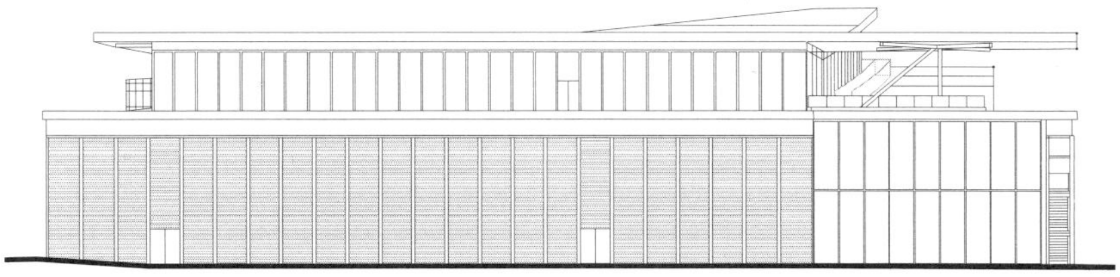

Elevation South

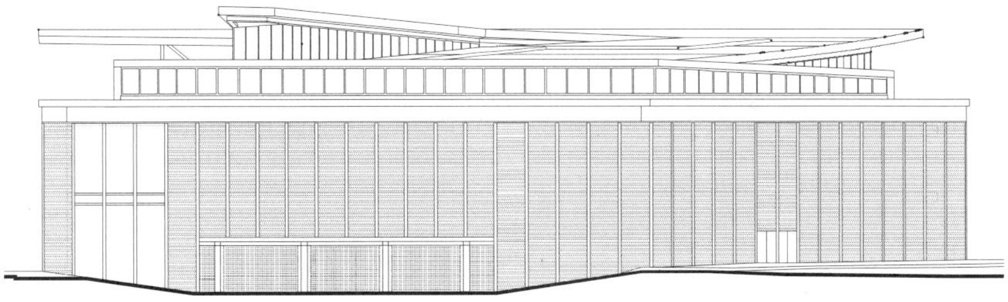

Elevation North

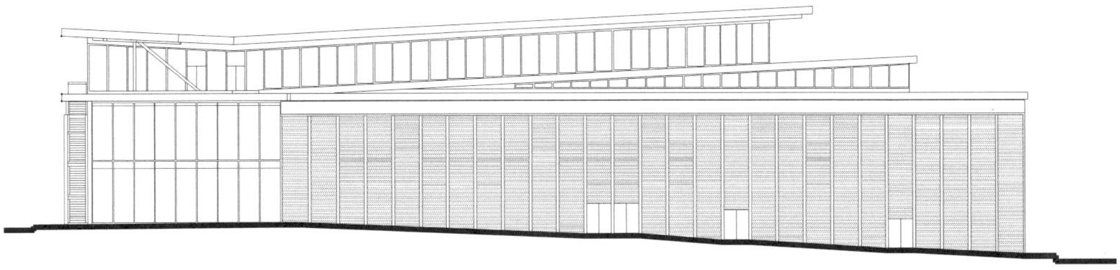

Elevation West

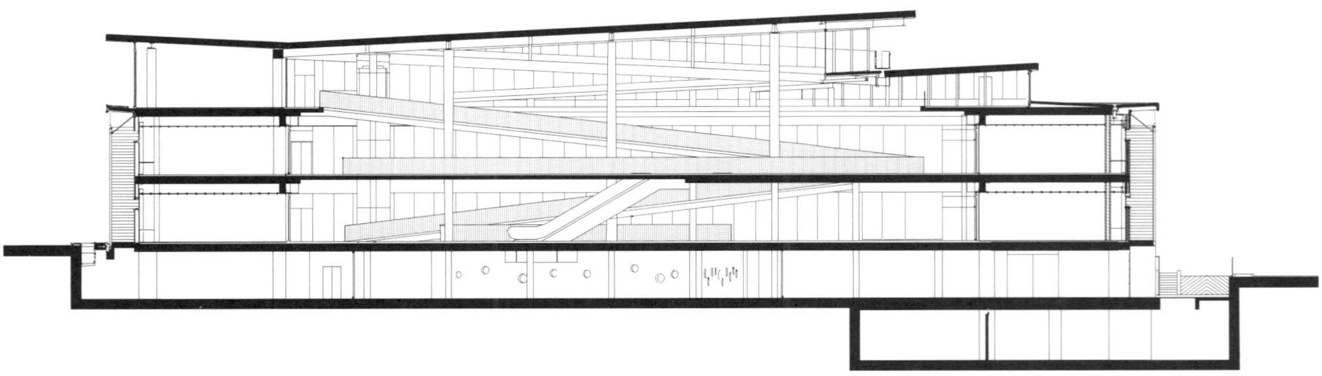

Section A A'

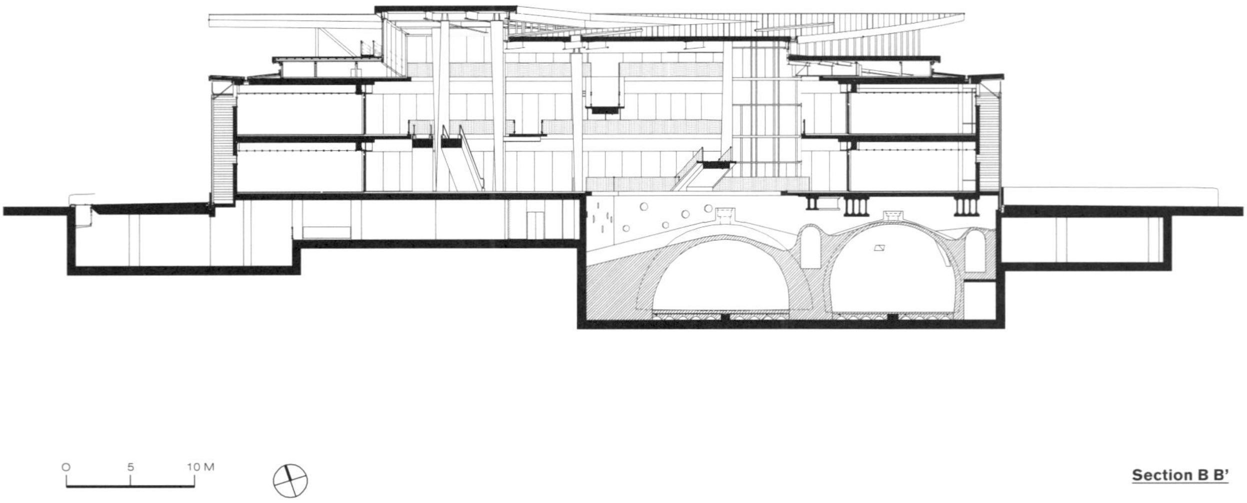

Section B B'

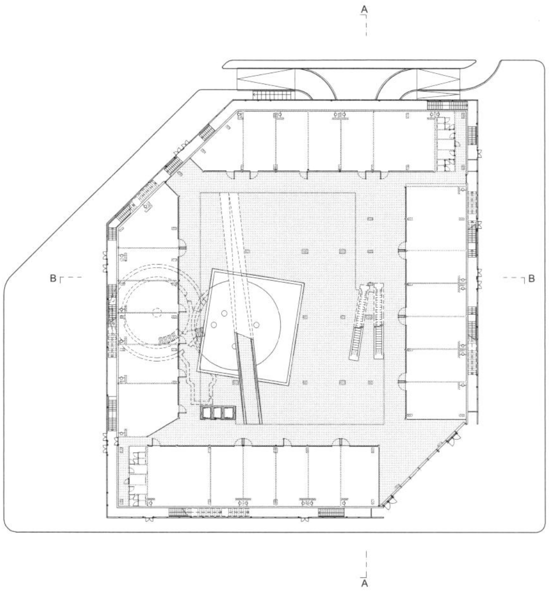

Ground floor plan

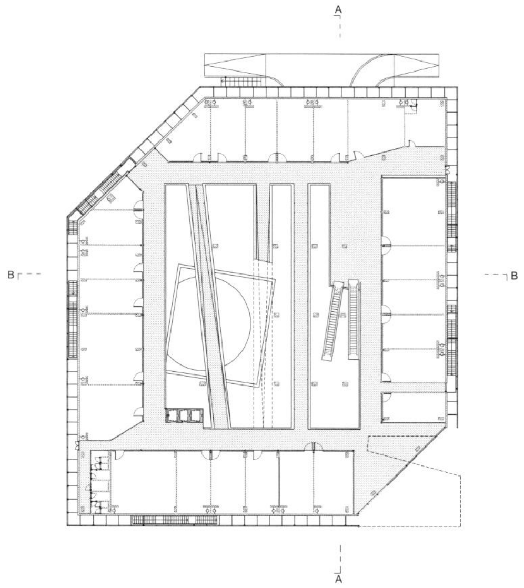

First floor plan

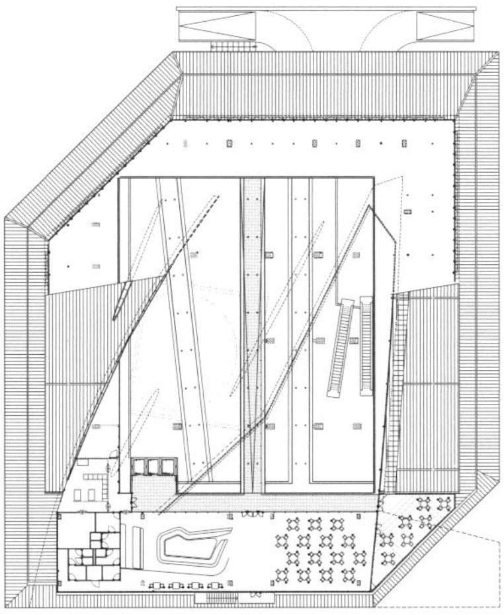

Second floor plan

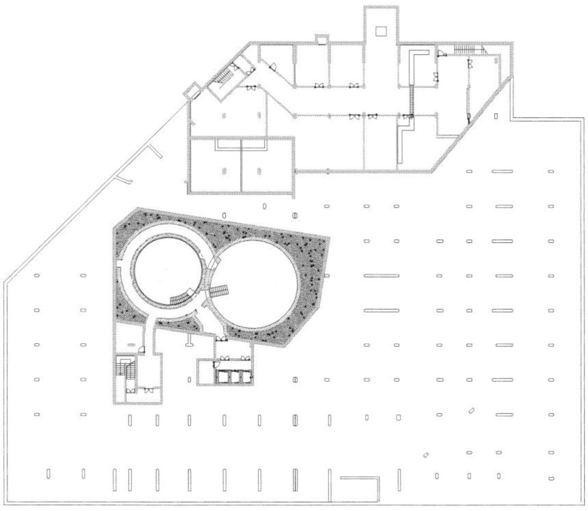

Basement floor plan

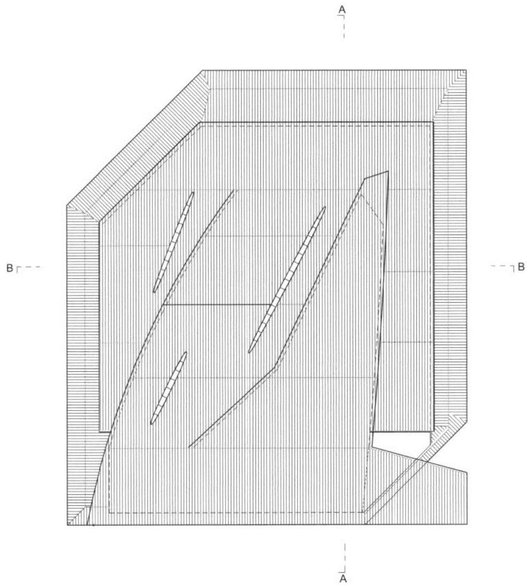

Roof plan

0 5 10 M

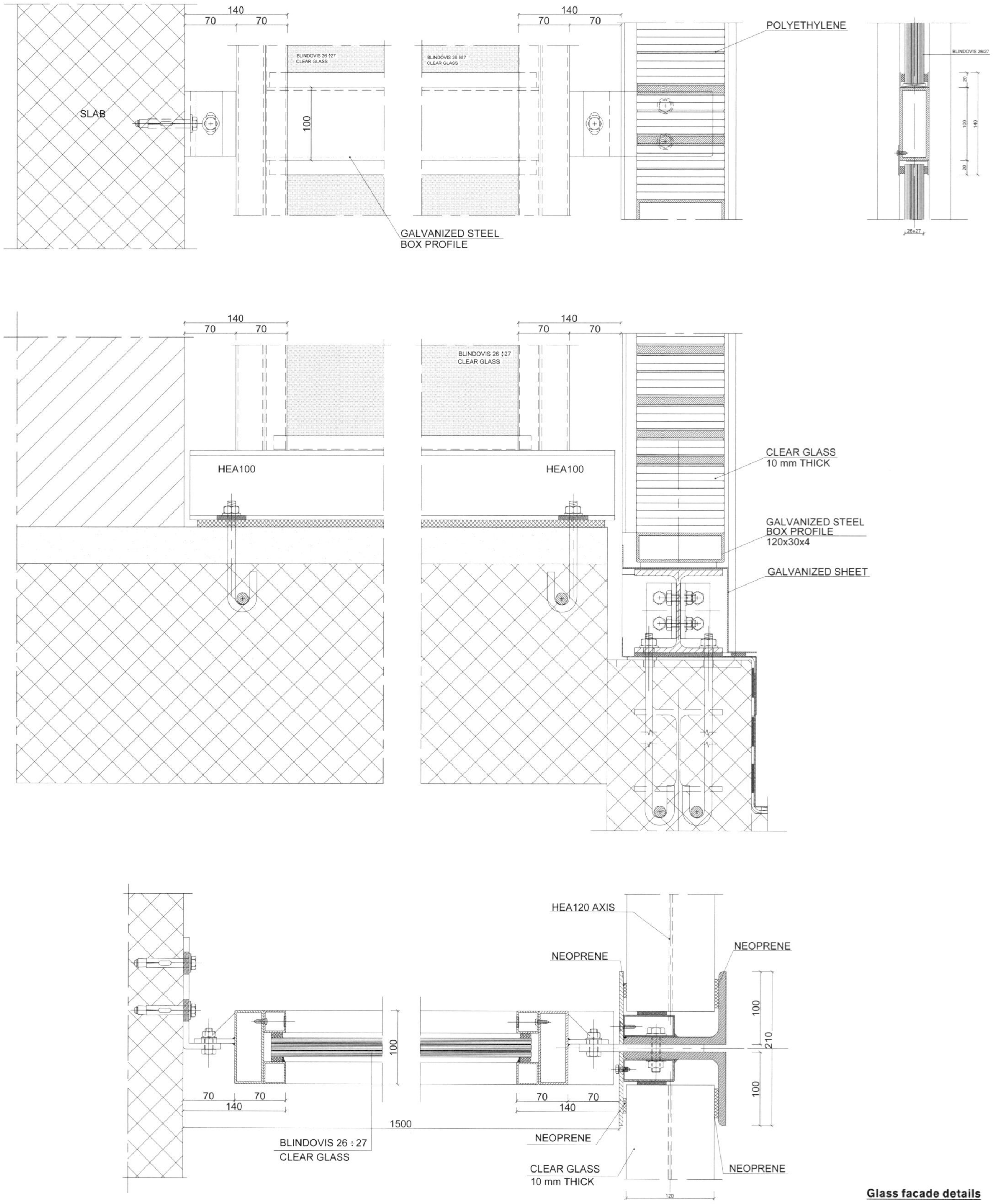

Glass facade details

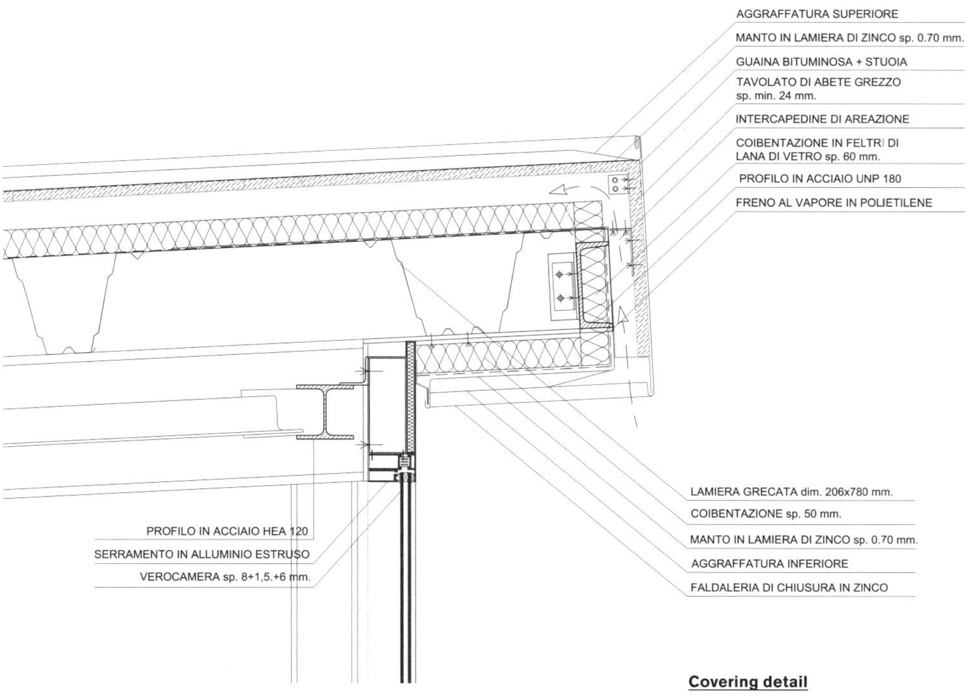

Covering detail

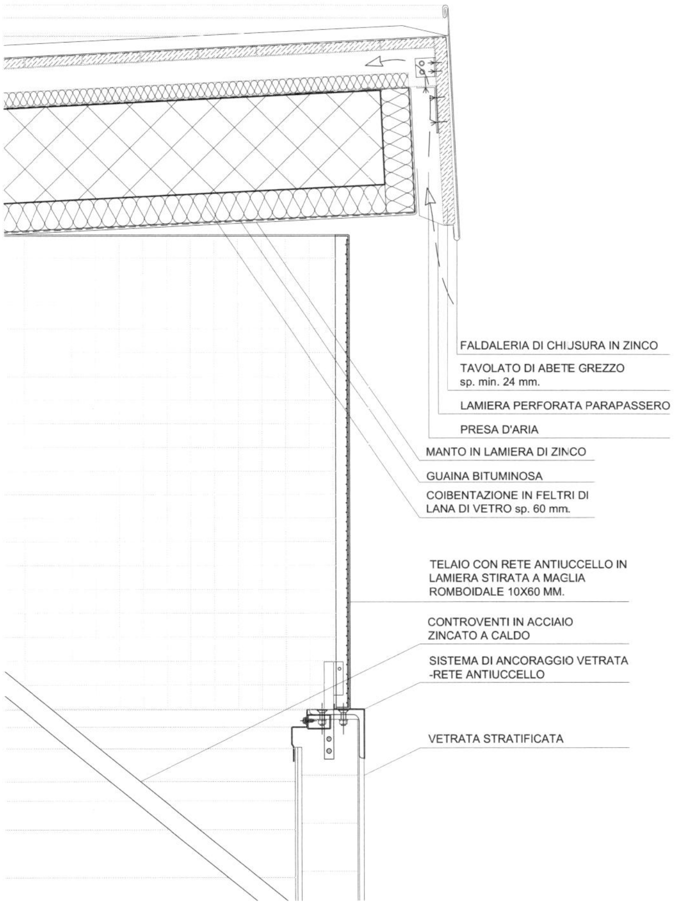

Glass-Front attack covering detail

LYON CONFLUENCE
LYON, FRANCE
2005–2010

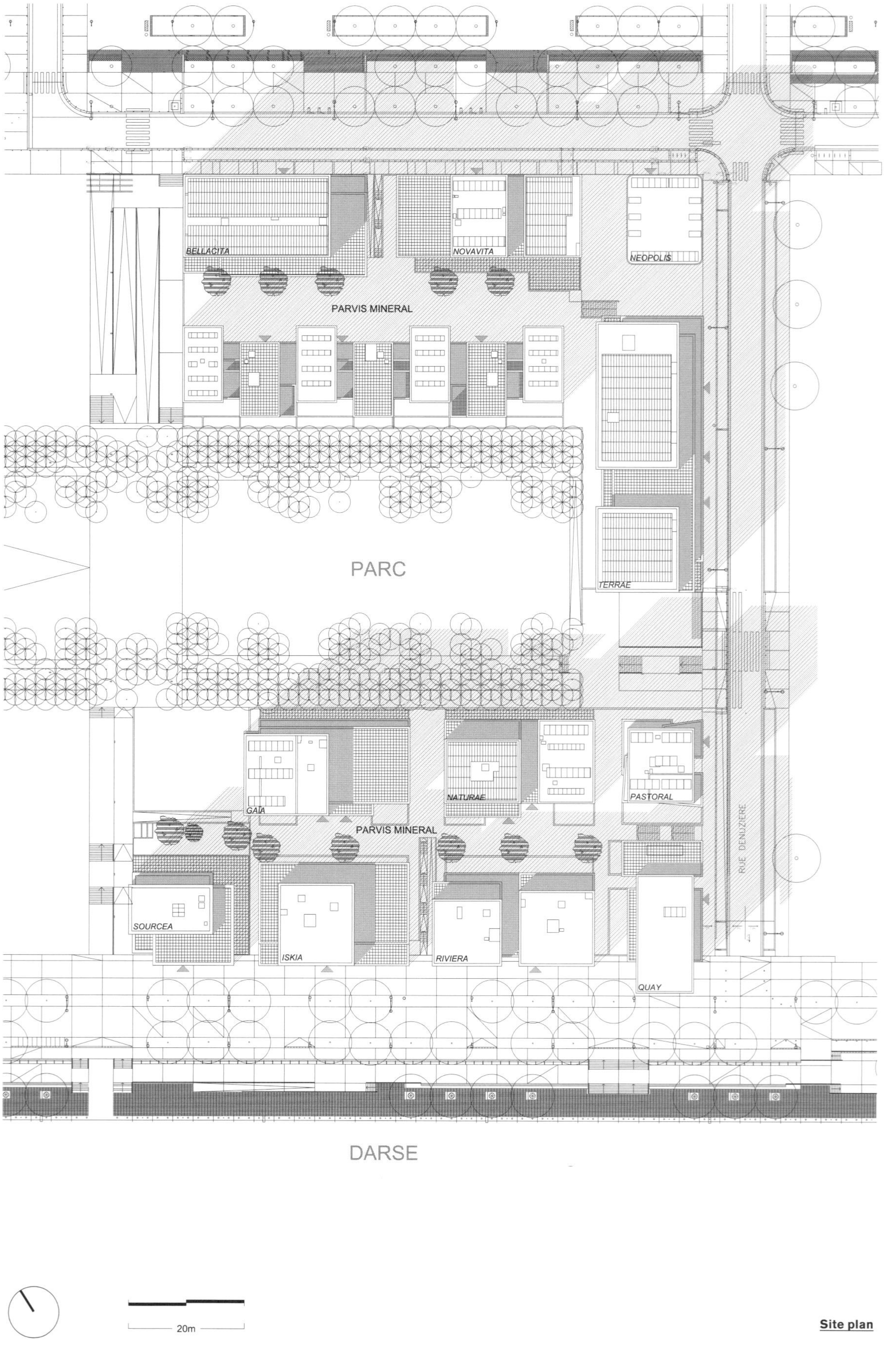

Site plan

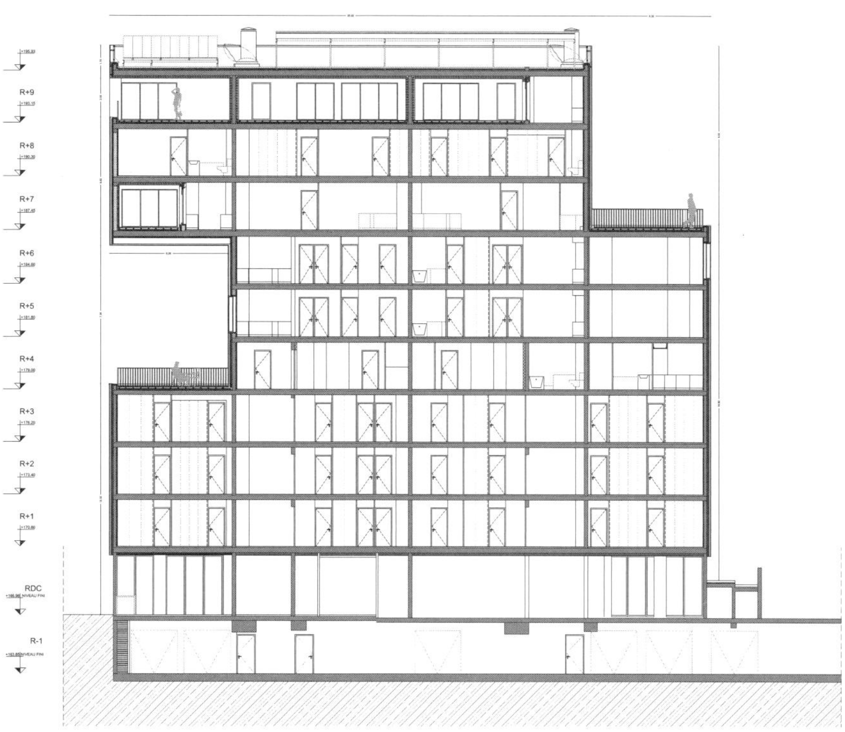

Longitudinal section

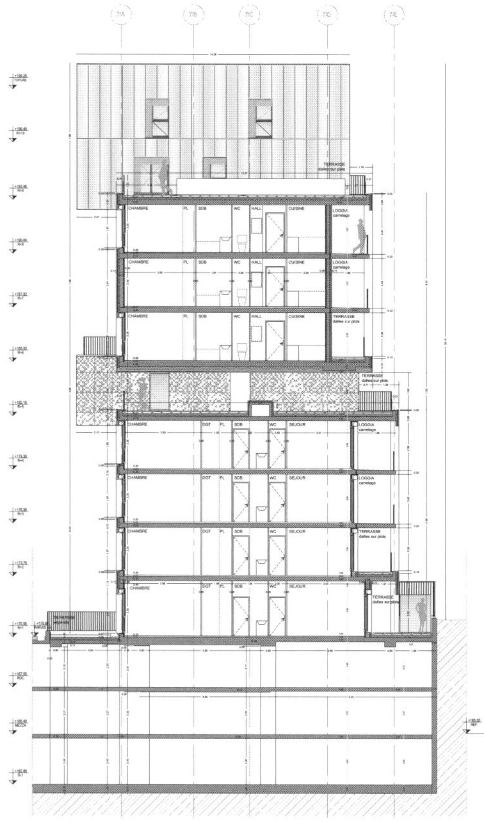

Transversal A section

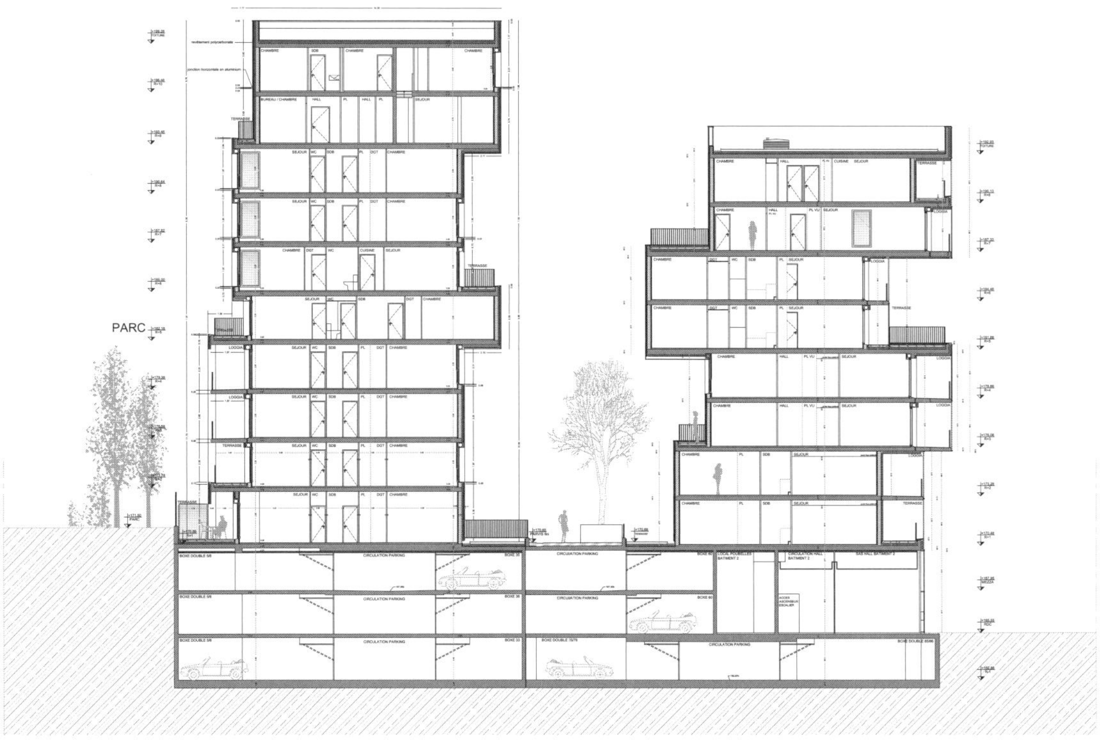

Transversal B section

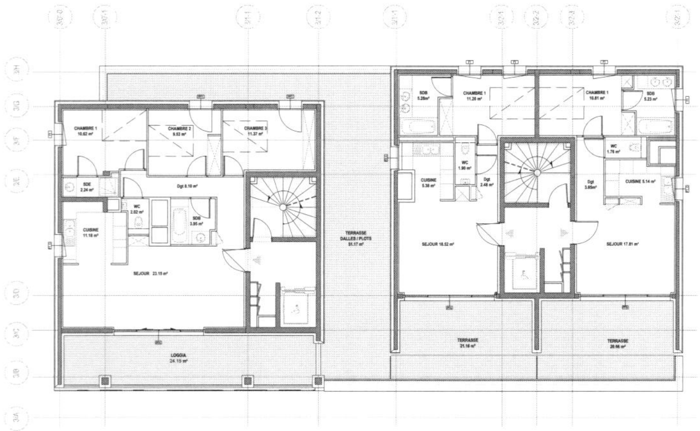

Plan Logement Cote Darse

Plan Logement Cote Nord

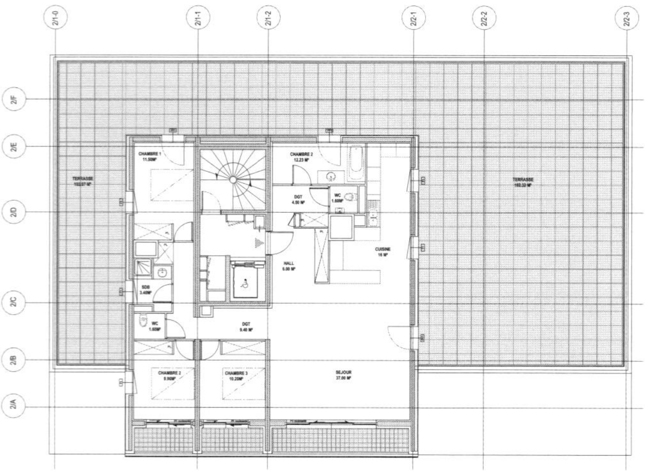

Plan Logement Sur Darse

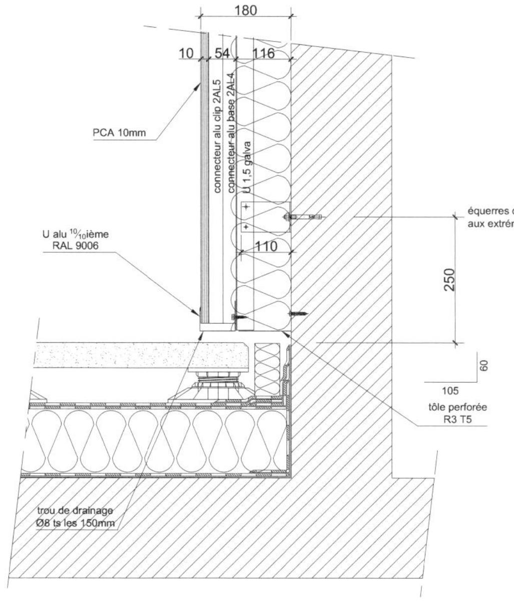

Polycarbonate façade detail

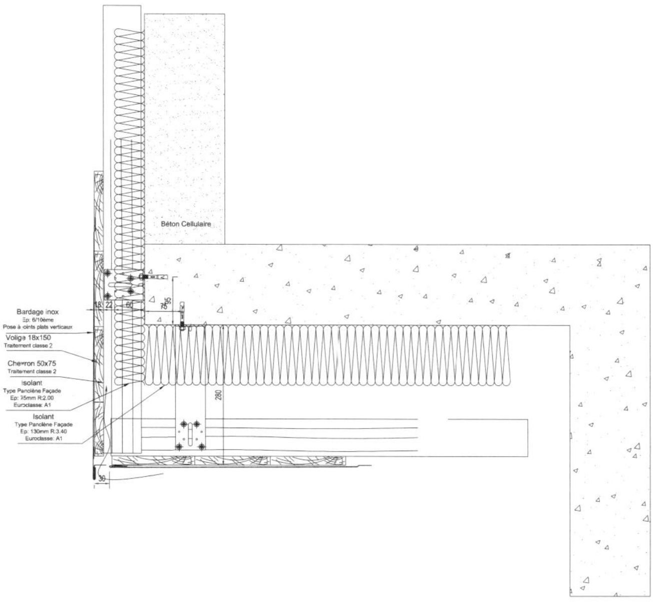

Polycarbonate façade detail

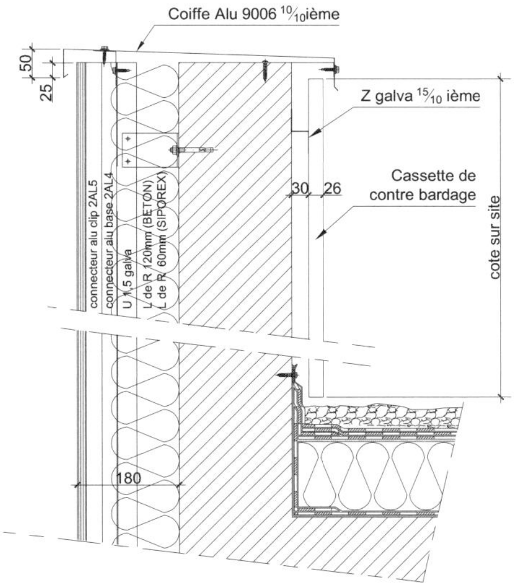

Inox façade detail

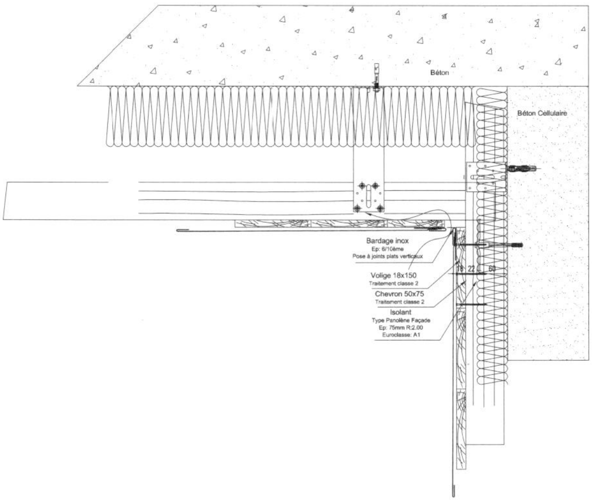

Inox façade detail

20 cm

ADMIRANT ENTRANCE BUILDING
EINDHOVEN, THE NETHERLANDS
2003–2010

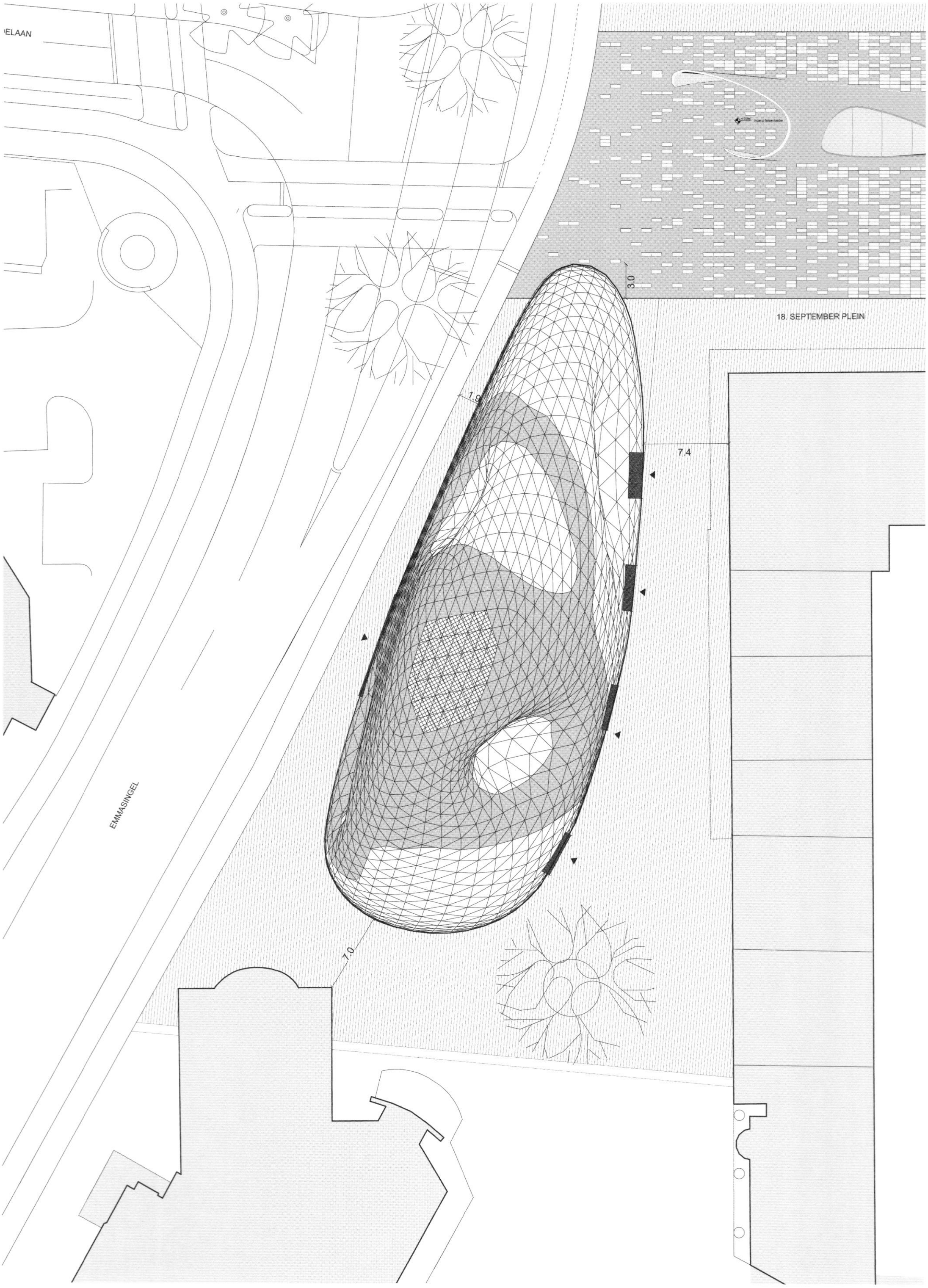

Site plan

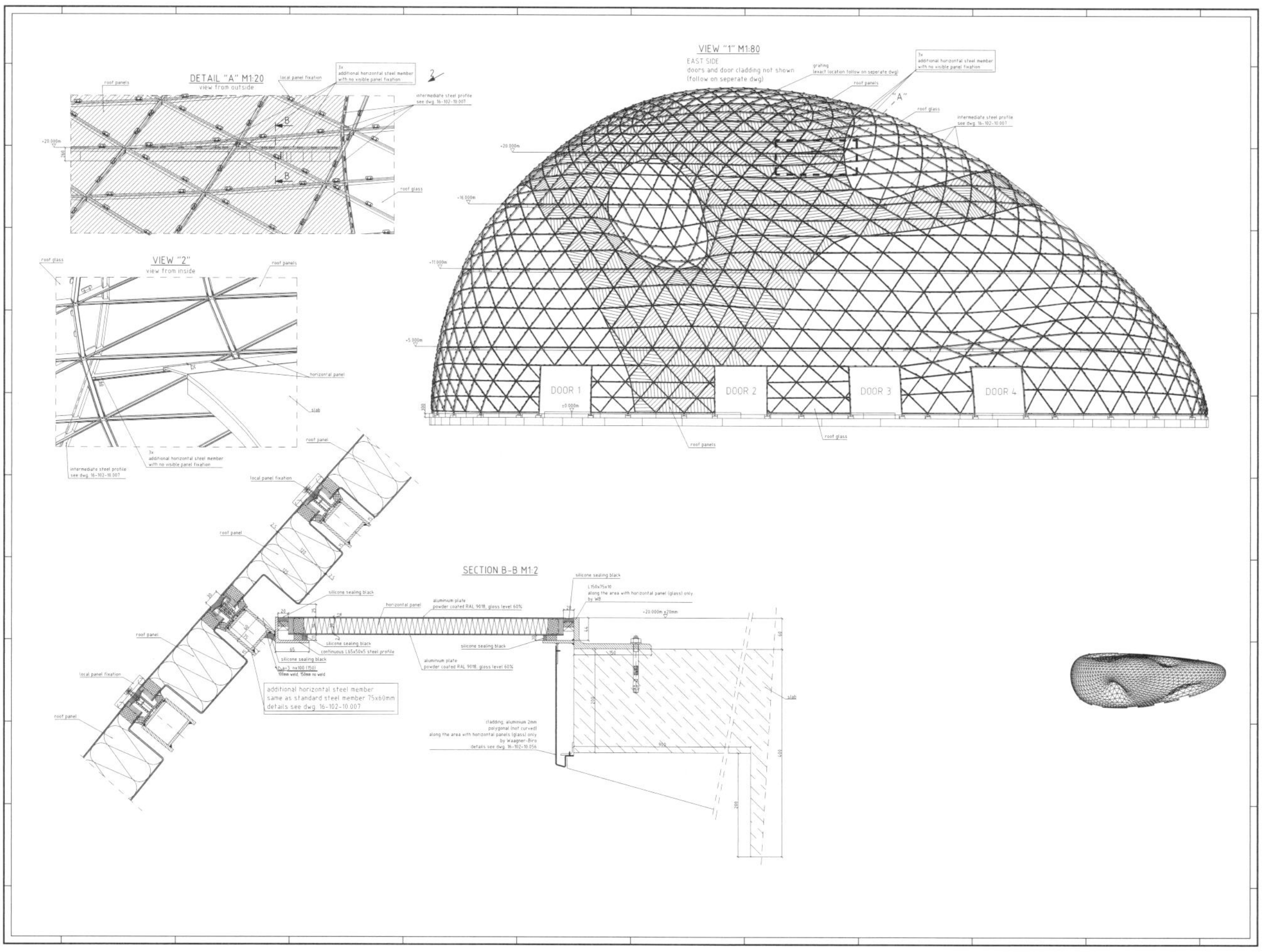
DETAIL "A" M1:20
view from outside
VIEW "2"
view from inside
VIEW "1" M1:80
EAST SIDE
doors and door cladding not shown
(follow on seperate dwg)
DOOR 1
DOOR 2
DOOR 3
DOOR 4
SECTION B-B M1:2
additional horizontal steel member
same as standard steel member 71x60mm
details see dwg. 16-102-10.007

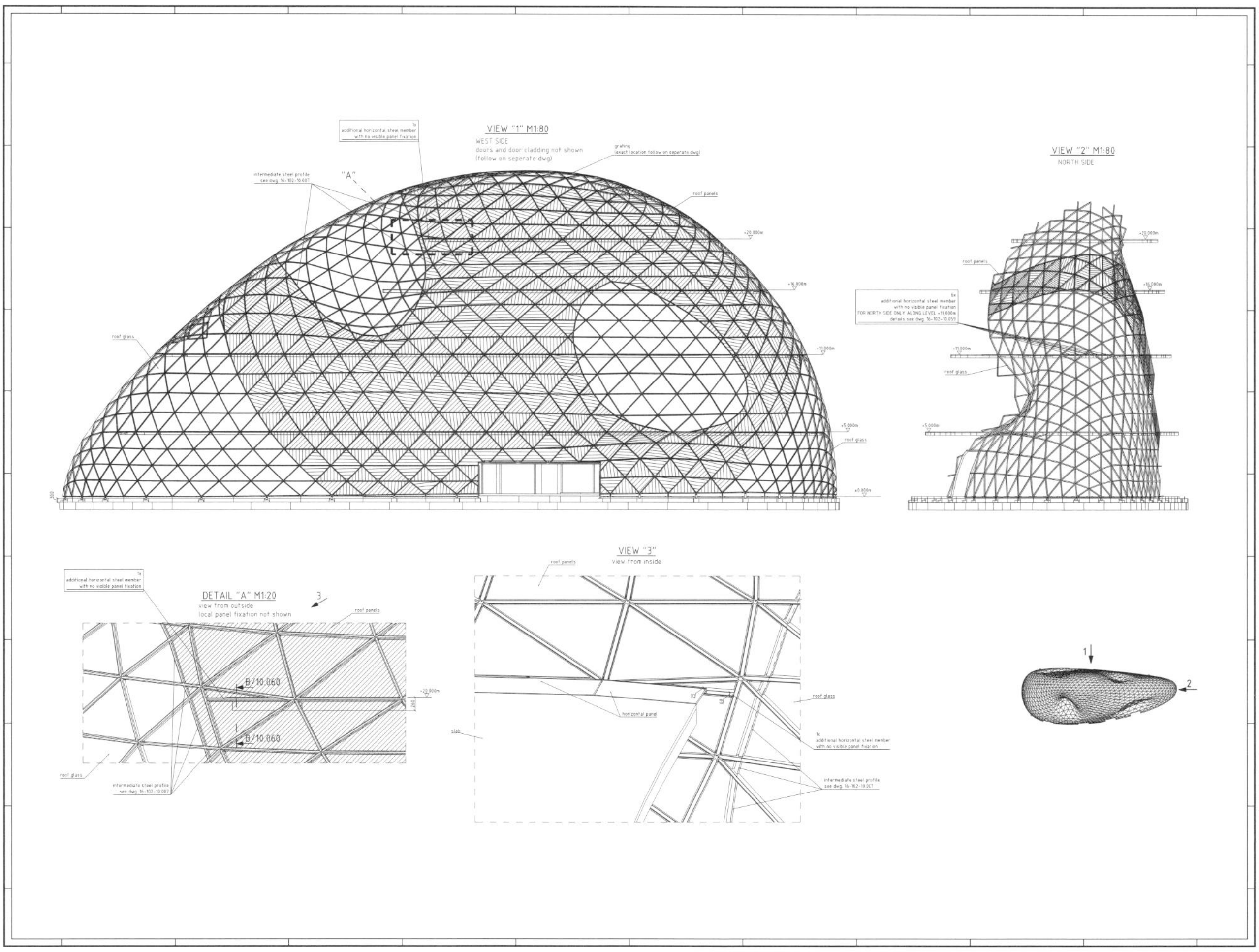
VIEW "1" M1:80
WEST SIDE
doors and door cladding not shown
(follow on seperate dwg)
VIEW "2" M1:80
NORTH SIDE
DETAIL "A" M1:20
view from outside
local panel fixation not shown
VIEW "3"
view from inside

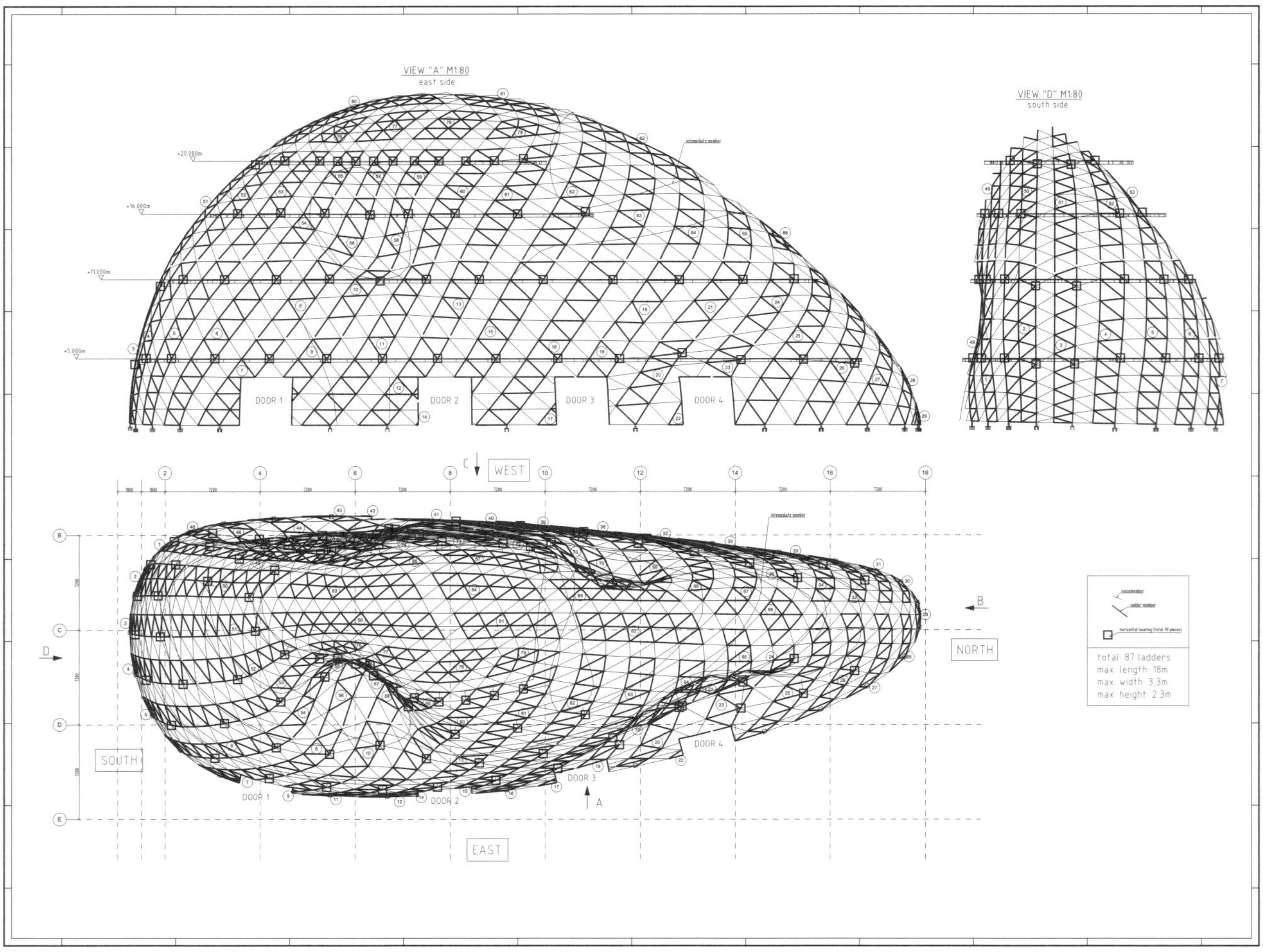
VIEW "A" M1:80
east side
+20.000m
+16.000m
+11.000m
+5.000m
DOOR 1
DOOR 2
DOOR 3
DOOR 4
VIEW "D" M1:80
south side
WEST
EAST
NORTH
SOUTH
total: 87 ladders
max. length: 18m
max. width: 3,3m
max. height: 2,3m

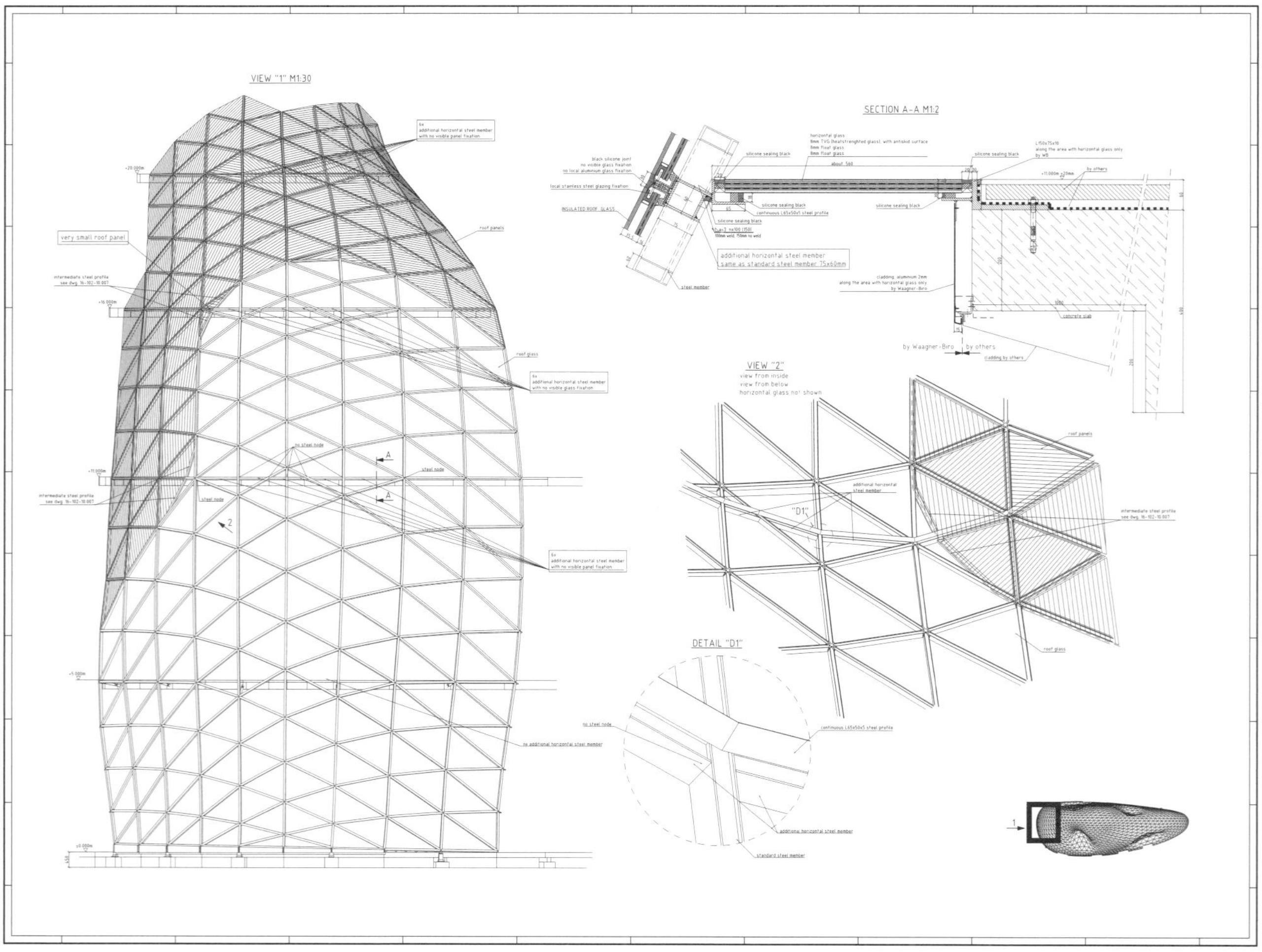
VIEW "1" M1:30
very small roof panel
SECTION A-A M1:2
additional horizontal steel member
same as standard steel member 75x60mm
by Waagner-Biro
by others
VIEW "2"
view from inside
view from below
horizontal glass not shown
"D1"
DETAIL "D1"

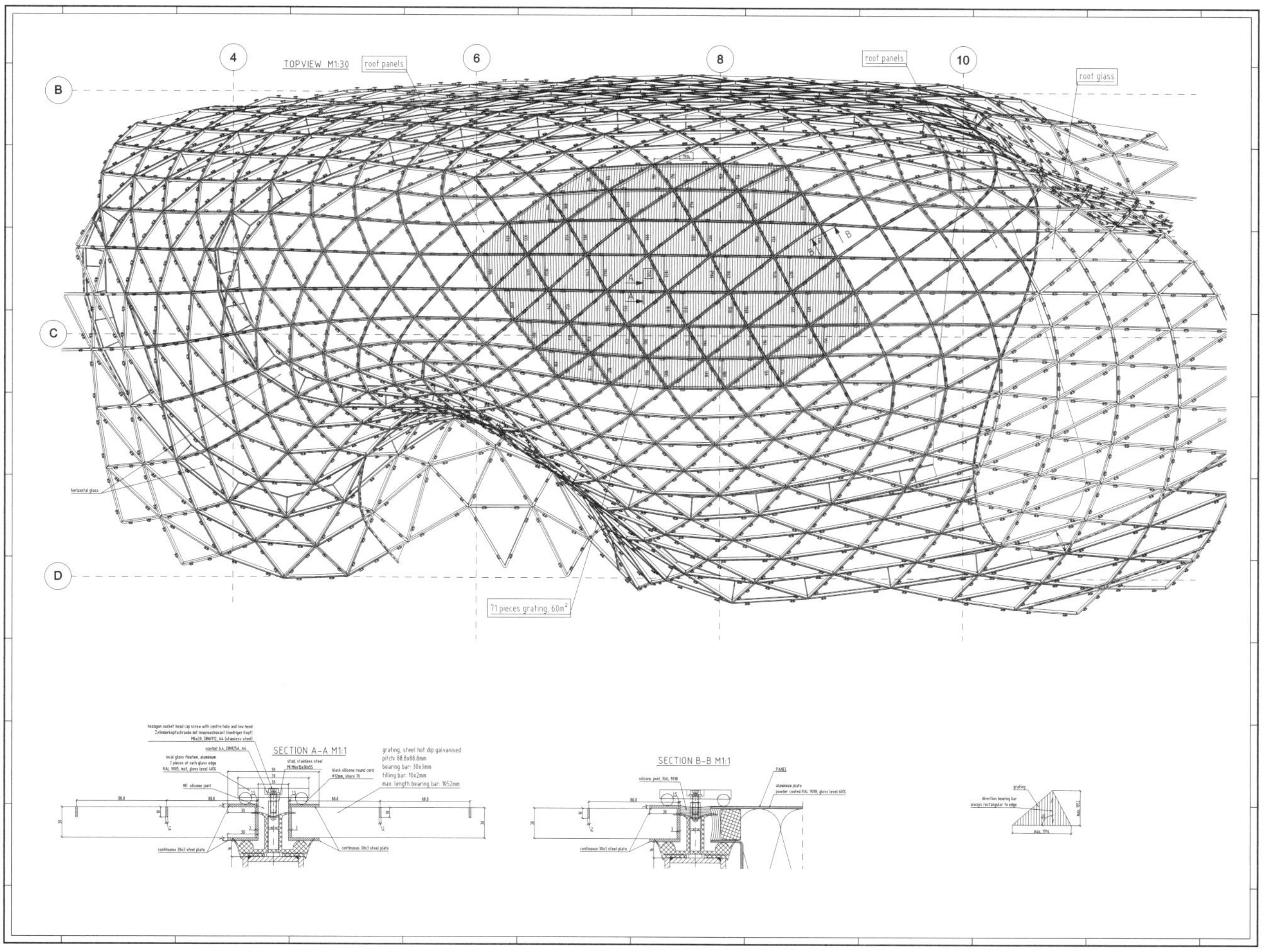

TOPVIEW M1:30
roof panels
roof panels
roof glass
4
6
8
10
B
C
D
71 pieces grating, 60m²
SECTION A-A M1:1
SECTION B-B M1:1
grating, steel hot dip galvanised

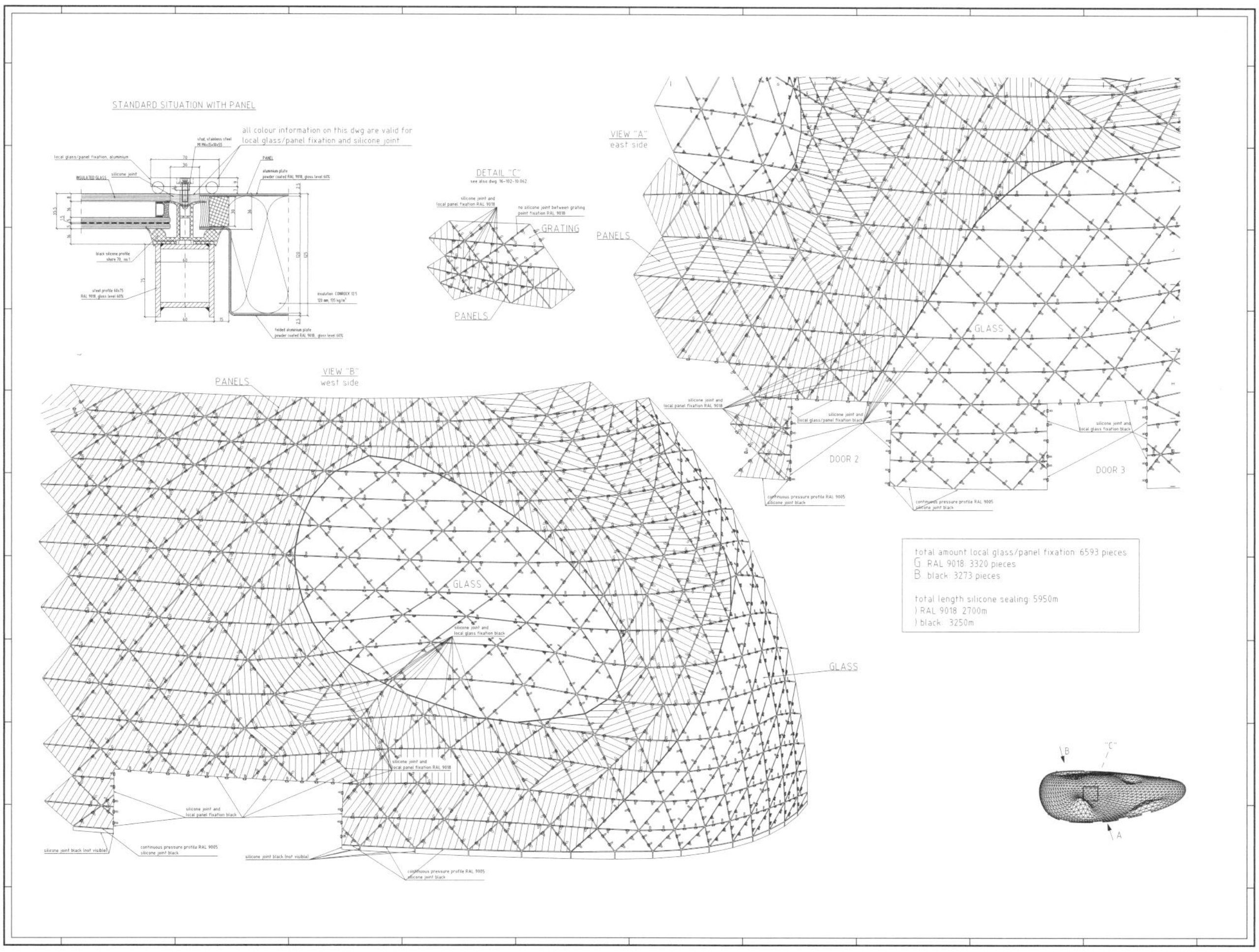

STANDARD SITUATION WITH PANEL
all colour information on this dwg are valid for
local glass/panel fixation and silicone joint
DETAIL "C"
GRATING
PANELS
VIEW "A"
east side
PANELS
GLASS
DOOR 2
DOOR 3
VIEW "B"
west side
PANELS
GLASS
GLASS
total amount local glass/panel fixation: 6593 pieces
G: RAL 9018: 3320 pieces
B: black: 3273 pieces
total length silicone sealing: 5950m
I RAL 9018: 2700m
I black: 3250m

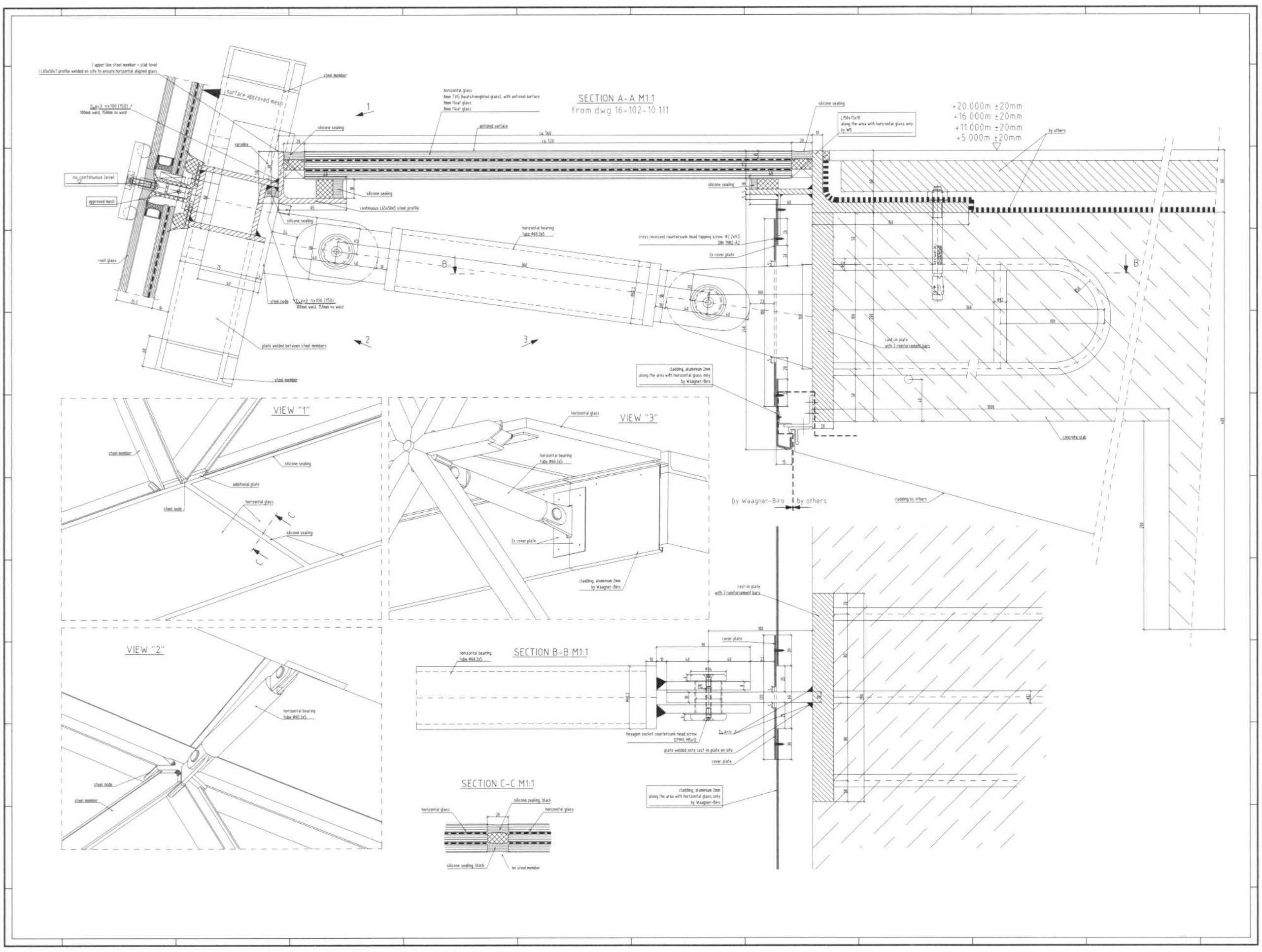
SECTION A-A M1:1
from dwg 16-102-10.111
+20.000m ±20mm
+16.000m ±20mm
+11.000m ±20mm
+5.000m ±20mm
VIEW "1"
VIEW "3"
VIEW "2"
SECTION B-B M1:1
SECTION C-C M1:1
by Waagner-Biro
by others

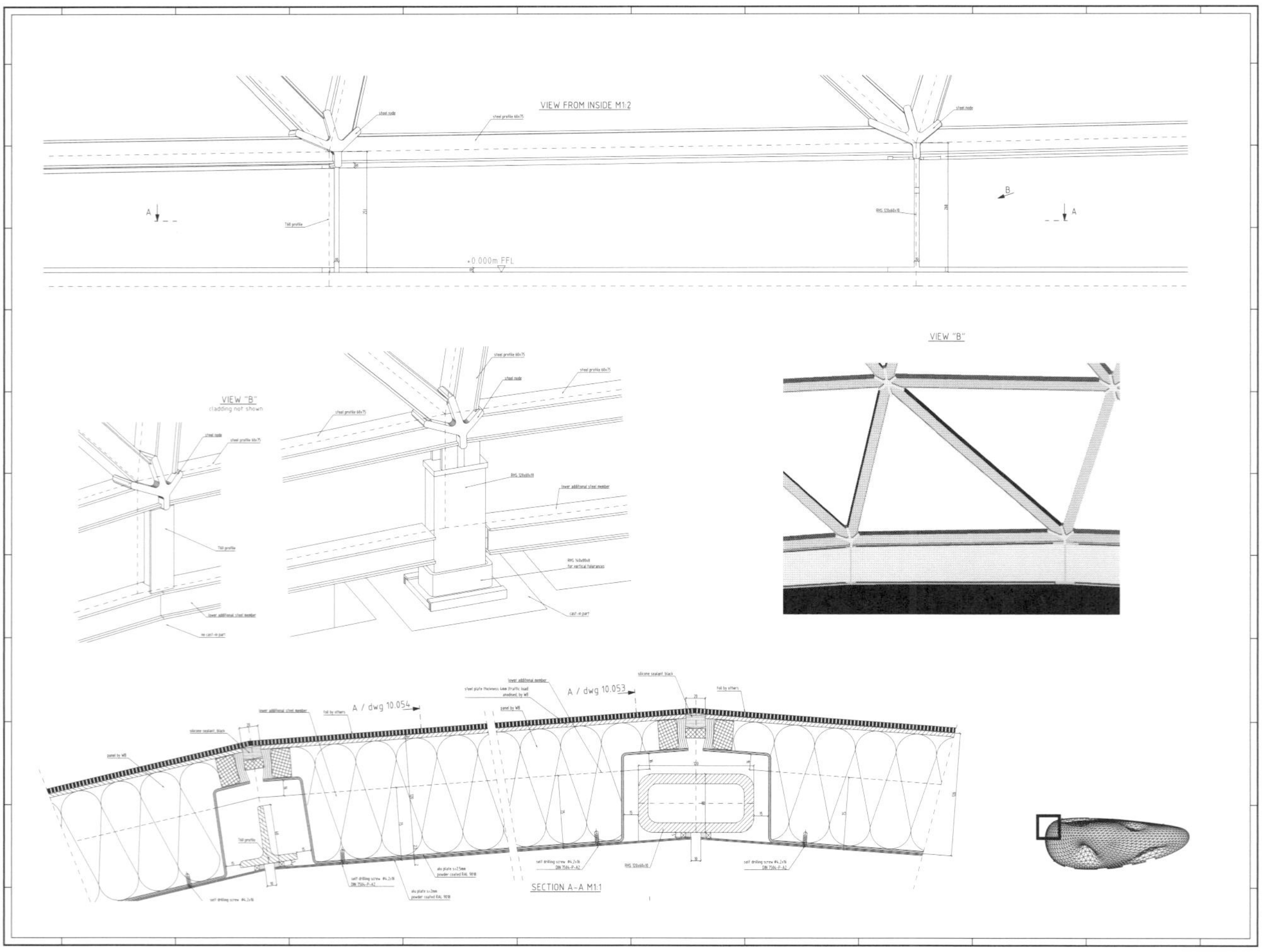
VIEW FROM INSIDE M1:2
+0.000m FFL
VIEW "B"
cladding not shown
VIEW "B"
A / dwg 10.054
A / dwg 10.053
SECTION A-A M1:1

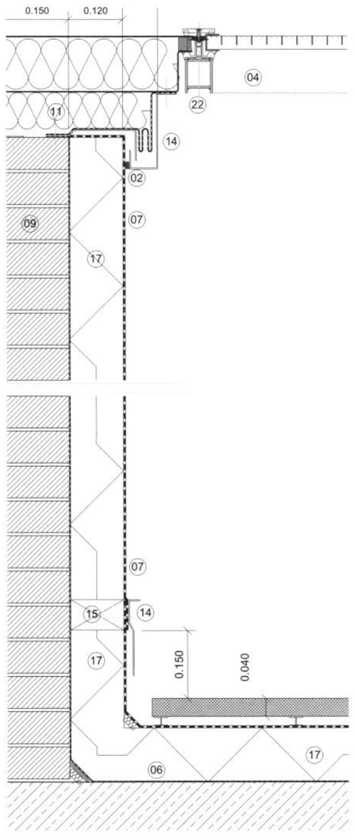

Detail 01 _ external wall at plant deck

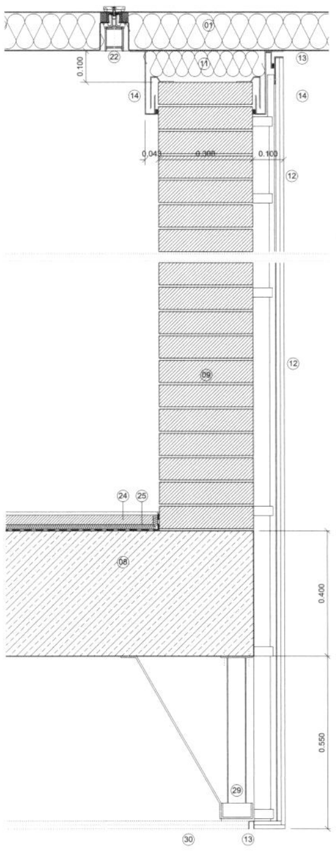

Detail 02 _ internal wall at plant room

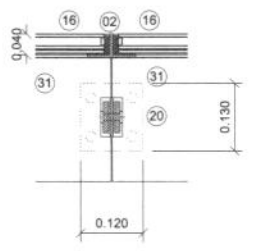

Detail 05 _ façade / floor slab interface _ section

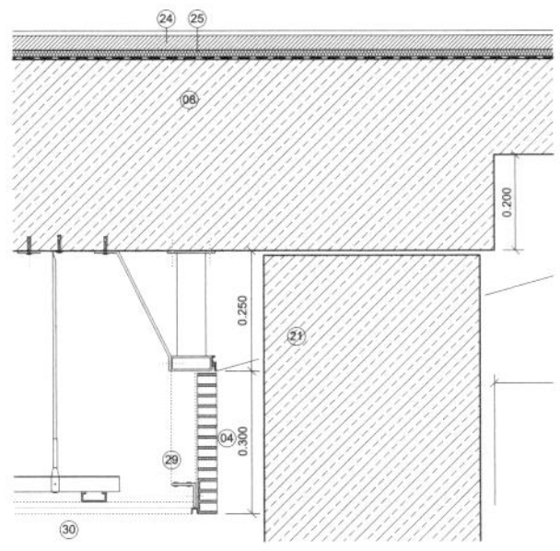

Detail 03 _ suspended ceiling, ventilation grill

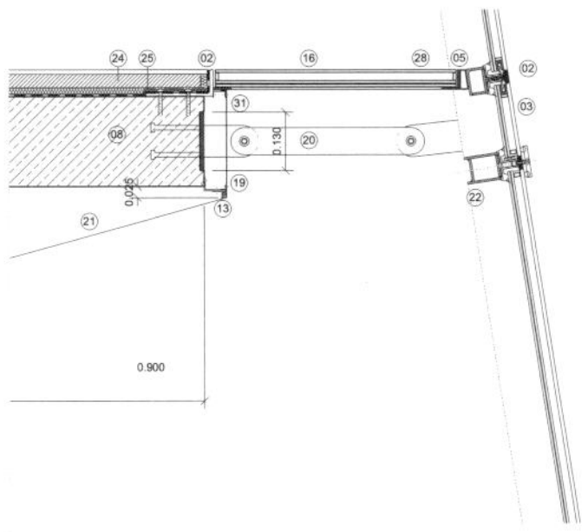

Detail 04 _ façade / floor slab interface _ cross section

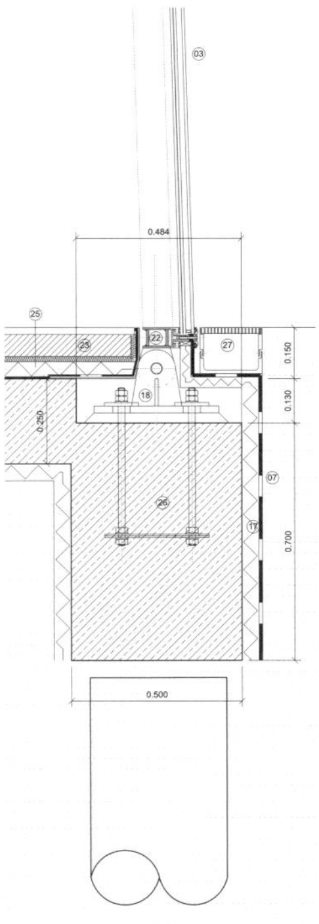

Detail 08 _ base condition façade

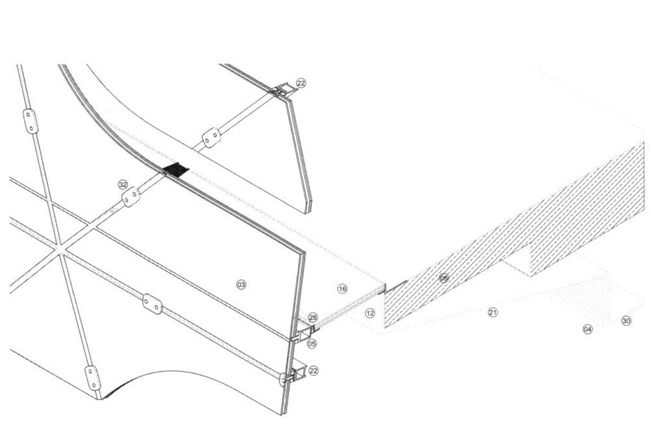

Detail 05 _ bearing horizontal ceiling - façade interface _ 3d

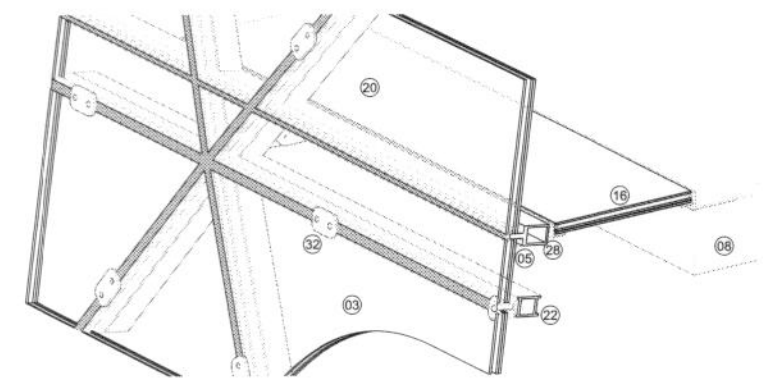

Detail 06 _ bearing horizontal ceiling - façade interface _ 3d

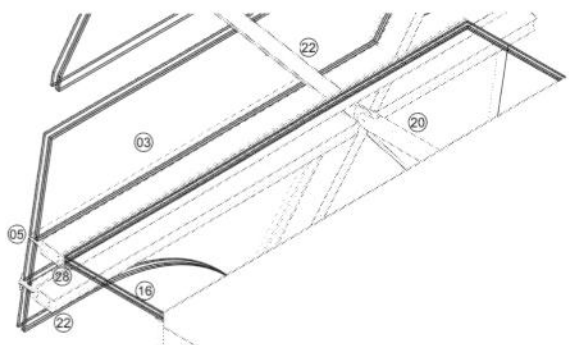

Detail 07 _ bearing horizontal ceiling - façade interface _ 3d

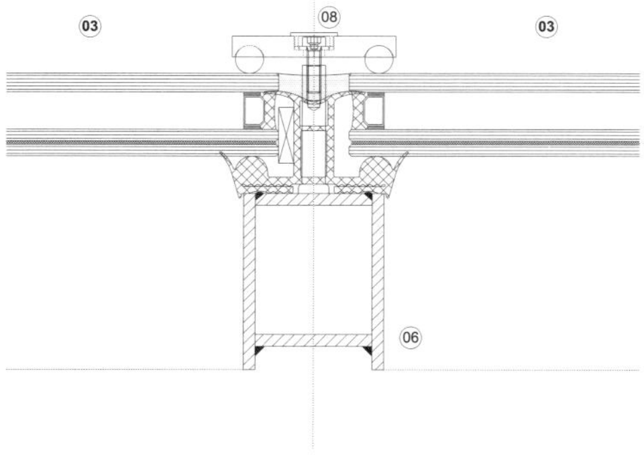

Detail 01 _ mechanical fixing glazing

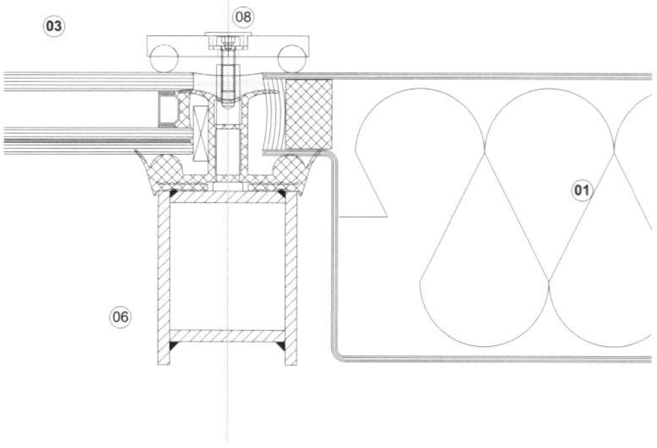

Detail 02 _ mechanical fixing glazing - insulated facade panel

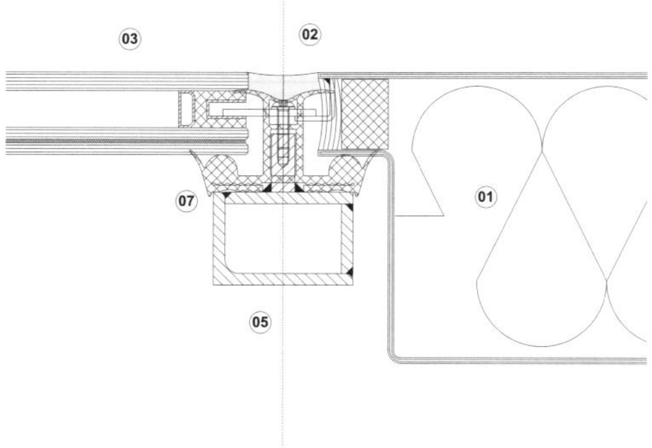

Detail 03 mechanical fixing glazing - insulated facade panel

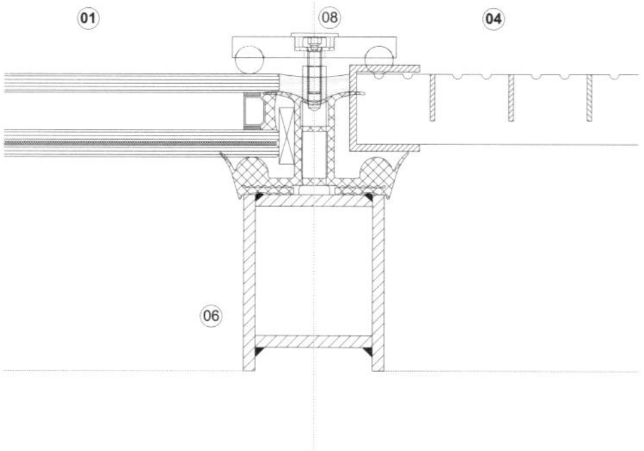

Detail 04 _ transition glazing - metal grill

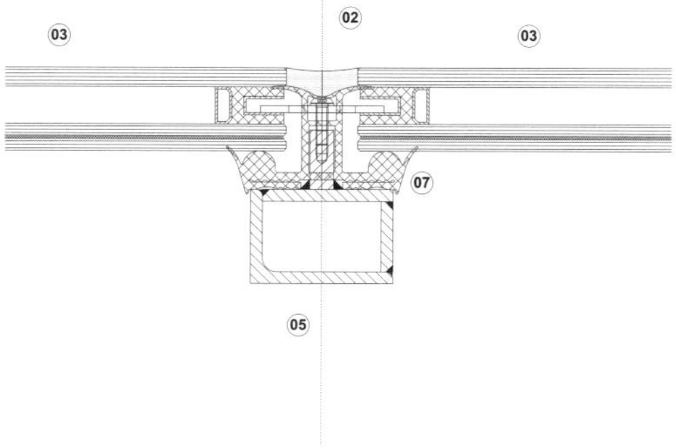

Detail 05 _ mechanical fixing of glass sheets at floorplate interfaces

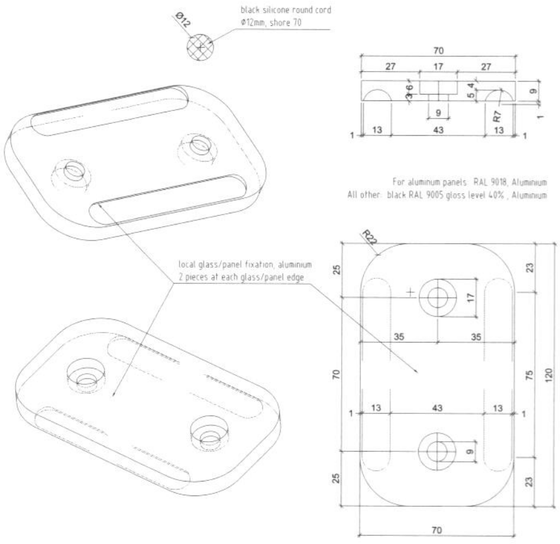

Detail 06 _ mechanical fixation

DETAIL "1"
view from inside
standard situation

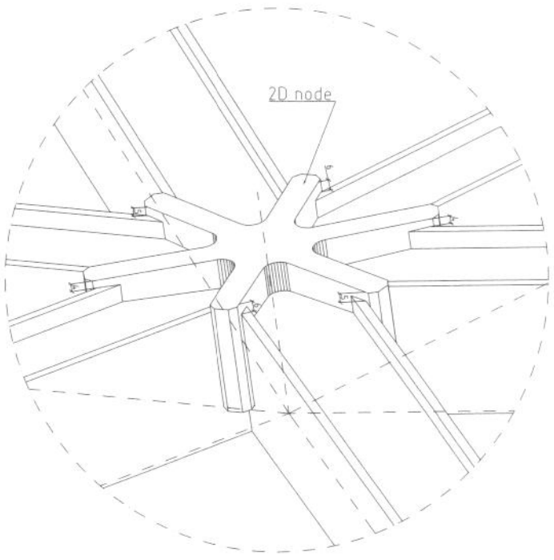

DETAIL "2"
view from inside

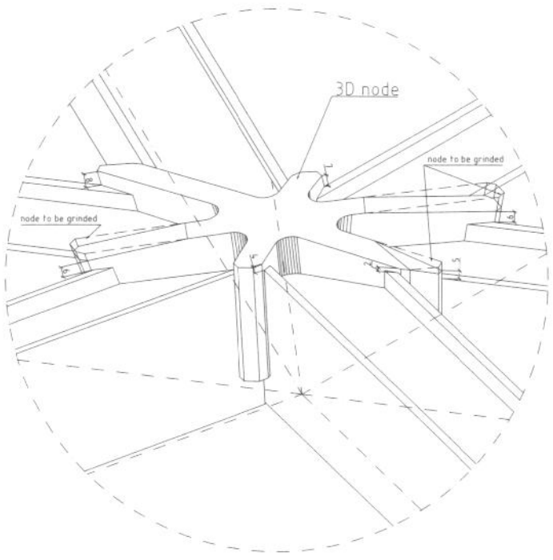

DETAIL "3"
view from inside

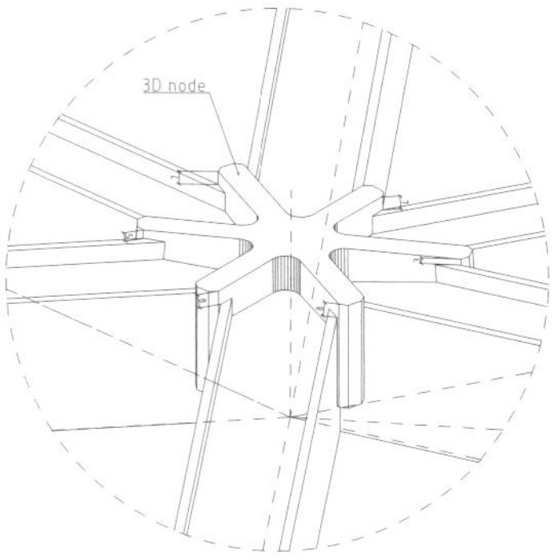

DETAIL "4"
view from inside

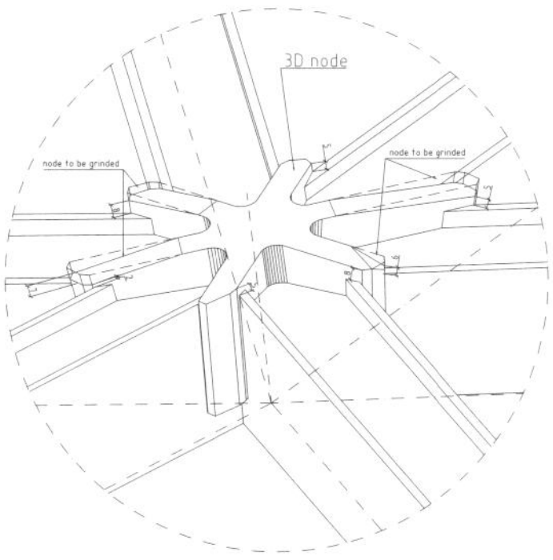

DETAIL "5"
view from inside

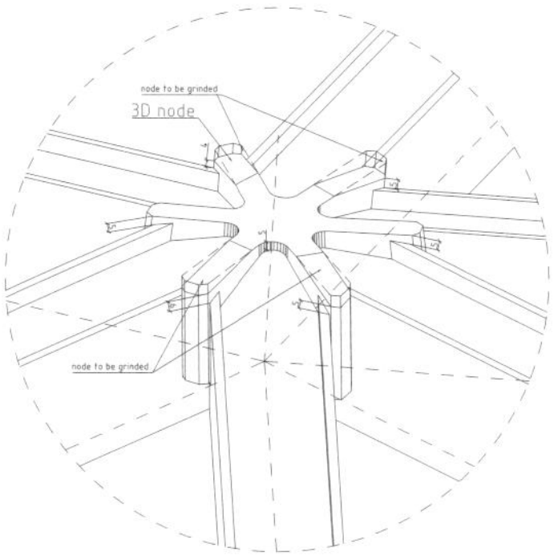

SECTION A-A M1:1

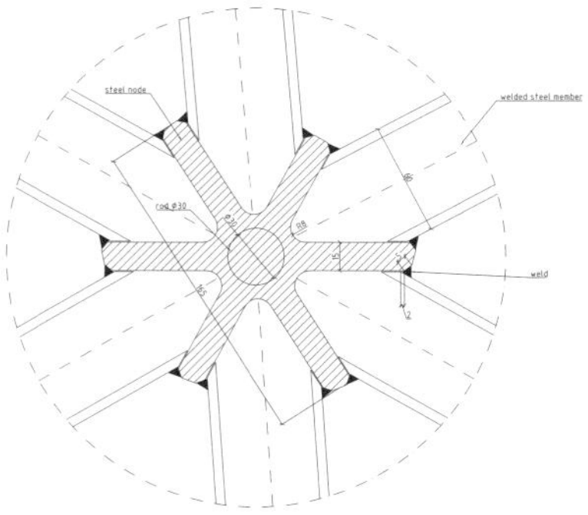

section through a special case node M1:2

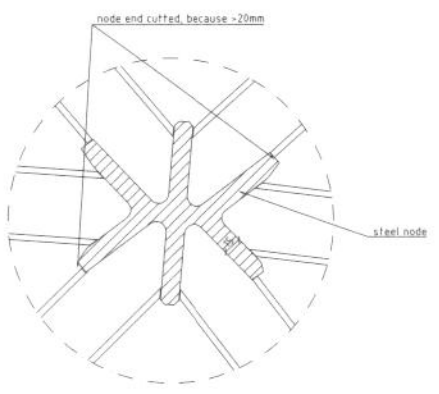

section through a special case node M1:2

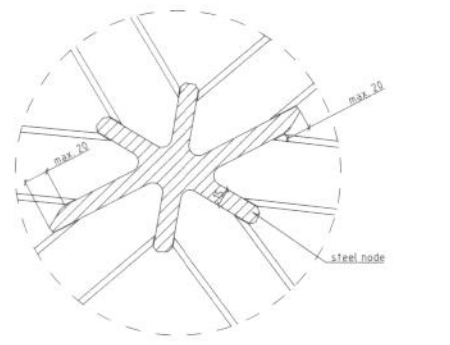

SECTION B-B M1:1

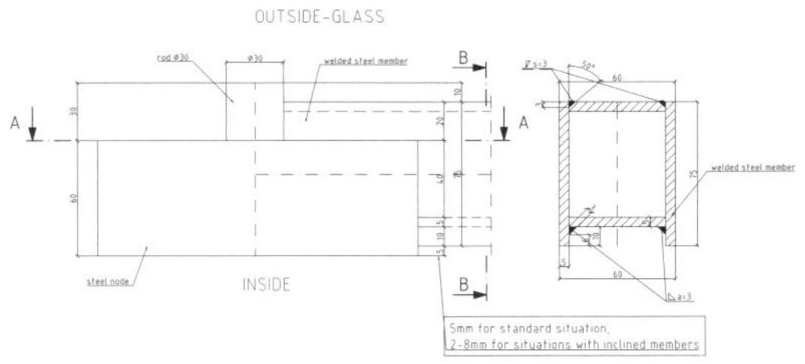

node	total amount about
standard 2D-node as in Detail "1"	40%
3D-node as in Detail "3"	40%
3D-node as in Detail "2","4","5"	20%

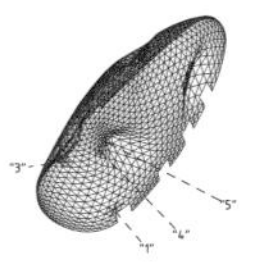

VIEW SOUTHEAST

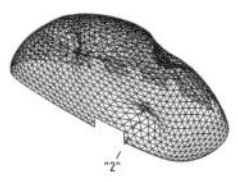

VIEW SOUTHWEST

PERES PEACE HOUSE
JAFFA, TEL AVIV, ISRAEL
1999–2009

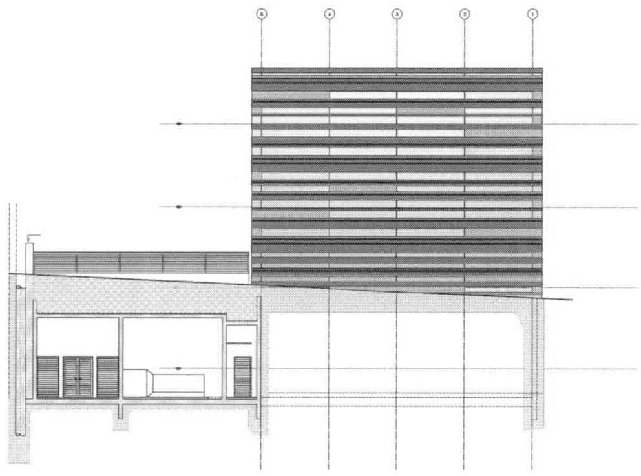

East facade

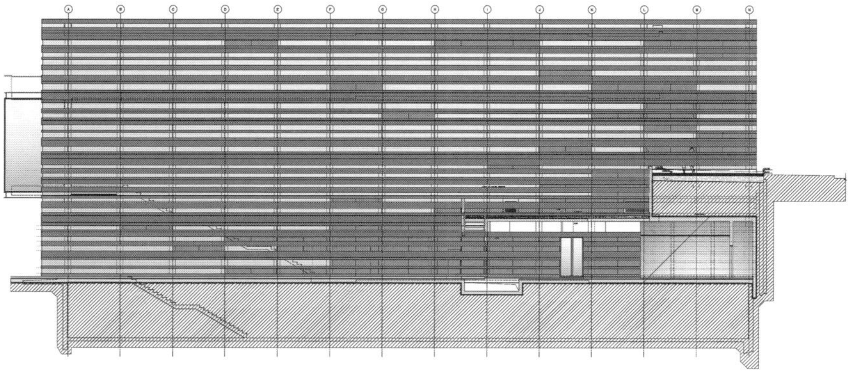

North facade

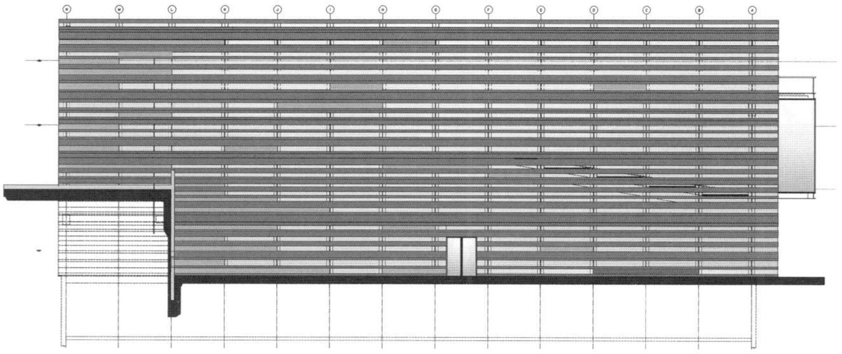

South facade

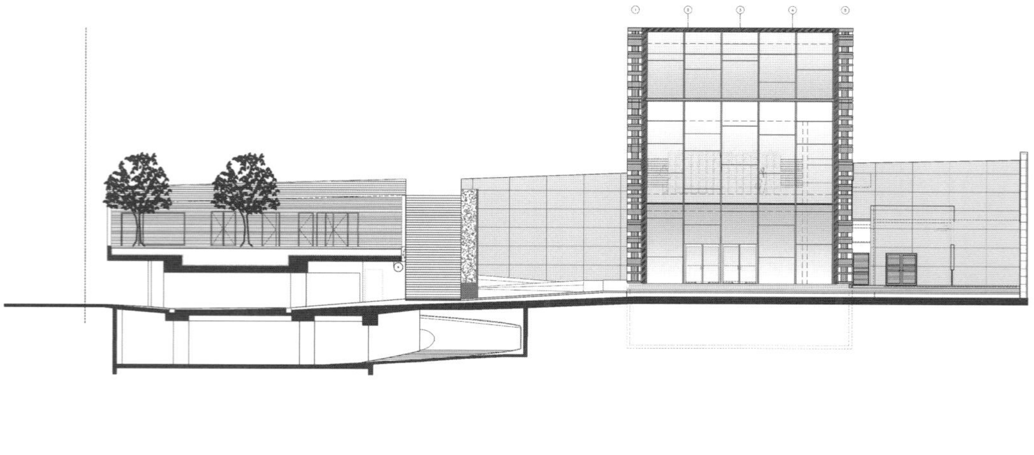

West facade

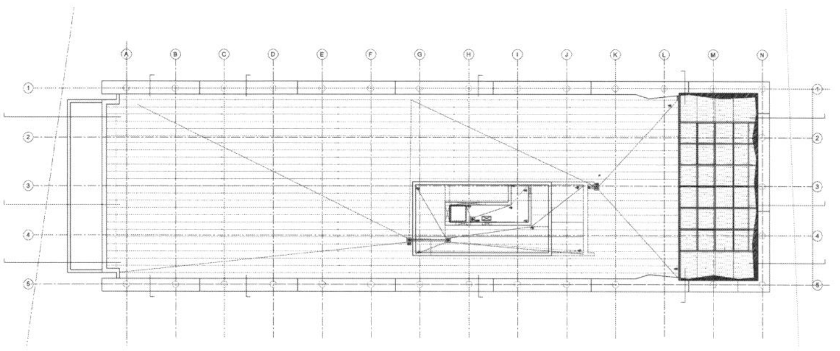

Roof plan

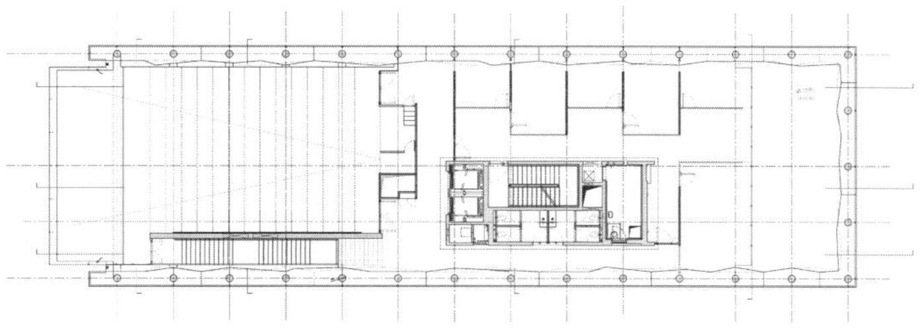

Level +7,95m plan

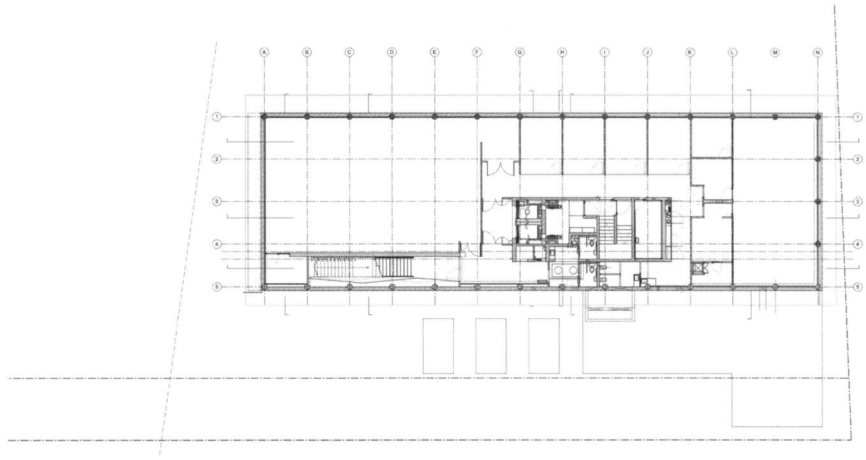

Level -4,00m plan

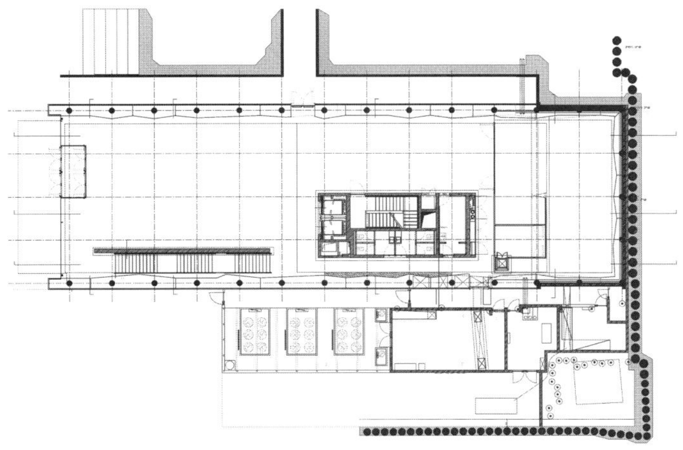

Ground floor plan

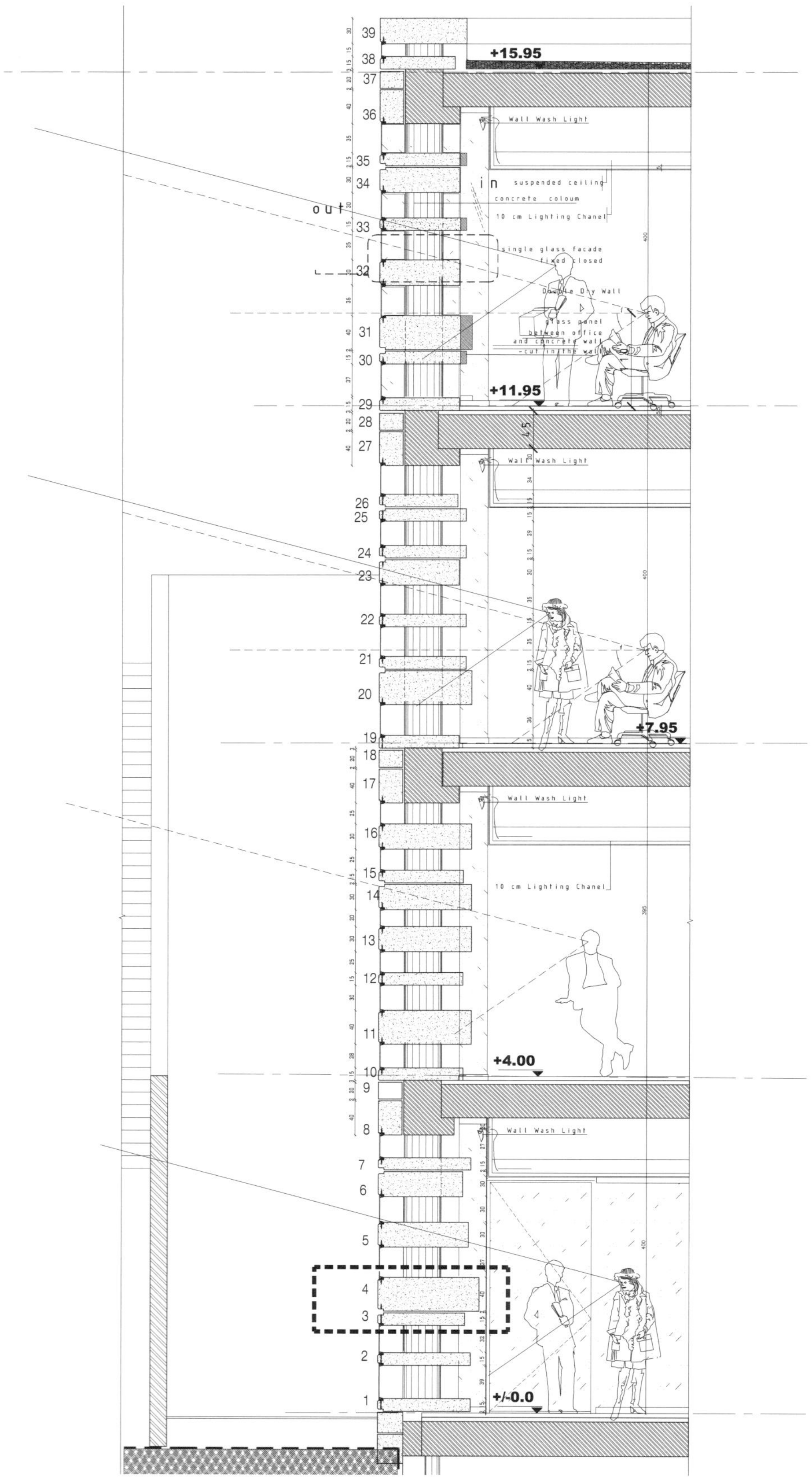

Section details

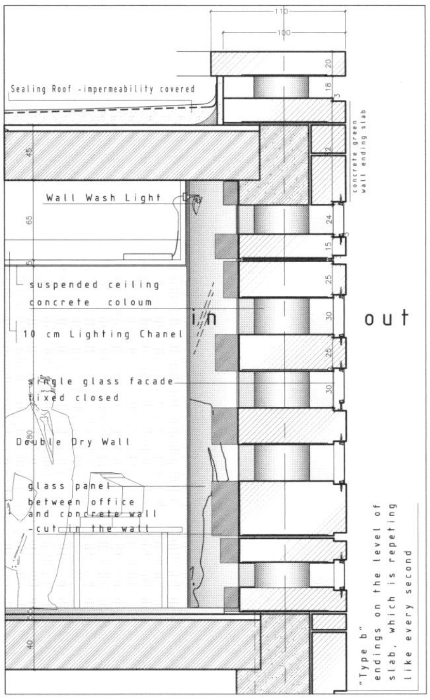

Section 1-1

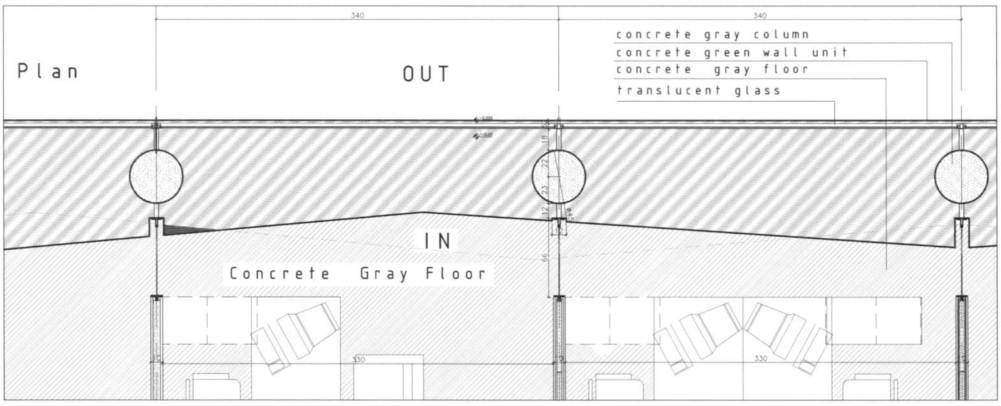

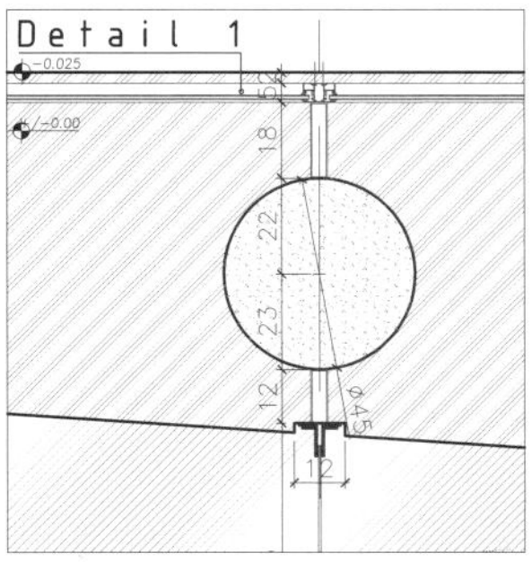

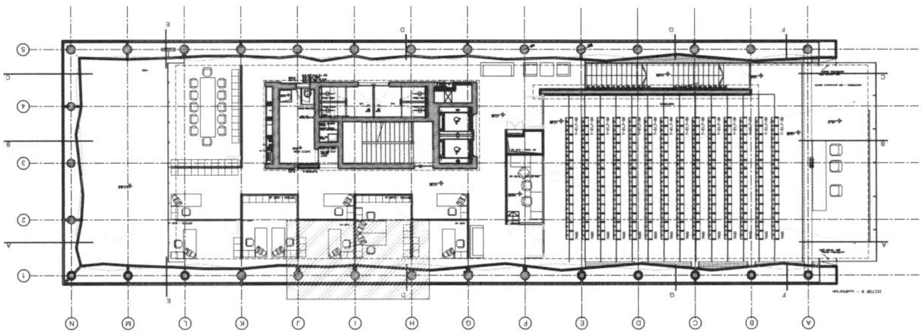

wall junction detail

ST. PAOLO CHURCH
FOLIGNO, ITALY
2001–2009

Site plan

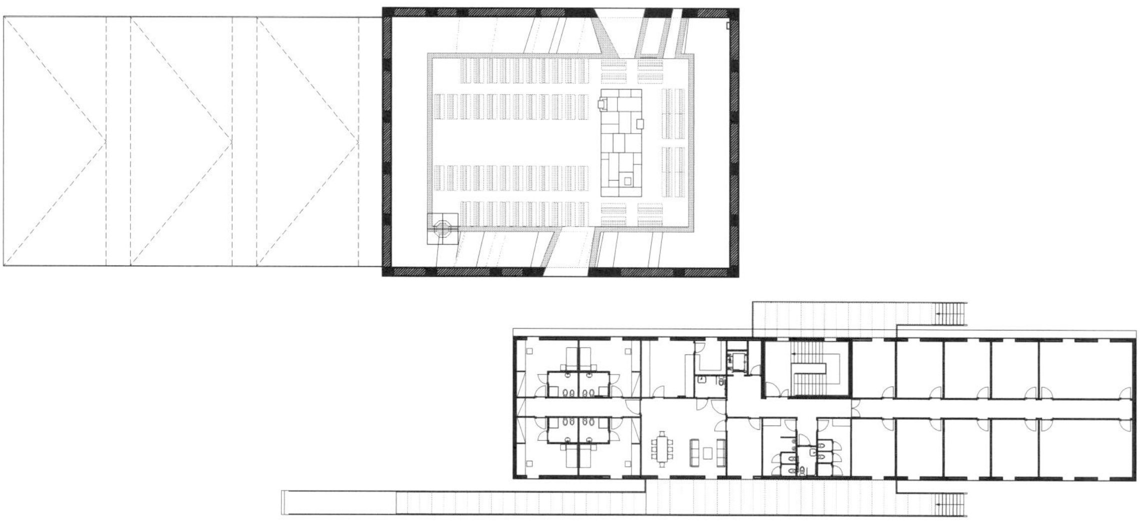

First floor plan

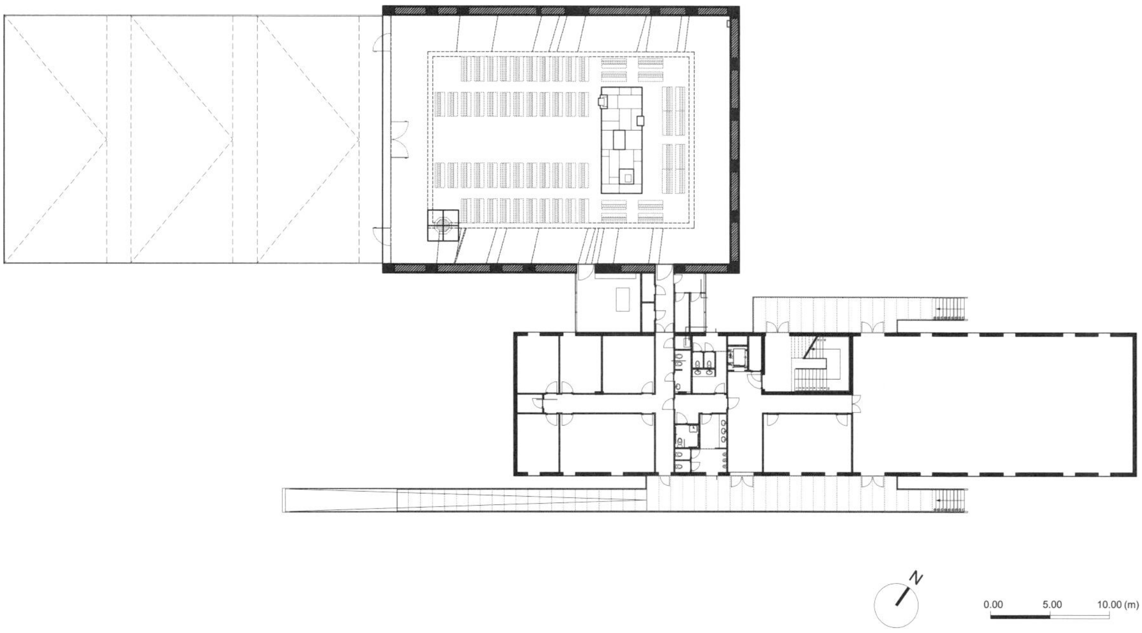

Ground floor plan

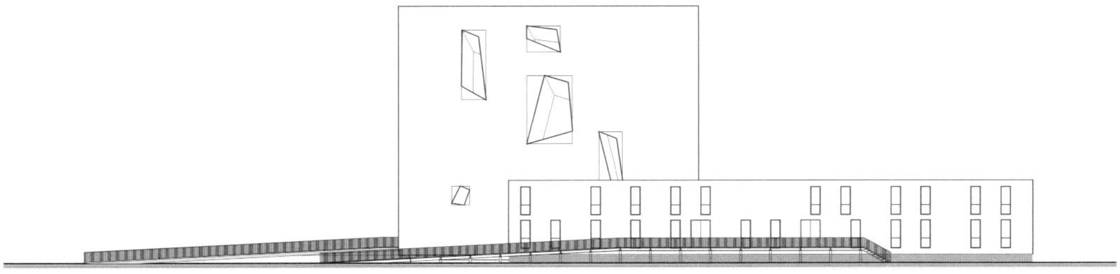

South elevation

West elevation

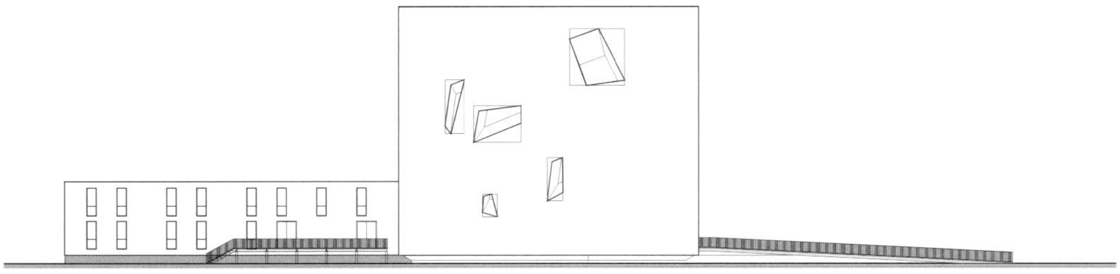

North elevation

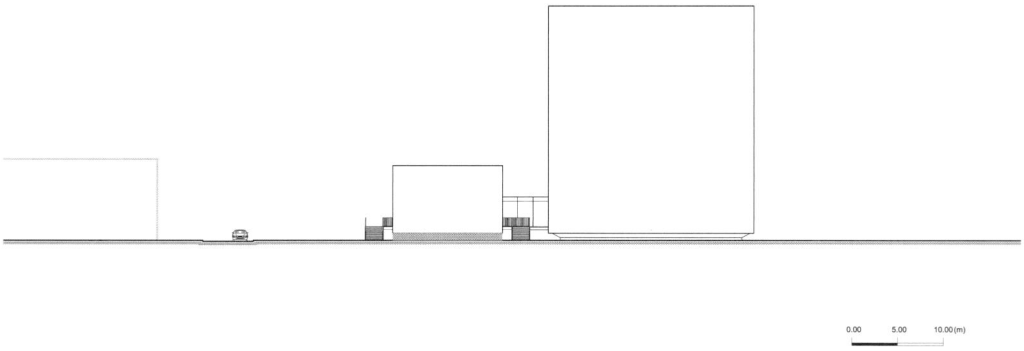

East elevation

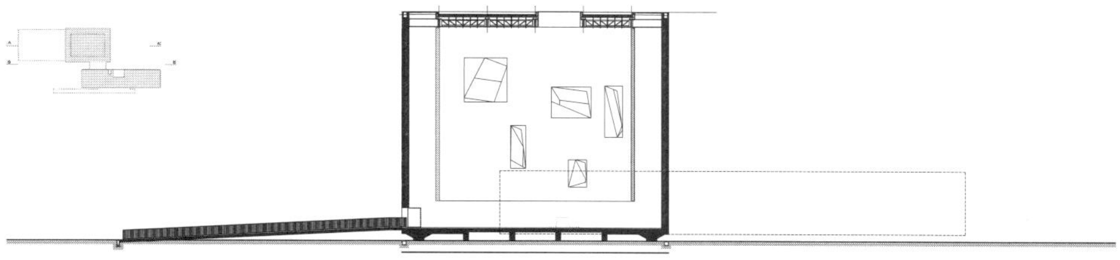

Section AA

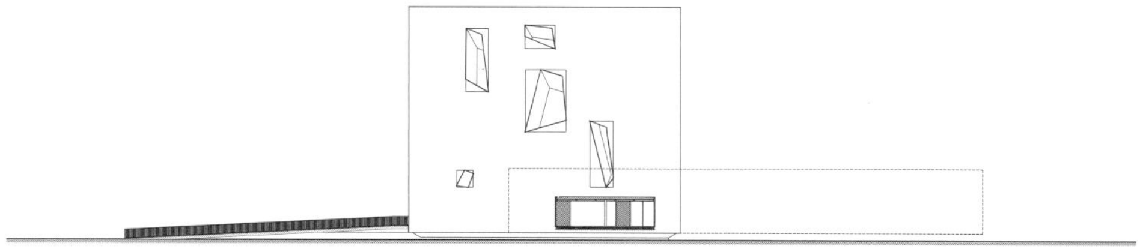

Section BB

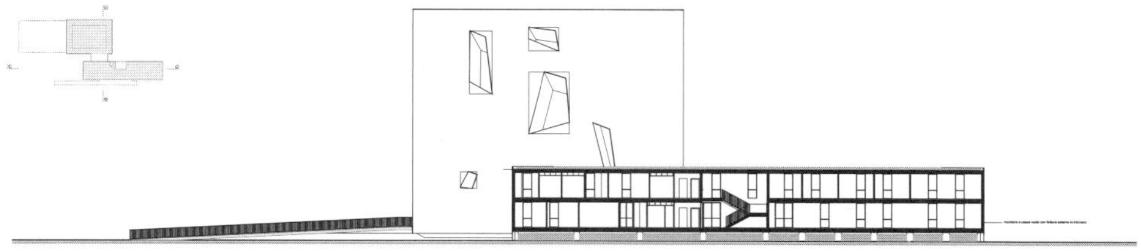

Section CC

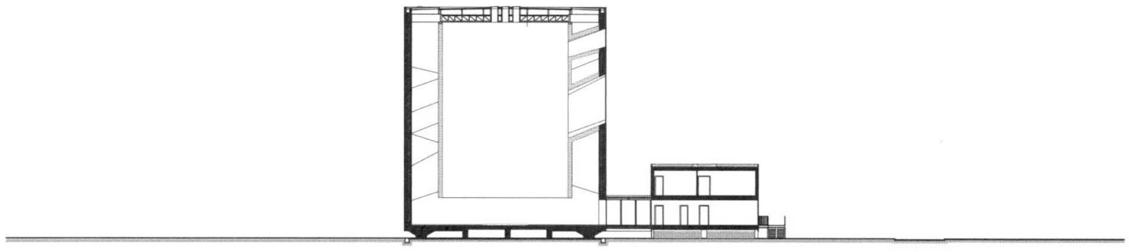

Section DD

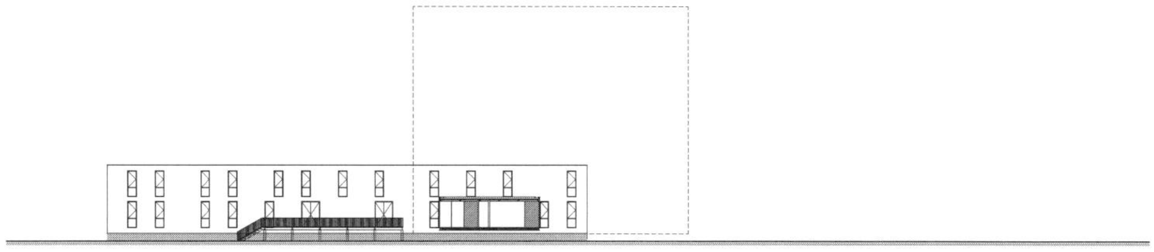

Section EE

MYZEIL
FRANKFURT AM MAIN, GERMANY
2002–2009

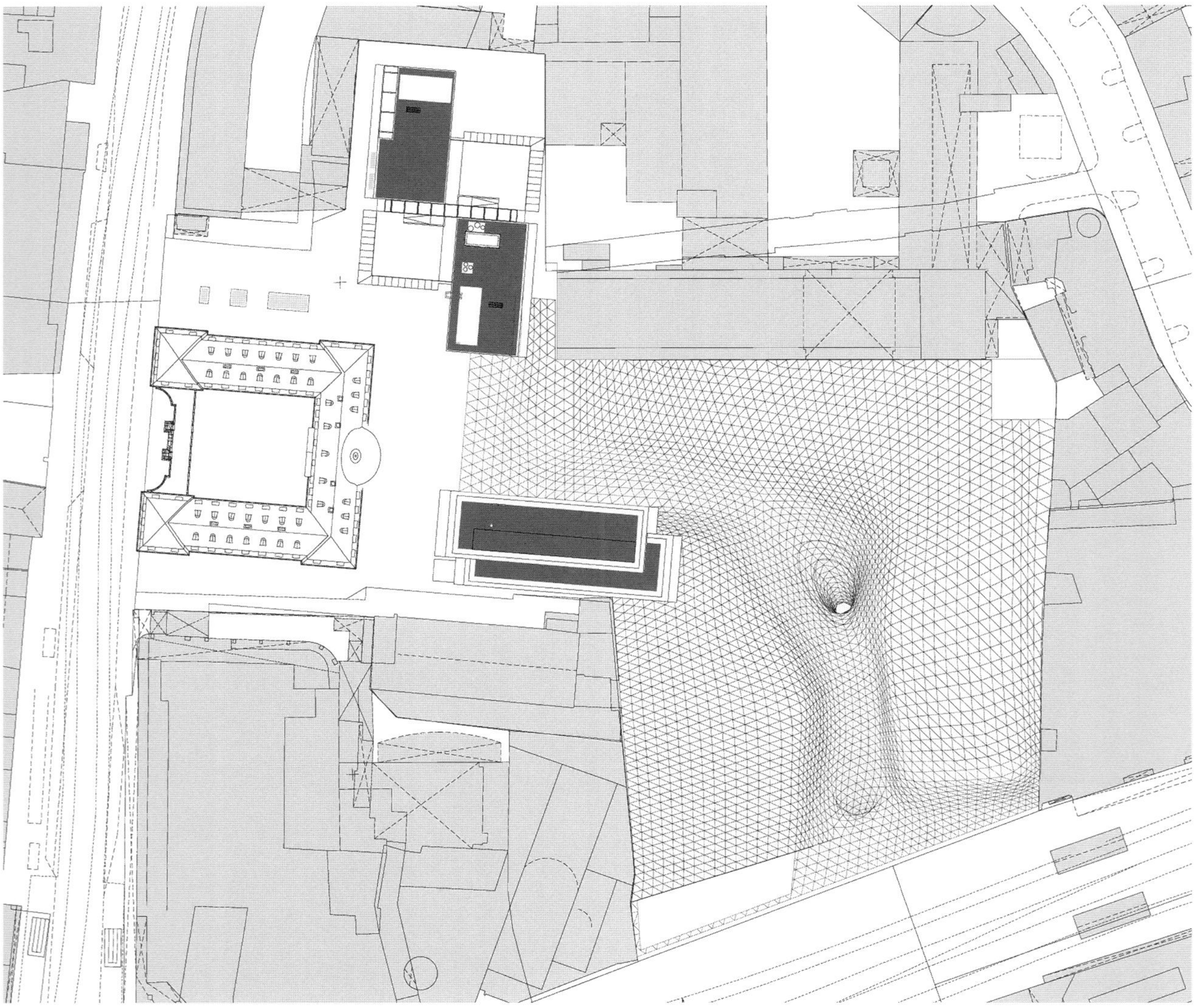

Site plan

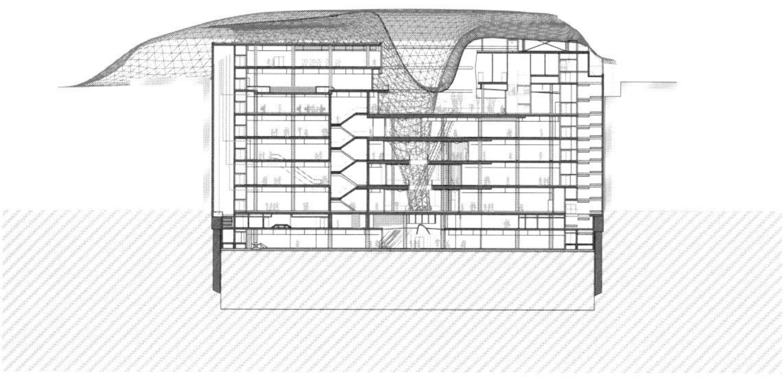

Section AA

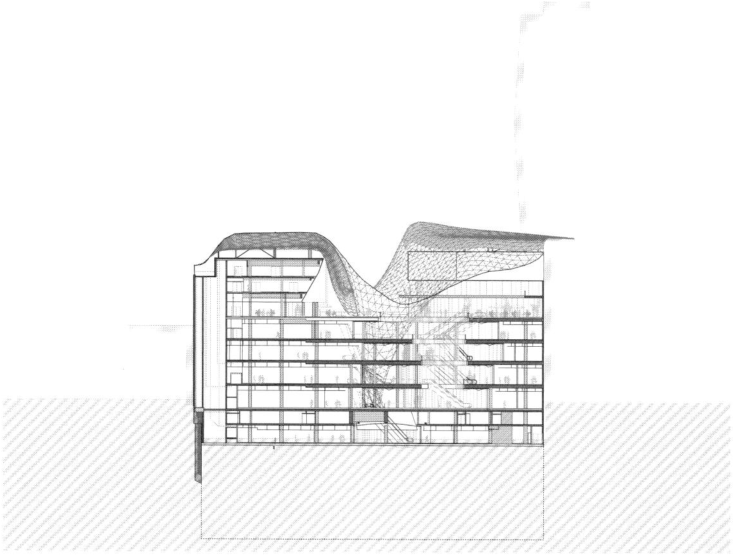

Section BB

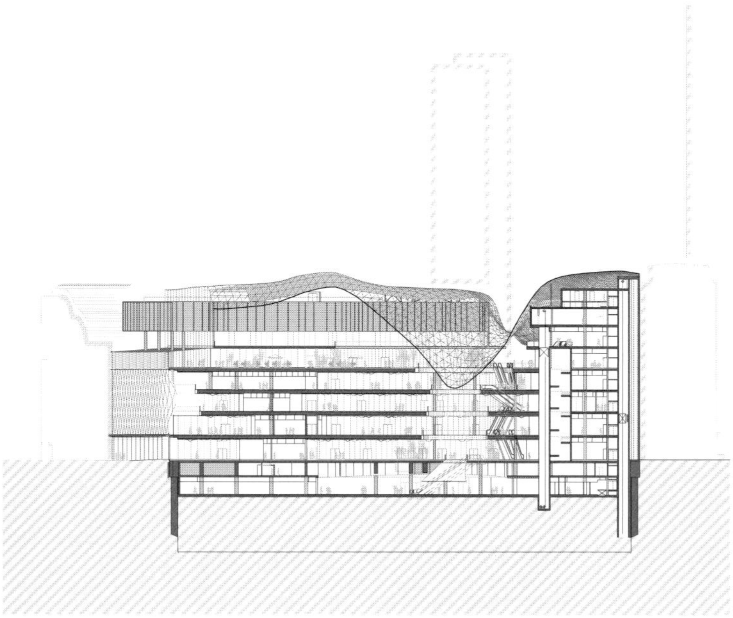

Section FF

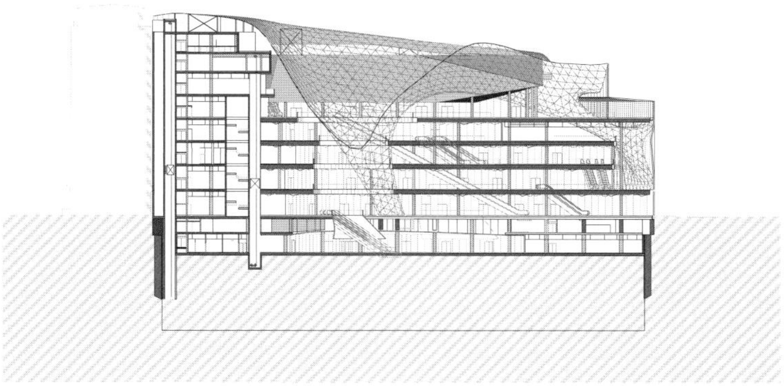

Section II

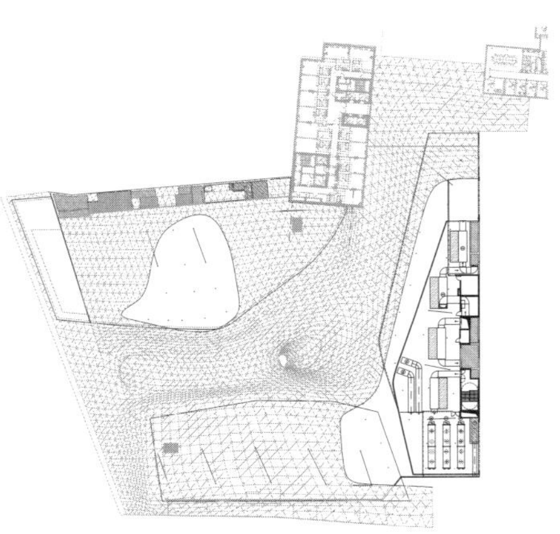

Eighth floor

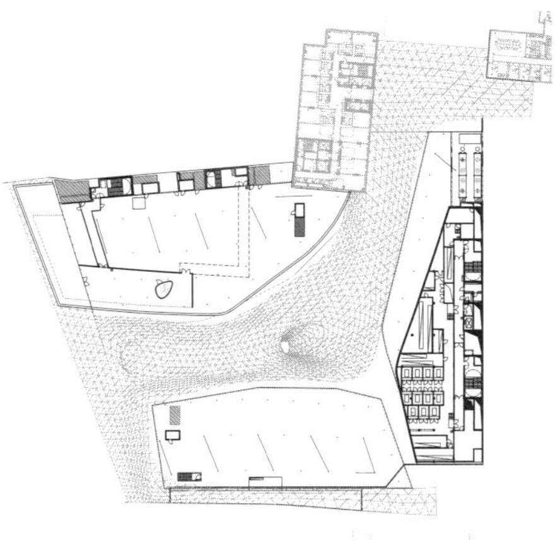

Seventh floor

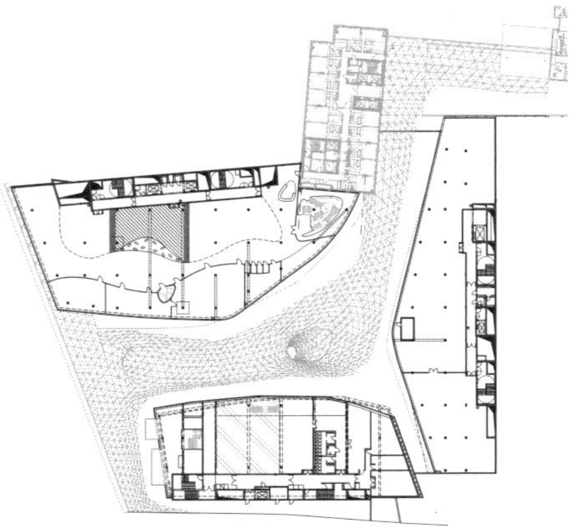

Sixth floor

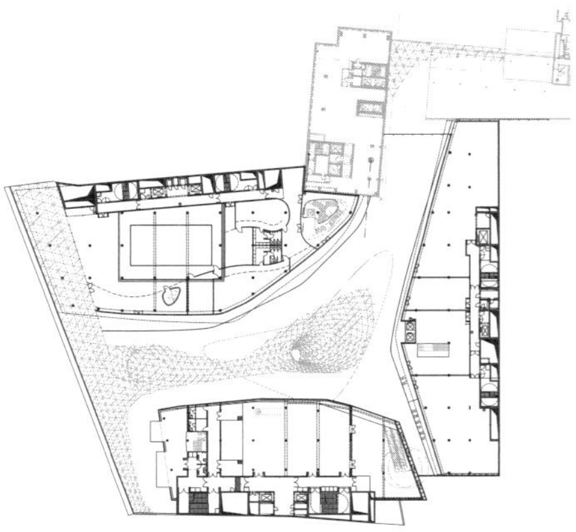

fifth floor

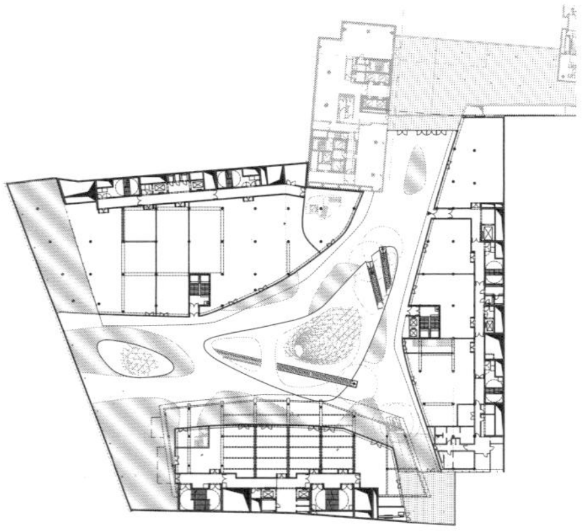

Fourth floor

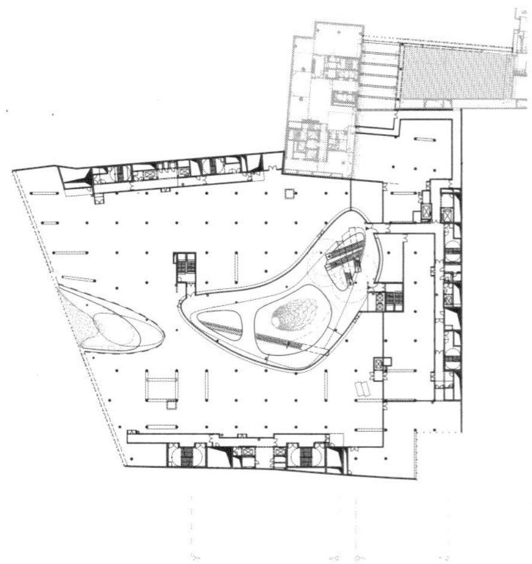

Thirth floor

Second floor

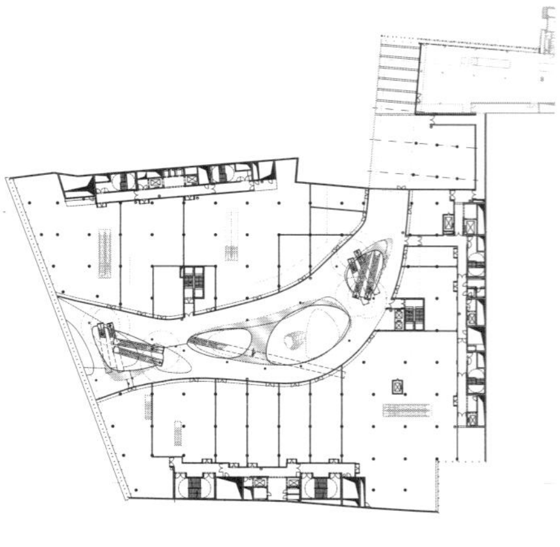

First floor

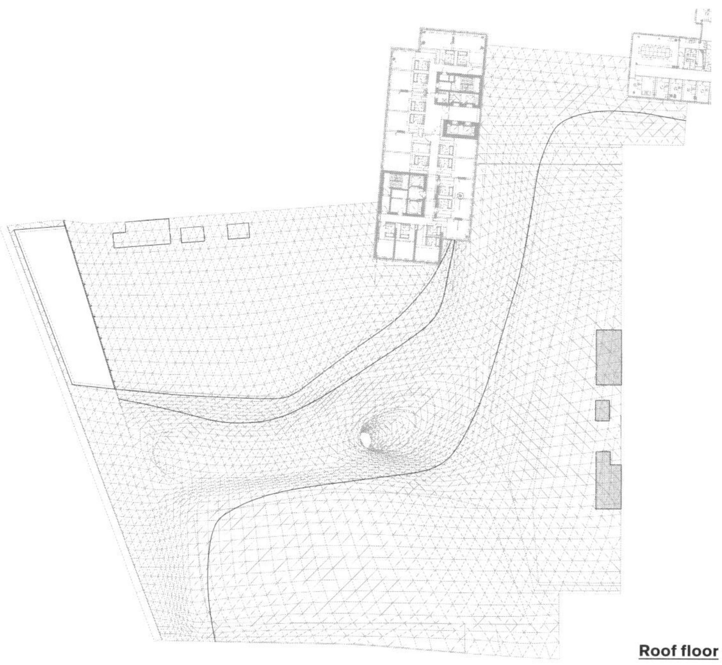

Roof floor

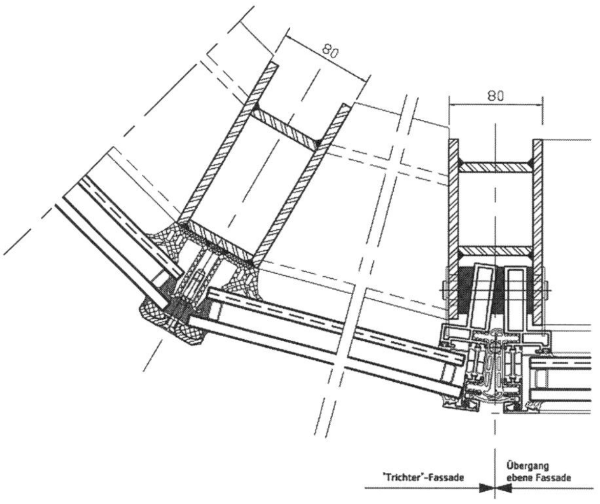

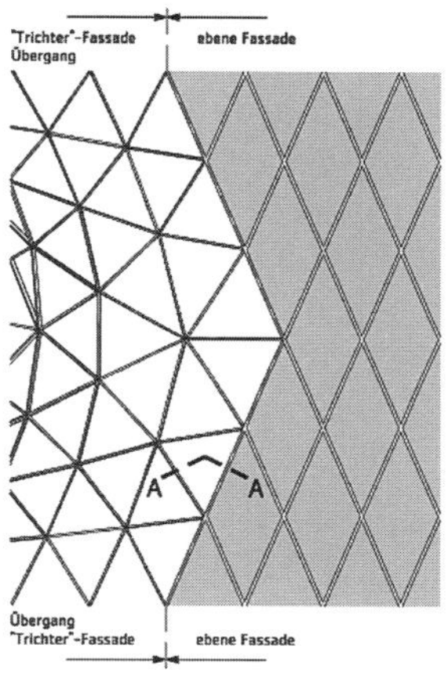

Section detail A-A
M. 1:2,5

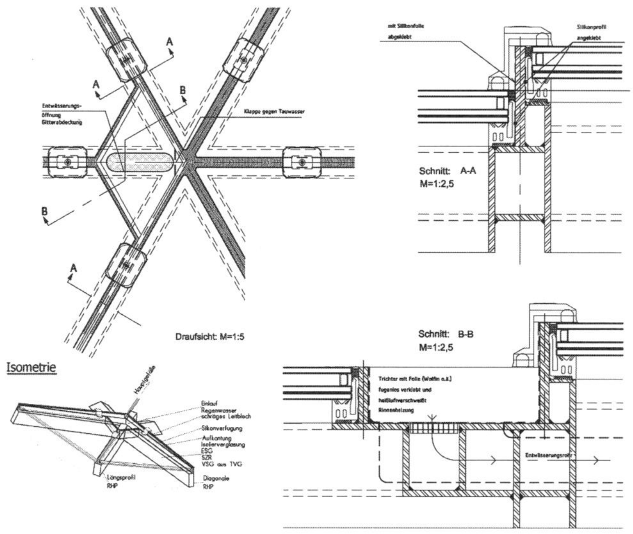

Detail Roof Drainage system towards Zeil
M. 1:5, M.1:2,5

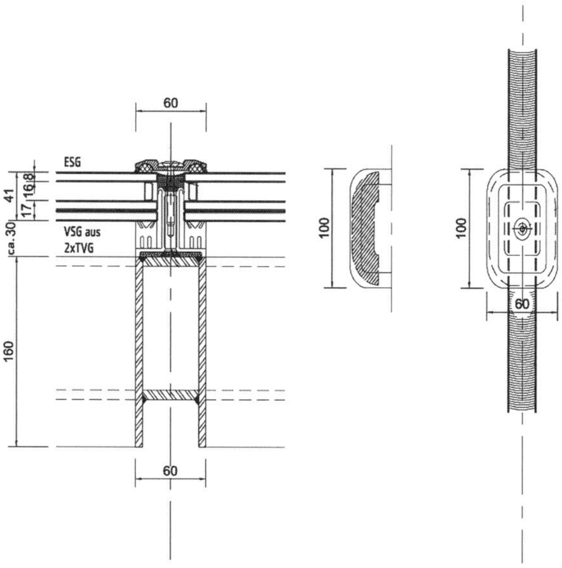

Detail Roof Glass Holder
M. 1:2

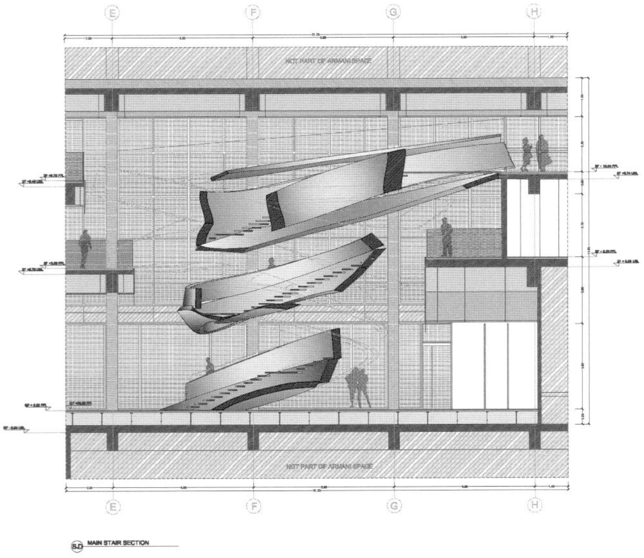

Main Stair Section SD

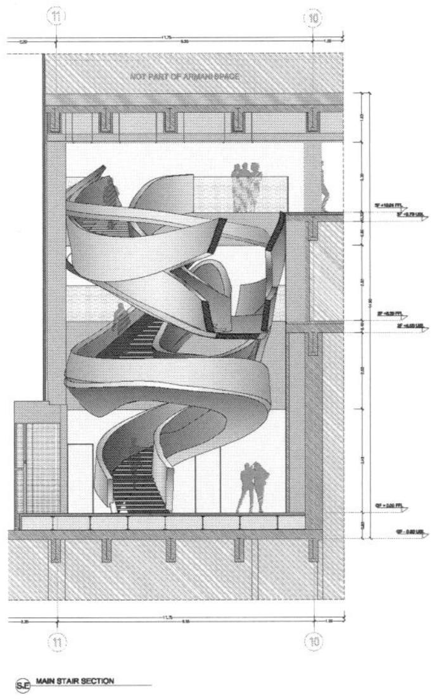

Main Stair Section SE

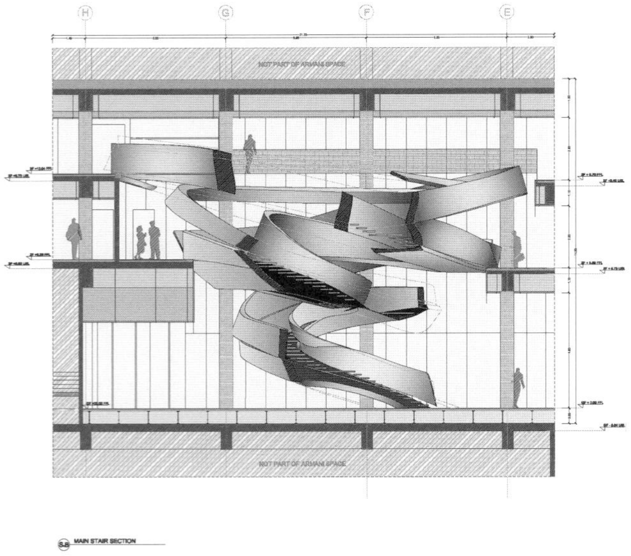

Main Stair Section SB

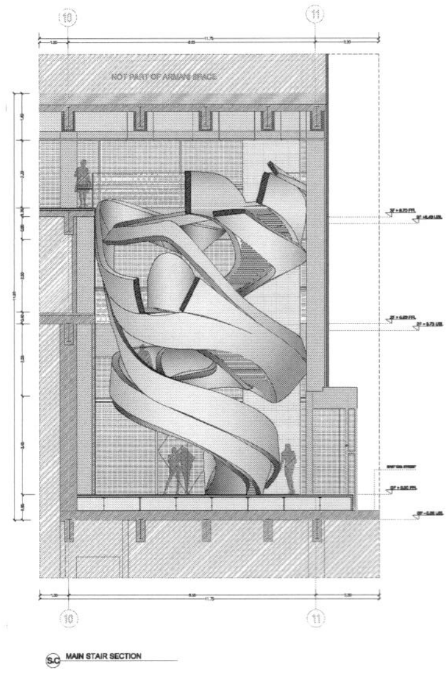

Main Stair Section SC

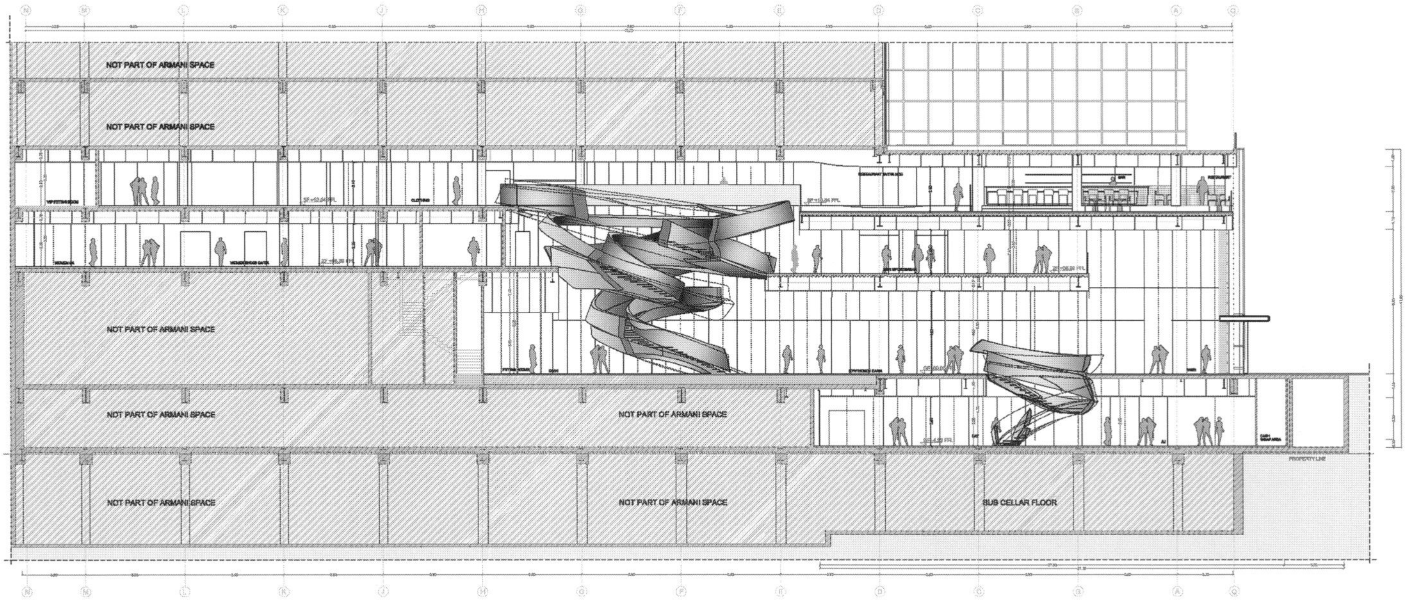

South East-West Section

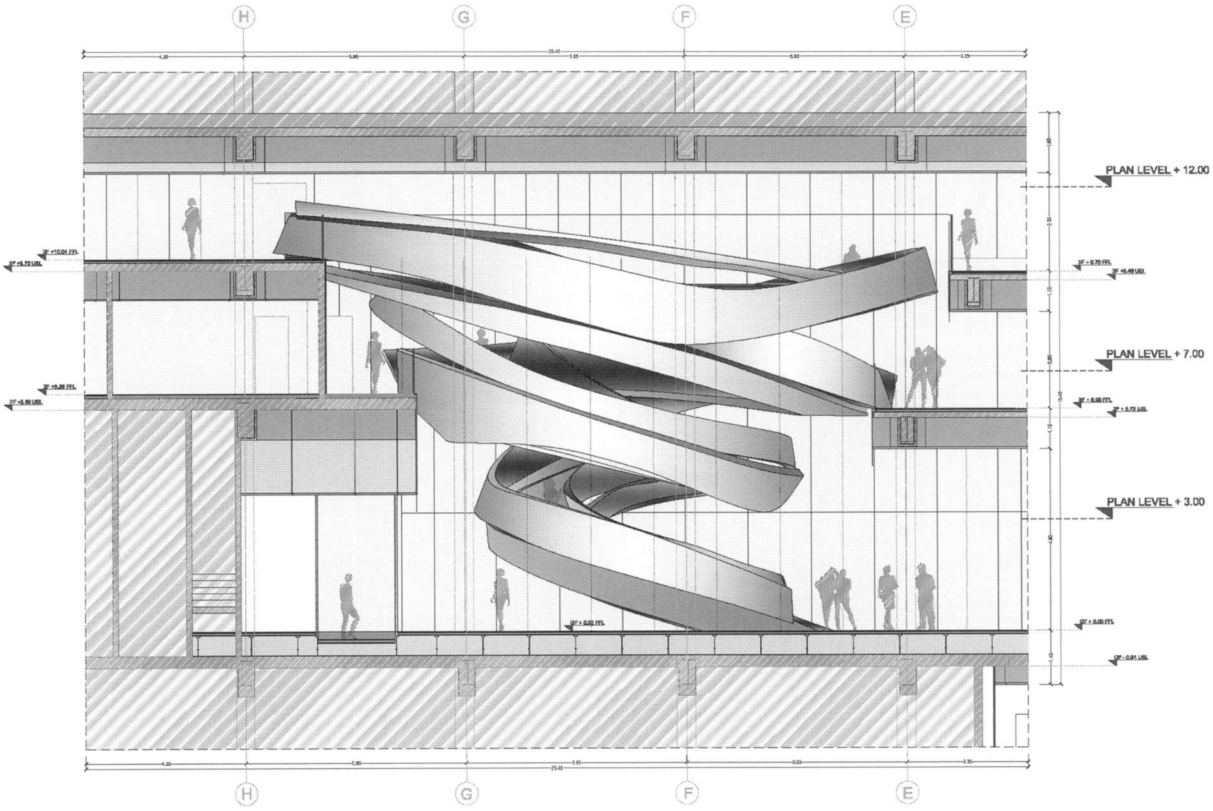

Main Stair Elevation

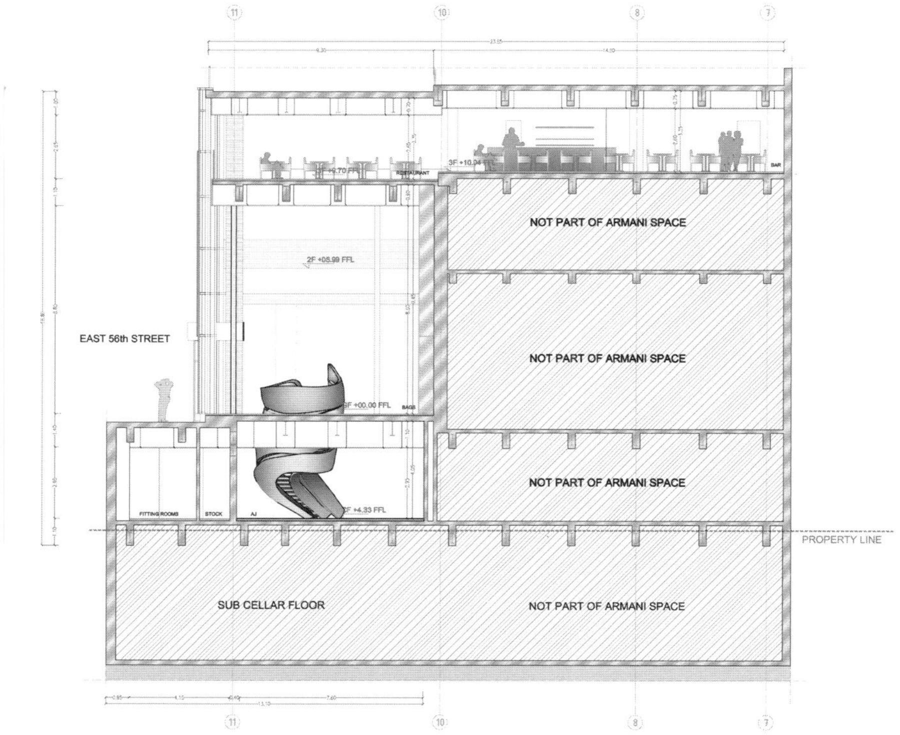

East North-South Section

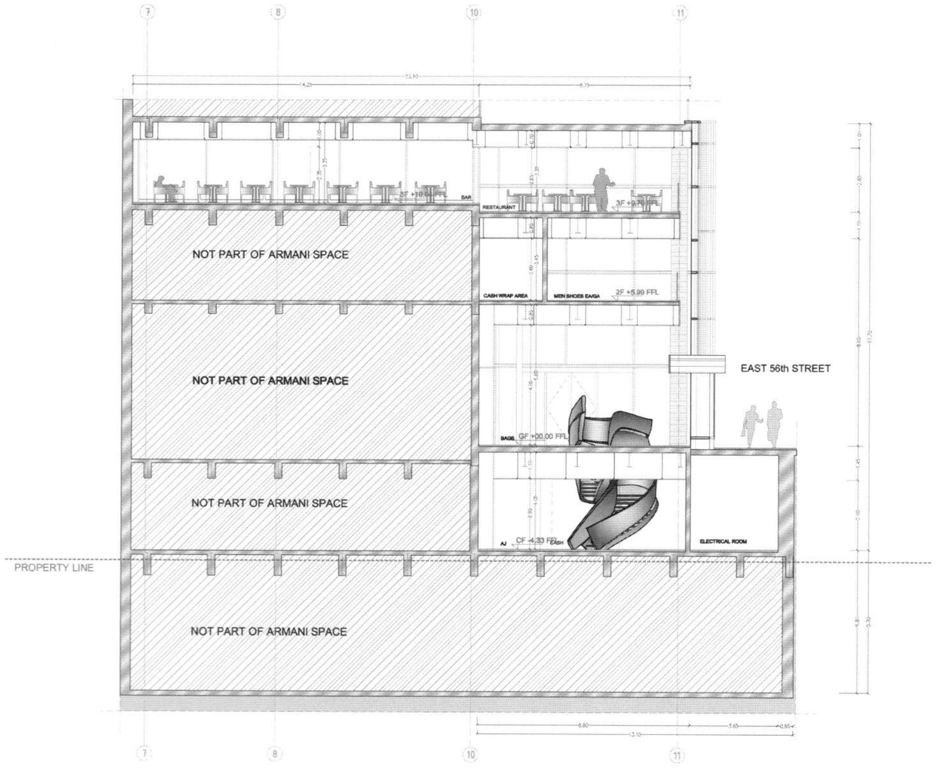

West North-South Section

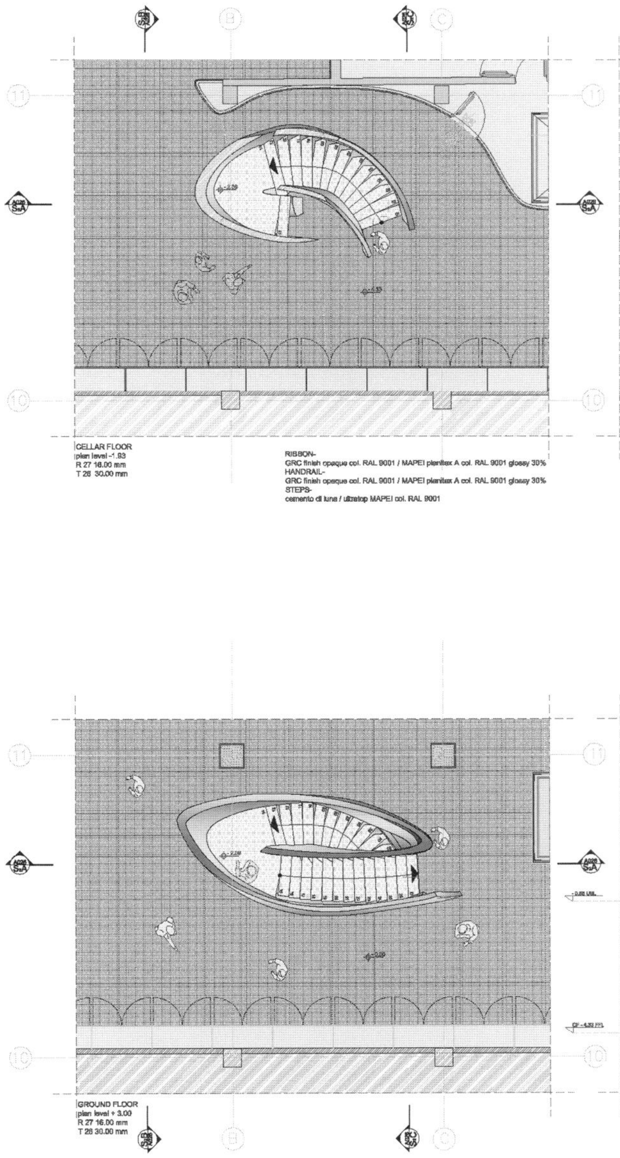

Main Stair Plans

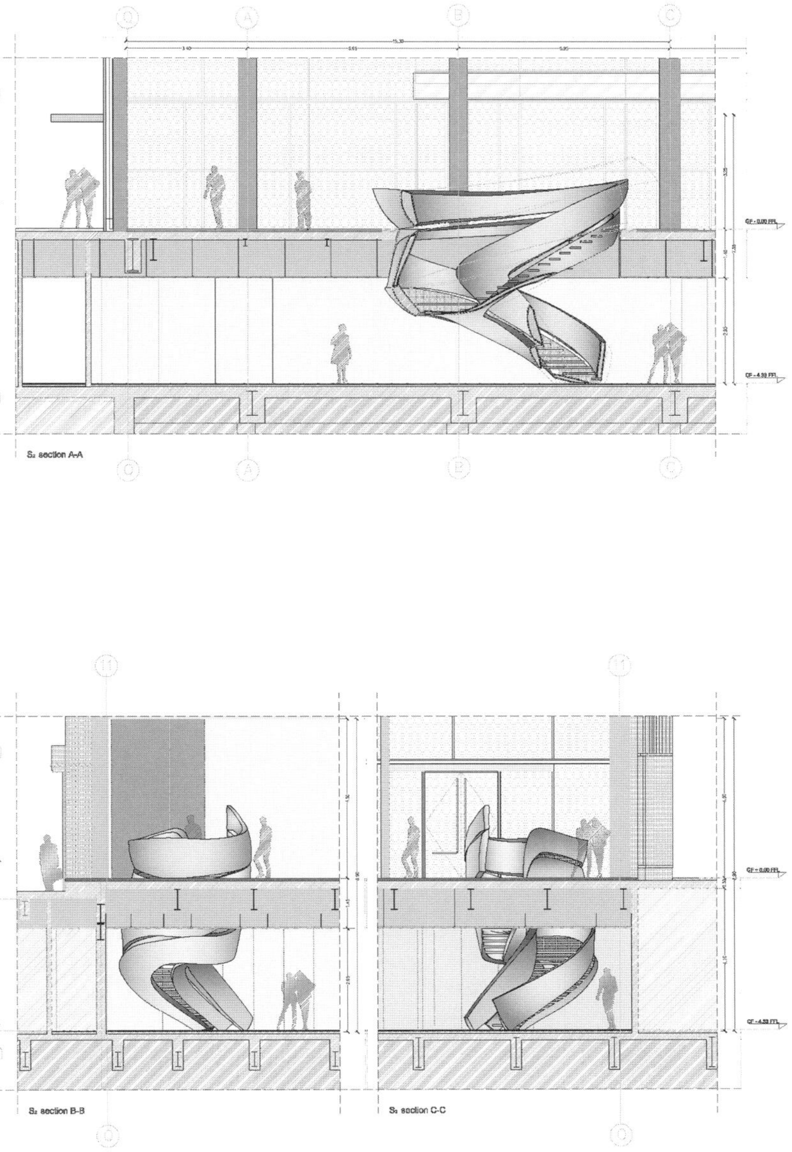

Main Stair Elevations

Elevation 56th Street

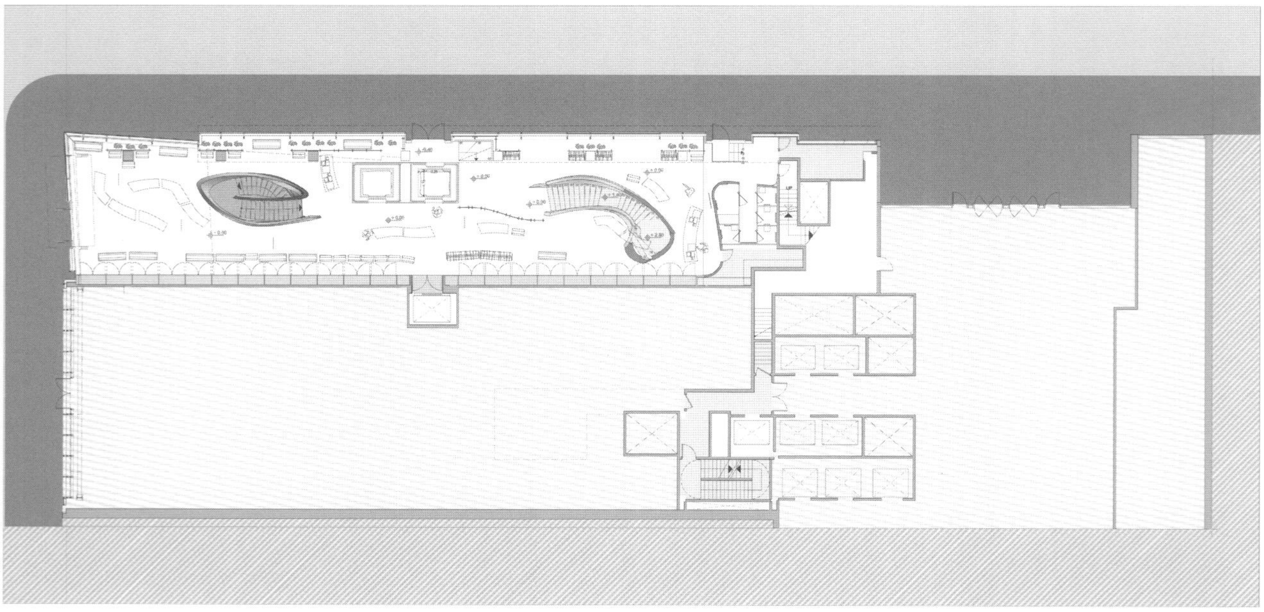

Ground floor

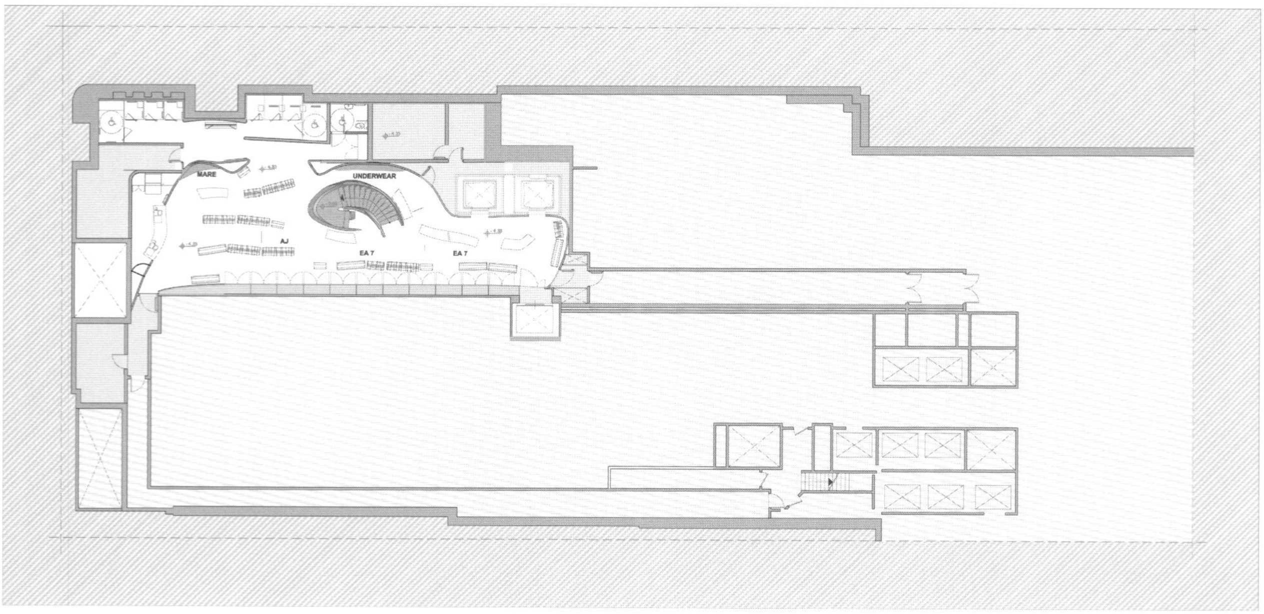

Cellar floor

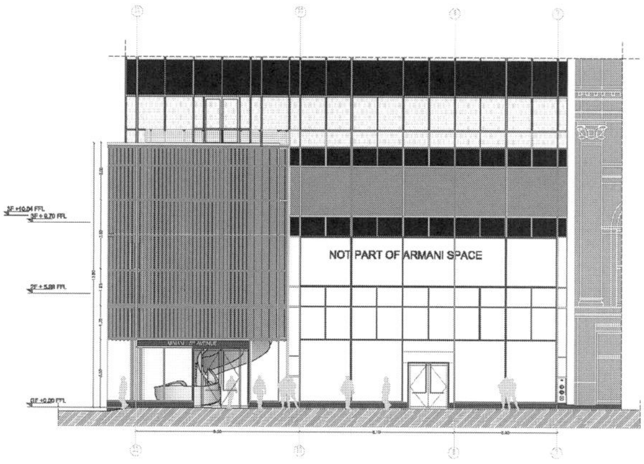

Elevation 5th Avenue

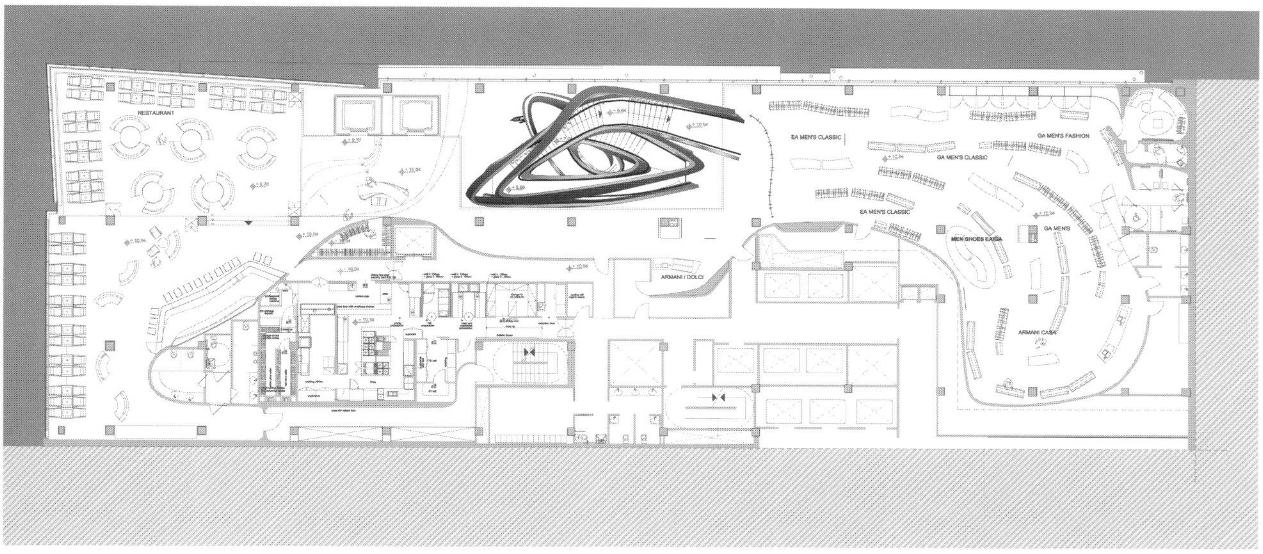

3rd floor

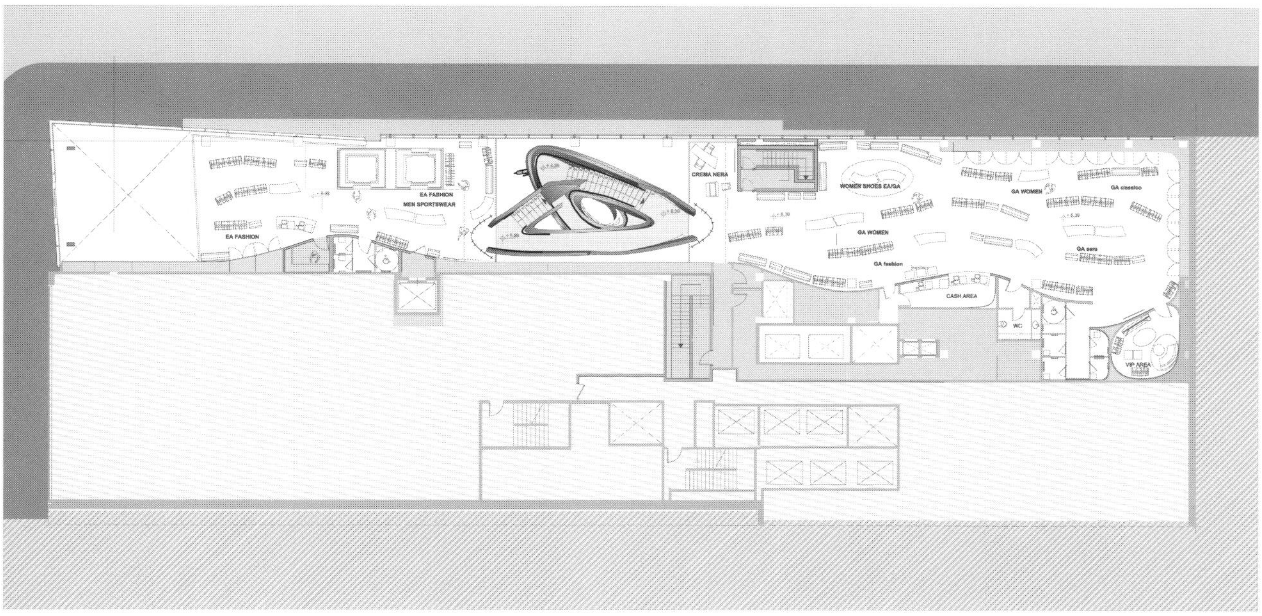

2nd floor

MAINZ MARKTHÄUSER 11-13

MAINZ, GERMANY
2003–2008

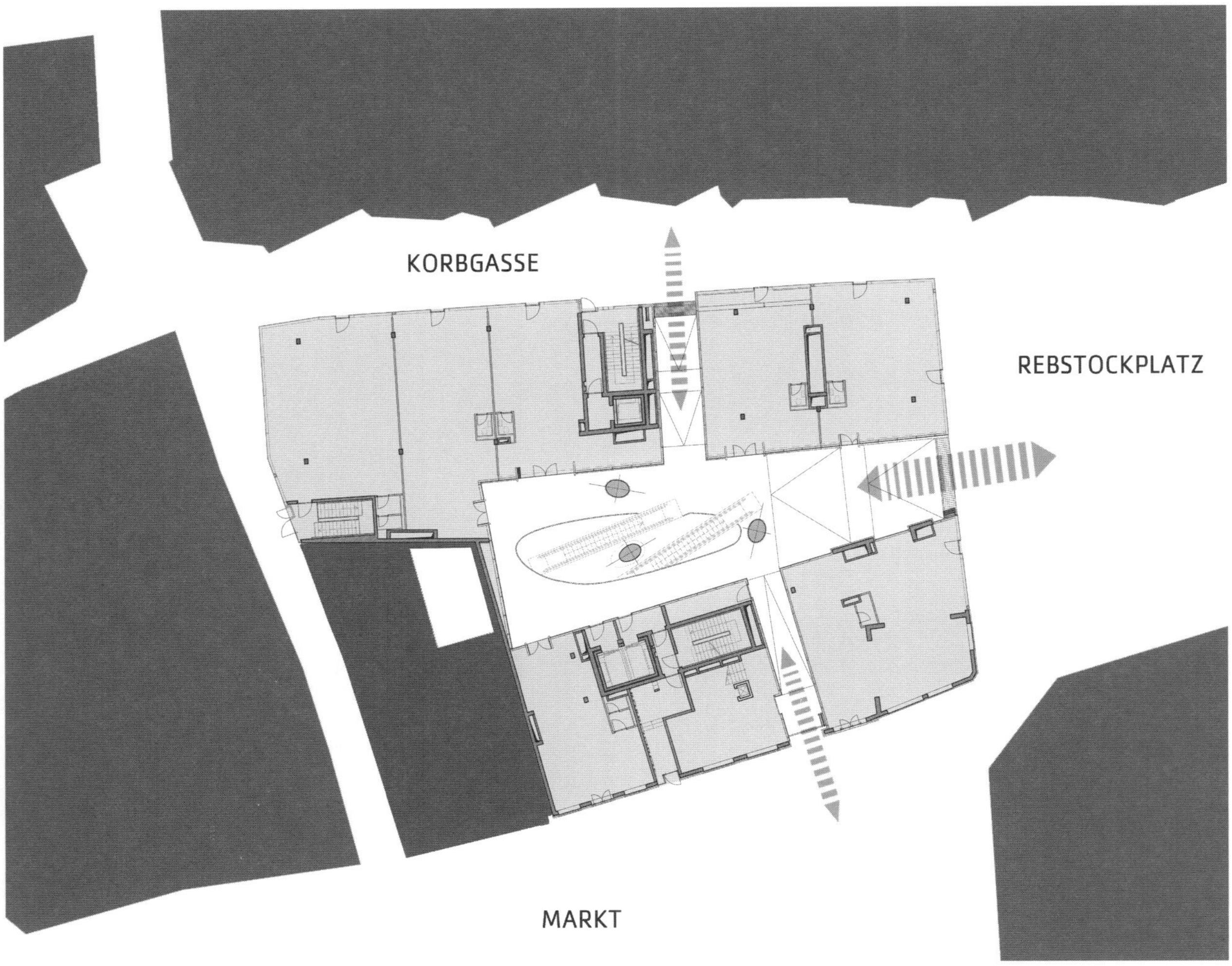

Site plan

-2 floor

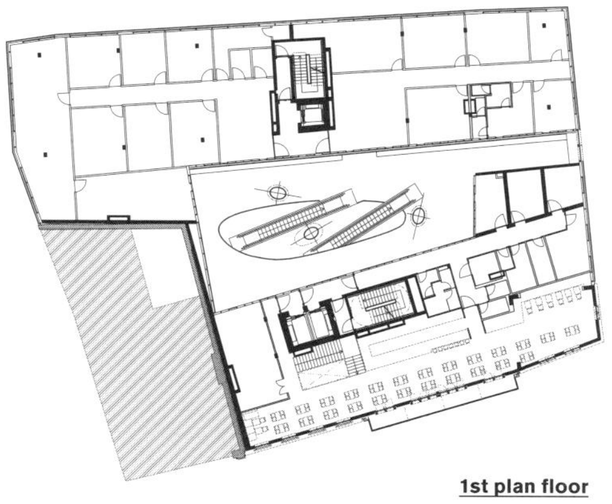

1st plan floor

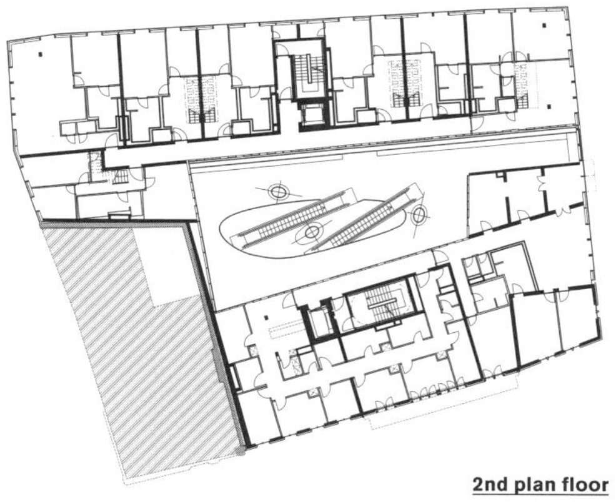

2nd plan floor

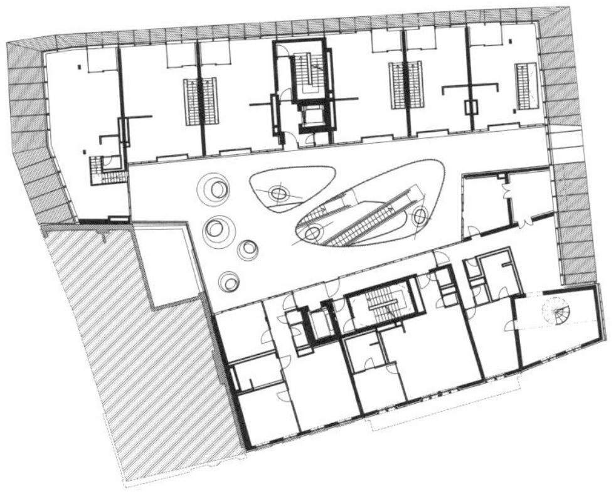

3rd plan floor

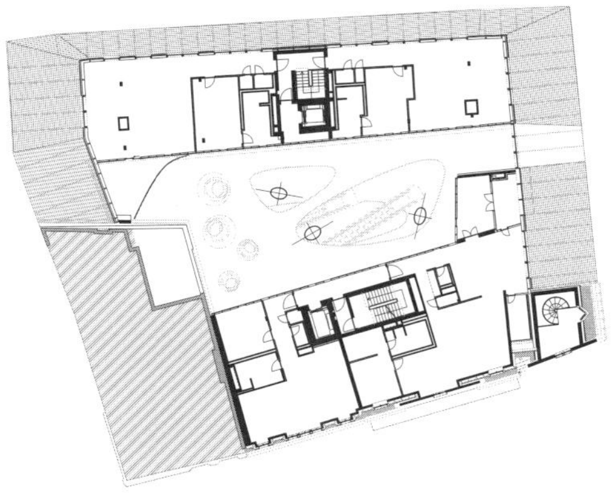

4th plan floor

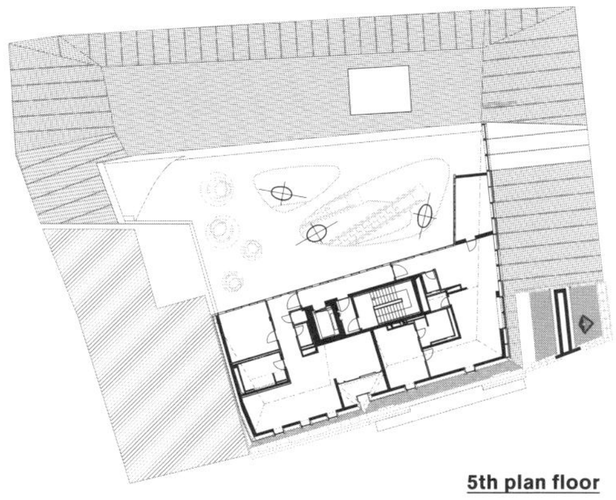

5th plan floor

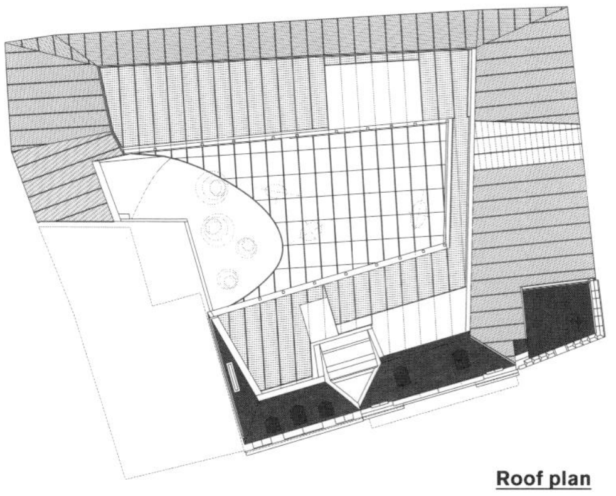

Roof plan

Ground floor

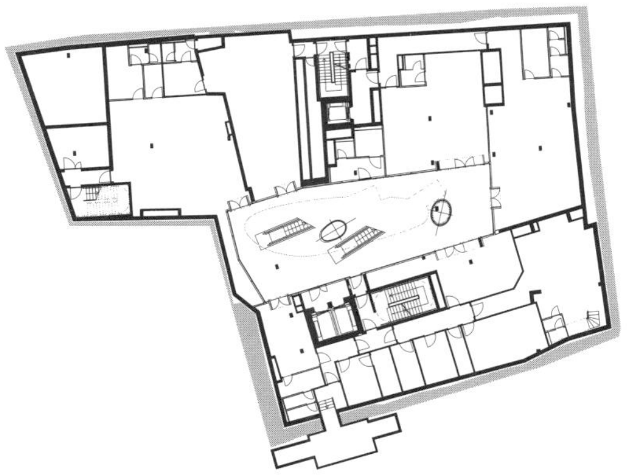

-1 floor

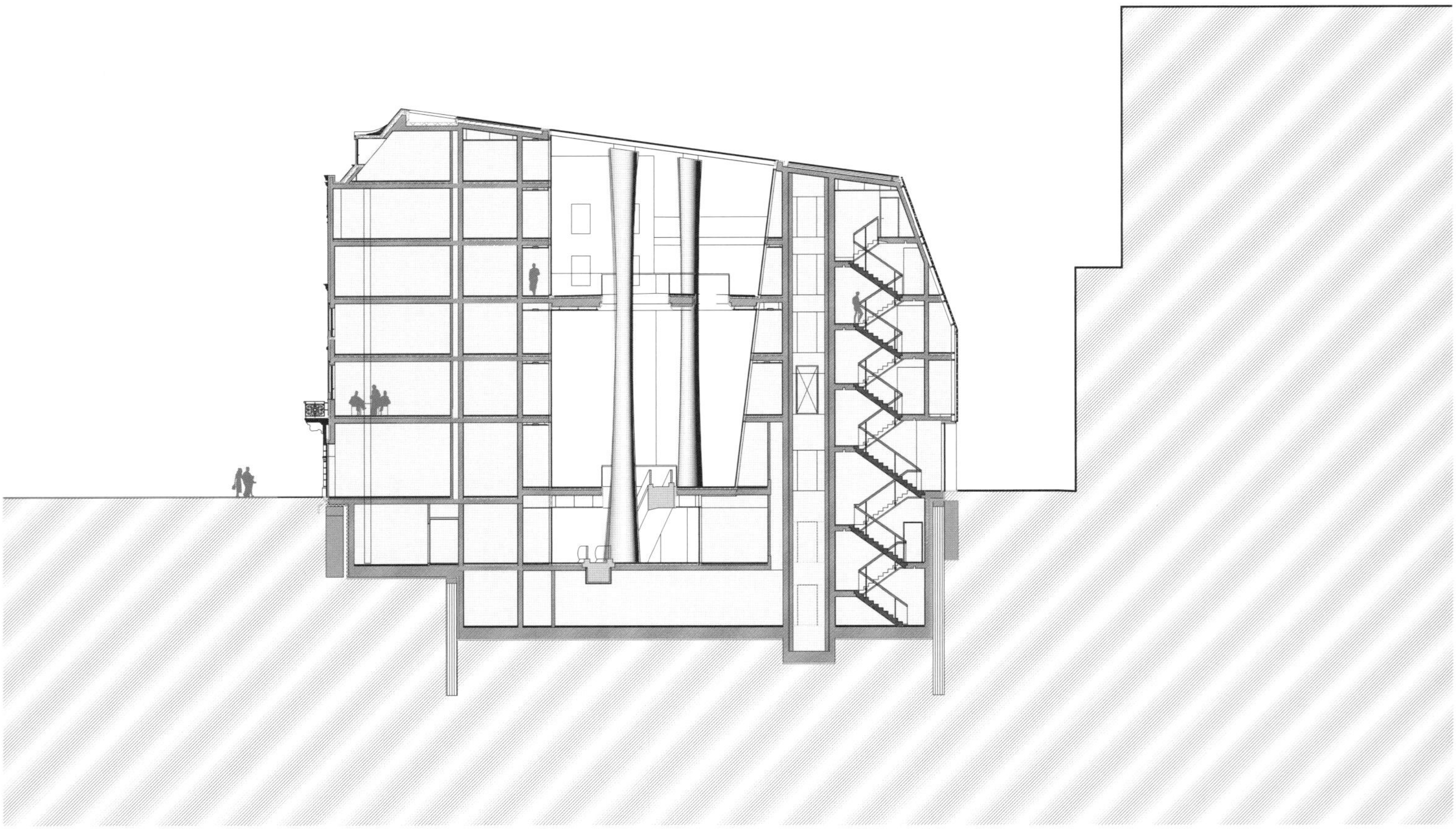

Section AA

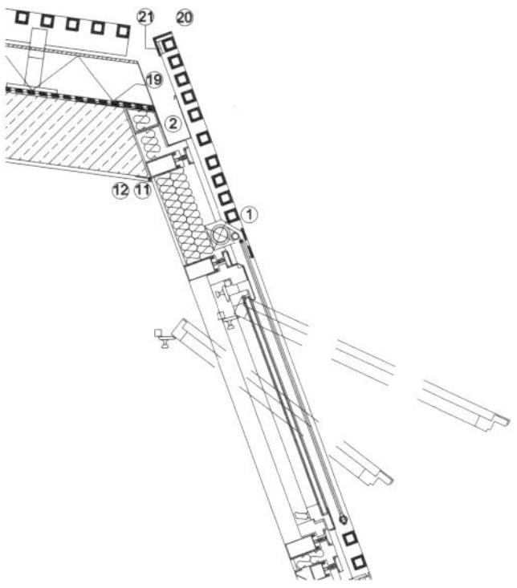

Detail 3 Cross section connection fins-element-facade-roof

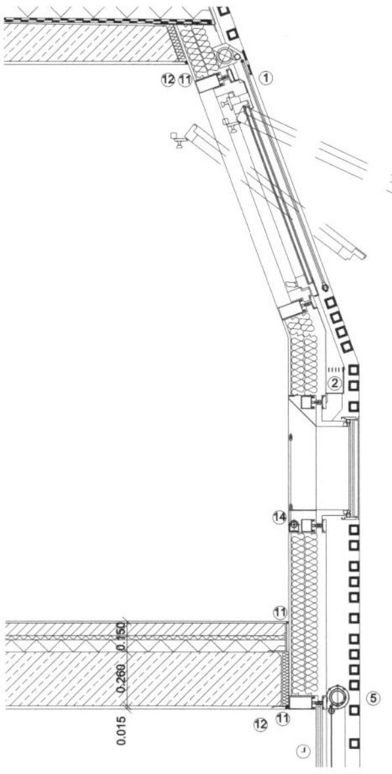

Detail 6 Cross section eaves fins-element-facade

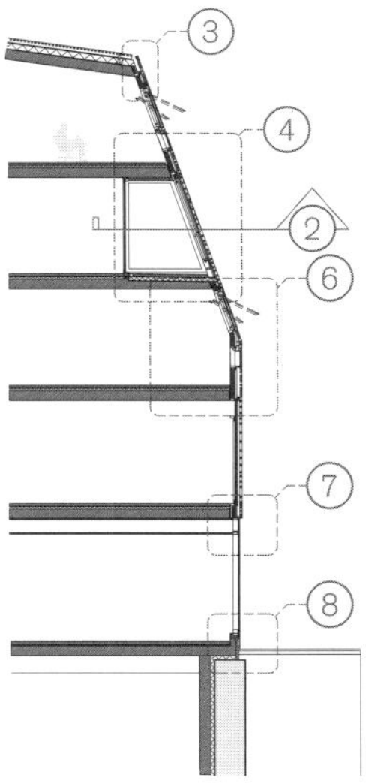

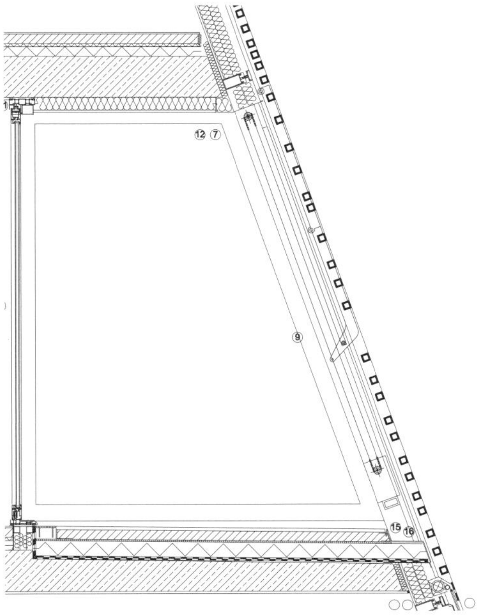

Detail 4 Cross section loggia 3

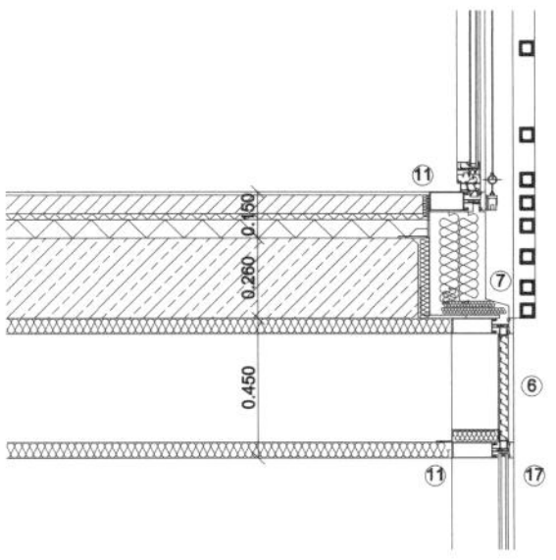

Detail 7 Cross section connection fins-element-facade

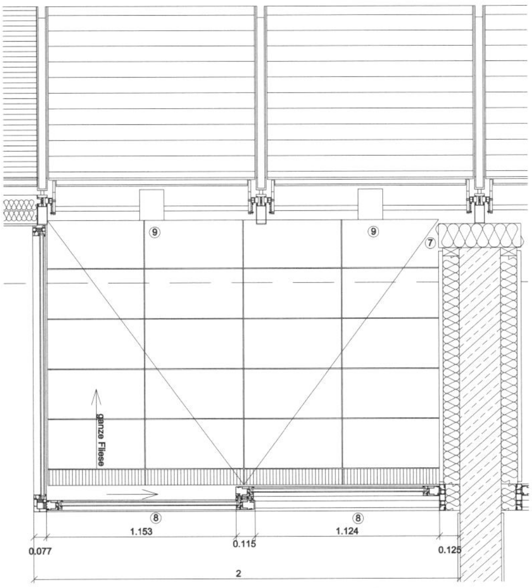

Detail 4 Cross section loggia 3

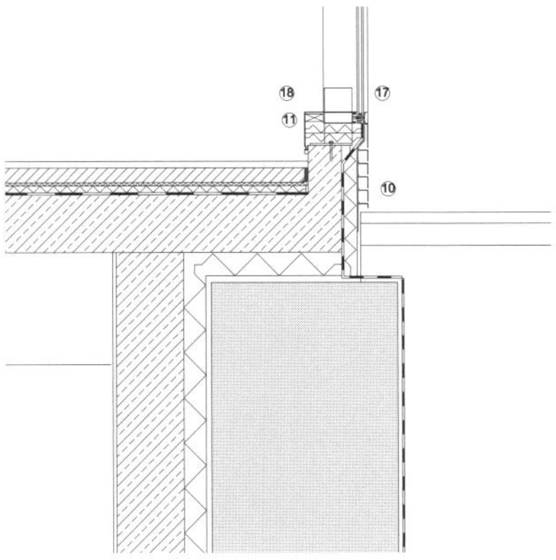

Detail 8 Cross section base point ground facade

Armored concrete	Natural stone	Insulation Layer	Sealing
Brickwork	Gypsum cardboard	Perimeter insulation	Printed glass
Existence	Prefabricated component	Break-off	Sunblind

ZENITH MUSIC HALL

(6,000-8,000 seats) AMIENS, FRANCE
2003–2008

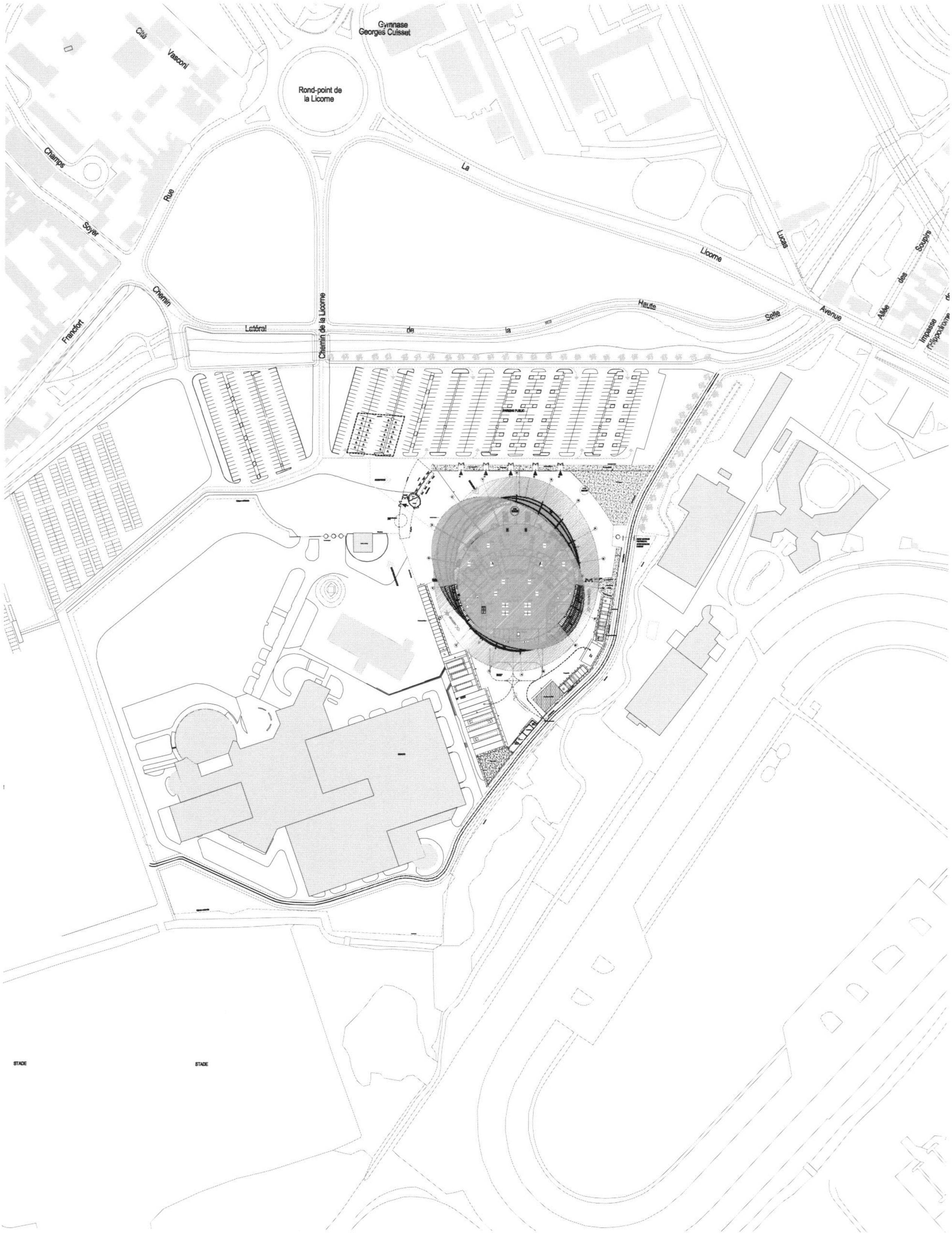

Site plan

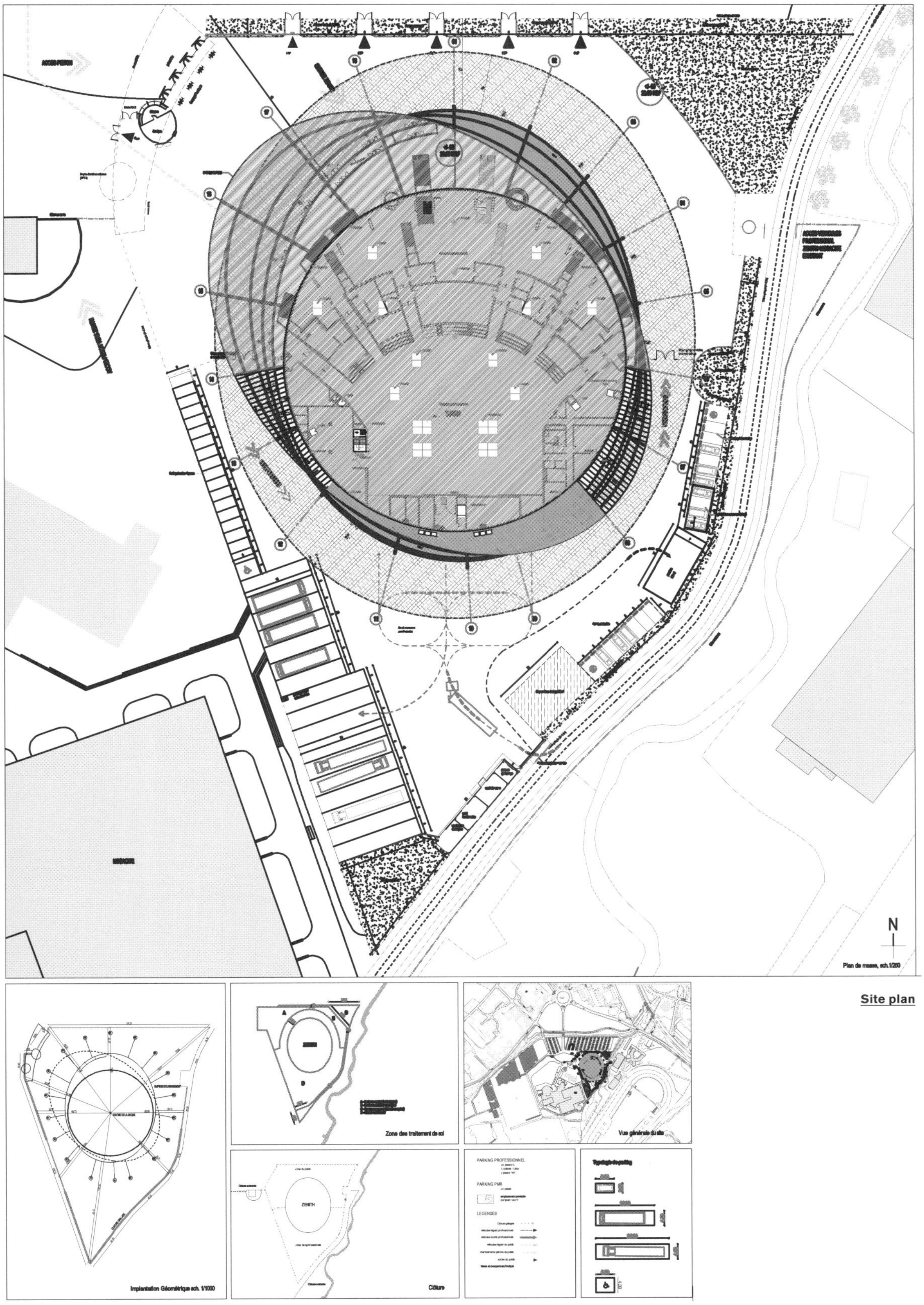
N
Plan de masse, ech.1/250
Implantation Géométrique ech. 1/1000
Zone des traitement de sol
Vue générale du site
ZENITH
Clôture
PARKING PROFESSIONNEL
PARKING PMR
LEGENDES
Typologie de parking

Site plan

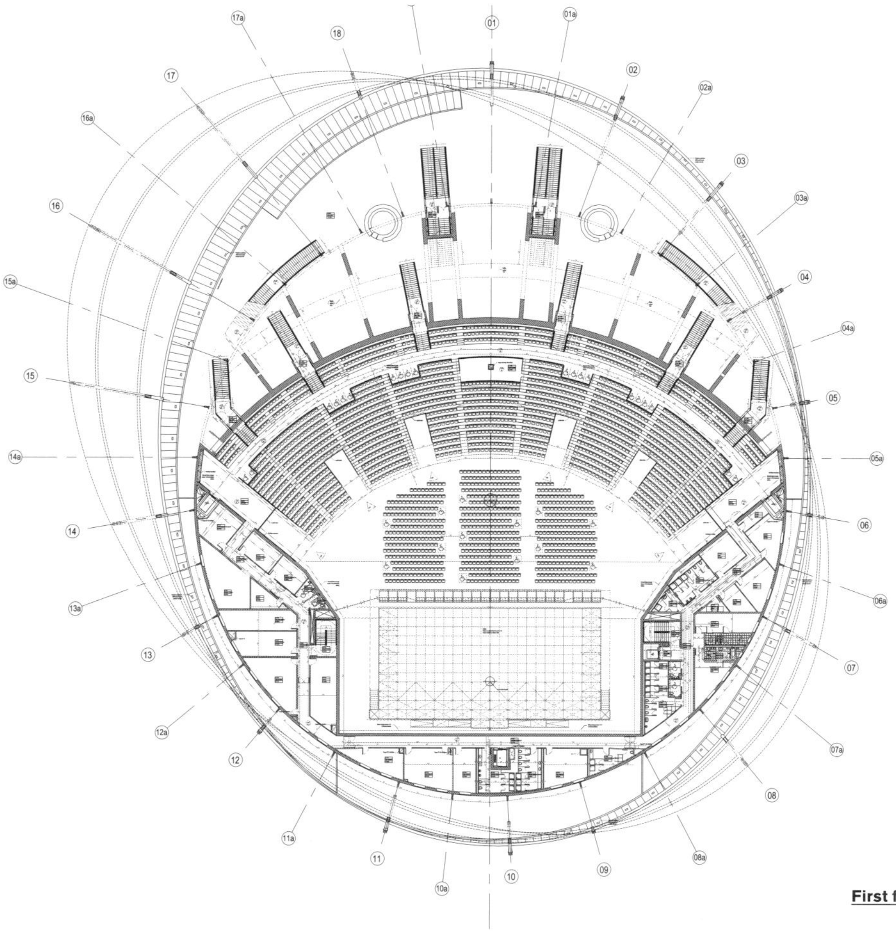

First floor

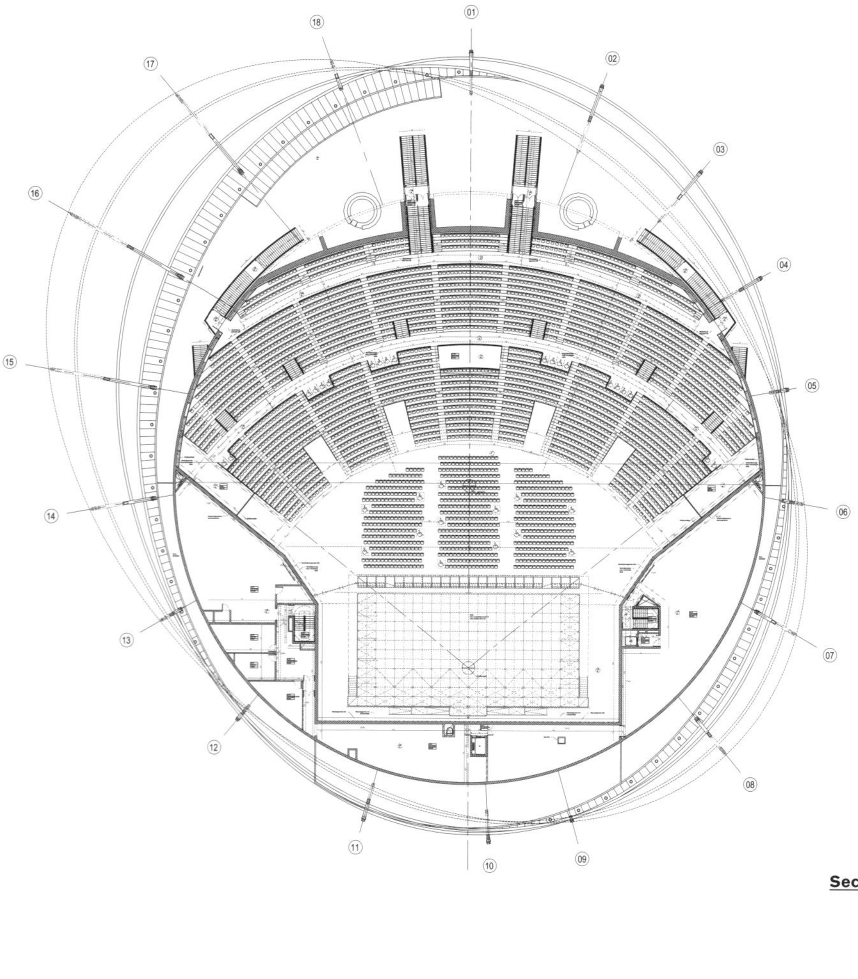

Second floor

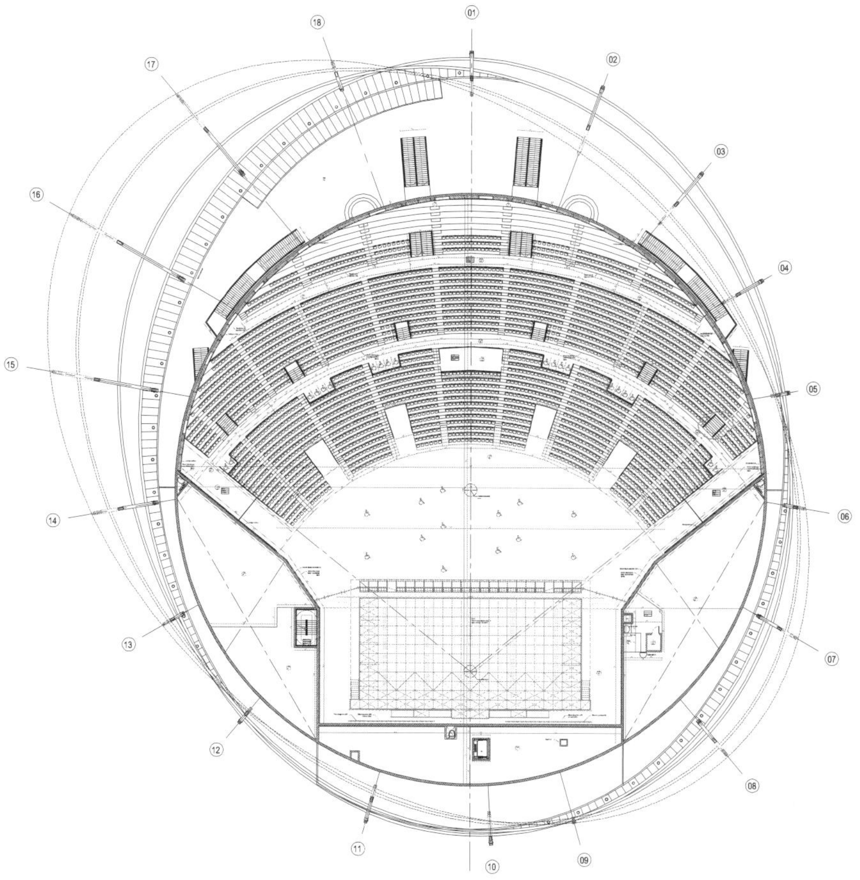

Third floor

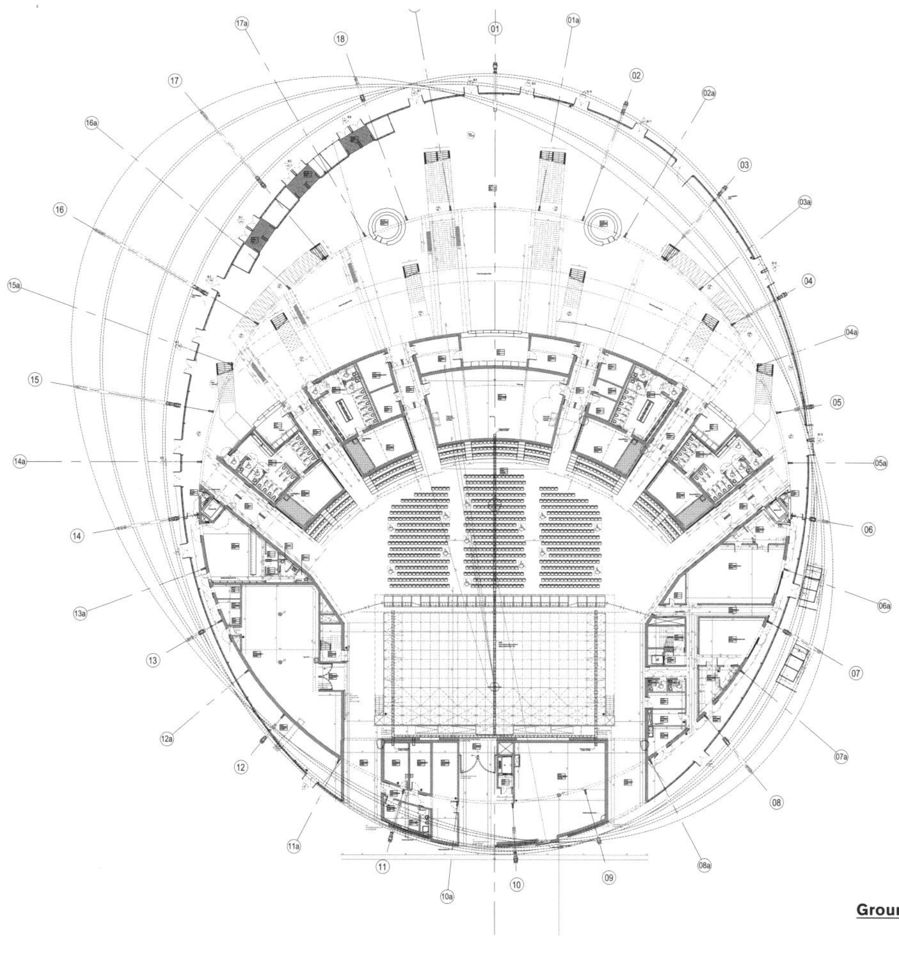

Ground floor

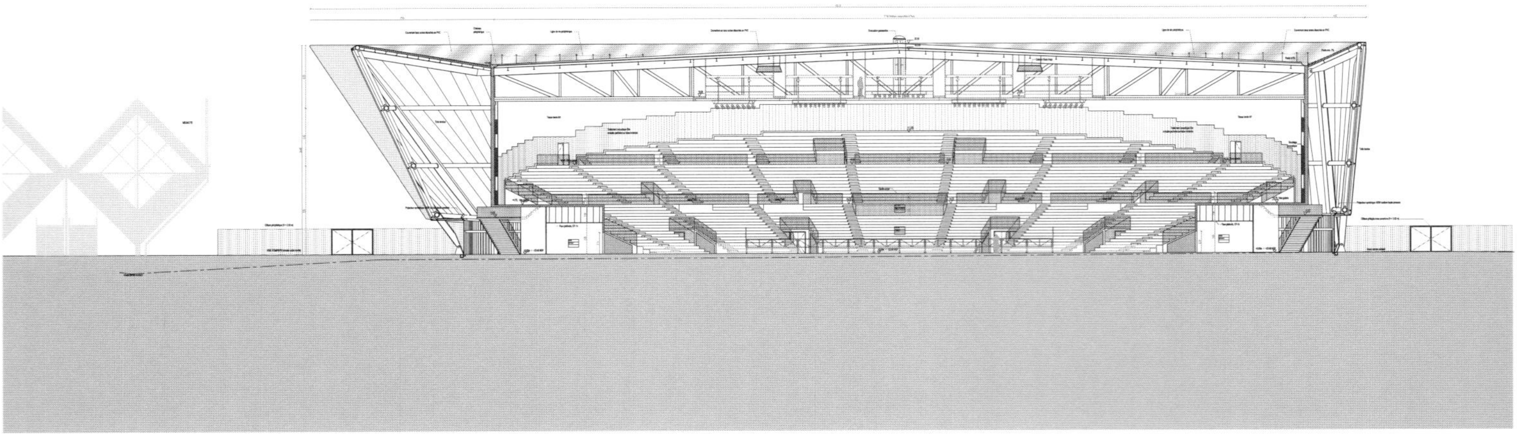

Transversal section

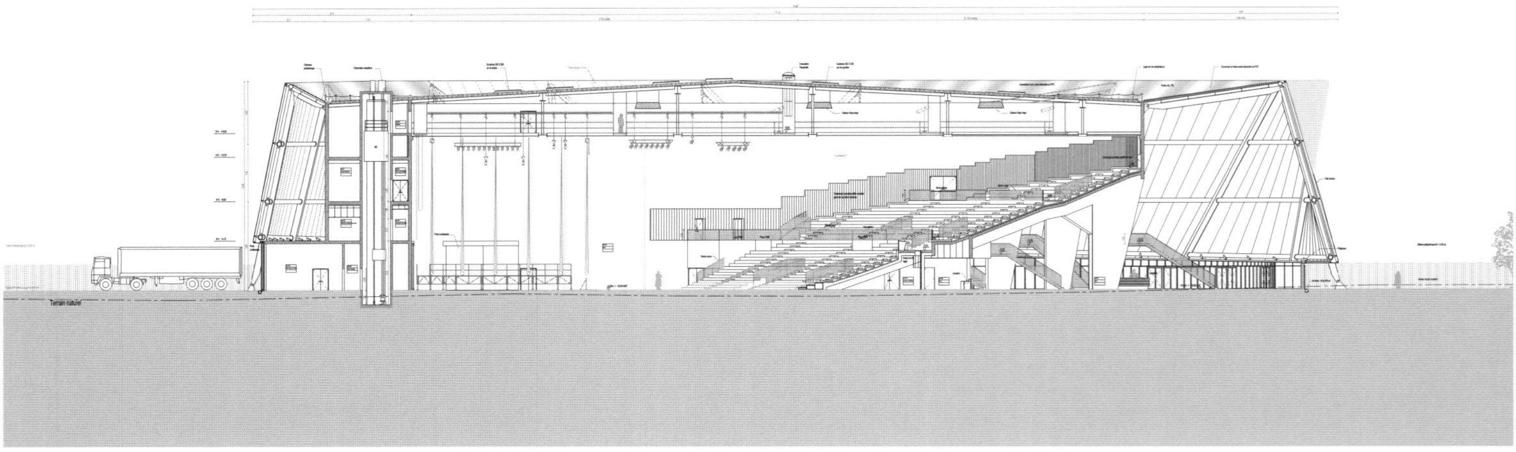

Longitudinal section

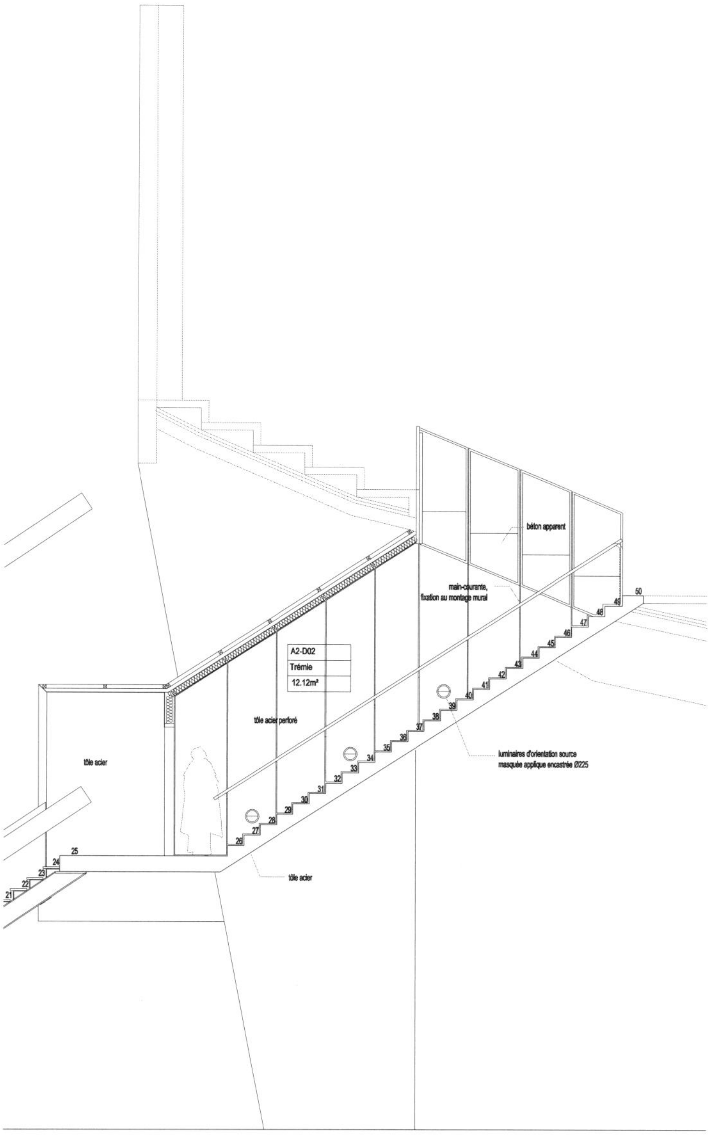
béton apparent
main-courante,
fixation au montage mural
A2-D02
Trémie
12.12m²
tôle acier perforé
tôle acier
luminaires d'orientation source
masquée applique encastrée Ø225
tôle acier
21 22 23 24 25 26 27 28 29 30 31 32 33 34 35 36 37 38 39 40 41 42 43 44 45 46 47 48 49 50

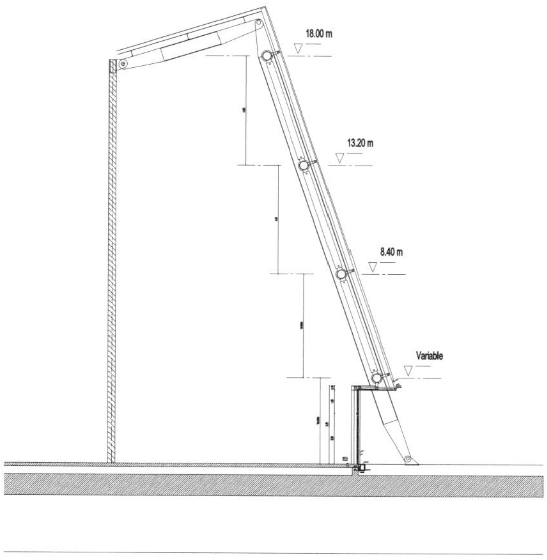
18.00 m
13.20 m
8.40 m
Variable

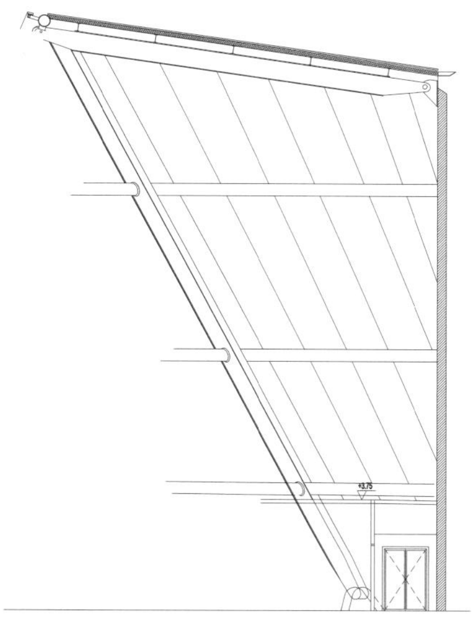

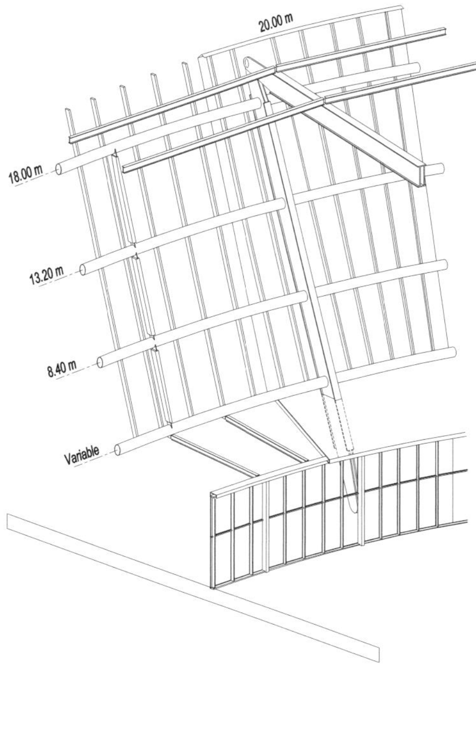
20.00 m
18.00 m
13.20 m
8.40 m
Variable

ZENITH MUSIC HALL
(10,000-12,000 seats) STRASBOURG, FRANCE
2003–2008

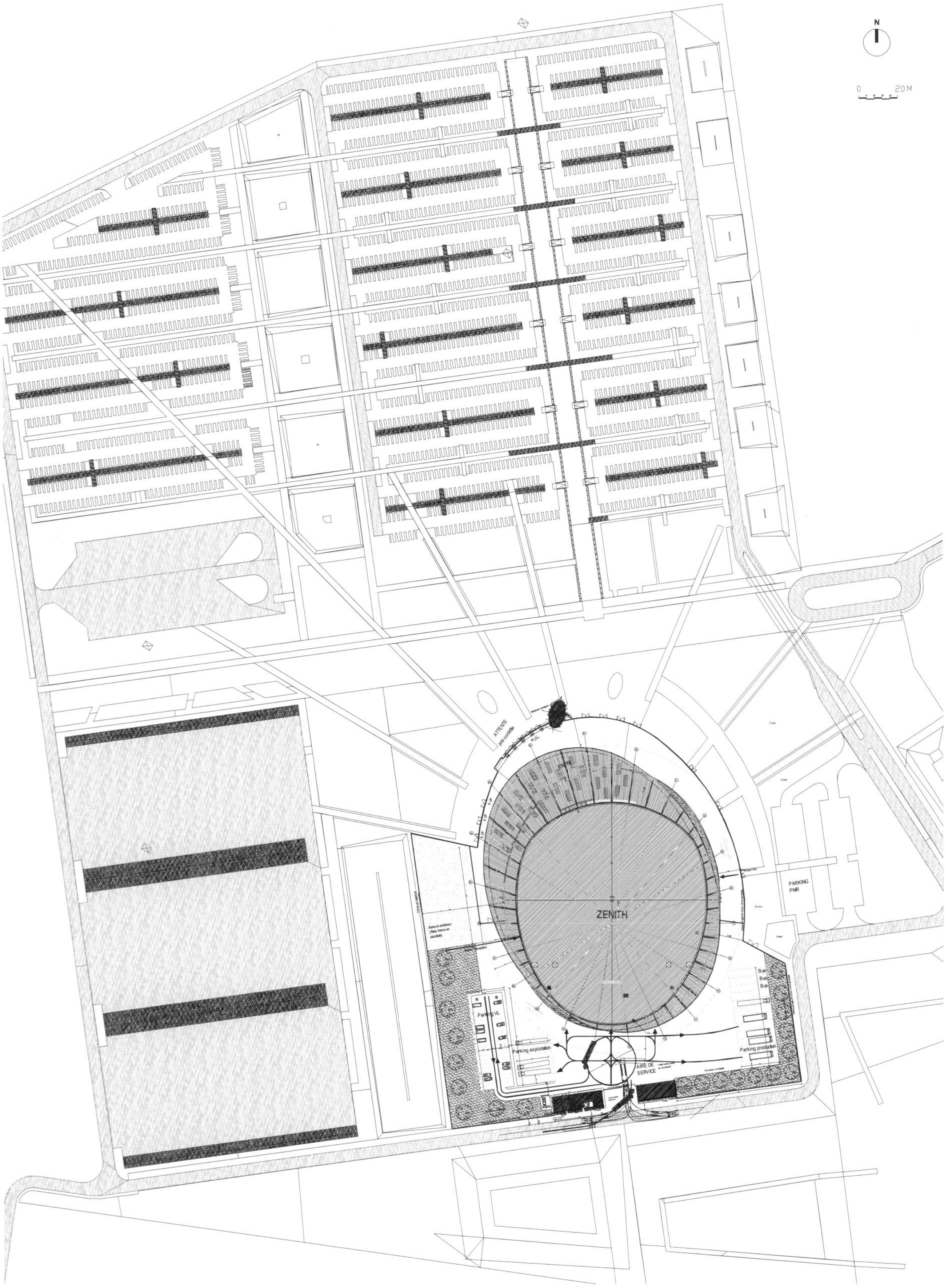

Site plan

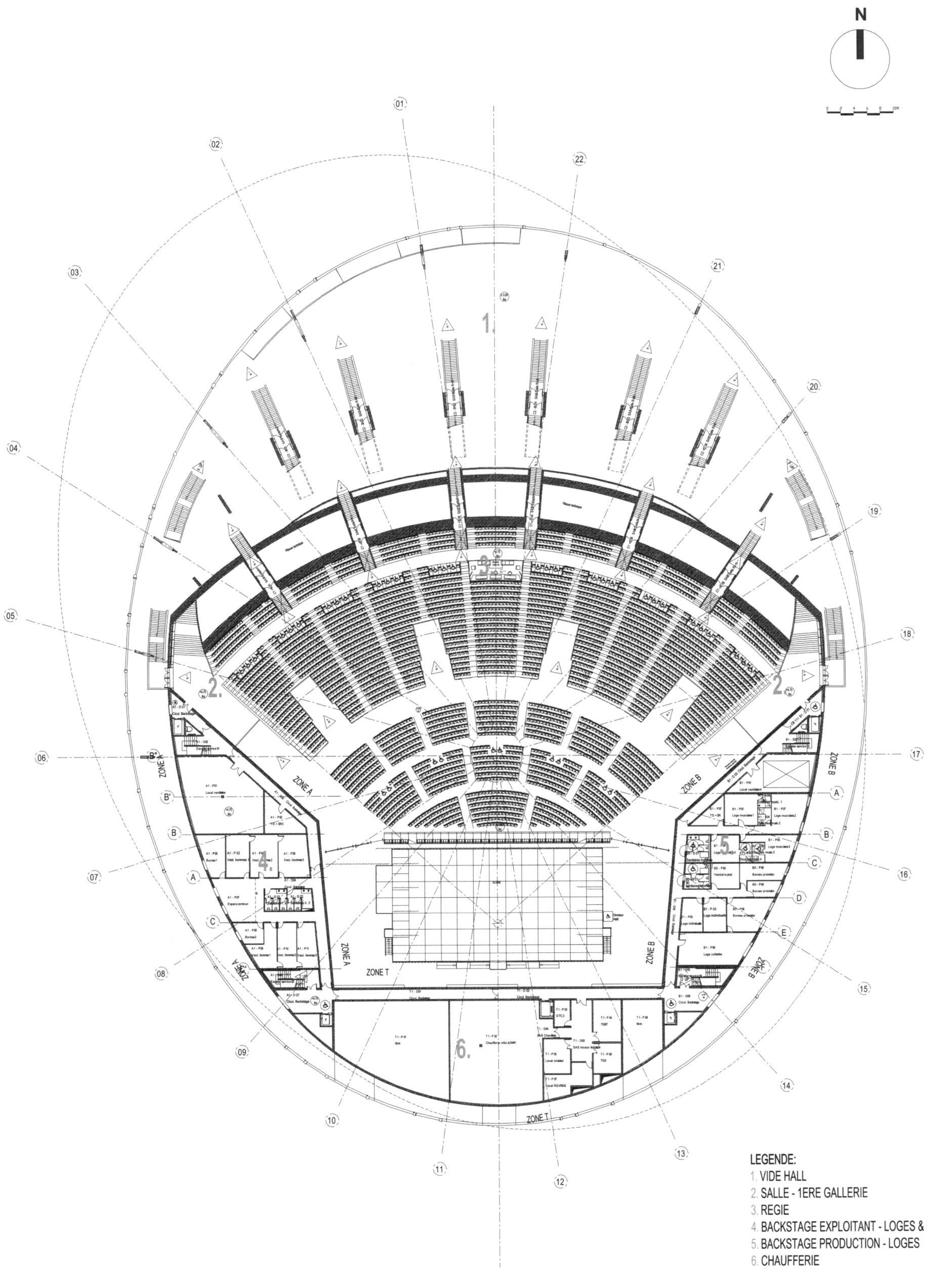

LEGENDE:
1. VIDE HALL
2. SALLE - 1ERE GALLERIE
3. REGIE
4. BACKSTAGE EXPLOITANT - LOGES & BUREAUX
5. BACKSTAGE PRODUCTION - LOGES
6. CHAUFFERIE

First floor

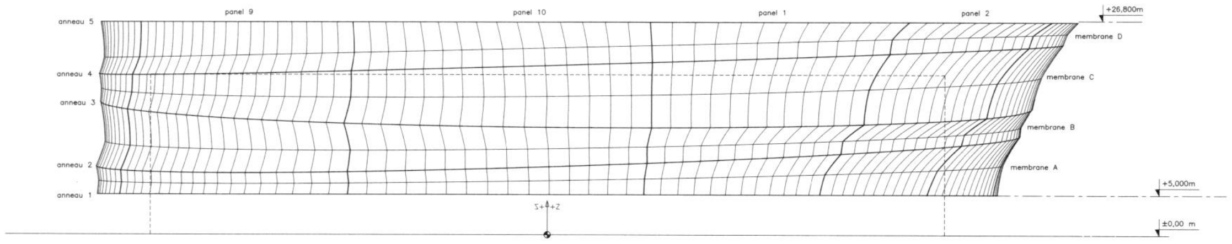

Elevation from North

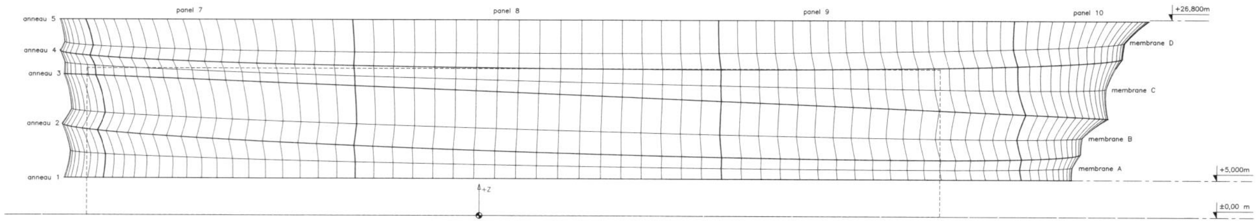

Elevation from East

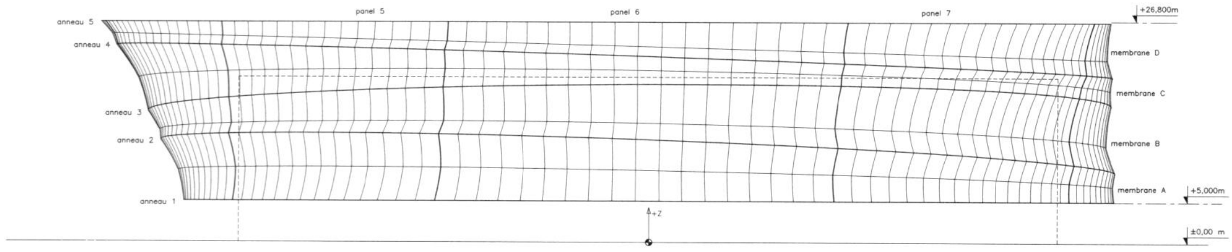

Elevation from South

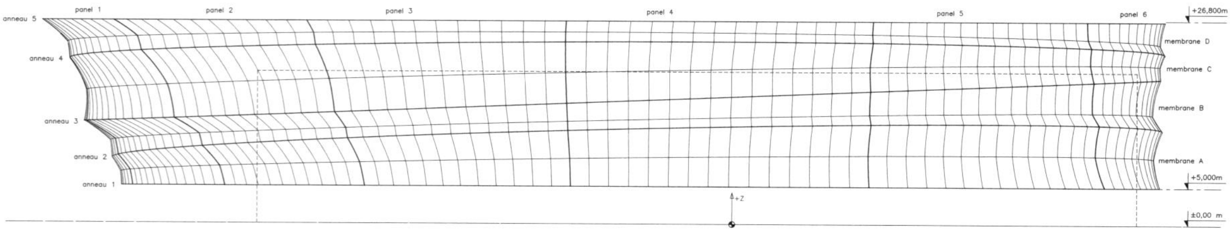

Elevation from West

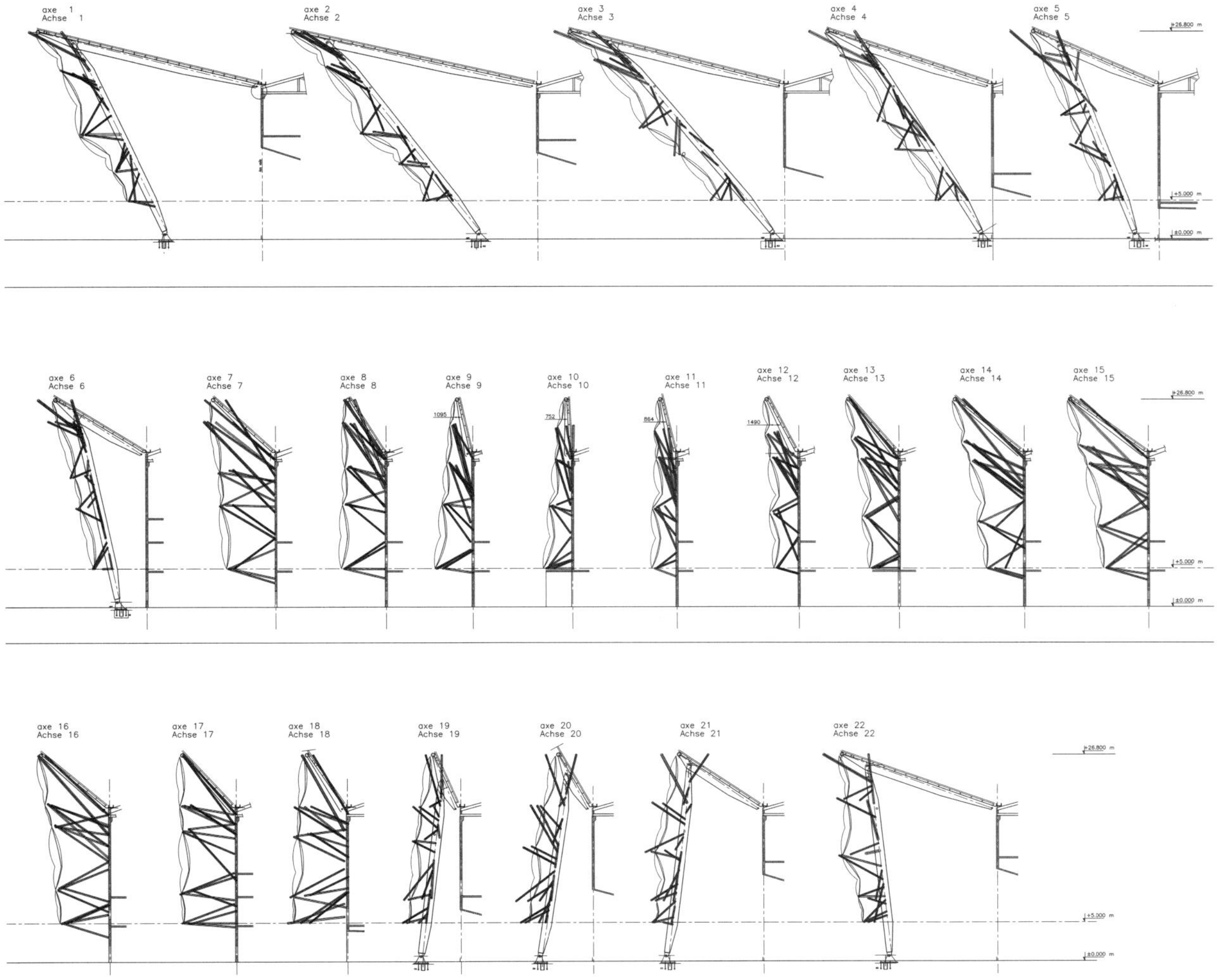

Anneau 5
section A–A

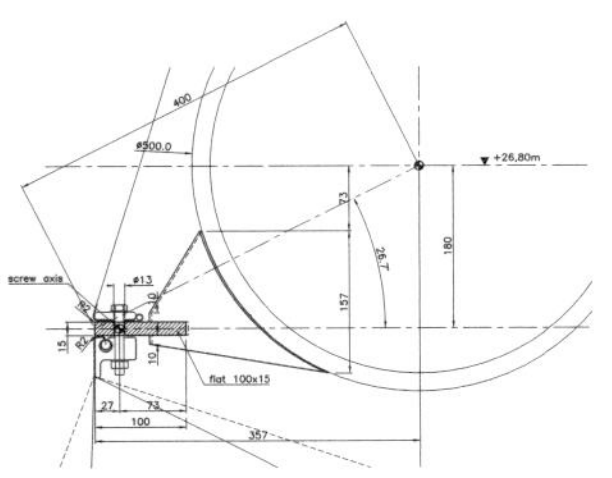

Anneau 4
section A–A

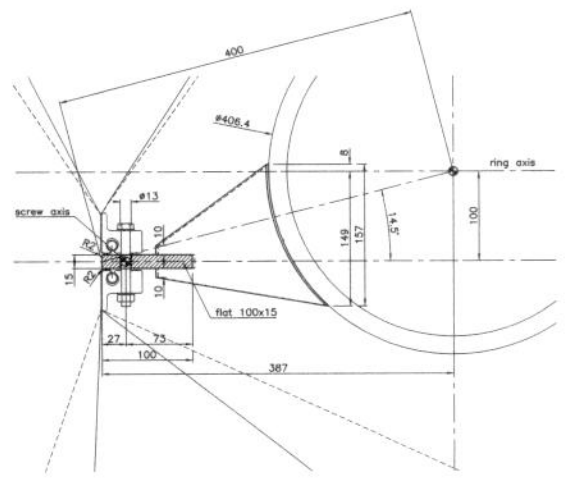

Anneau 3
section A–A

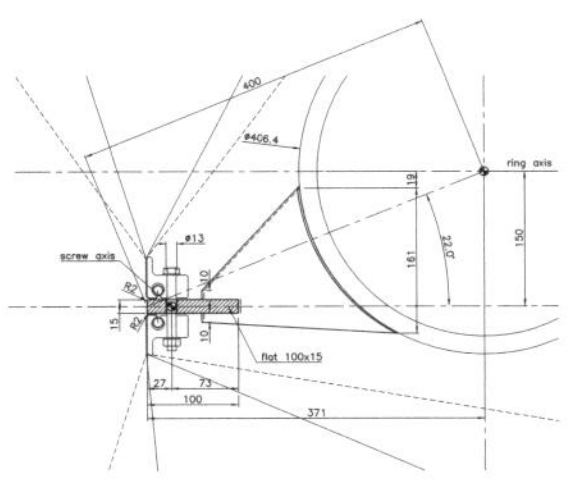

Anneau 2
section A–A

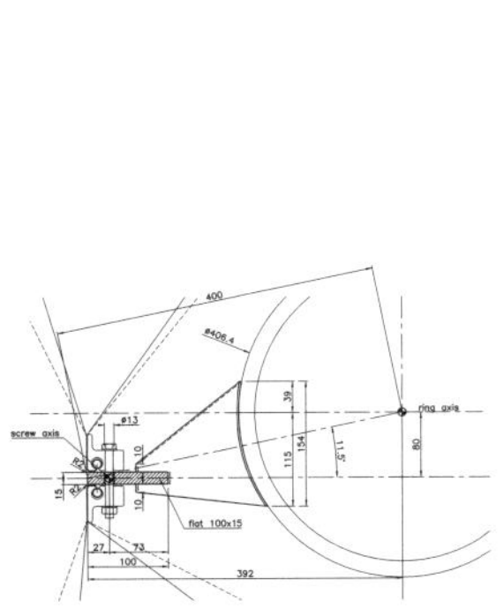

Anneau 1
section A–A

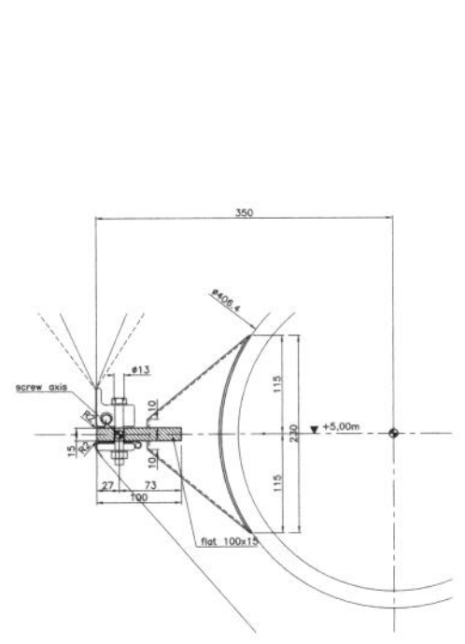

direct view on Anneau
example flat connection

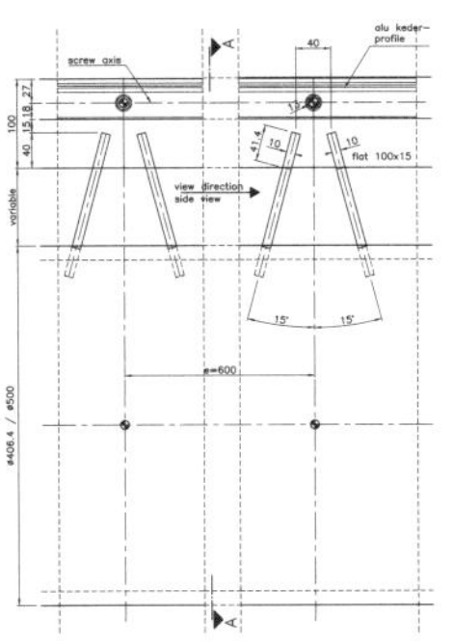

Detail anneau 5 (angle 30°)

Detail anneau 2–4

Detail cable A–D

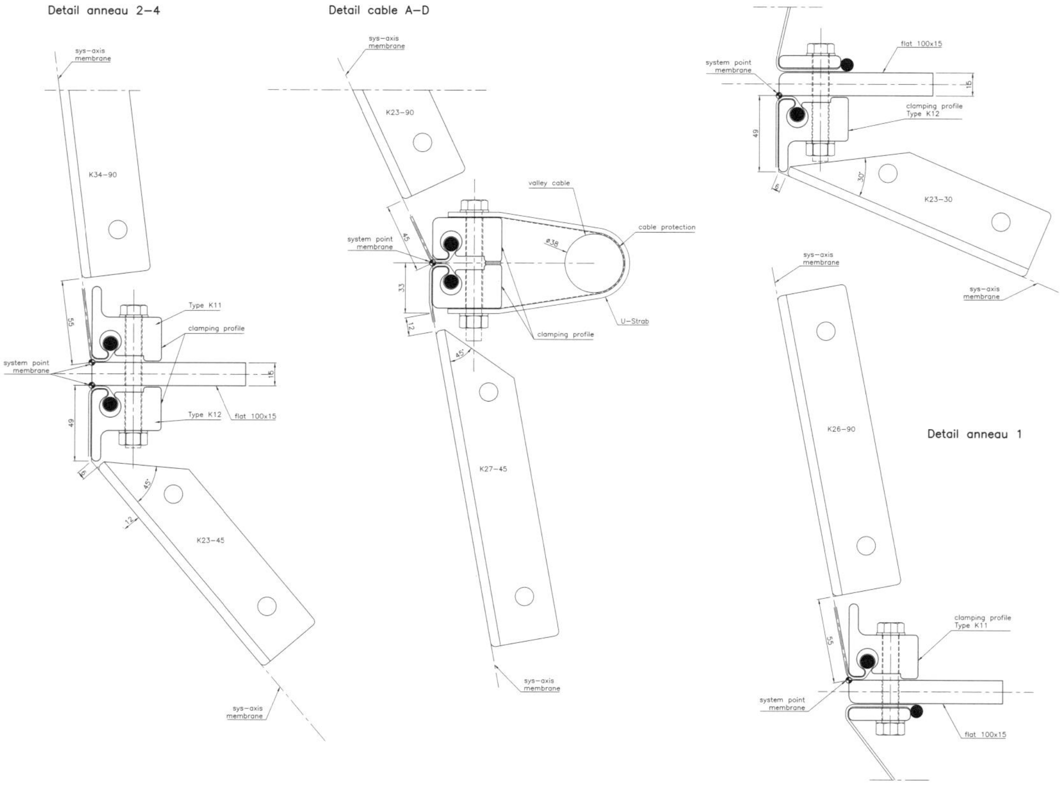

Vertical membrane joint - Clamping profiles

isometric view from inside

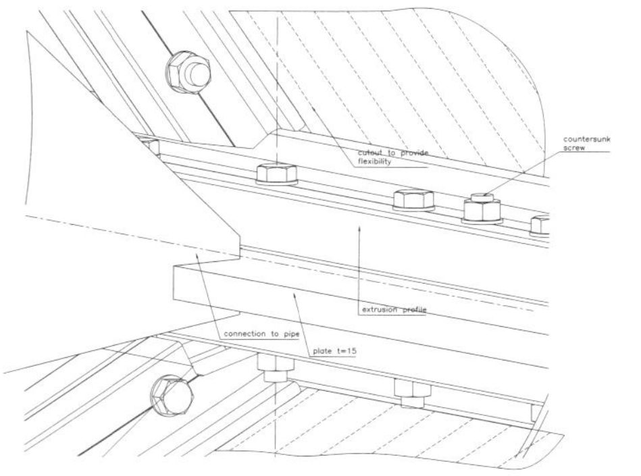

isometric view from inside
valley cable to vertical clamping

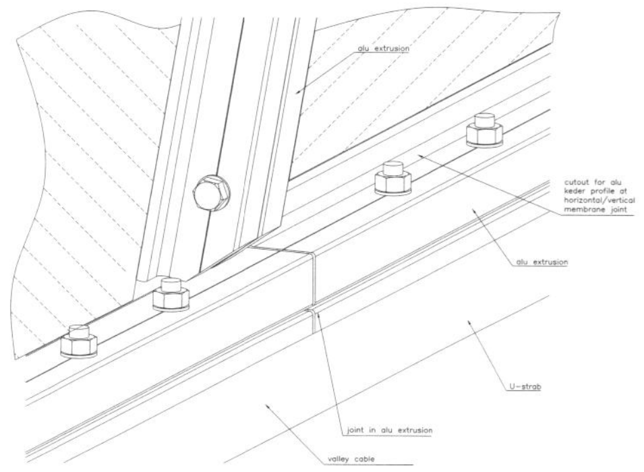

isometric view from outside
steel ring to vertical clamping

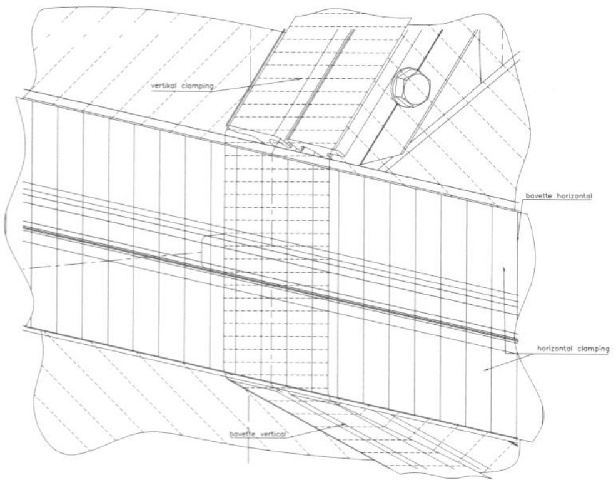

isometric view from outside

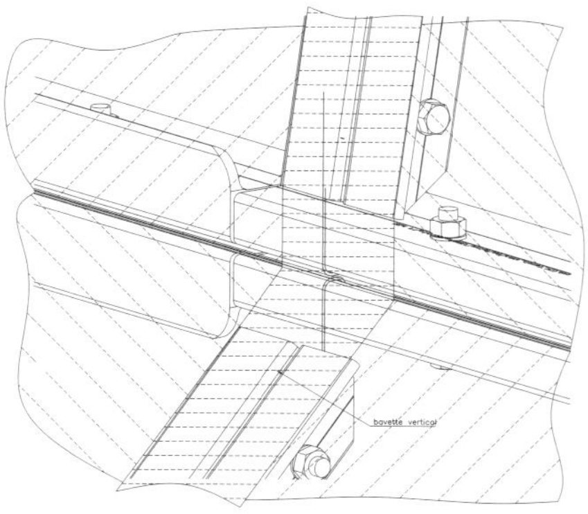

Top View

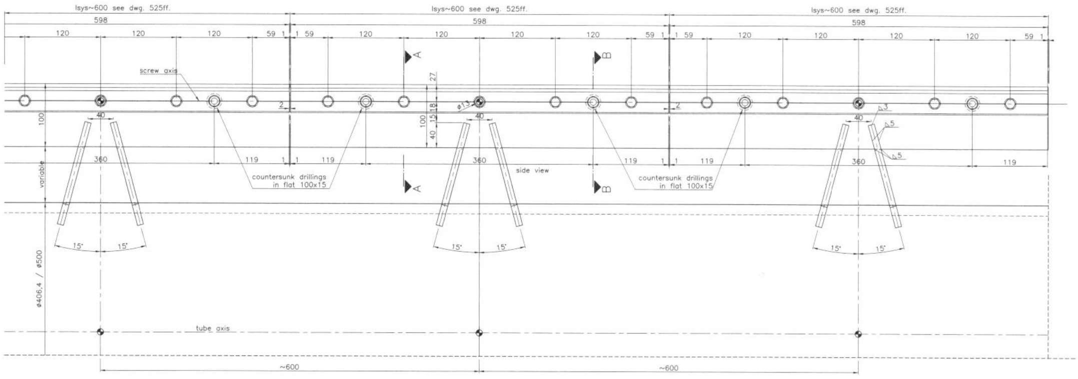
lsys~600 see dwg. 525ff.
598
120
59
119
screw axis
countersunk drillings in flat 100x15
side view
variable
ø406,4 / ø500
15°
tube axis
~600
A
B

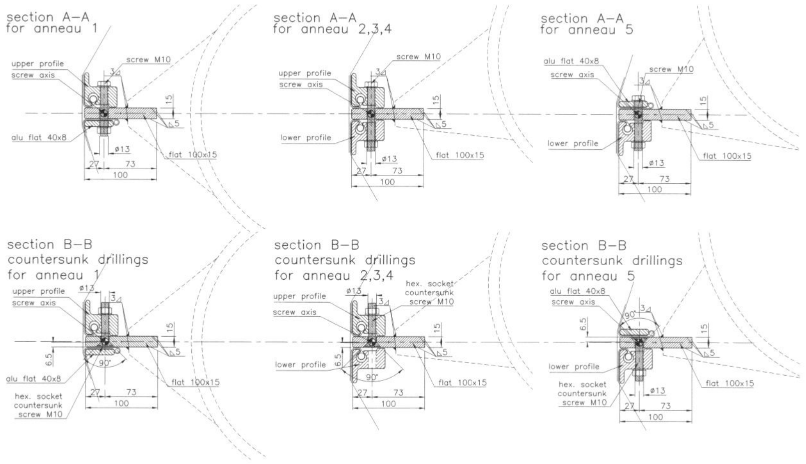
section A–A for anneau 1
section A–A for anneau 2,3,4
section A–A for anneau 5
upper profile
screw axis
screw M10
alu flat 40x8
lower profile
flat 100x15
ø13
27
73
100
15
section B–B countersunk drillings for anneau 1
section B–B countersunk drillings for anneau 2,3,4
section B–B countersunk drillings for anneau 5
hex. socket countersunk screw M10
90°
6,5

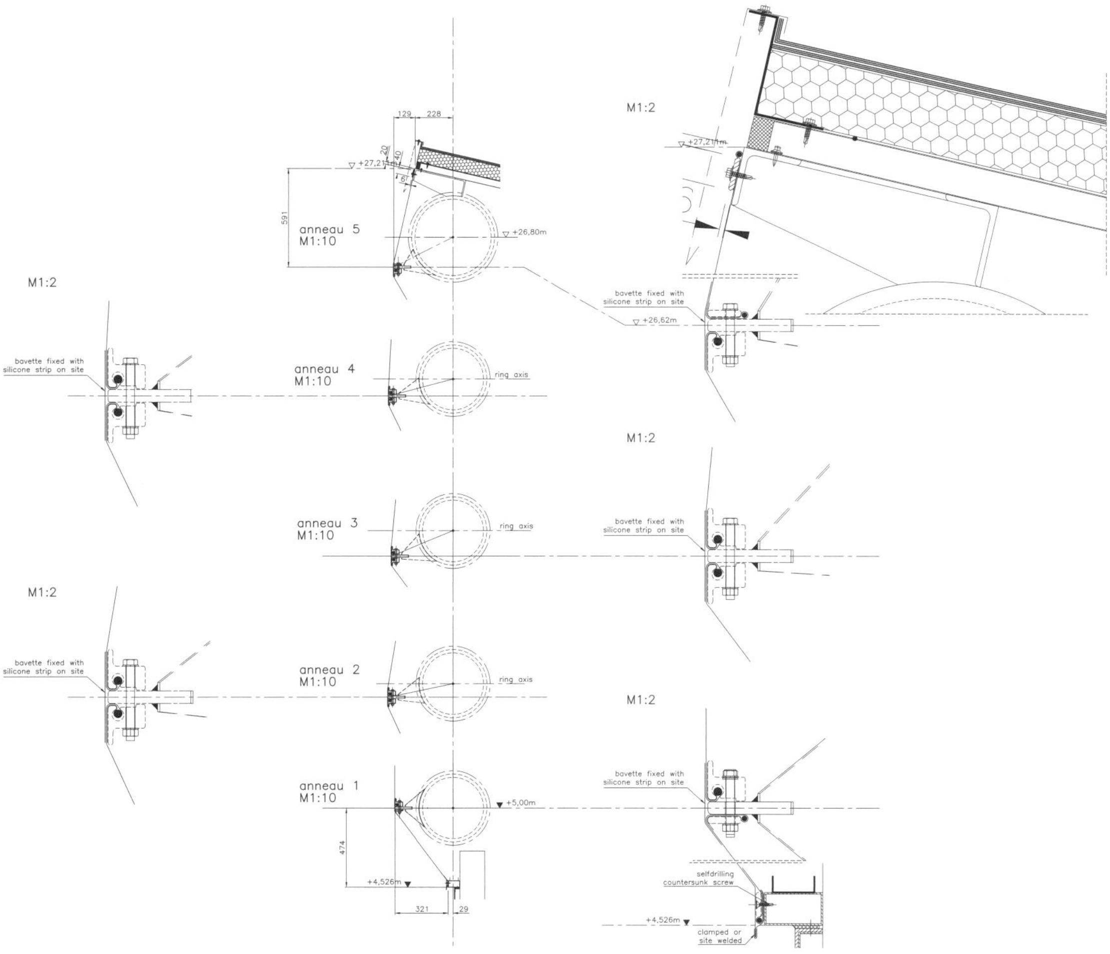
M1:2
anneau 5
M1:10
anneau 4
M1:10
anneau 3
M1:10
anneau 2
M1:10
anneau 1
M1:10
bavette fixed with silicone strip on site
ring axis
+27,21m
+26,80m
+26,62m
+5,00m
+4,526m
591
474
321
29
selfdrilling countersunk screw
clamped or site welded

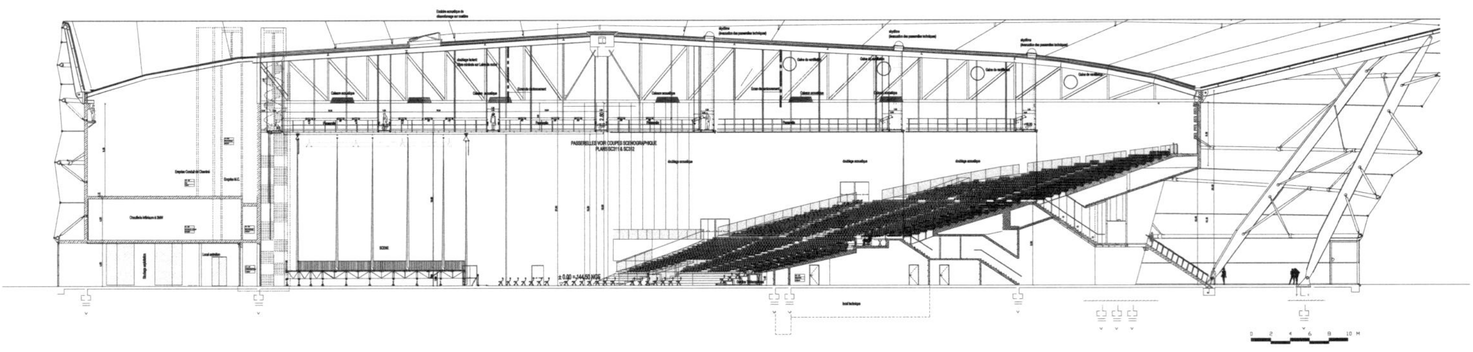

Longitudinal section

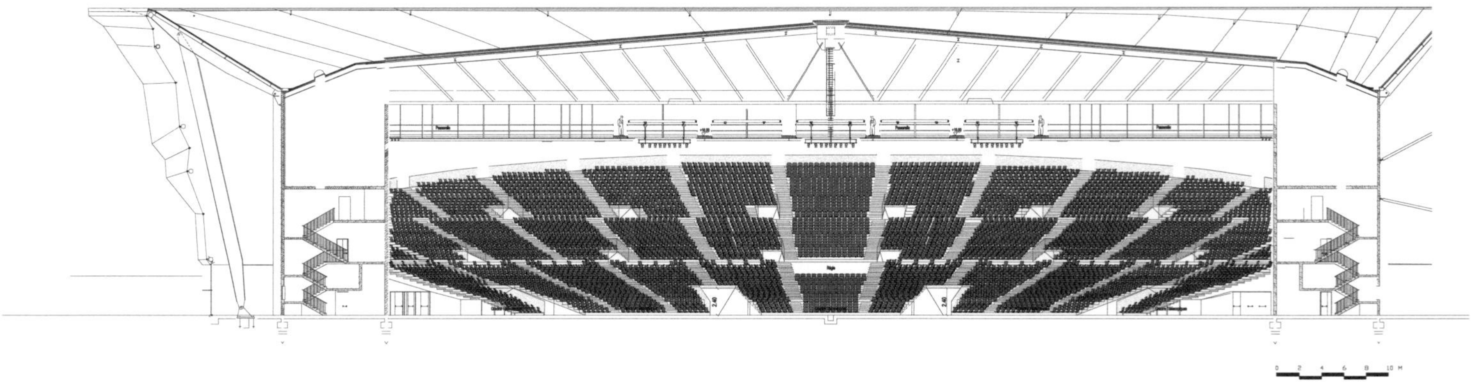

Transversal section

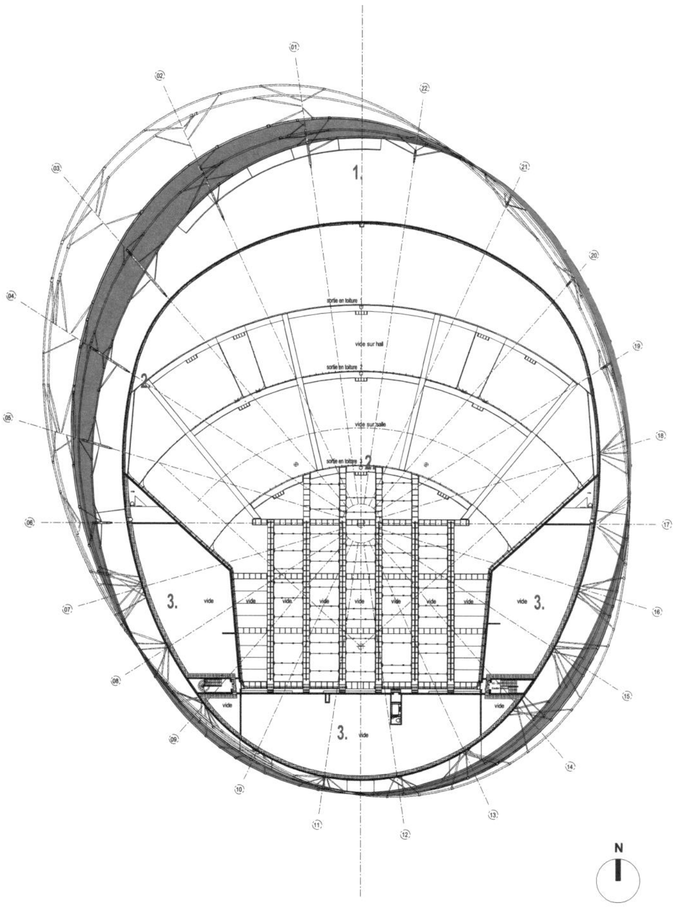

N

LEGENDE:
1. VIDE HALL
2. GRILL
3. VIDE

Fourth floor

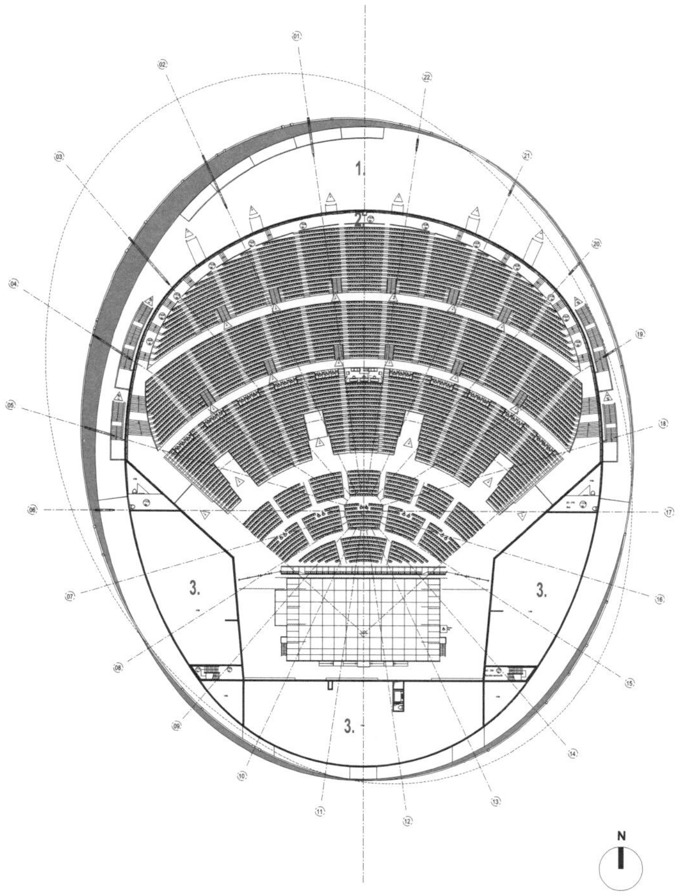

N

LEGENDE:
1. VIDE HALL
2. GALLERIE PERIPHERIQUE 5 (max +13.46)
3. VIDE

Third floor

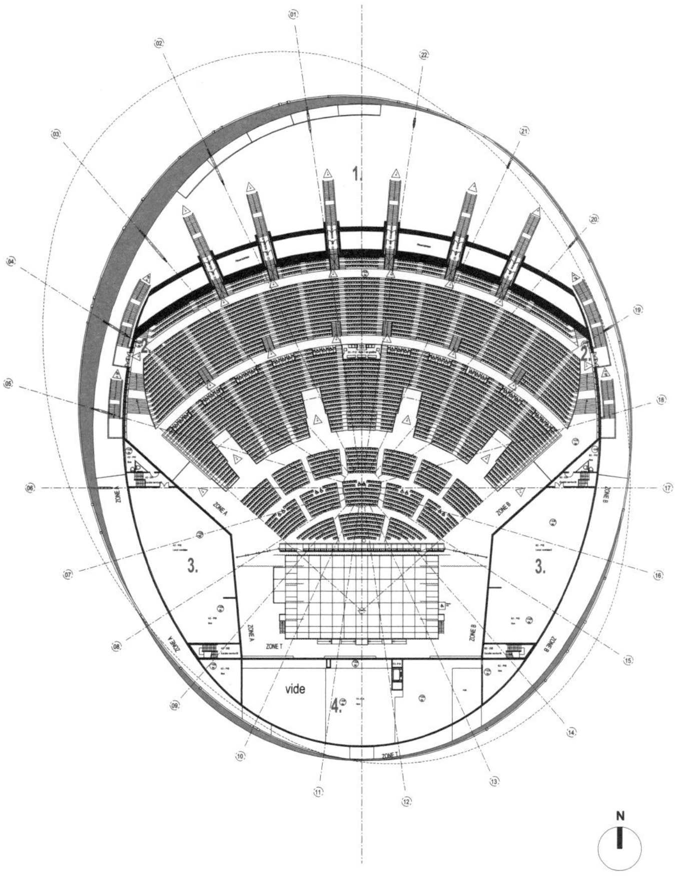

N

LEGENDE:
1. VIDE HALL
2. SALLE - SECONDE GALLERIE
3. LOCAUX CTA
4. NON AFFECTE

Second floor

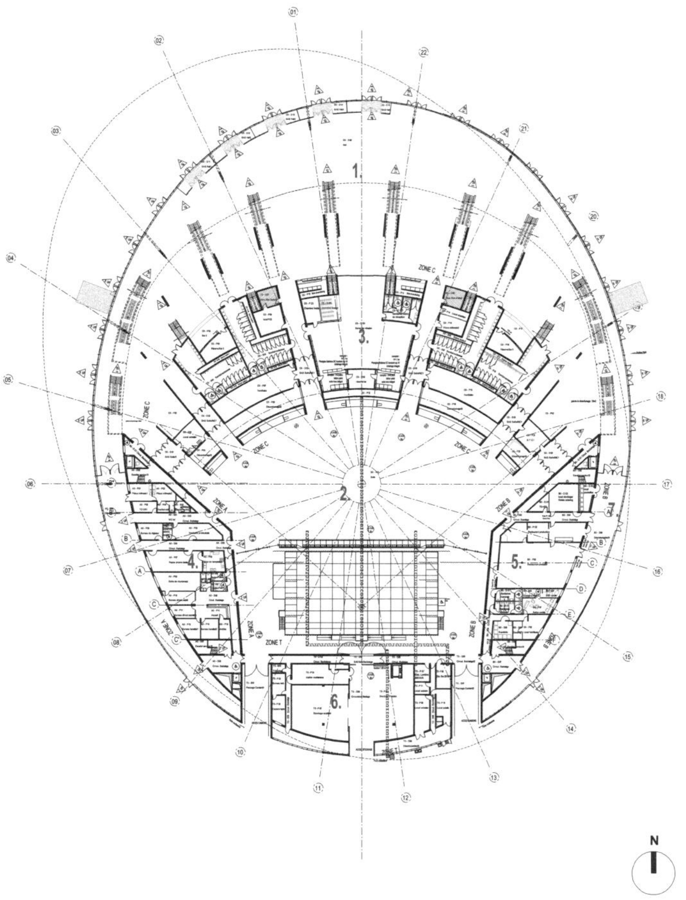

N

LEGENDE:
1. HALL
2. SALLE
3. SALON VIP
4. BACKSTAGE EXPLOITANT
5. BACKSTAGE PRODUCTION
6. LOCAL STOCKAGE
7. DEAMBULATOIRES

Gorund floor

Intersection of vertical connection and valley cable clamping M1:2

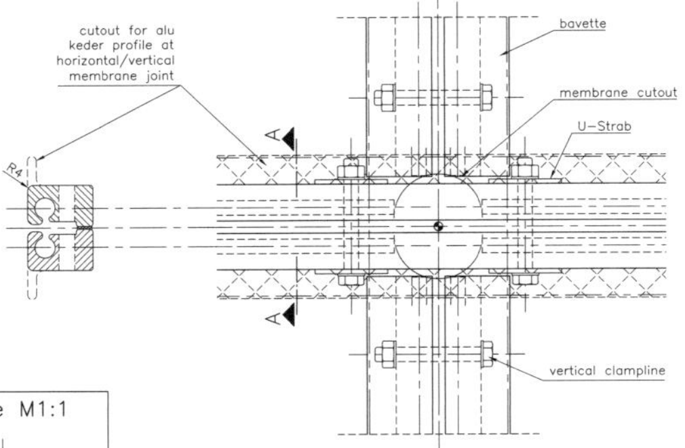

standard alu-profile M1:1

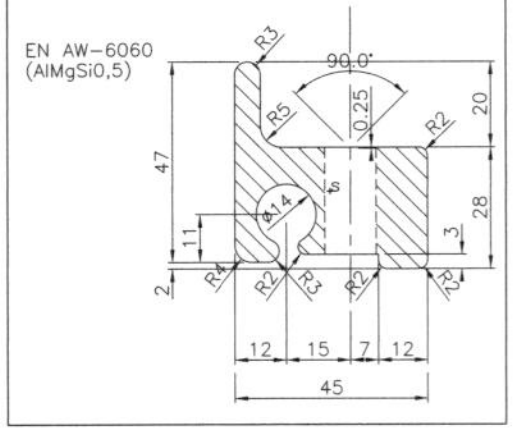

Vertical conneciton between panels

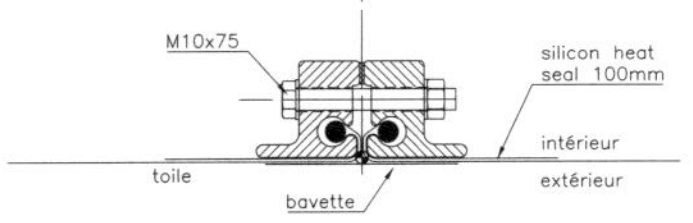

geometry information for Typ A,B,C (elements) M1:1

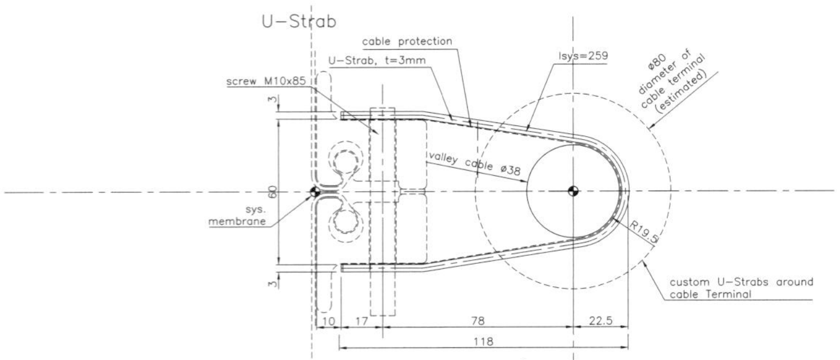

pressure elements

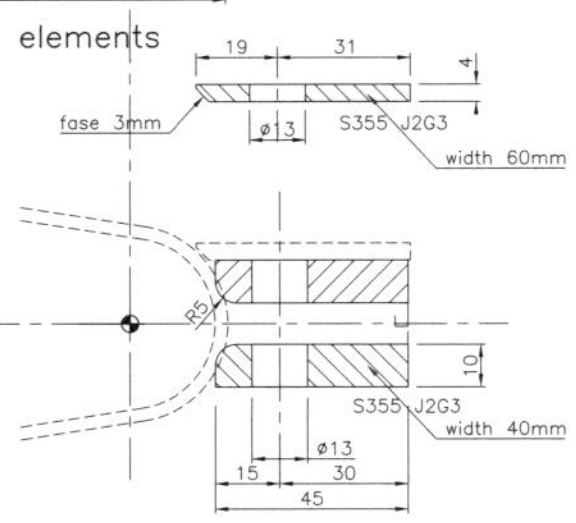

cable clamp

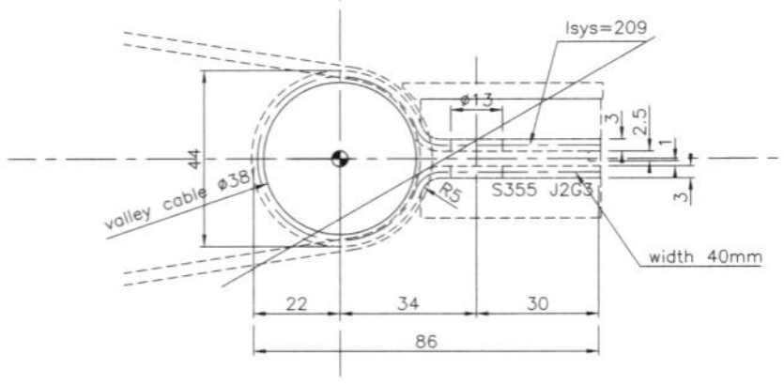

Typ A M1:2

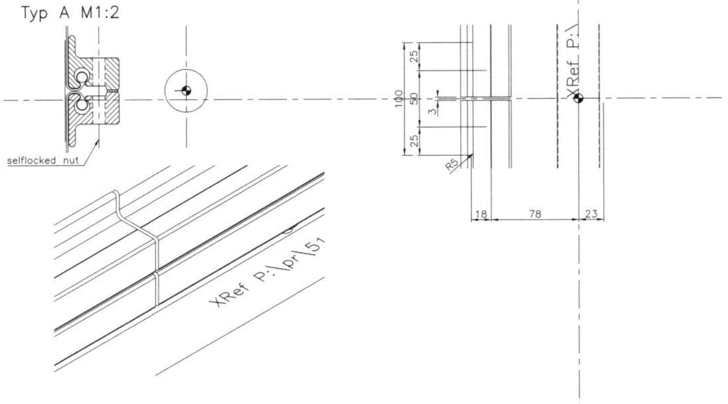

Typ B M1:2 (with ring clamp)

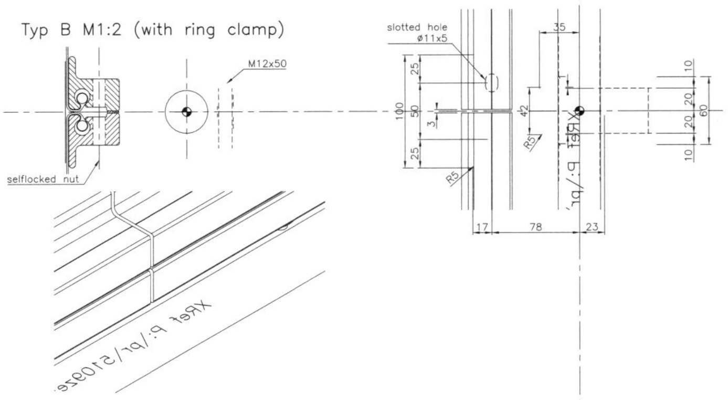

Typ C M1:2

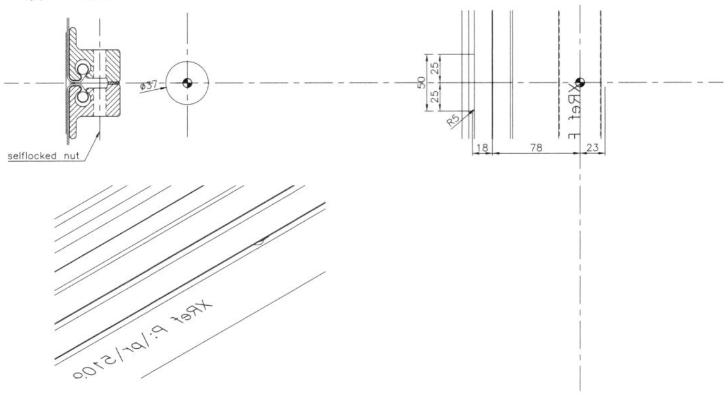

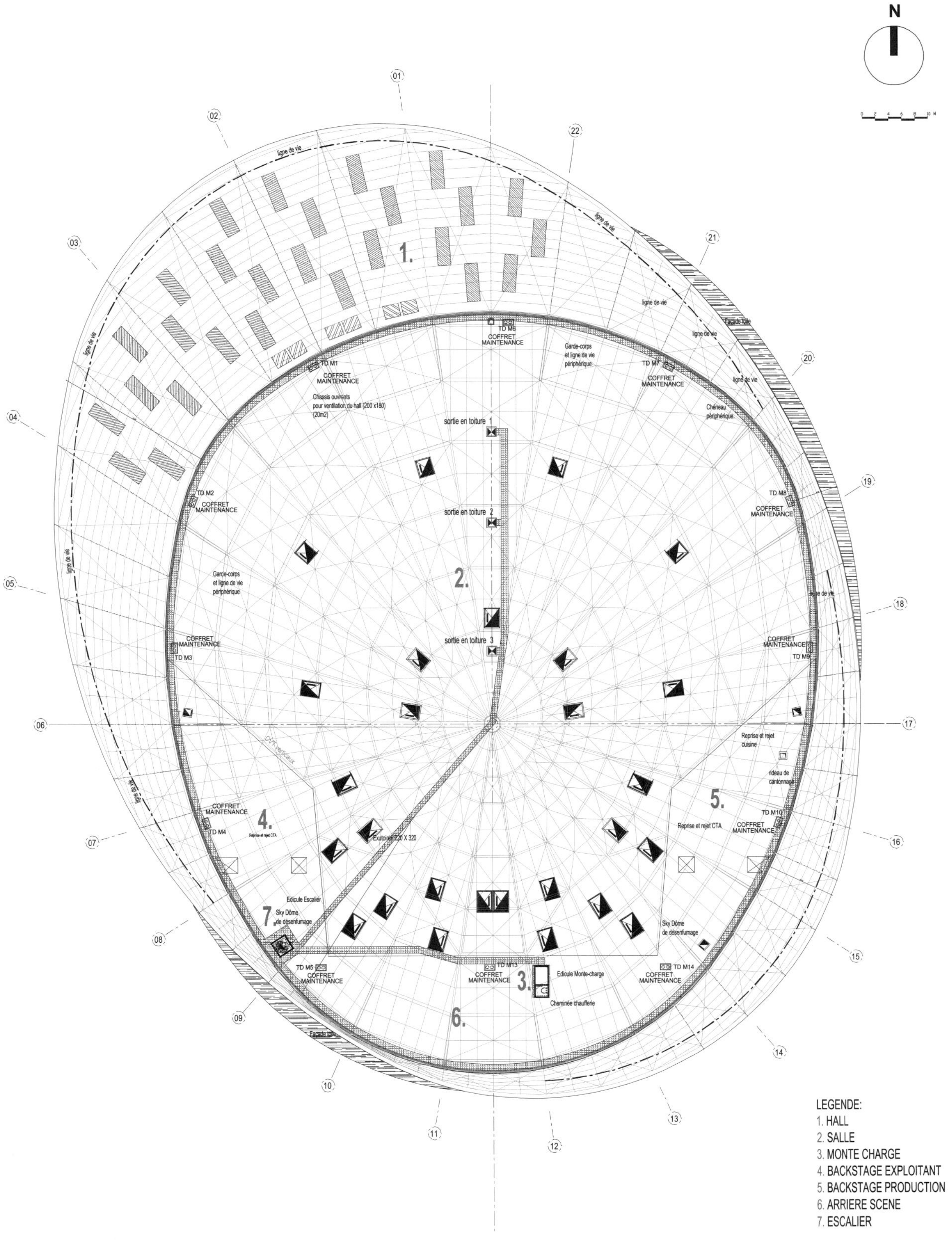

LEGENDE:
1. HALL
2. SALLE
3. MONTE CHARGE
4. BACKSTAGE EXPLOITANT
5. BACKSTAGE PRODUCTION
6. ARRIERE SCENE
7. ESCALIER

Roof floor

DE CECCO OPERATIONAL HEADQUARTERS

PESCARA, ITALY
2001–2008

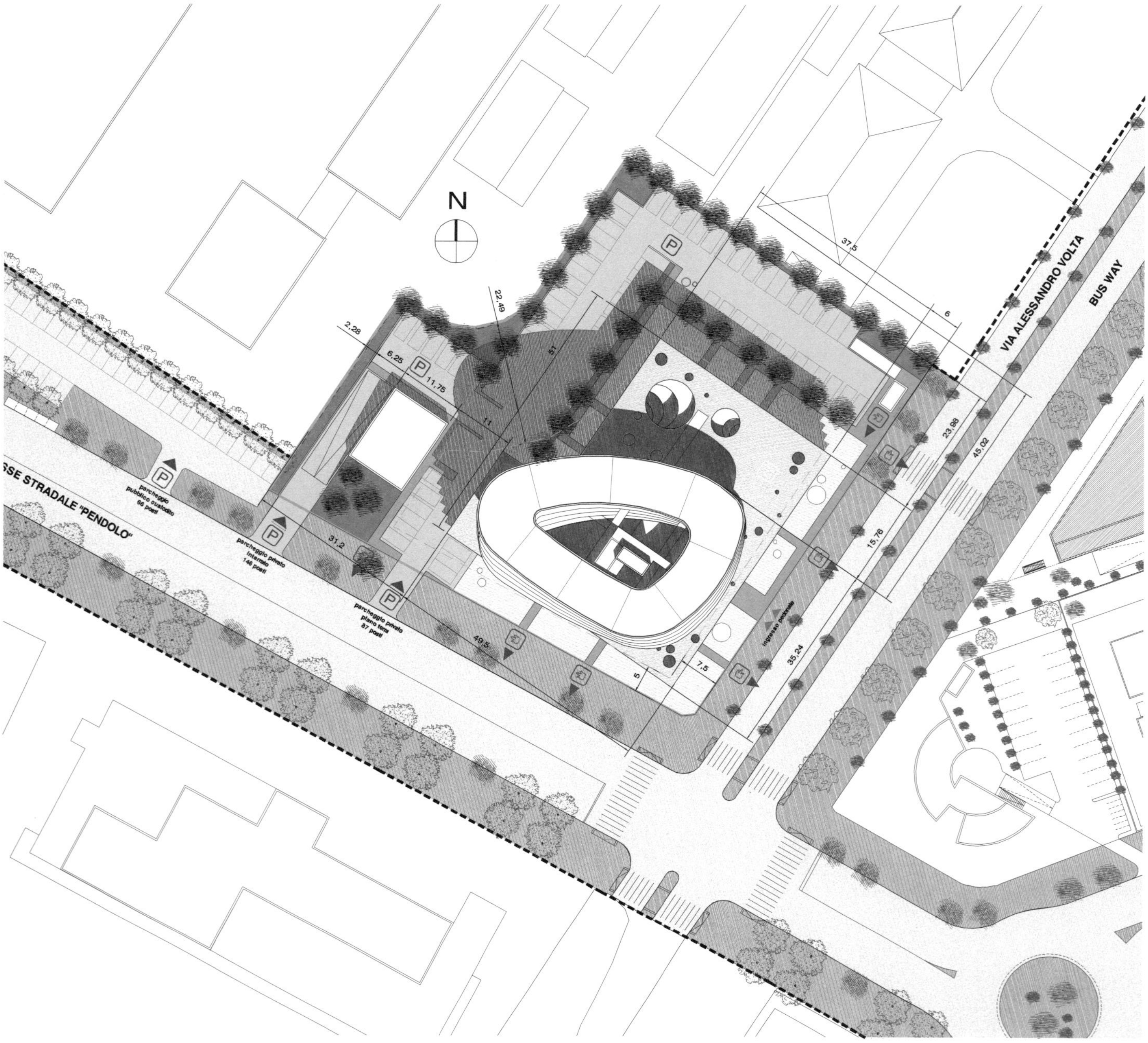

Site plan

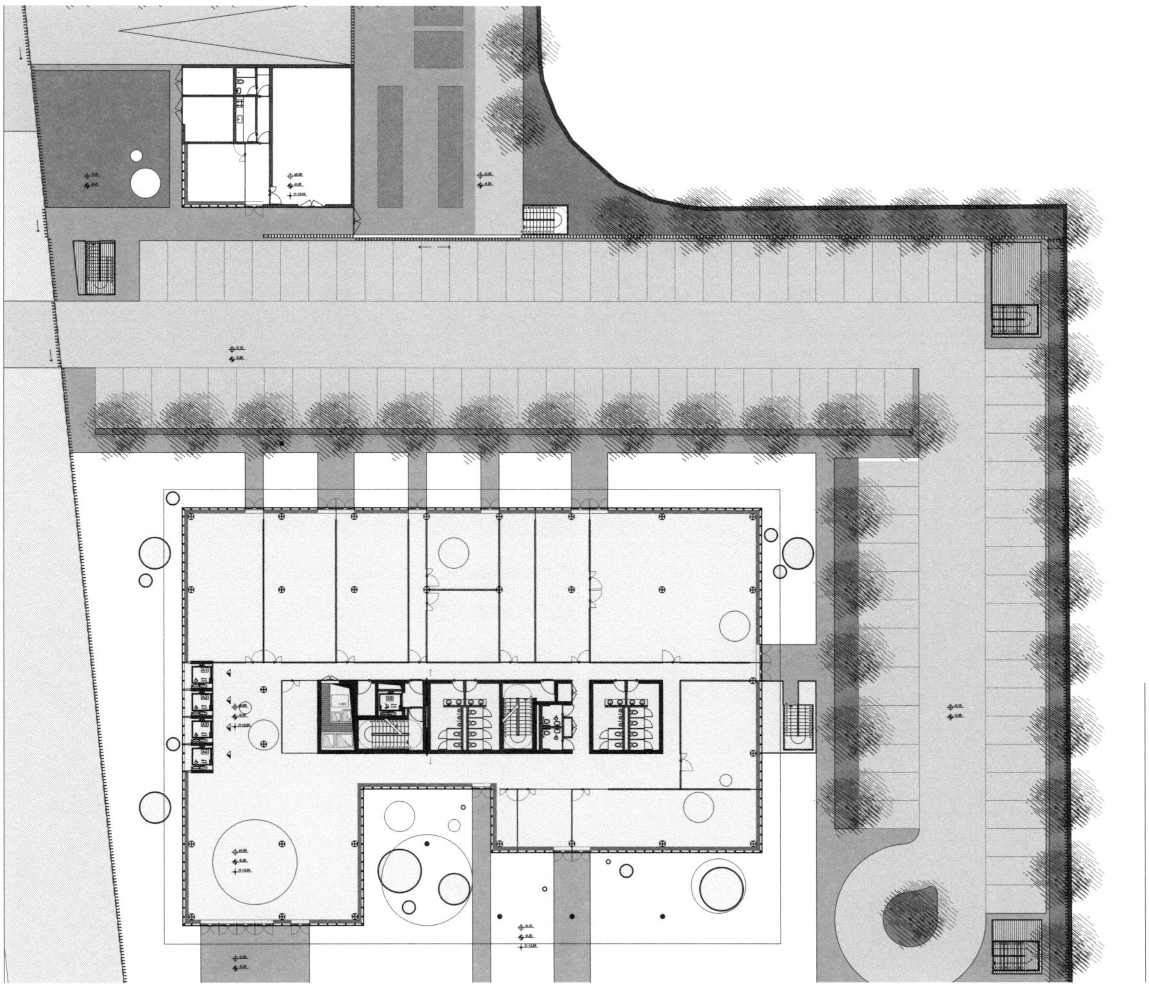

Ground floor

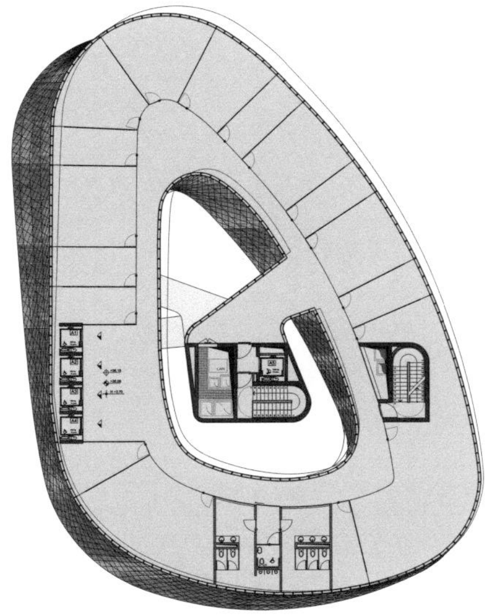

Tenth floor

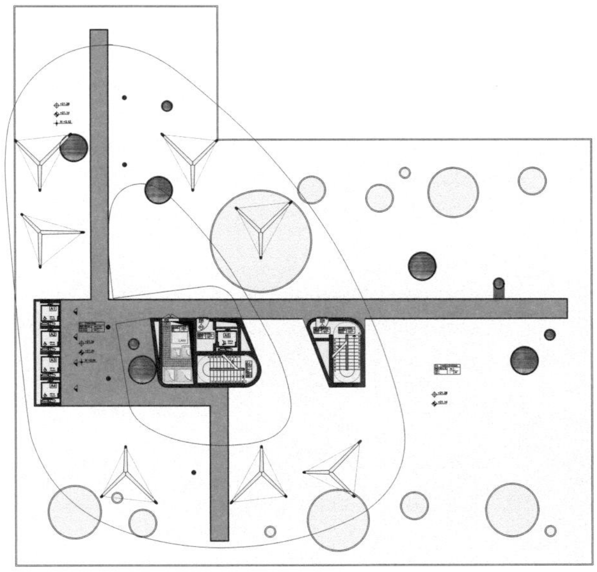

Sixth floor

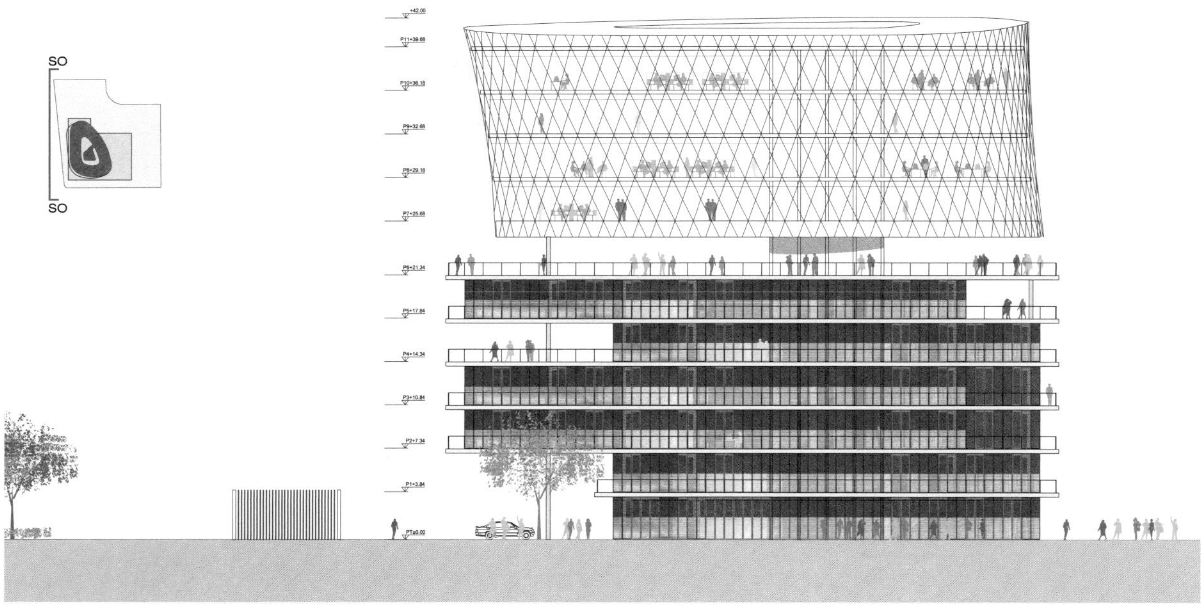
SO
SO
+42.00
P11+39.68
P10+36.18
P9+32.68
P8+29.18
P7+25.68
P6+21.34
P5+17.84
P4+14.34
P3+10.84
P2+7.34
P1+3.84
PT±0.00

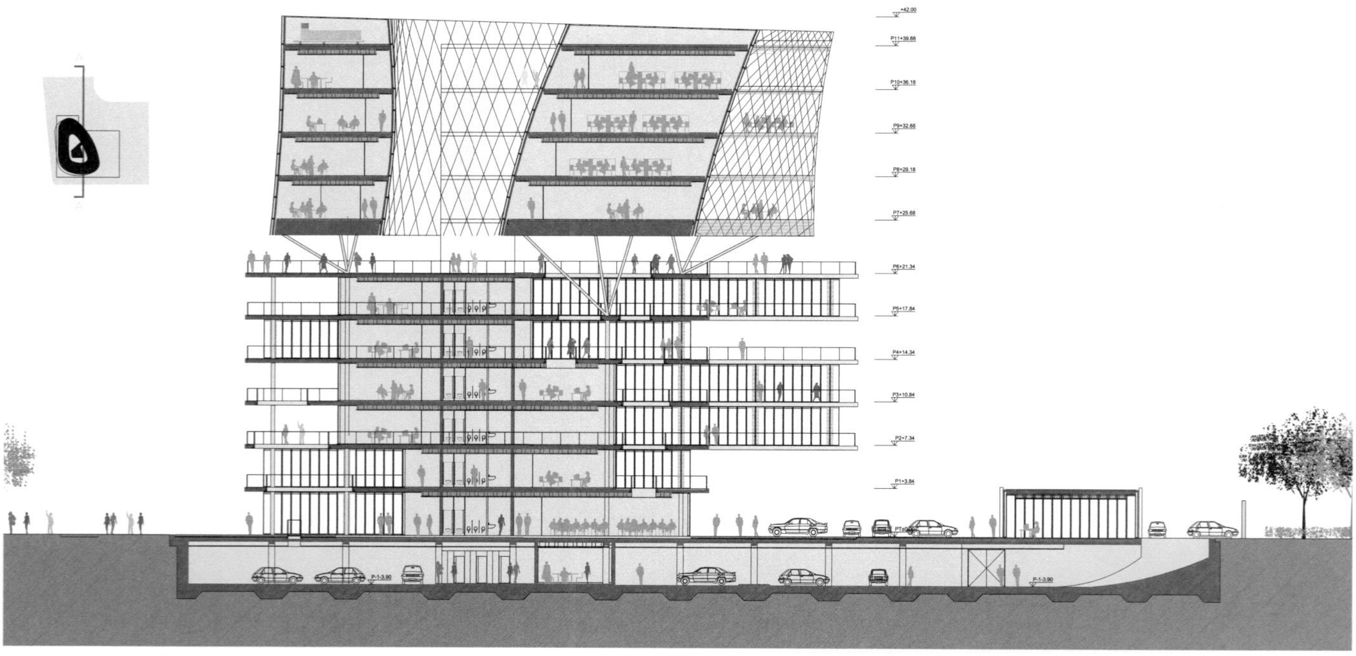
+42.00
P11+39.68
P10+36.18
P9+32.68
P8+29.18
P7+25.68
P6+21.34
P5+17.84
P4+14.34
P3+10.84
P2+7.34
P1+3.84

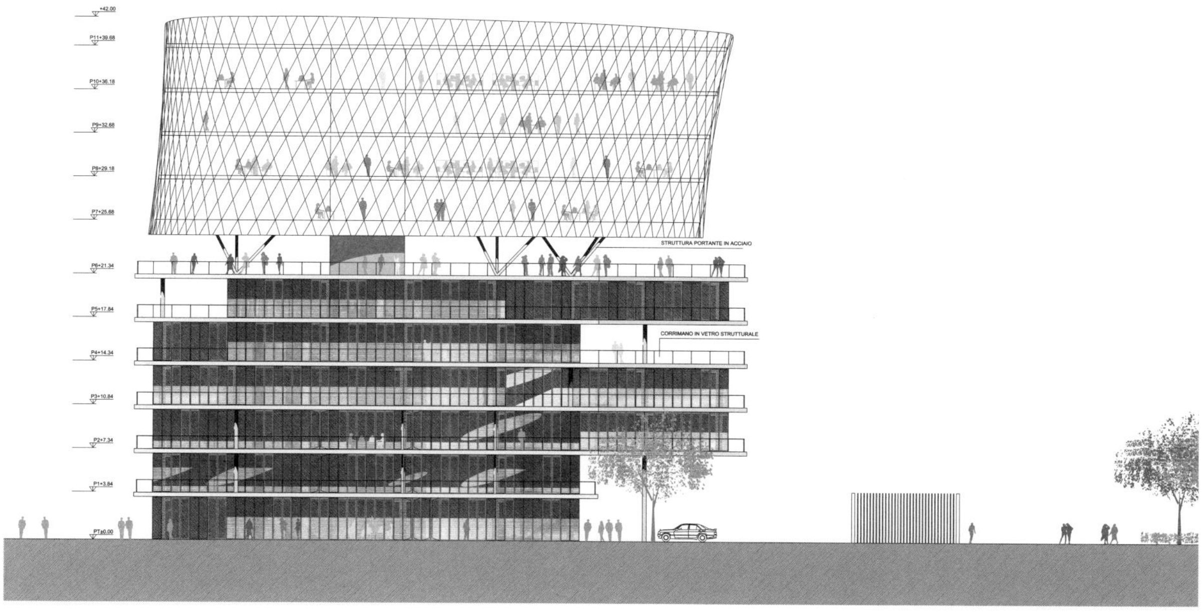
+42.00
P11+39.68
P10+36.18
P9+32.68
P8+29.18
P7+25.68
STRUTTURA PORTANTE IN ACCIAIO
P6+21.34
P5+17.84
CORRIMANO IN VETRO STRUTTURALE
P4+14.34
P3+10.84
P2+7.34
P1+3.84
PT±0.00

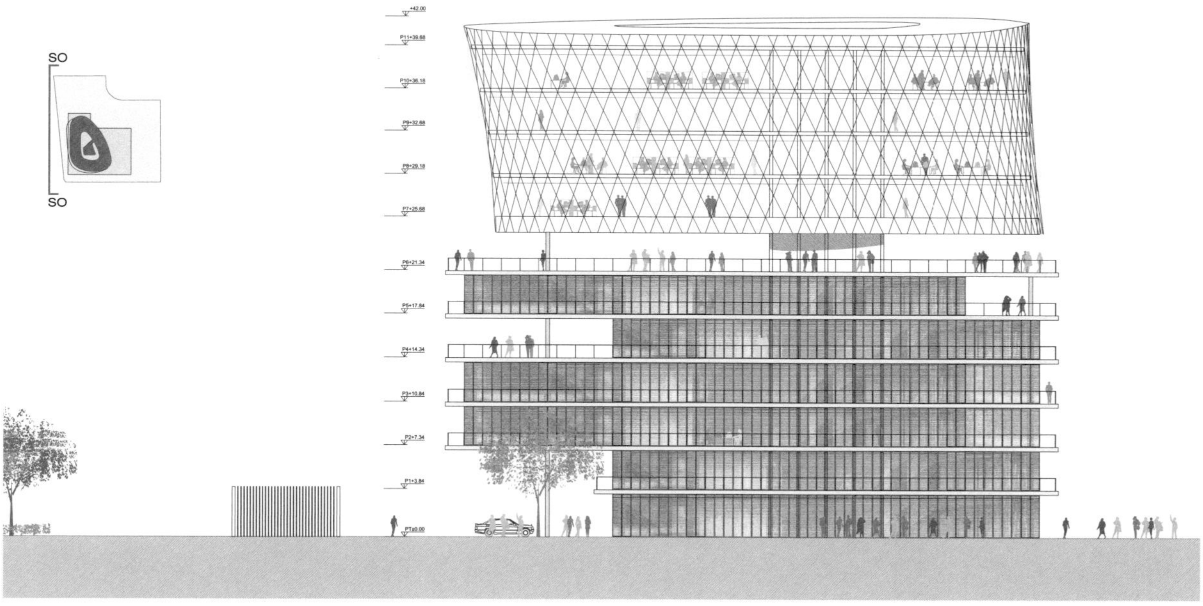
SO
SO
+42.00
P11+39.68
P10+36.18
P9+32.68
P8+29.18
P7+25.68
P6+21.34
P5+17.84
P4+14.34
P3+10.84
P2+7.34
P1+3.84
PT±0.00

NEW TRADE FAIR
RHO-PERO, MILAN, ITALY
2002–2005

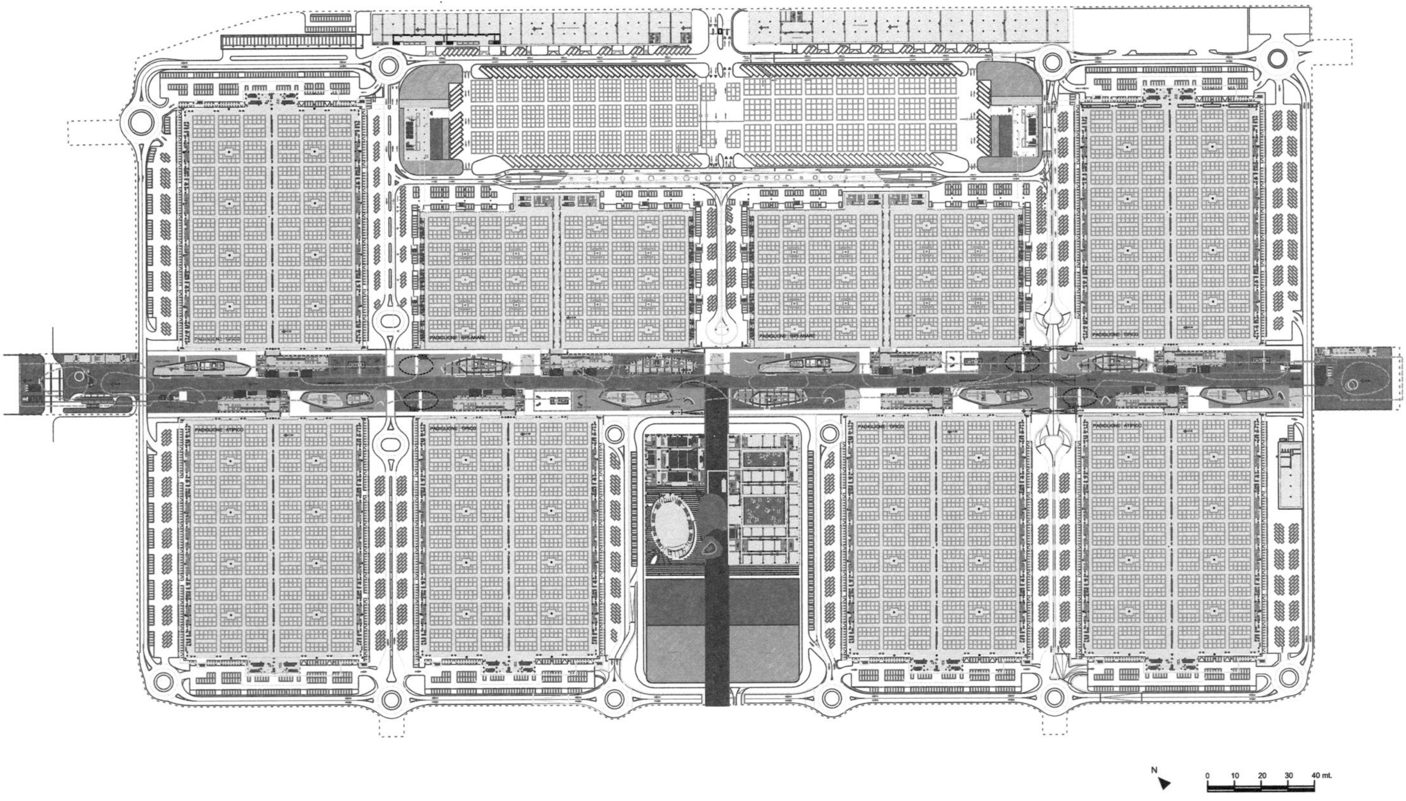

Site plan

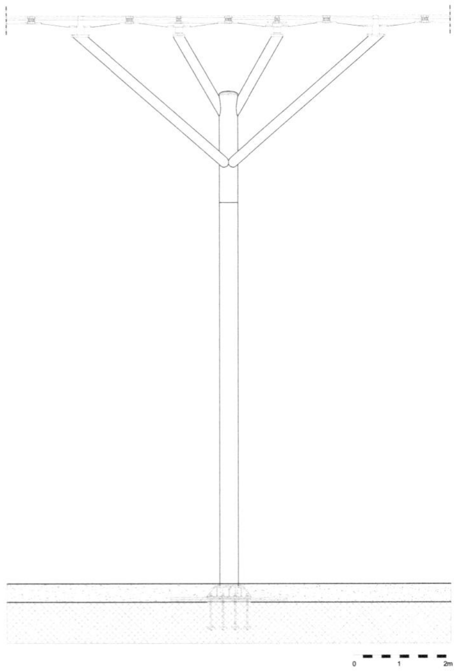

Roof pillar

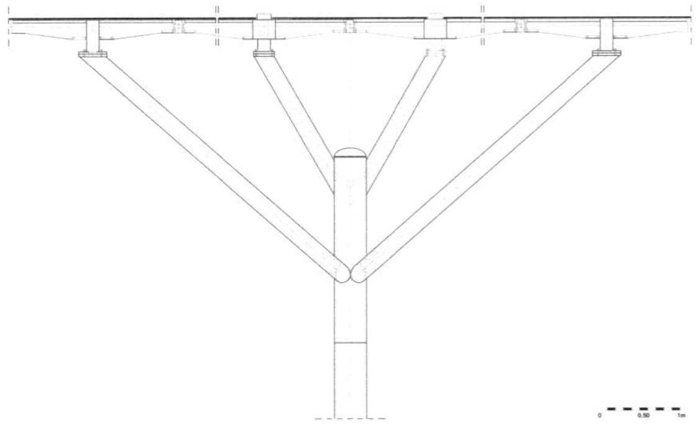

Roof pillar

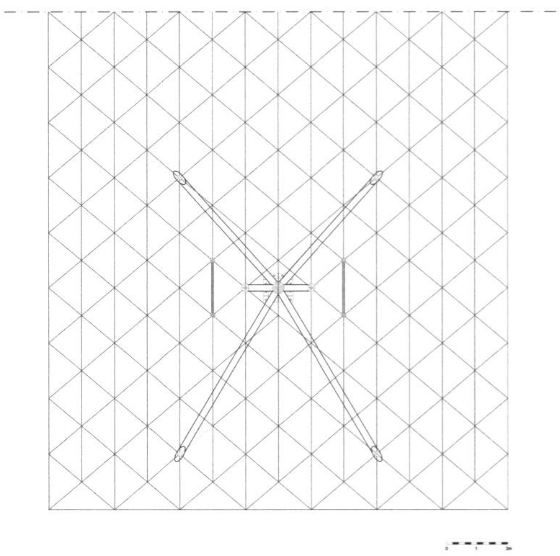

Roof pillar. View from above

Service centre

Plan level +6.50 m

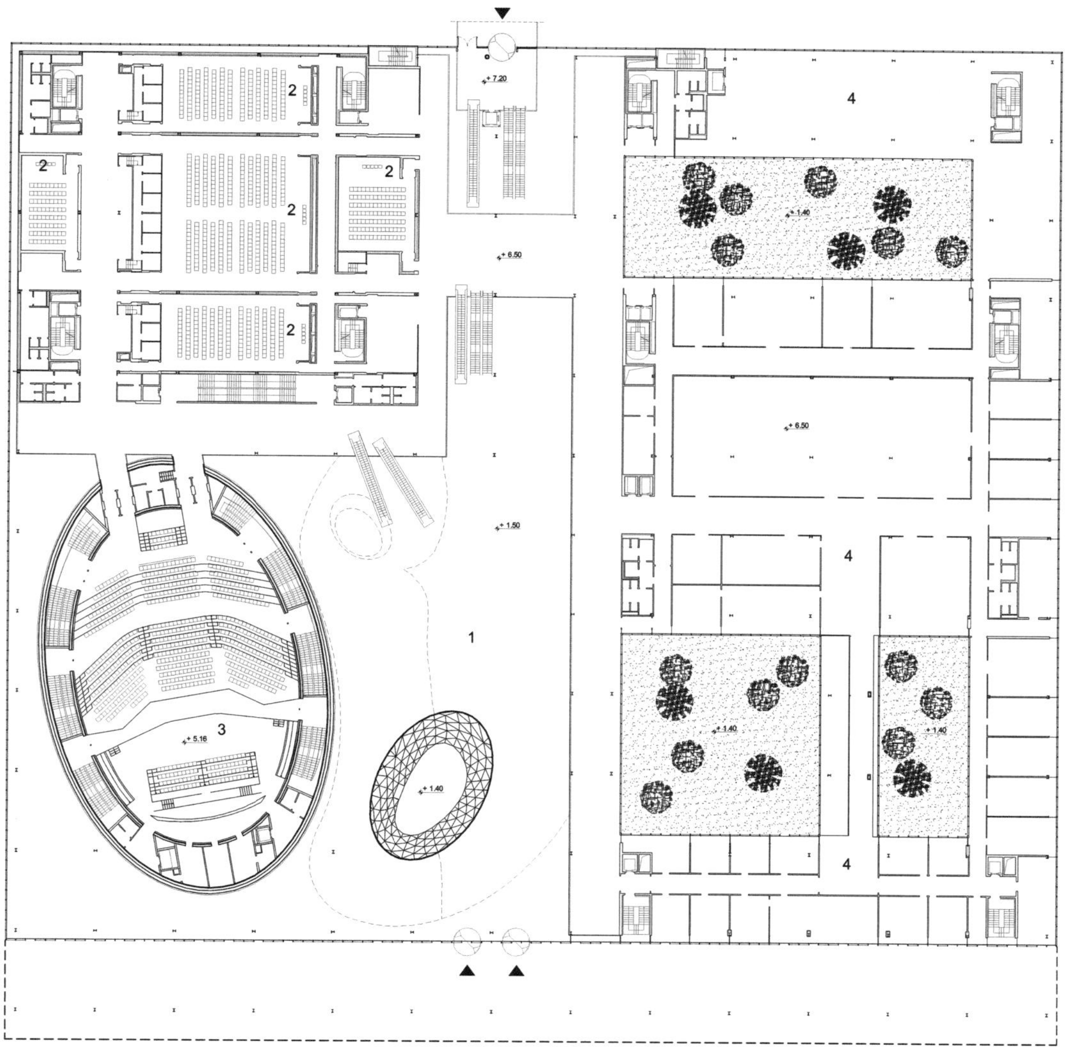

1. Hall
2. Conference room
3. Auditorium
4. Service centre

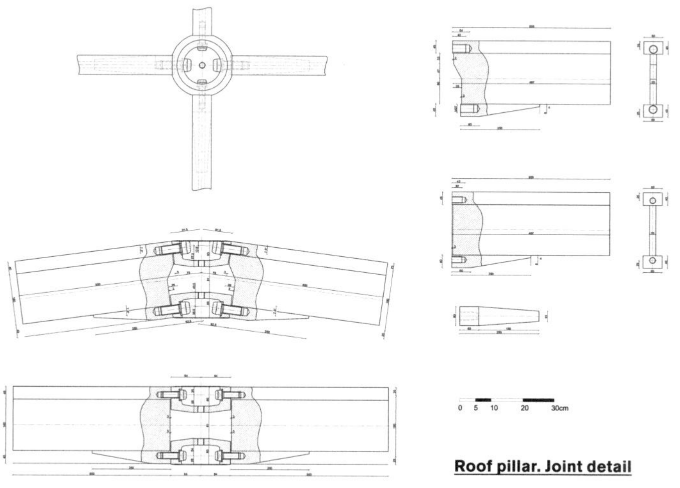

Roof pillar. Joint detail

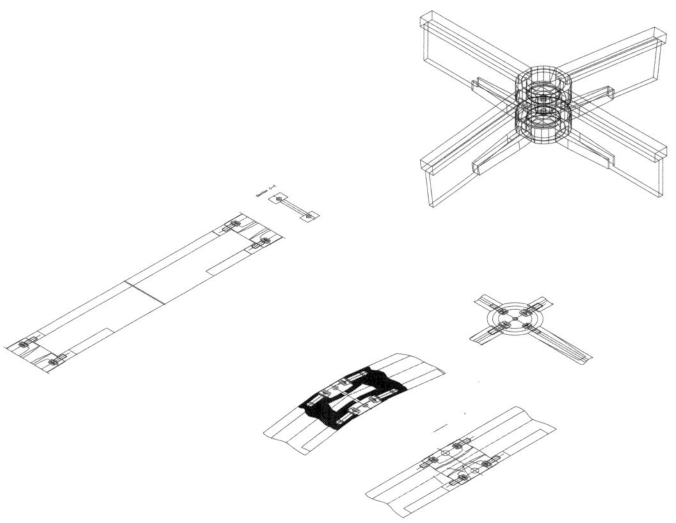

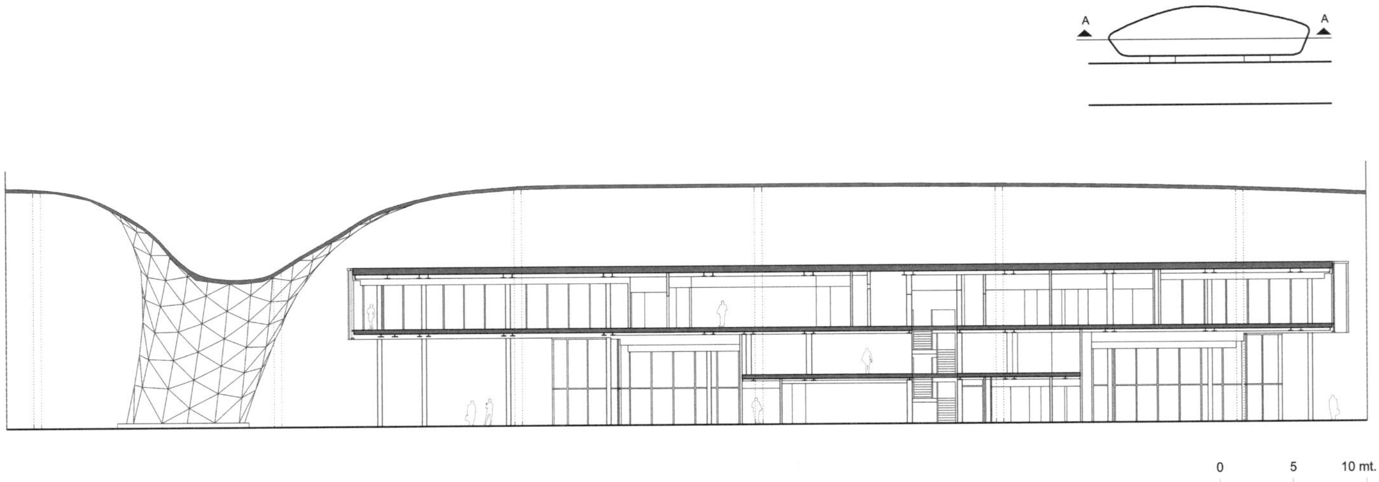

Section AA

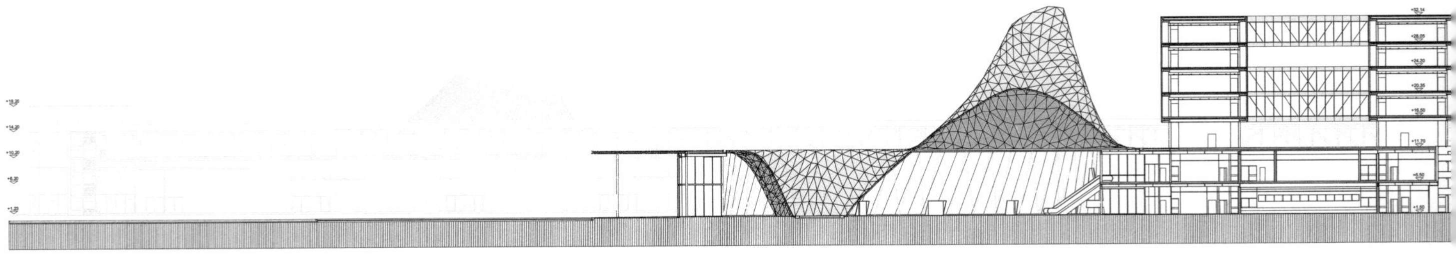

Transversal section, Central axis, Service centre

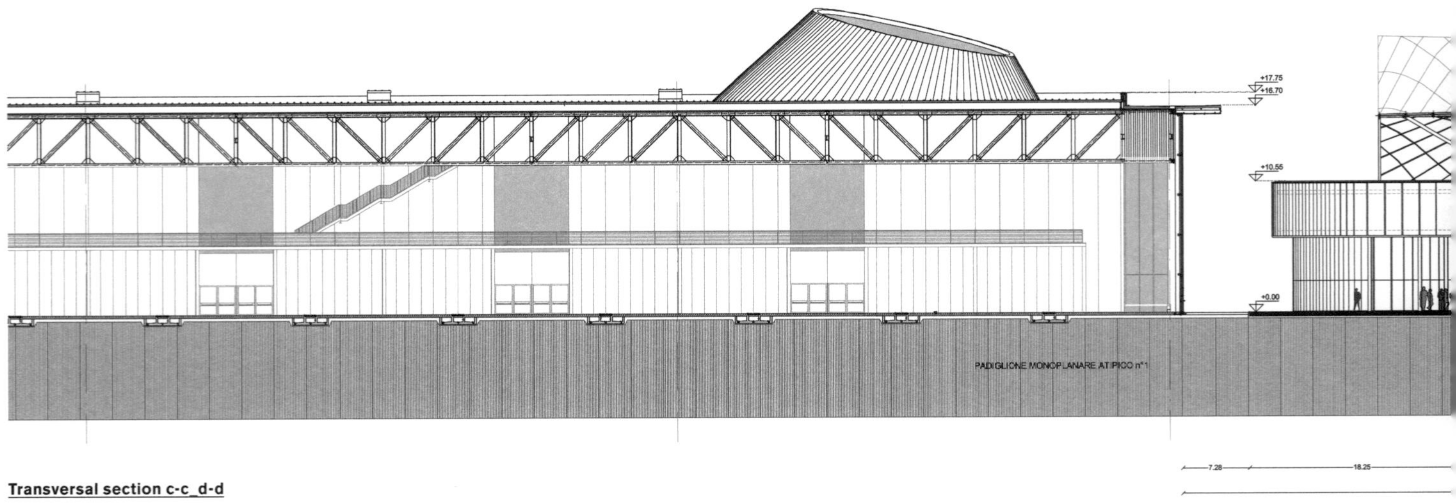

Transversal section c-c_d-d

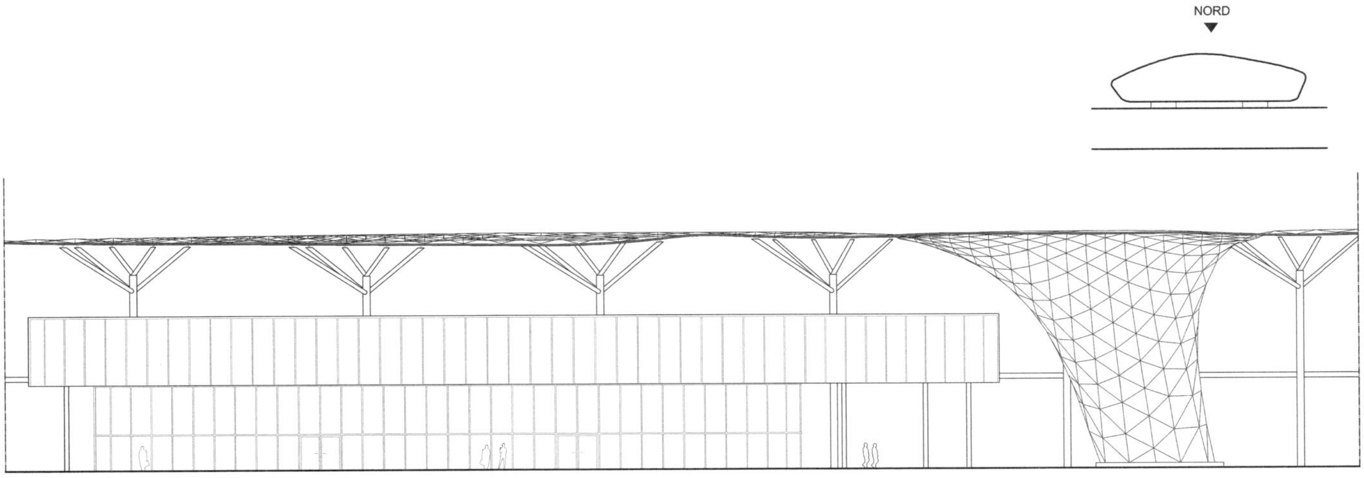

North Elevation

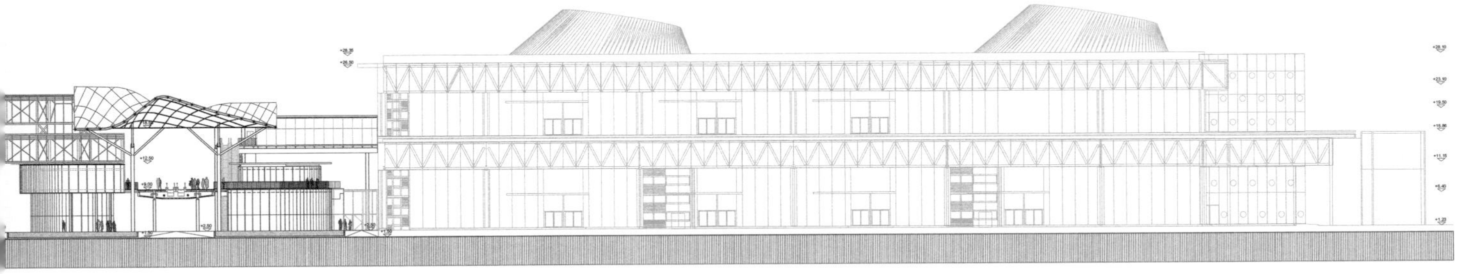

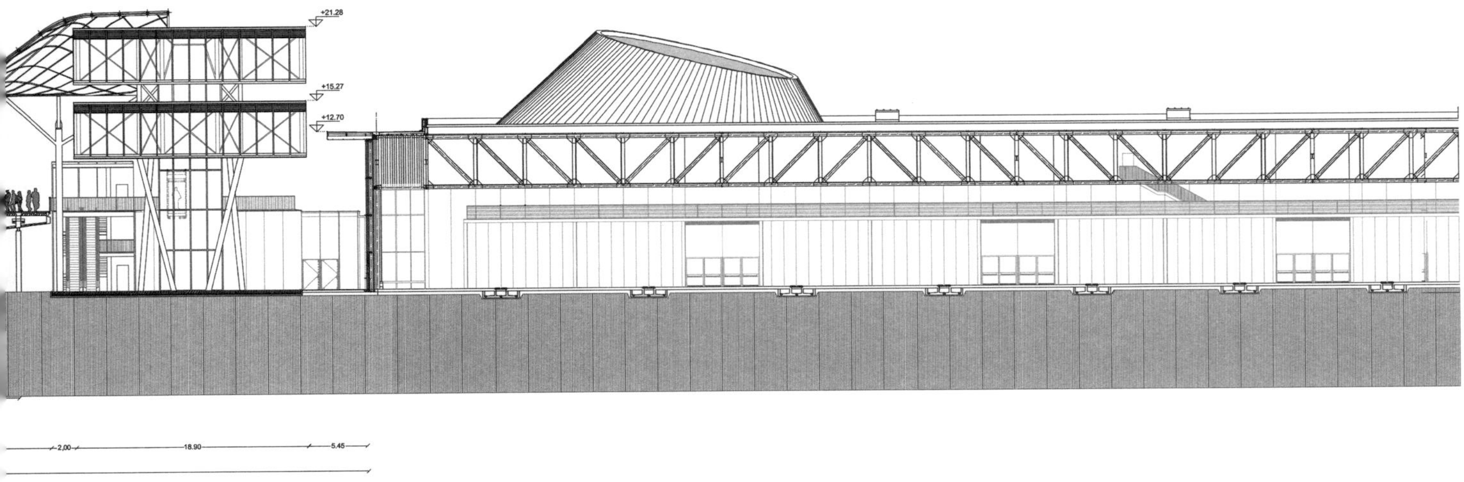

NARDINI RESEARCH CENTRE AND AUDITORIUM
BASSANO DEL GRAPPA, VICENZA, ITALY
2002–2004

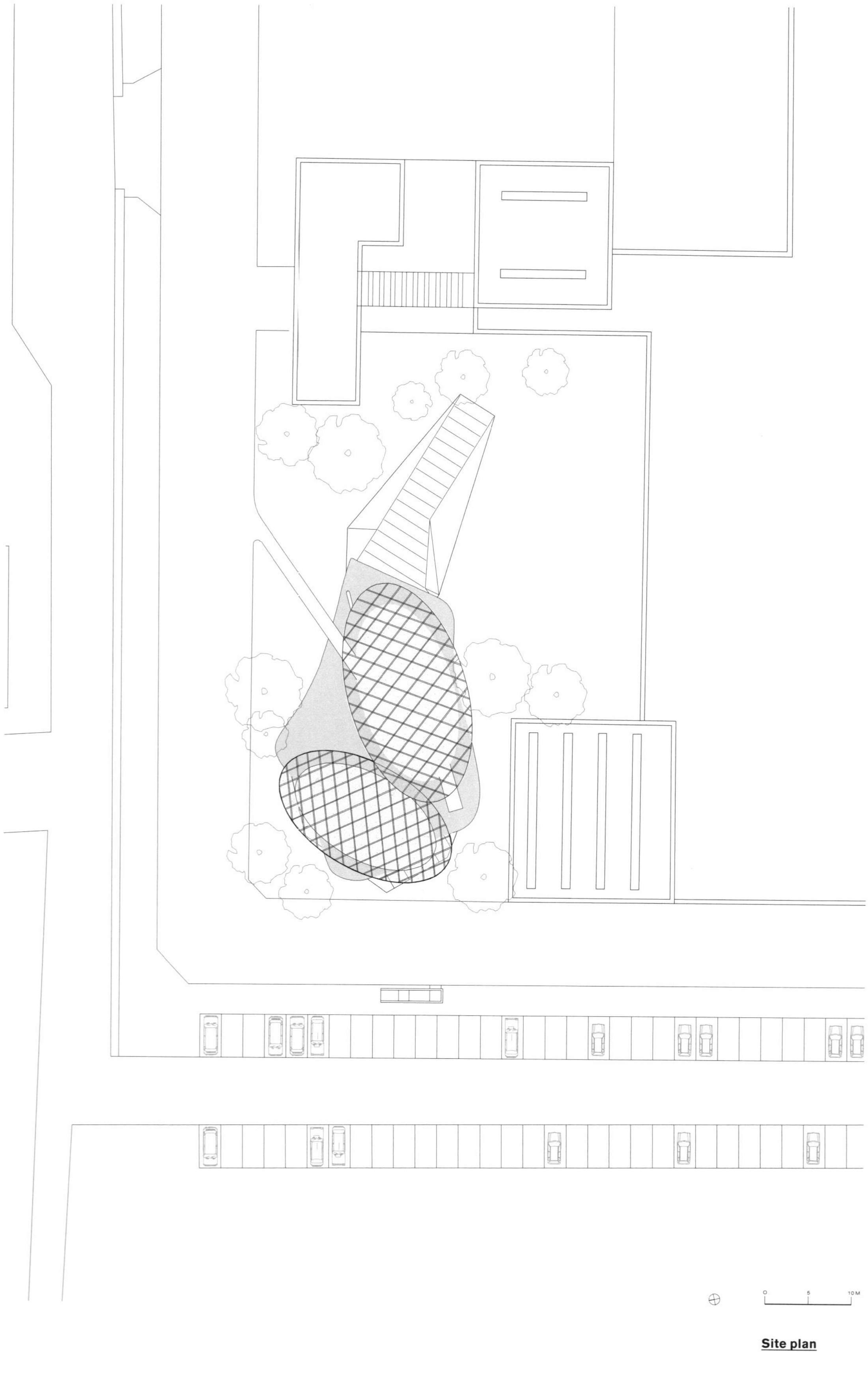

Site plan

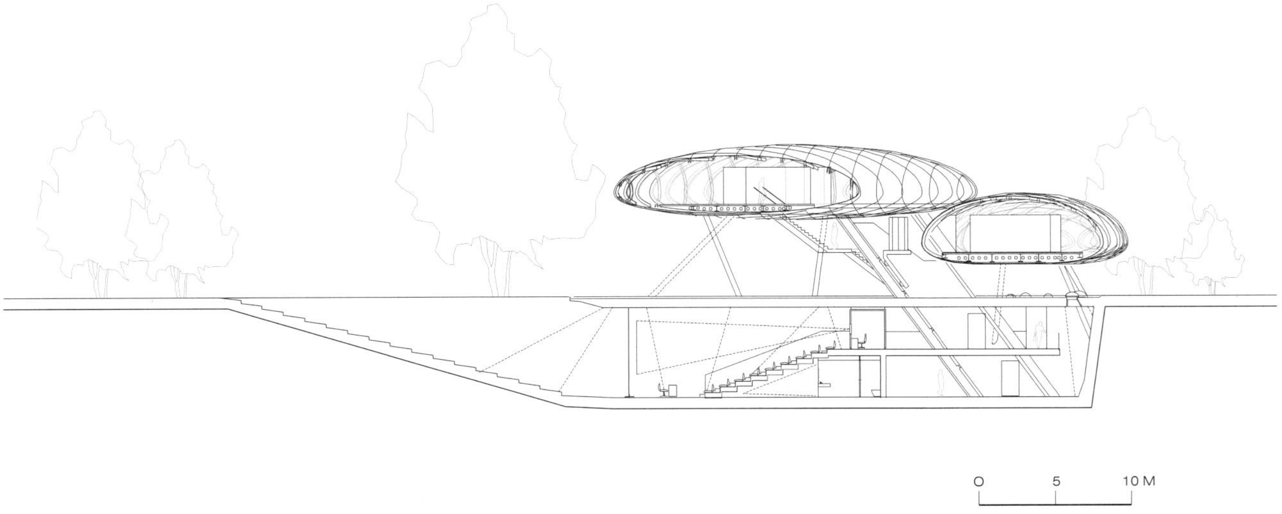
0
5
10 M

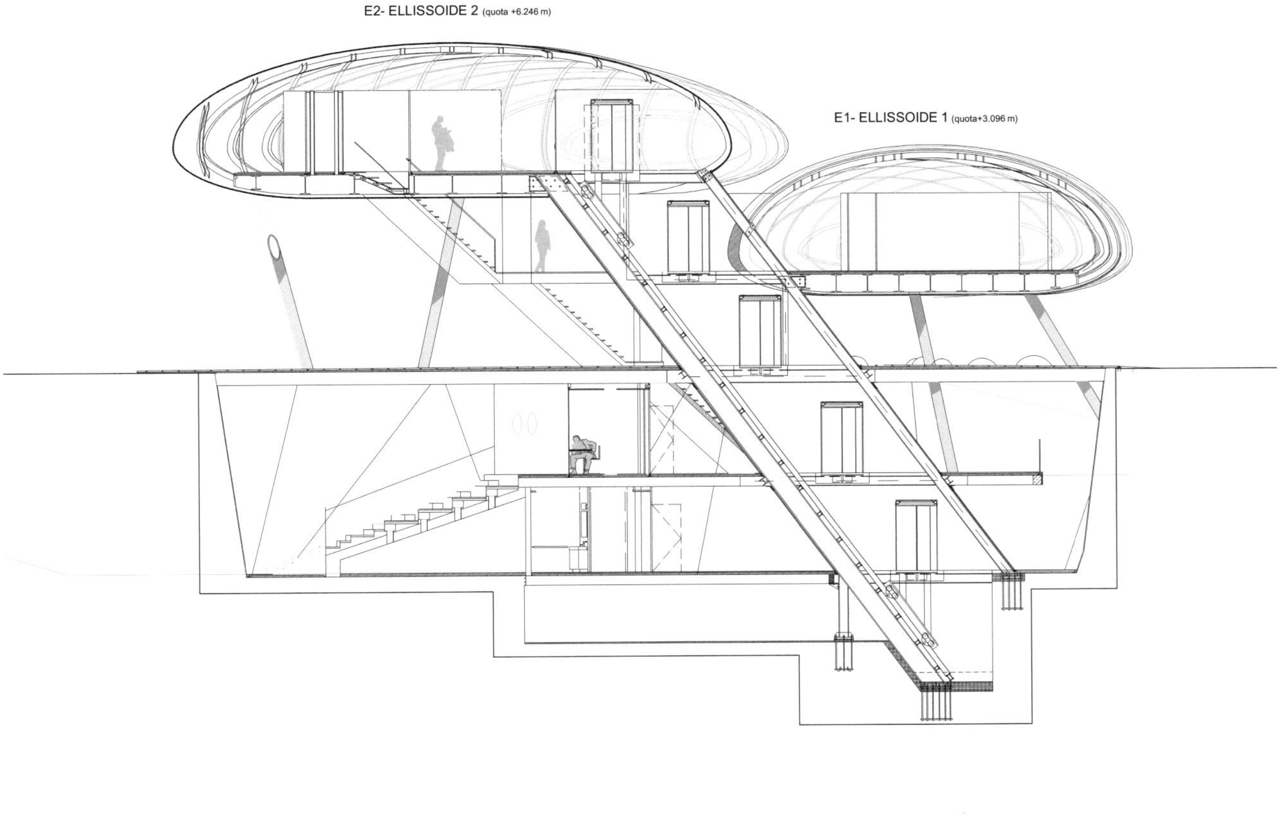
E2- ELLISSOIDE 2 (quota +6.246 m)
E1- ELLISSOIDE 1 (quota+3.096 m)

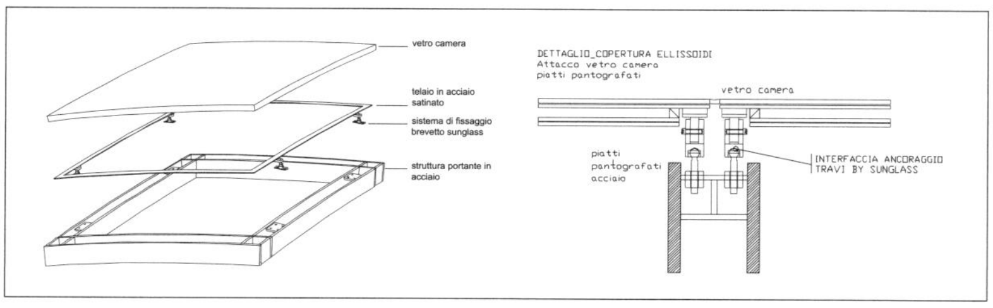

Glass joint detail

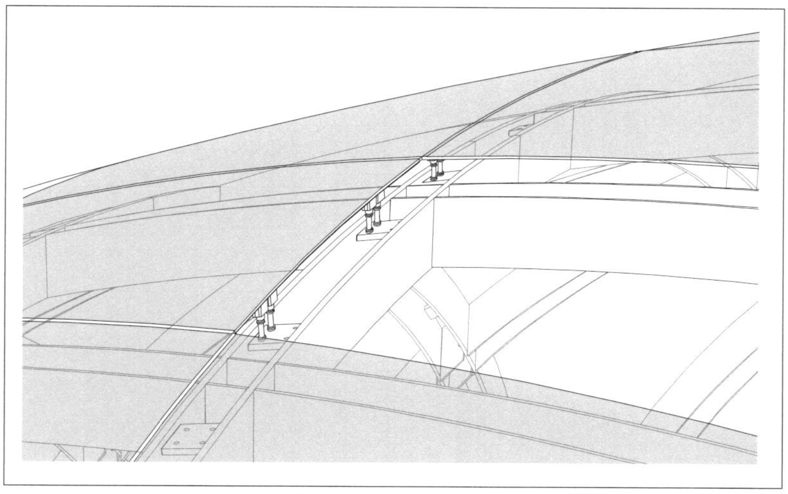

Glass structure detail

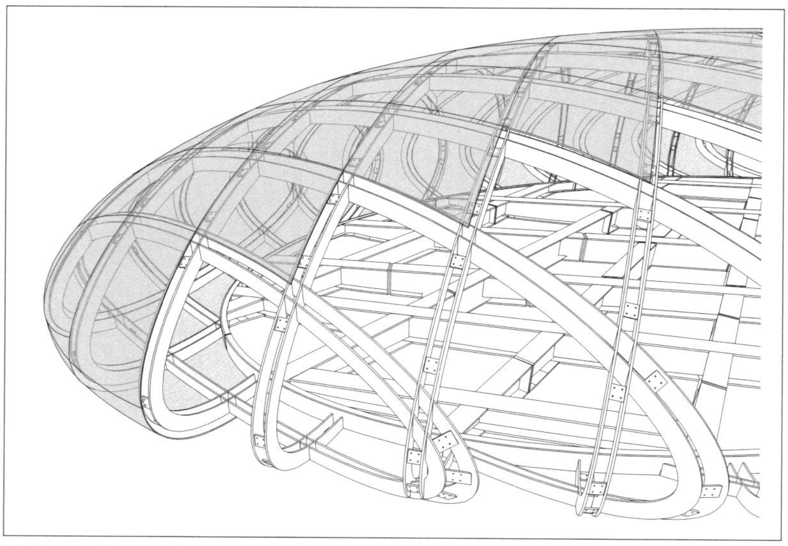

Ribs detail

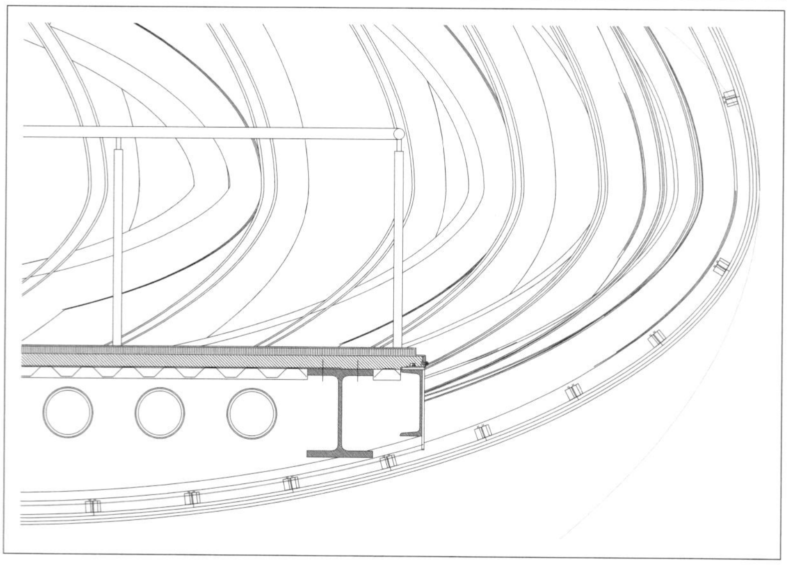

Section detail

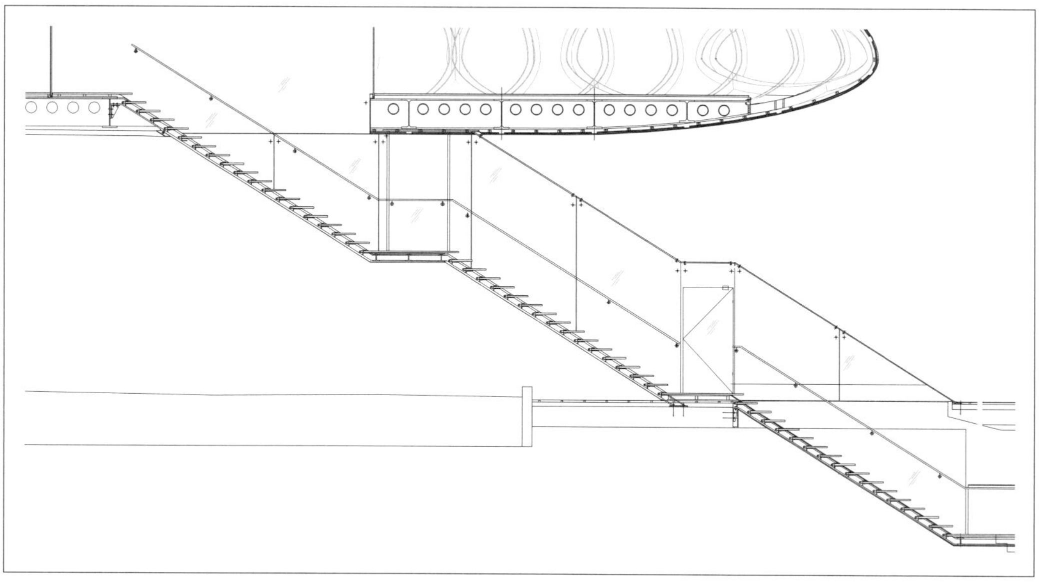

Stair detail

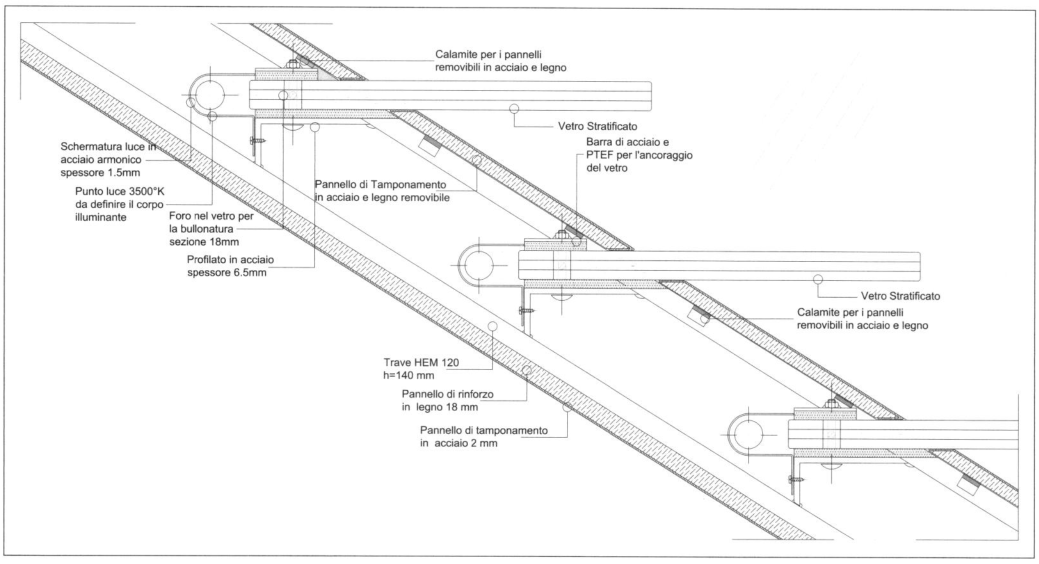

Section stair

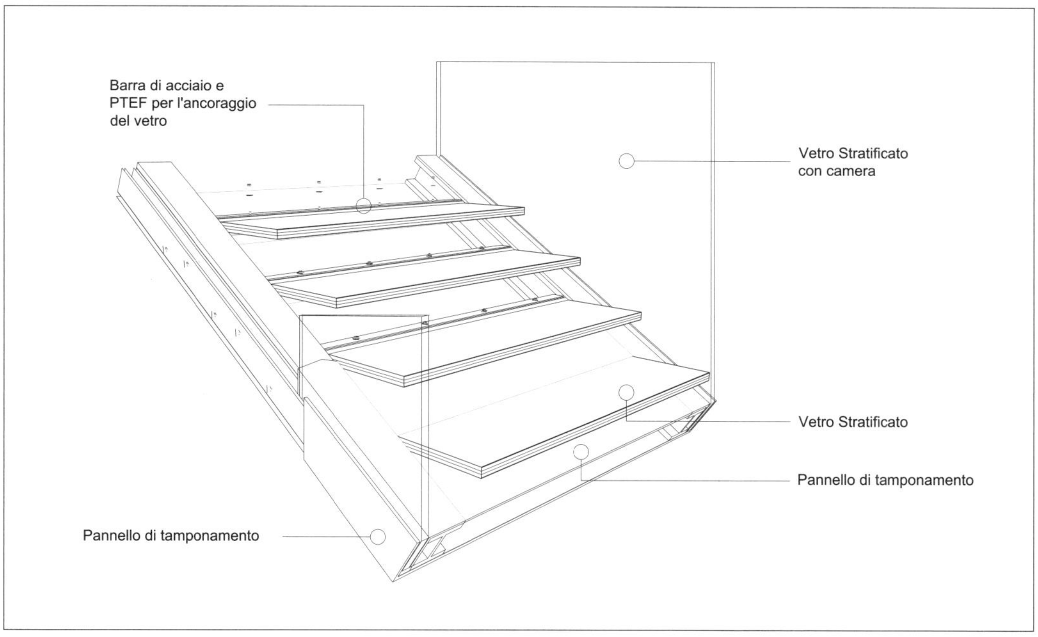

Stair 3D

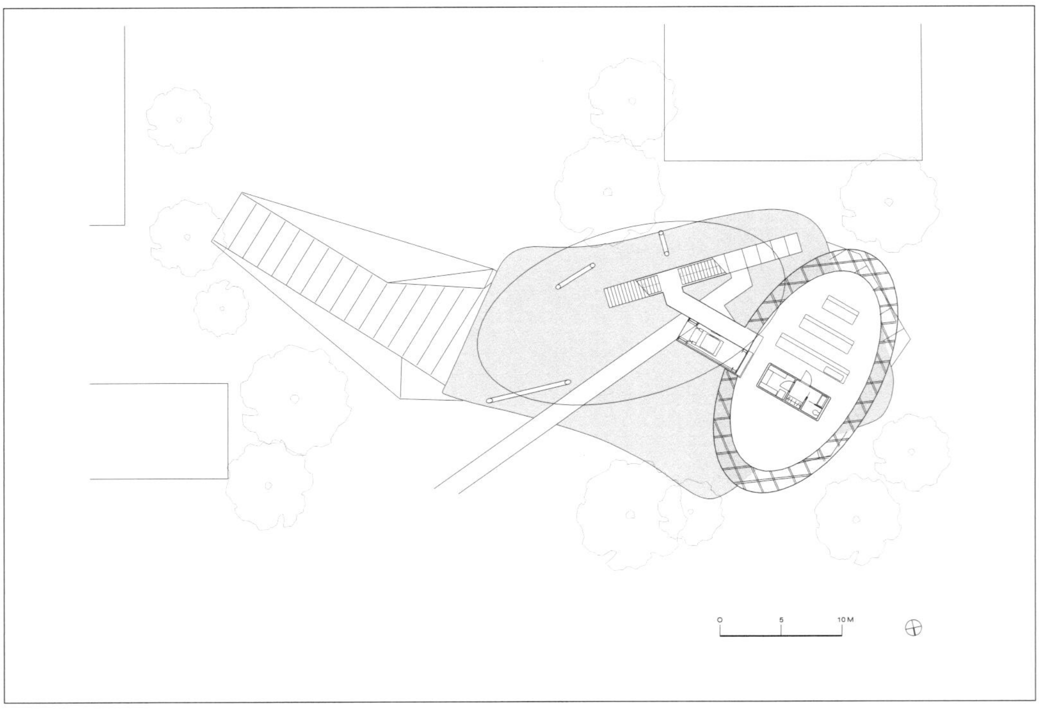

Plan level +3.10

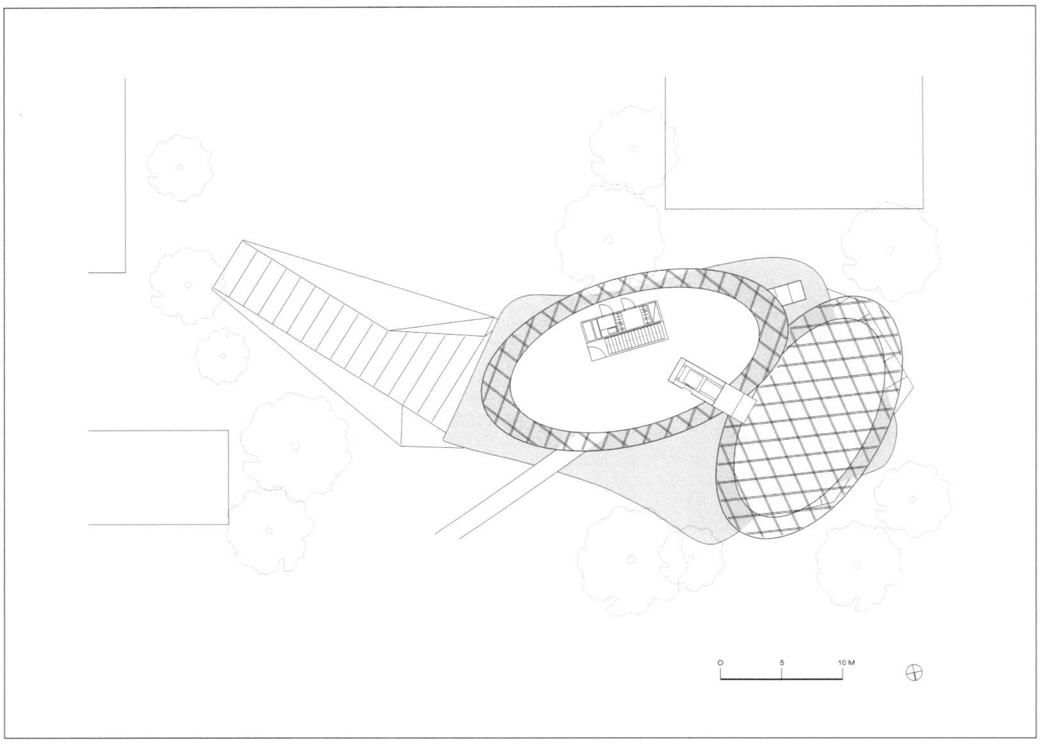

Plan level +6.25

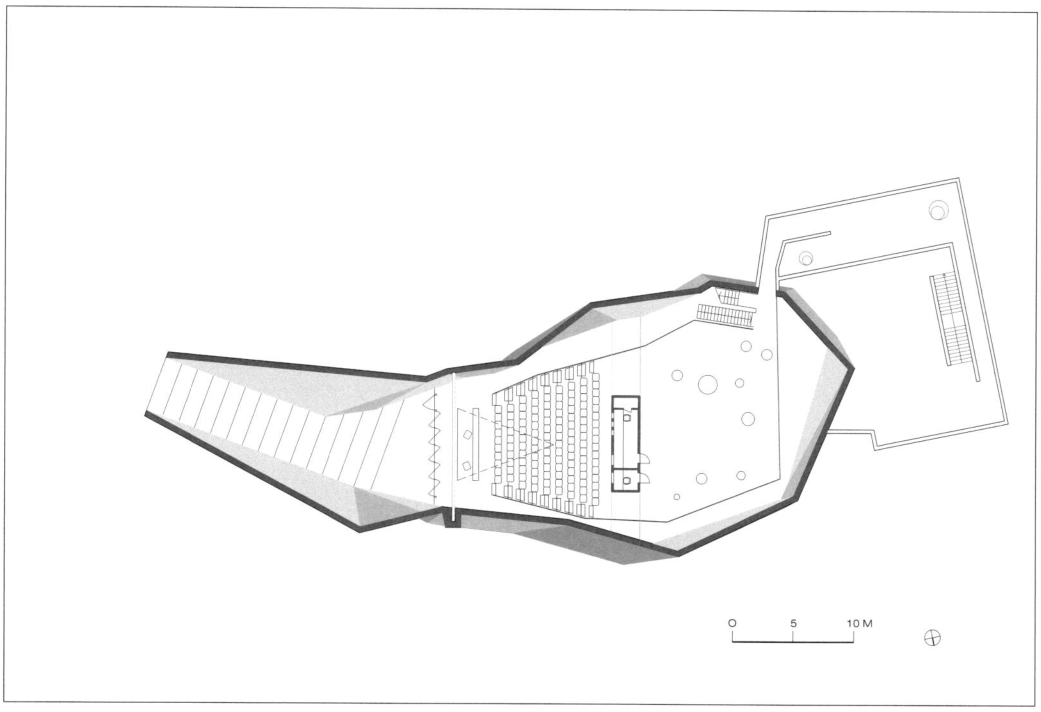

Auditorium plan

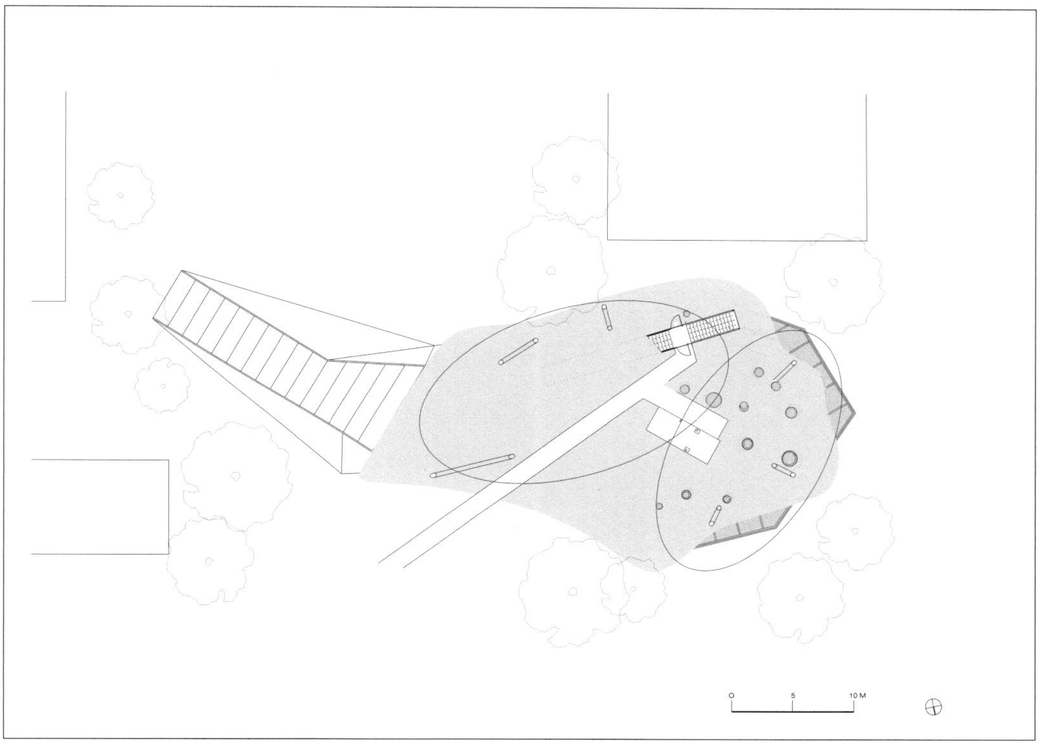

Ground floor plan

FERRARI OPERATIONAL HEADQUARTERS AND RESEARCH CENTRE

MARANELLO, MODENA, ITALY
2001–2004

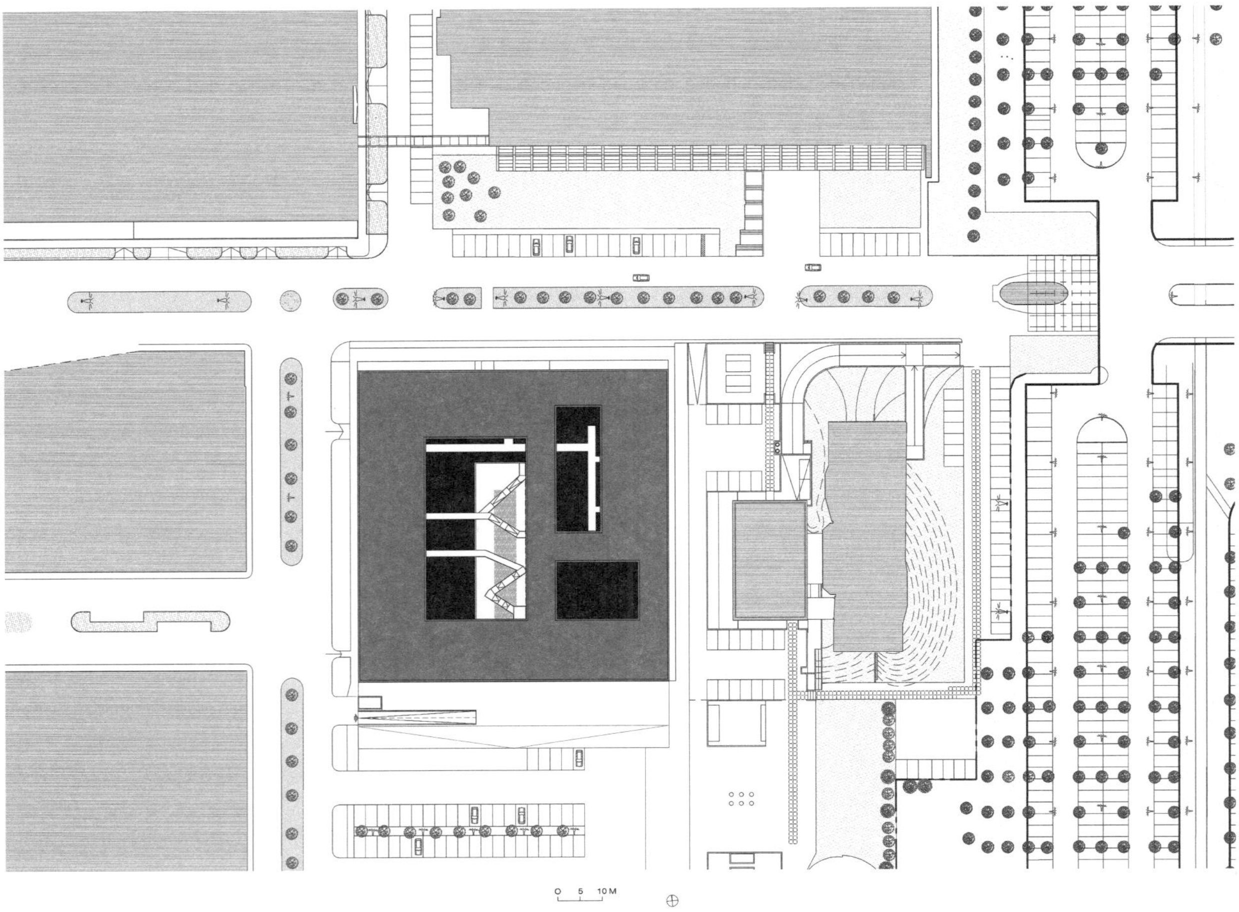

Site plan

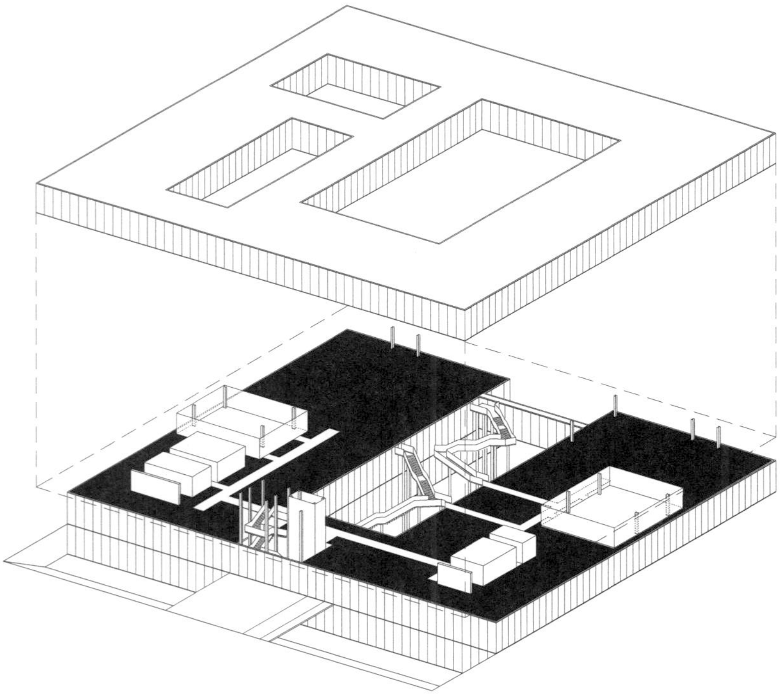

3D view / isometric view

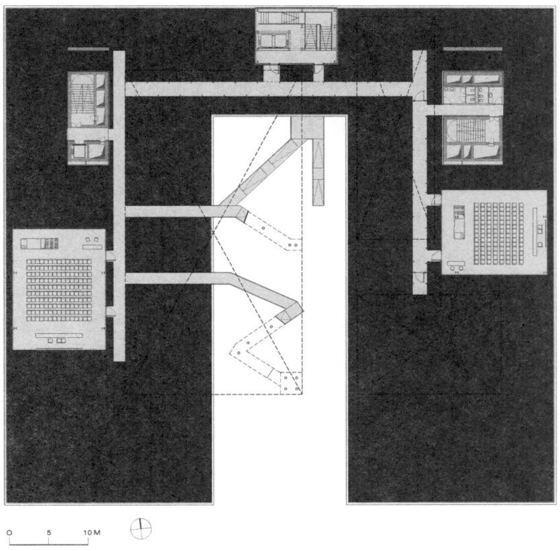

Level +2

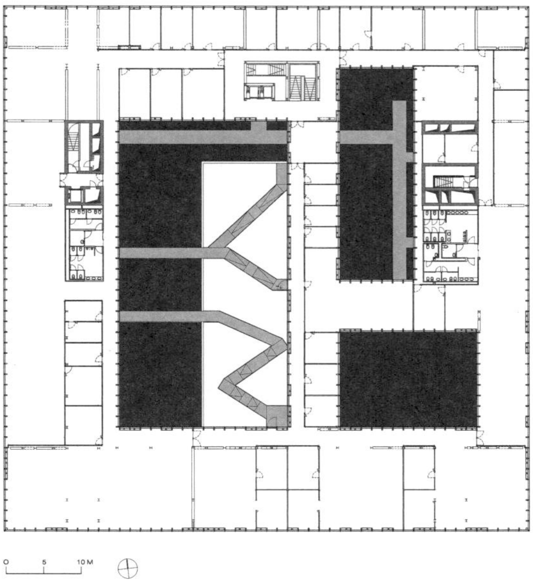

Level +1

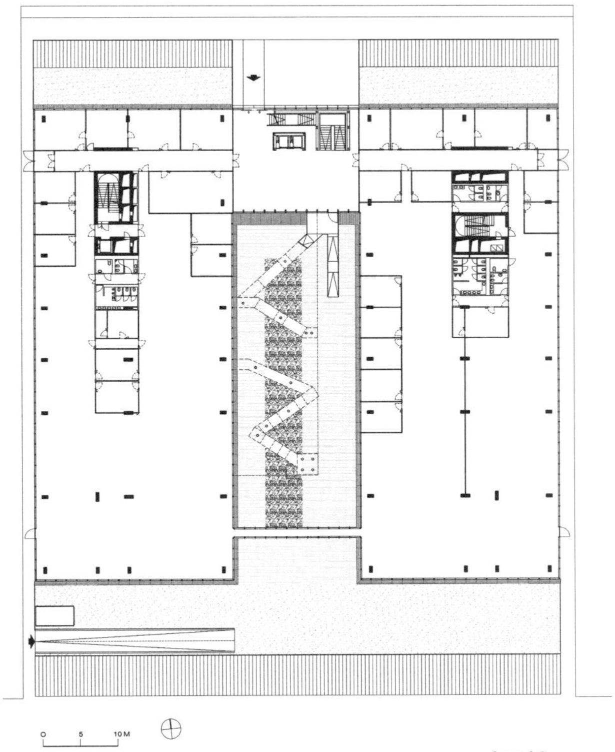

Level 0

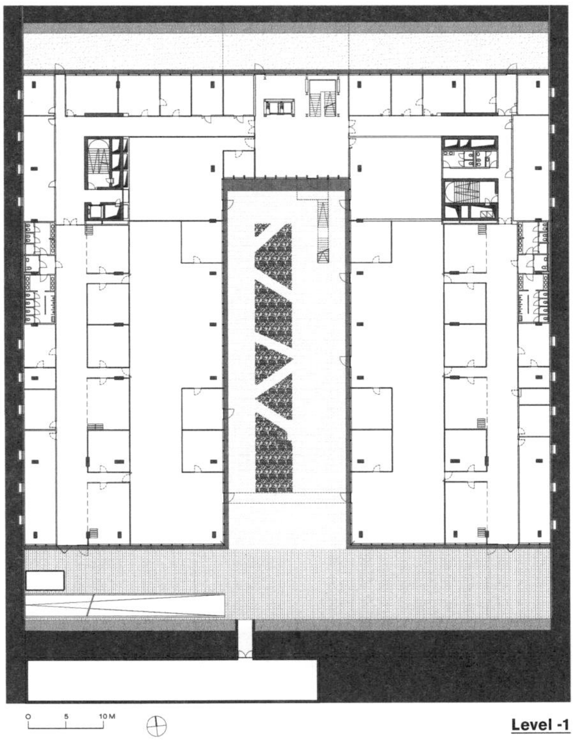

Level -1

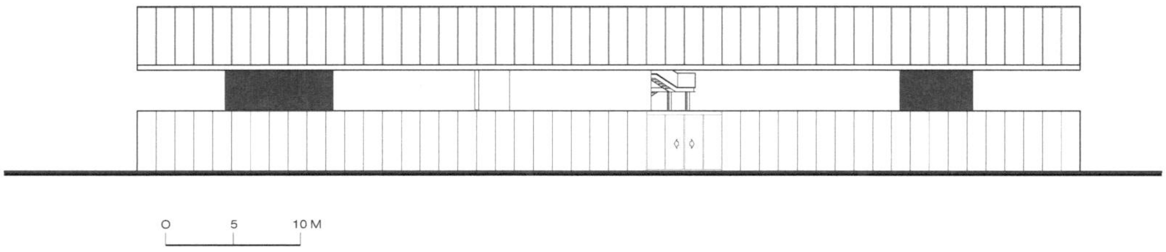

North elevation

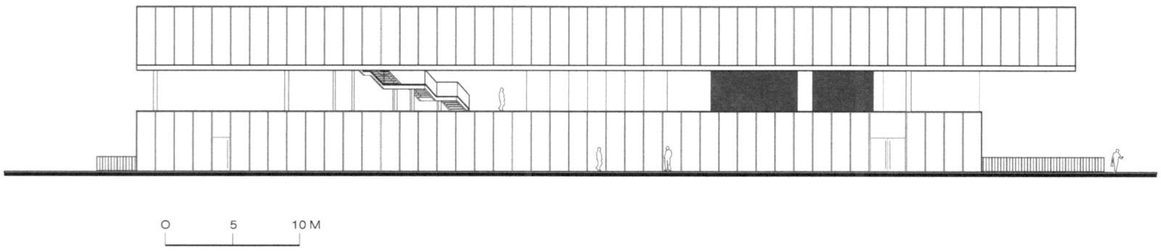

East elevation

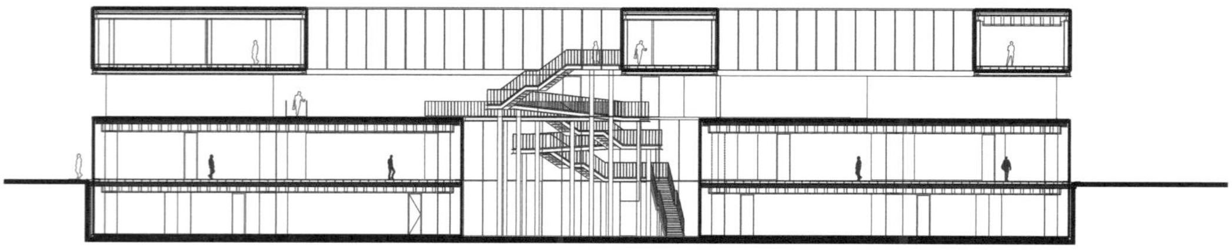

Section A

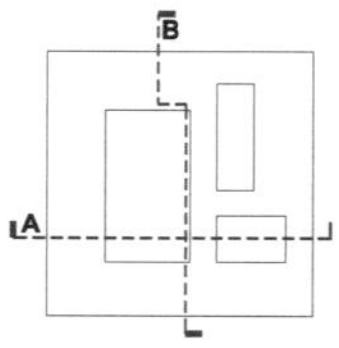

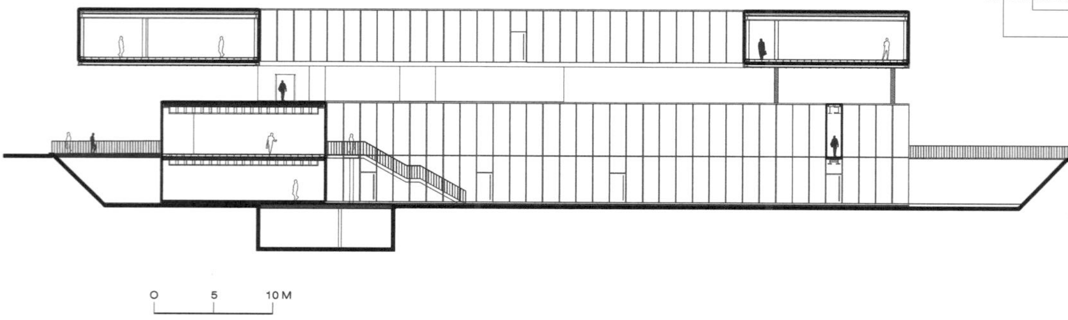

Section B

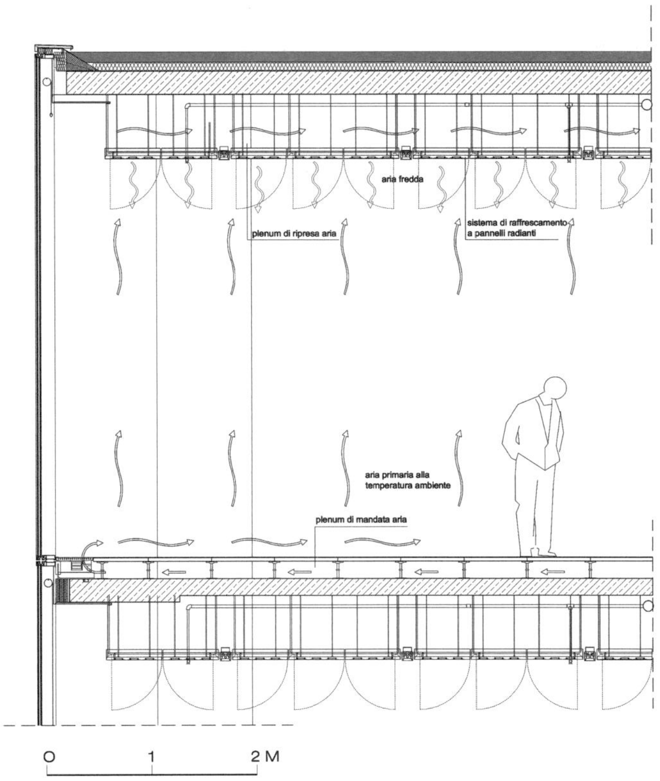

Summer

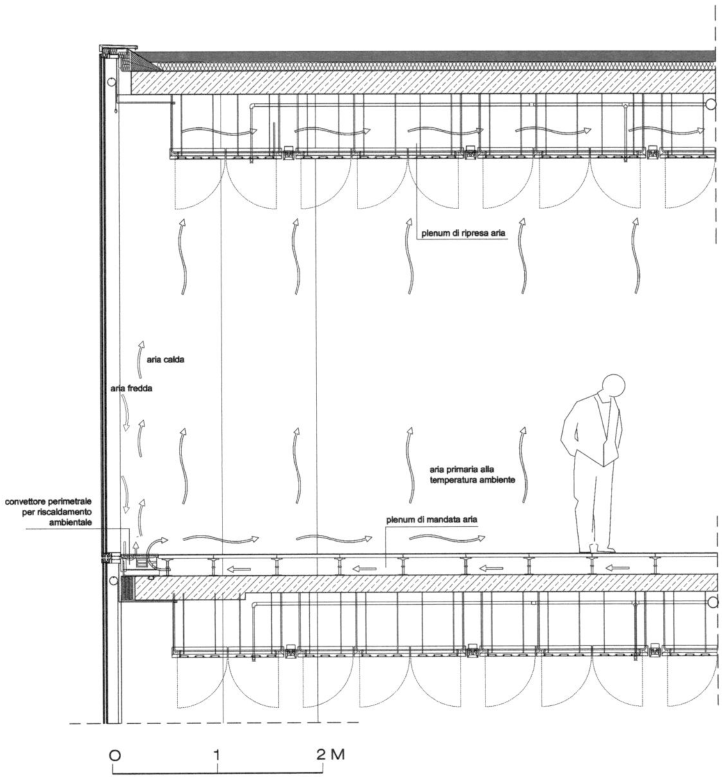

Winter

SHENZHEN BAO'AN INTERNATIONAL AIRPORT TERMINAL 3

SHENZHEN, CHINA
2008–Ongoing

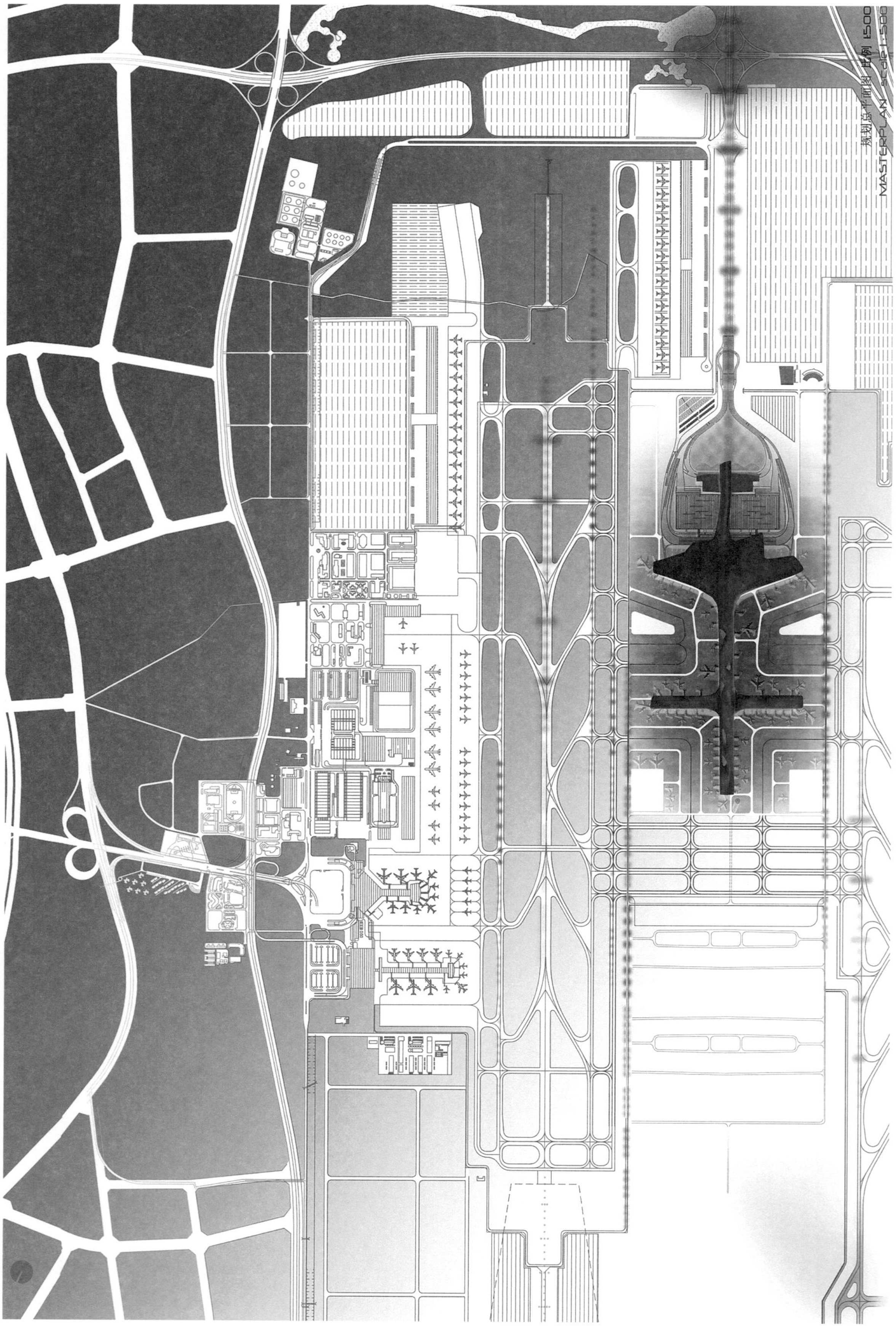

Site plan

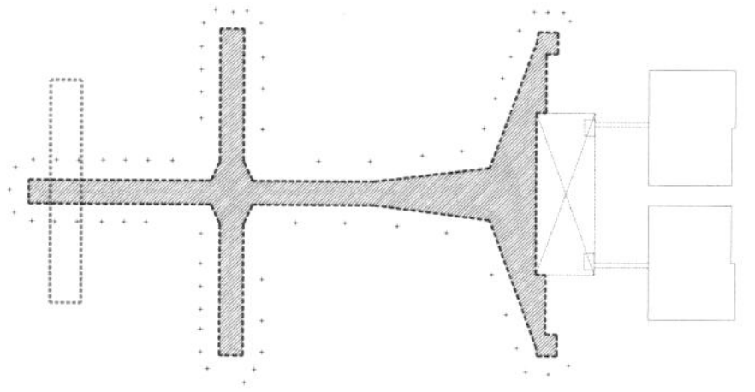

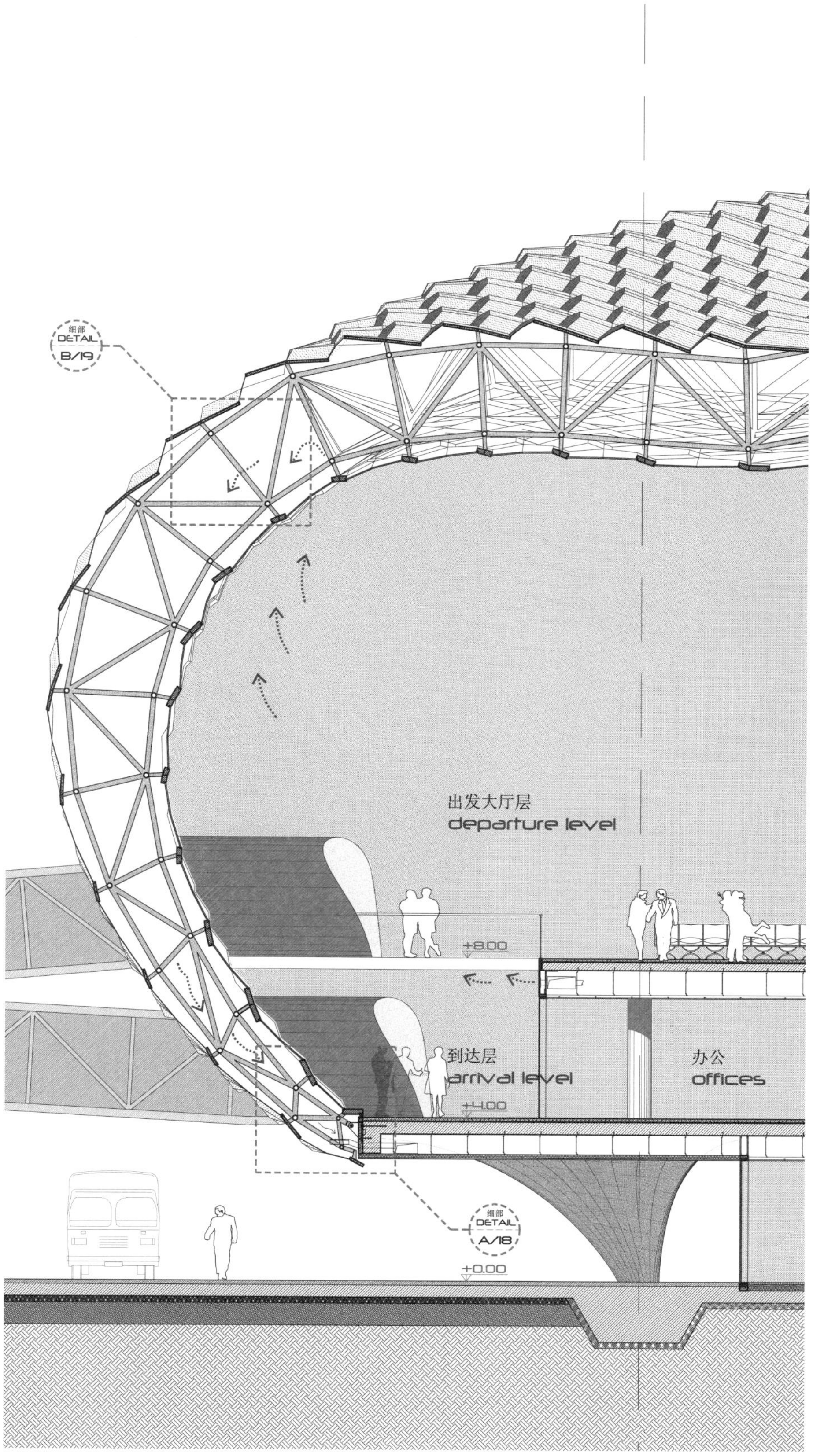

细部
DETAIL
B/19
出发大厅层
departure level
+8.00
到达层
arrival level
+4.00
办公
offices
细部
DETAIL
A/18
+0.00

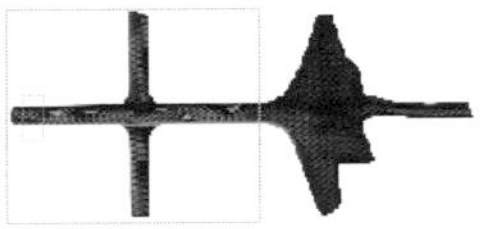

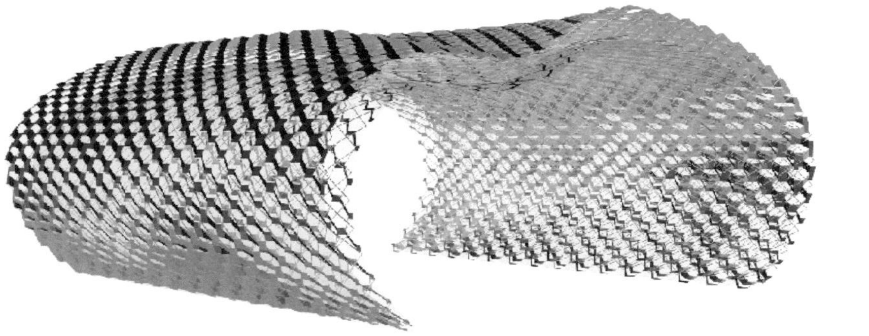

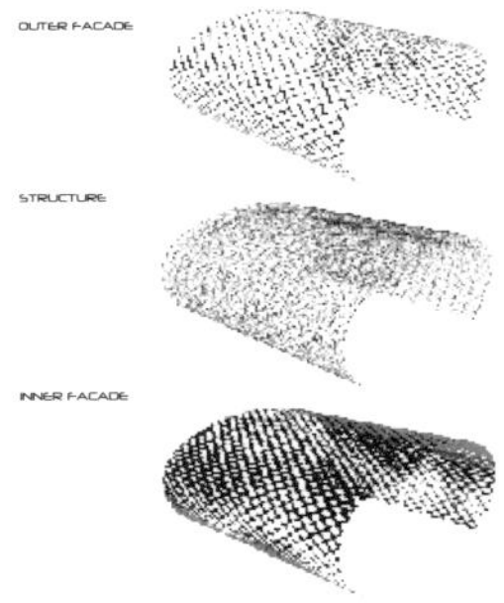

FACADE EXTRACT CONCOURSE

The building envelope covers the terminal like a beautifully woven piece of cloth with variable loop sizes. There is no differentiation between façade and roof. The hole building envelope has been merged to one continuous sculptural element. It has been carefully crafted to give the building an almost magic appearance of soft transition from concave and convex, from transparent to opaque. The two façade layers converge and reject one another in a subtle way. Offering ever changing perspectives for the beholder both exterior and interior.

The structure between the two façade layers forms a homogenous mesh of slender metal sections that spans without any columns from one side of the Terminal Concourse to the other.

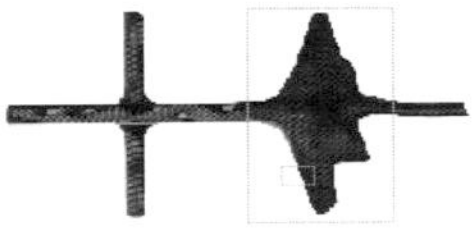

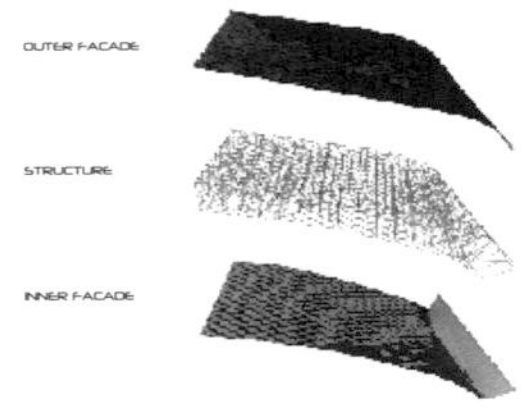

At the check-in hall the roof construction forms a generous canopy thus creating a grand welcoming gesture to the people arriving from the street side. The façades are inclined in order to minimize reflection and achieve the greatest possible transparency. From the first moment of arrival there is a visual connection from the street kerb through the check in hall onto the runway. This makes orientation very easy for the user which is a key issue for buildings of transportation. At this point the roof is at its highest level creating a generous open space. This is further amplified by the carefully sculptured columns that rise up to the roof structure.

BUILDING GEOMETRY

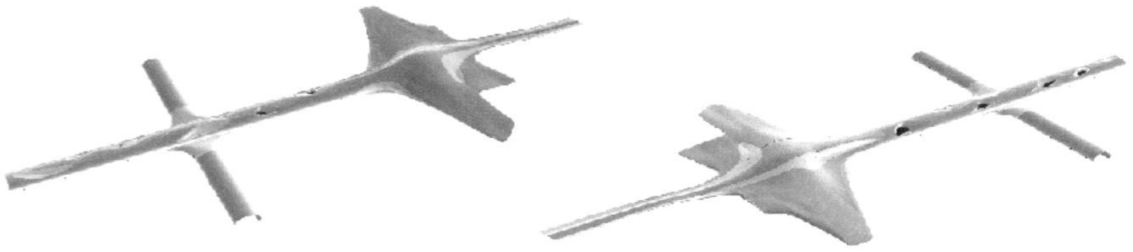

The building envelope has been first conceived as a sculptural artifact. To translate the free form into a defined geometry that can be build with todays construction methods and within a reasonable budget is one of the key challenges for a unique project like this one.

Over many years now we have developed and refined techniques to translate complex shapes into optimized building geometries. Today state of the art computer tools allow us to do this as a largely automated process. So called Parametric design tools allow us to handle huge and complex geometries in order to establish a continuous dataflow from early design stages to shop drawings and eventually production.

Standard Modules _ 25,000 mq

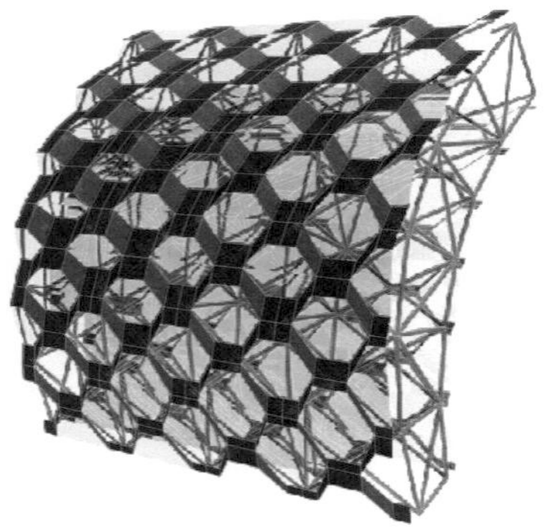

Amended Standard Modules _ 32,500 mq

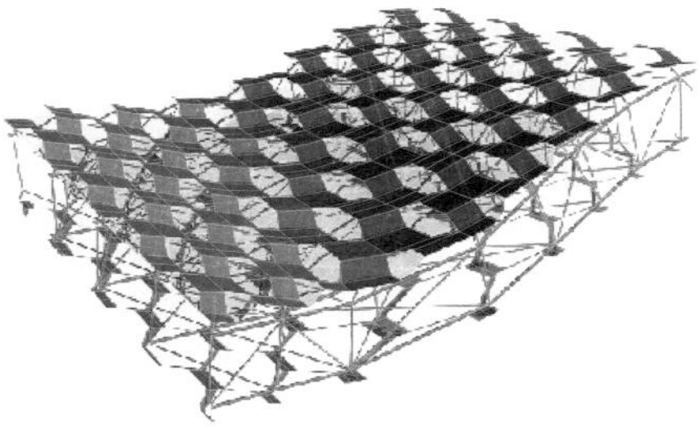

Special Purpose Cladding _ 18,000 mq

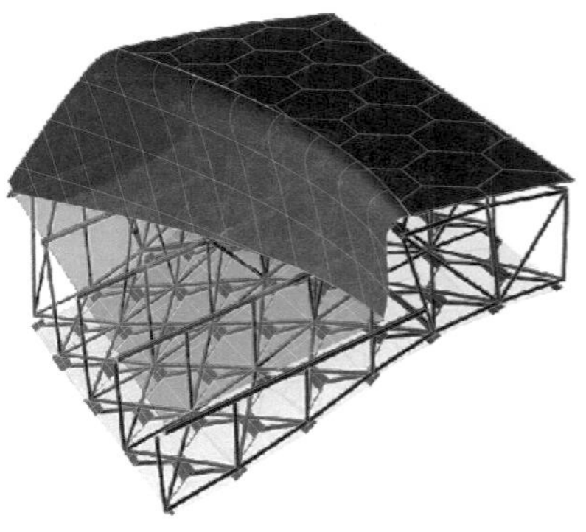

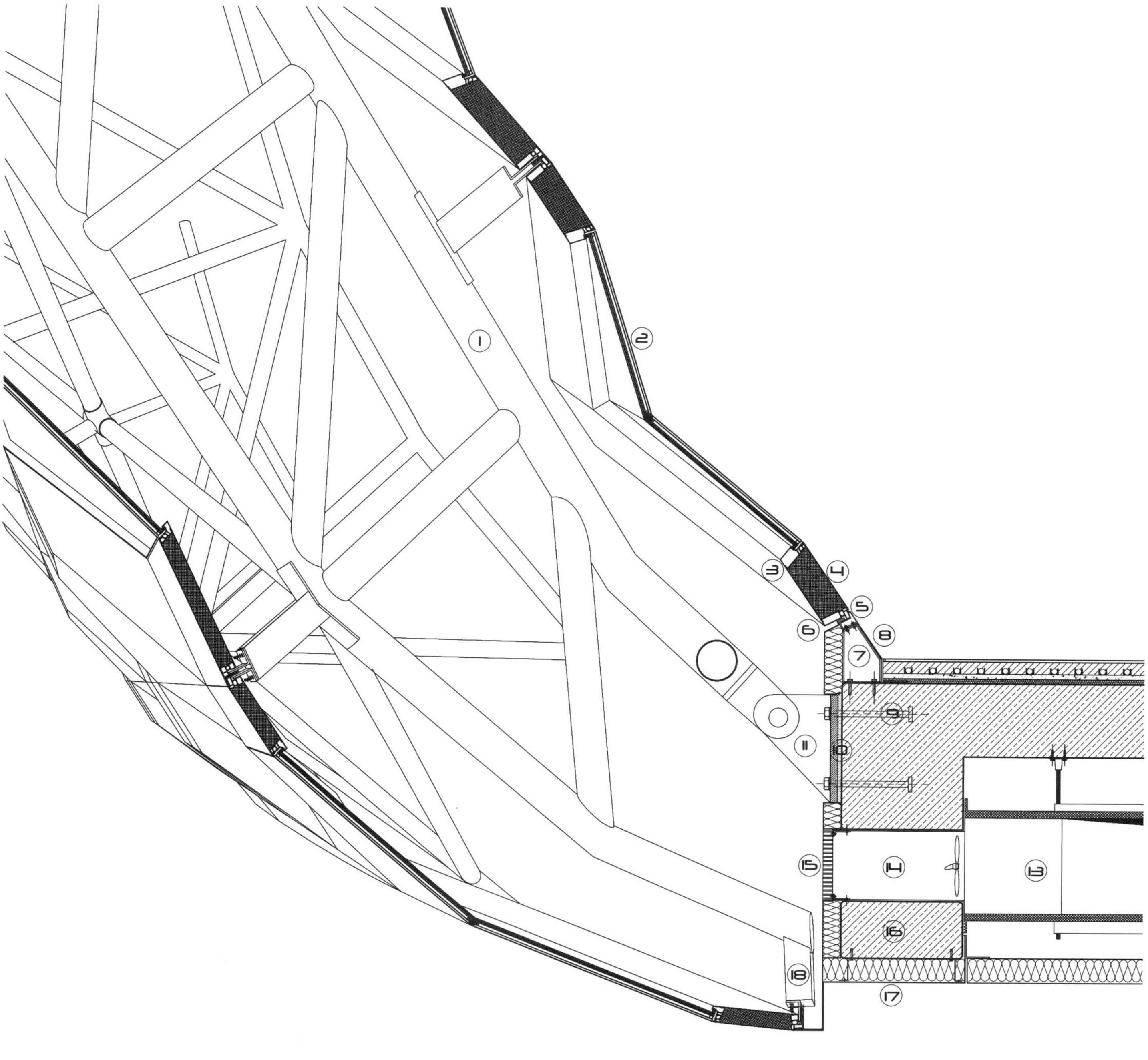

(1) Steel Framework assembled from circular hollow steel sections d=120mm

(2) Fixed Glazing made from one layer of toughened and two layers of laminated glass sheets

(3) aluminium profile along panel edge with neoprene support for glazing

(4) Prefabricated panel made from powdercoated, folded aluminium sheet with foamcore

(5) aluminium profile along panel edge with fastening srew thread

(6) Adjustable Aluminium clamp, bolted to bracket

(7) steel support to panel fixation at 3.60m intervalls bolted to RC-slab

(8) metal skirting

(9) cast-in anchor bolts

(10) 20 mm steel plate fixed to anchor bolts

(11) Steel bracket with 100 mm hinge bearing welded to anchor plate

(12) leveling course of special mortar to allow for tolerance compensation

(13) Airduct connected to air handling unit

(14) air exhaustion to discharge heat gain

(15) Aluminium Louvres

(16) Reinforced concrete edgebeam (to transfer loads to columns at 9.00 m intervalls)

(17) suspended Aluminium cladding to close of facade cavity.

(18) Steel Brackett, welded to steel framework for panel fixation

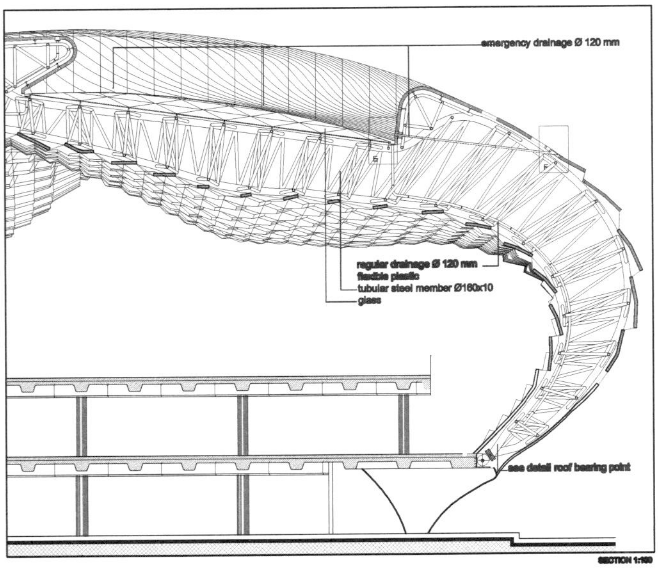

SECTION 1:100

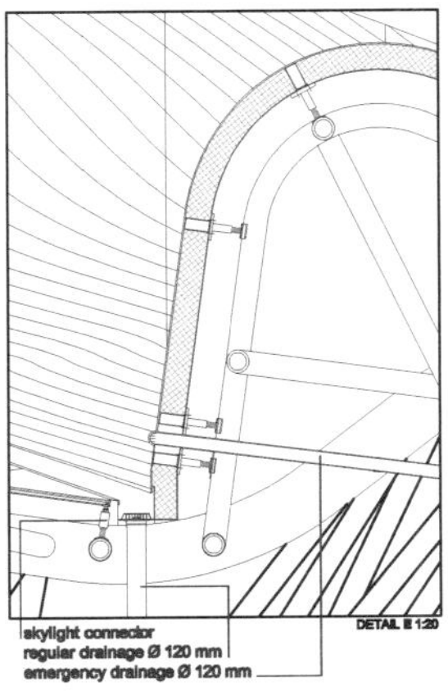

DETAIL E 1:20

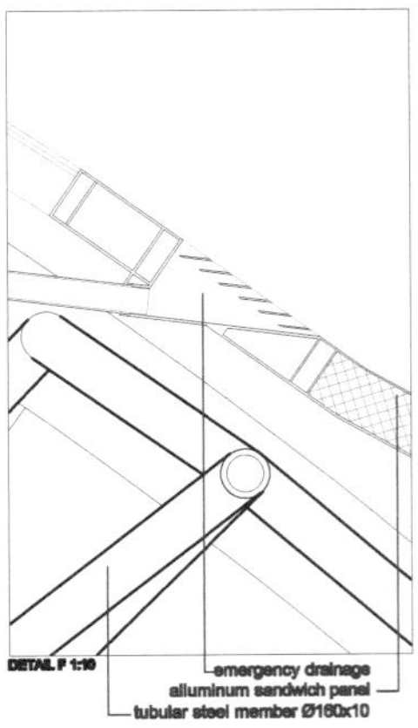

DETAIL F 1:10

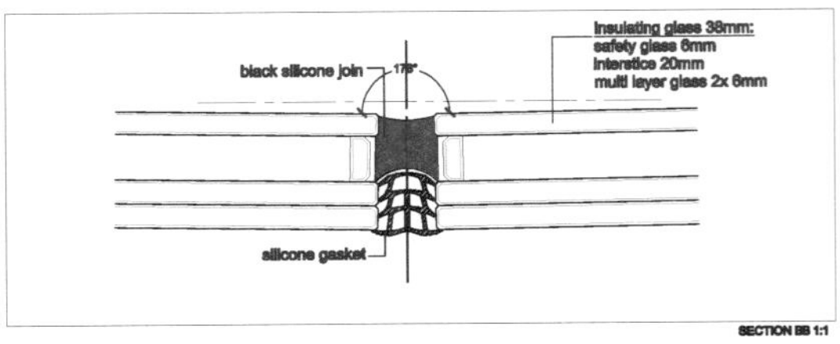

SECTION BB 1:1

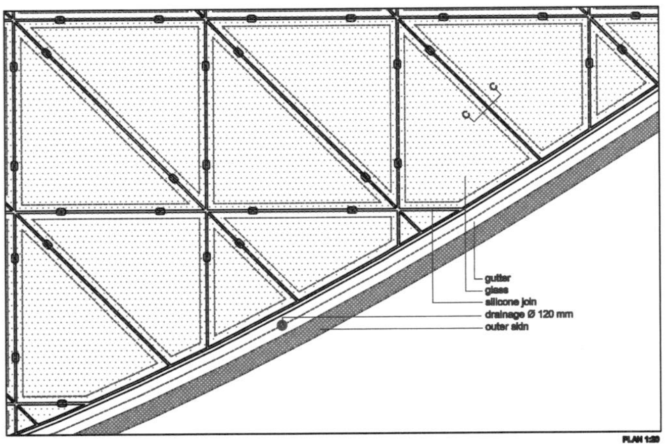

PLAN 1:20

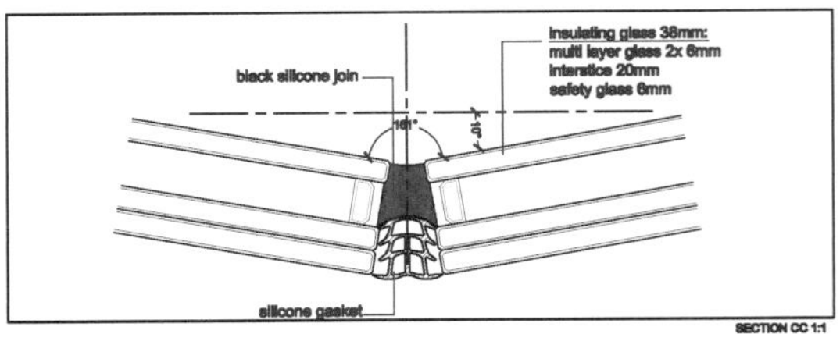

SECTION CC 1:1

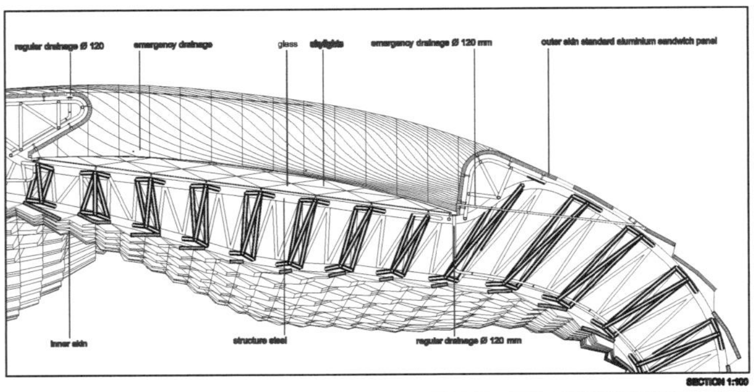

SECTION 1:100

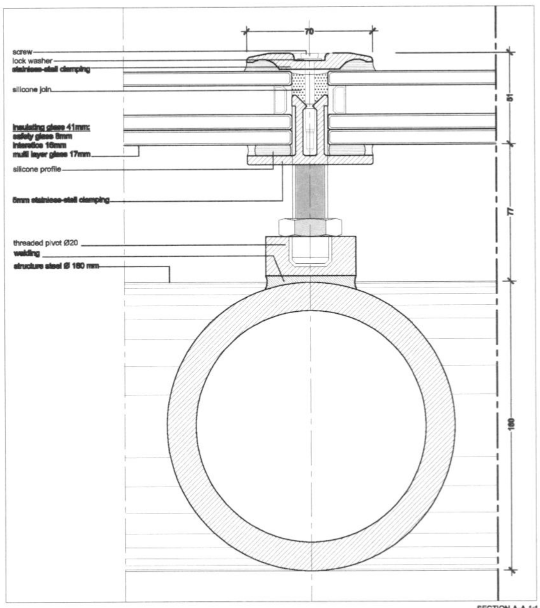

SECTION A-A 1:1

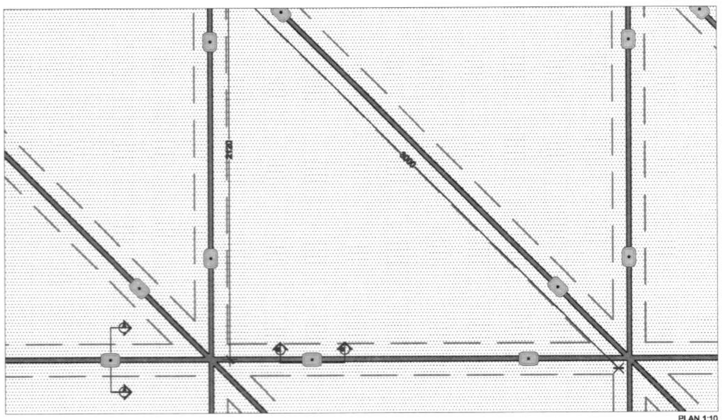
PLAN 1:10

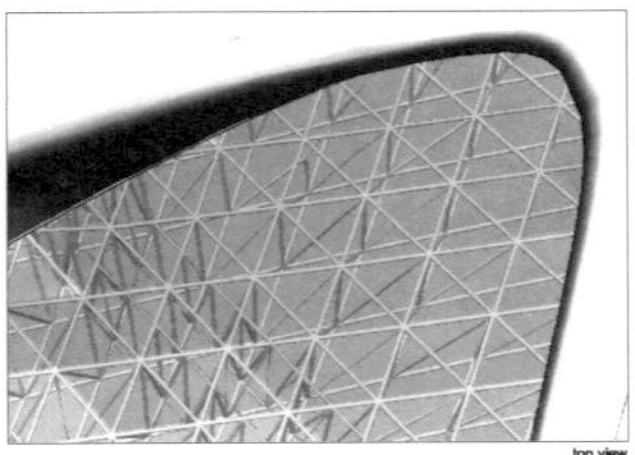
top view

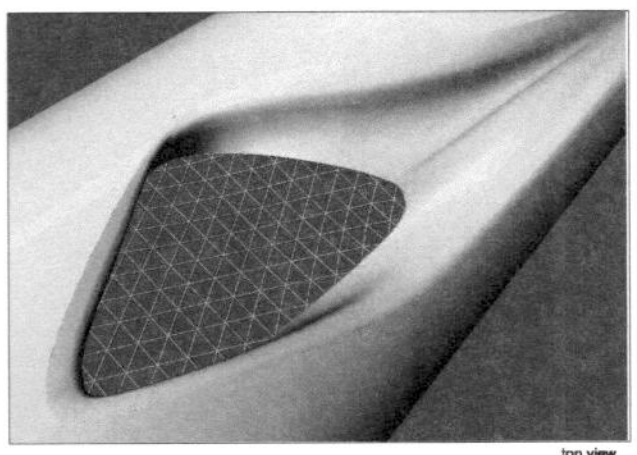
top view

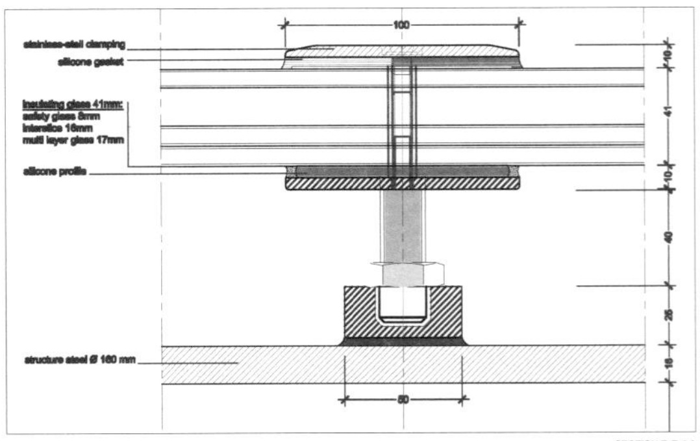

SECTION B-B 1:1

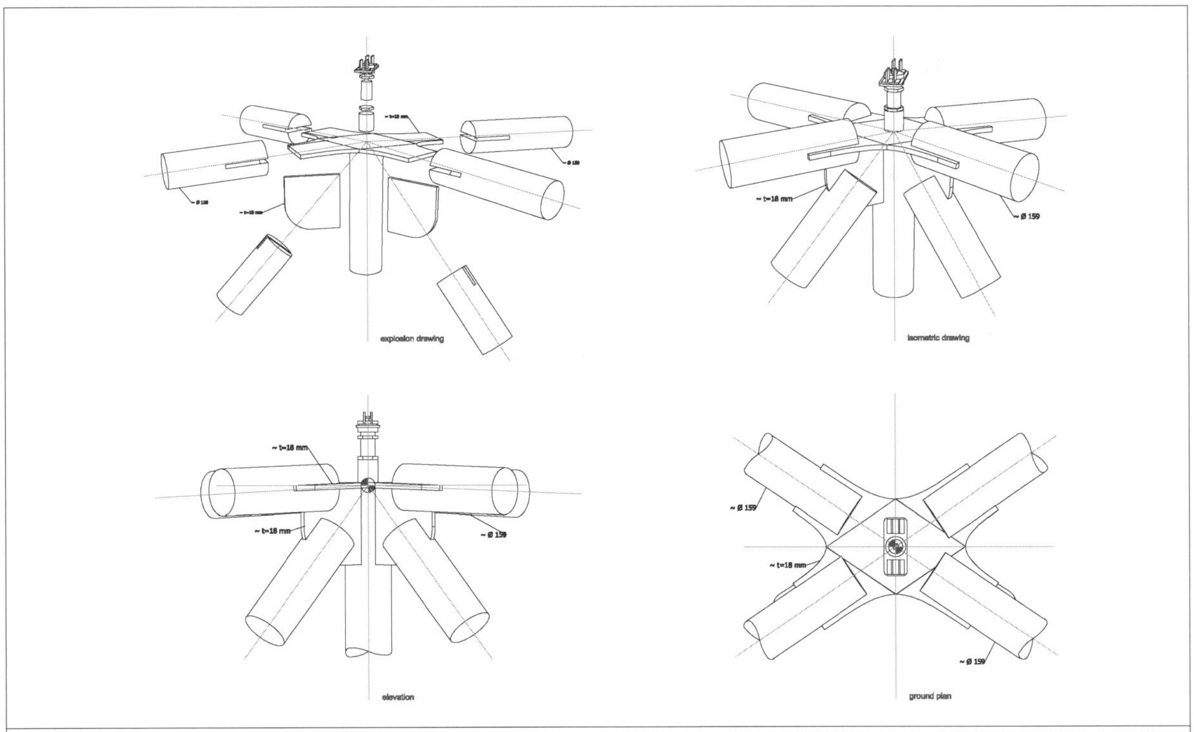

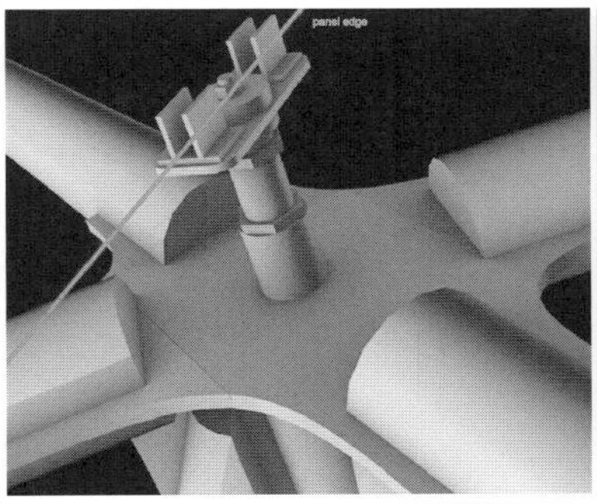

DETAILS INNER SKIN PANEL

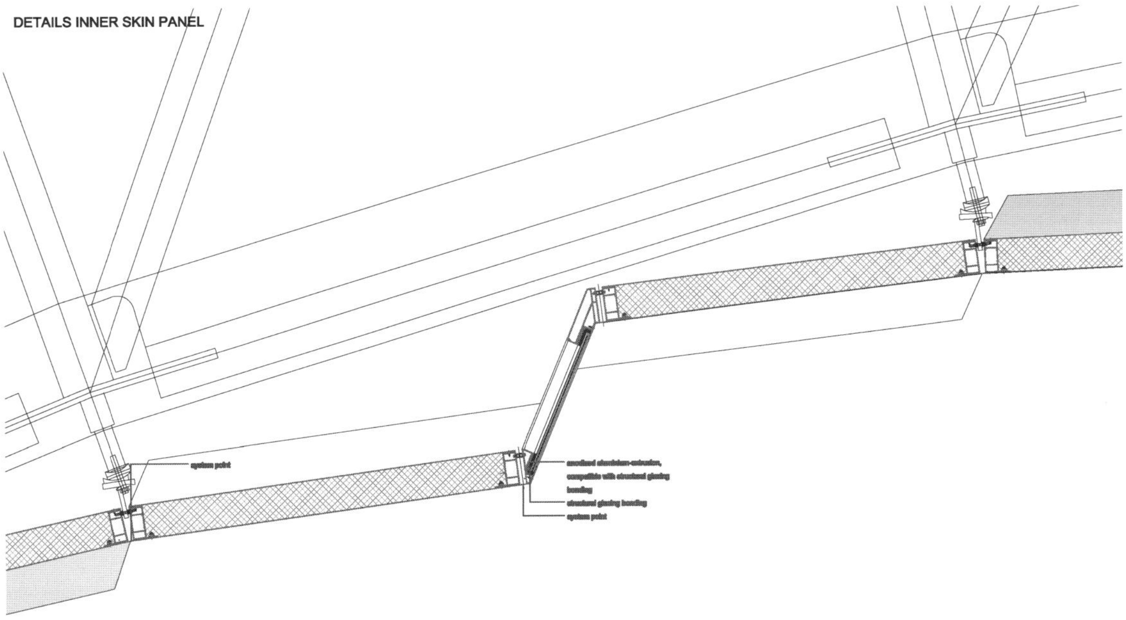

PANEL DETAILS 1/5

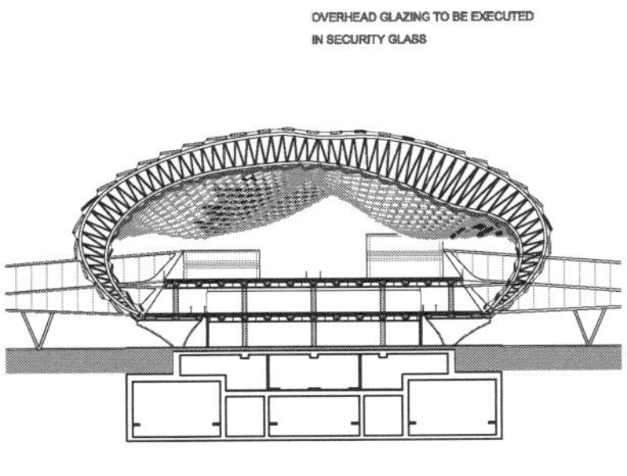

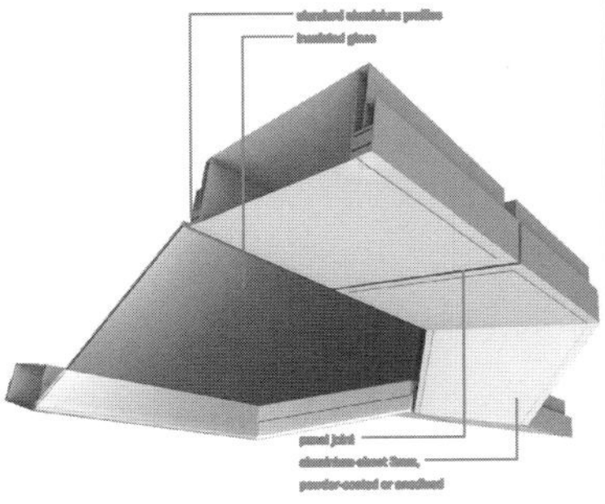

EUR NEW CONGRESS CENTRE

ROME, ITALY
1998–ongoing

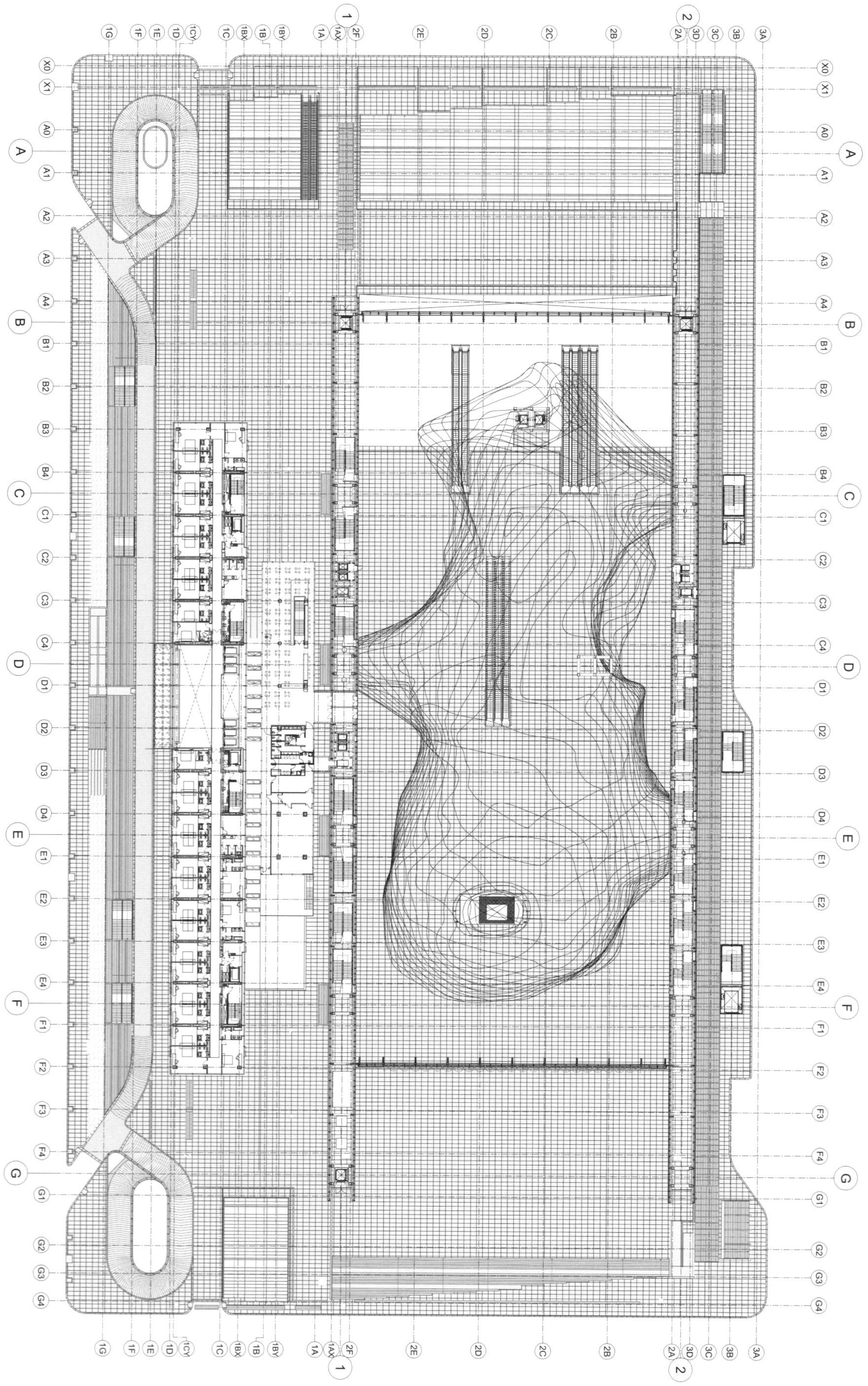

First level

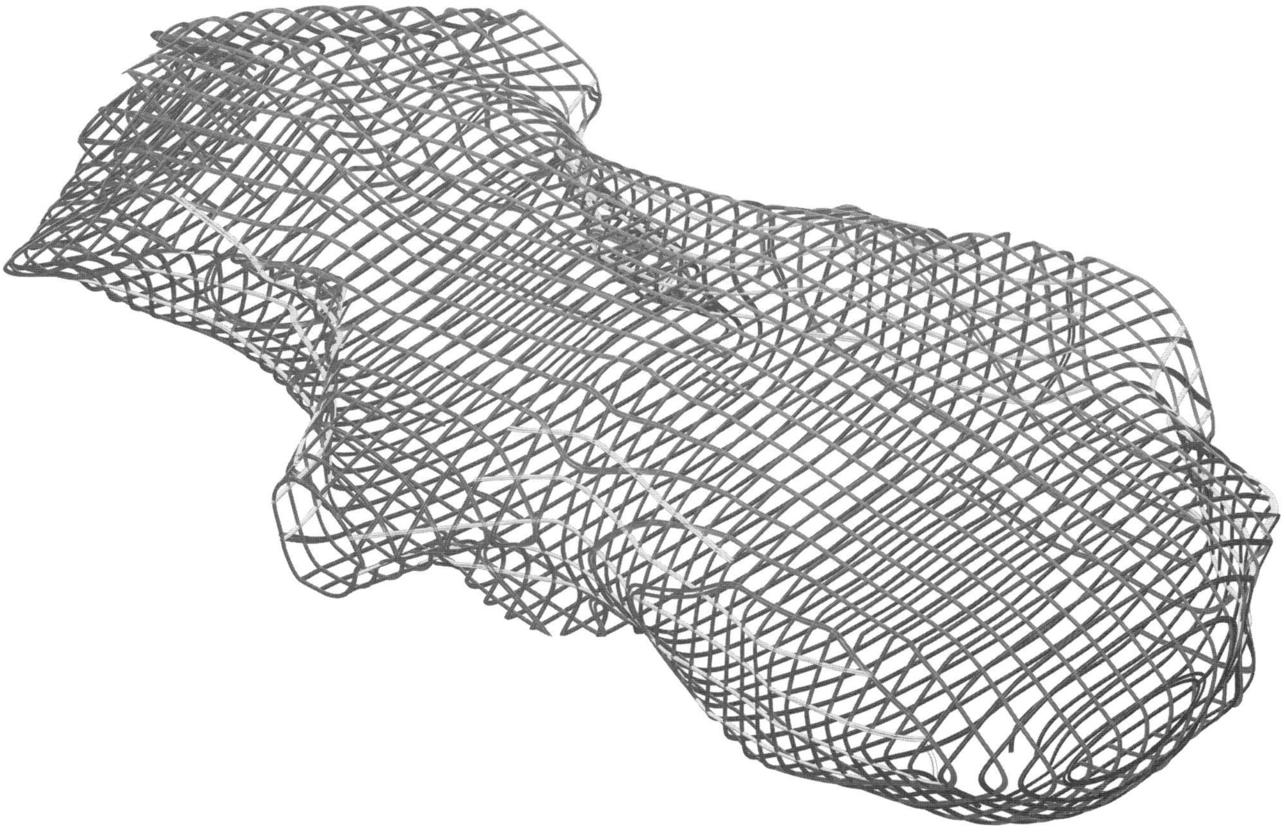

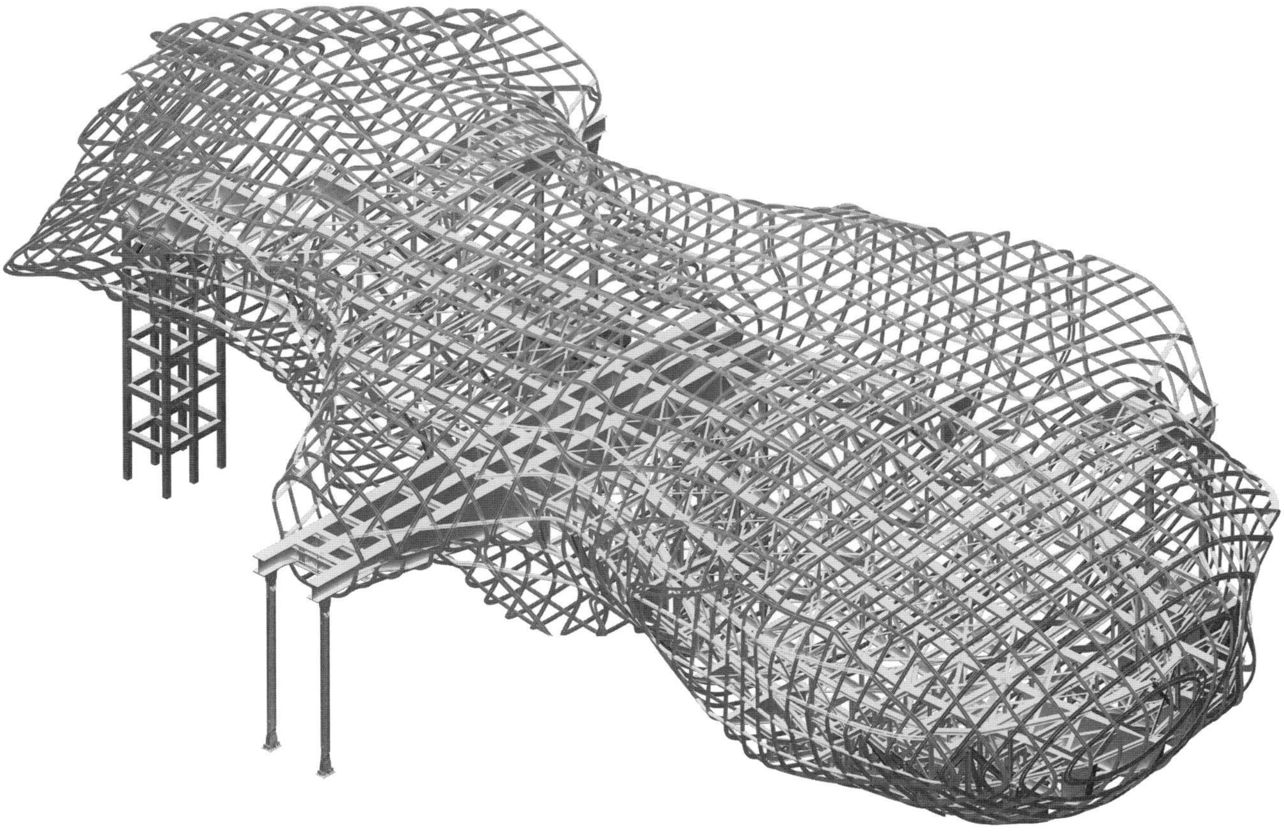

Cloud structure

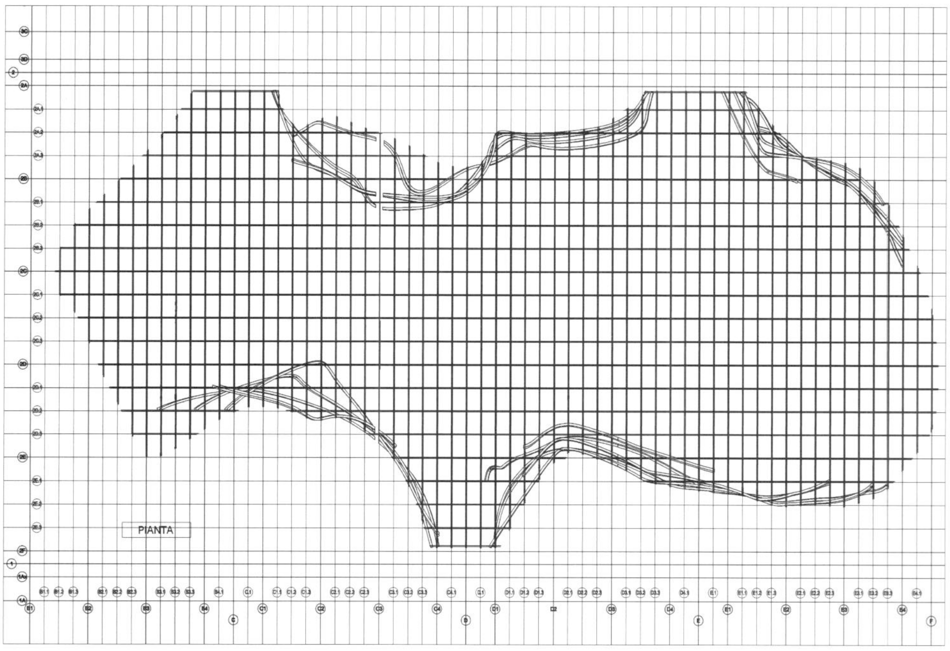

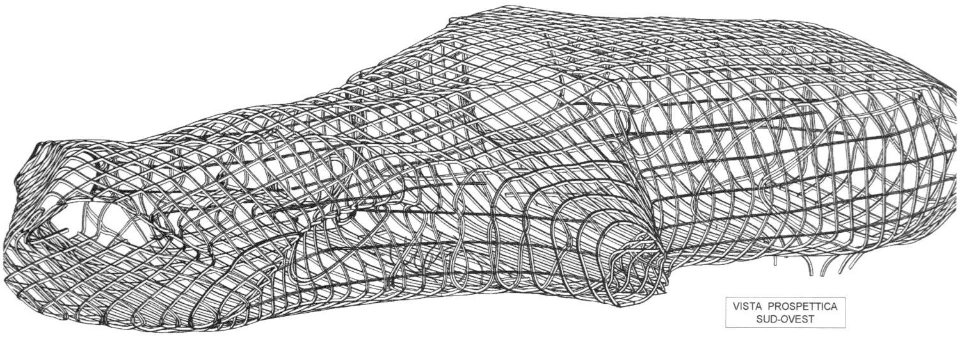

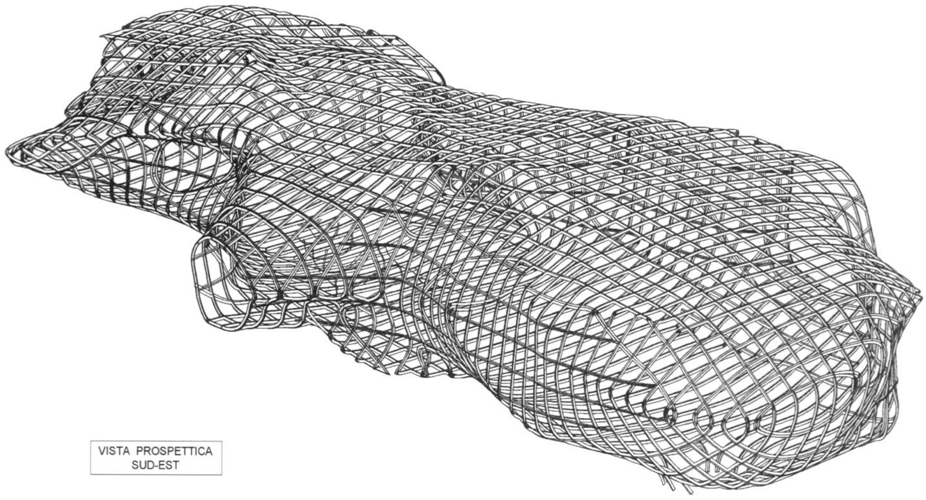

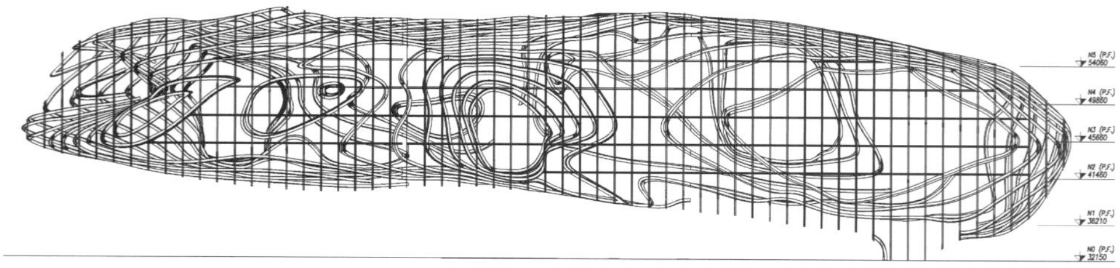

Cloud structure

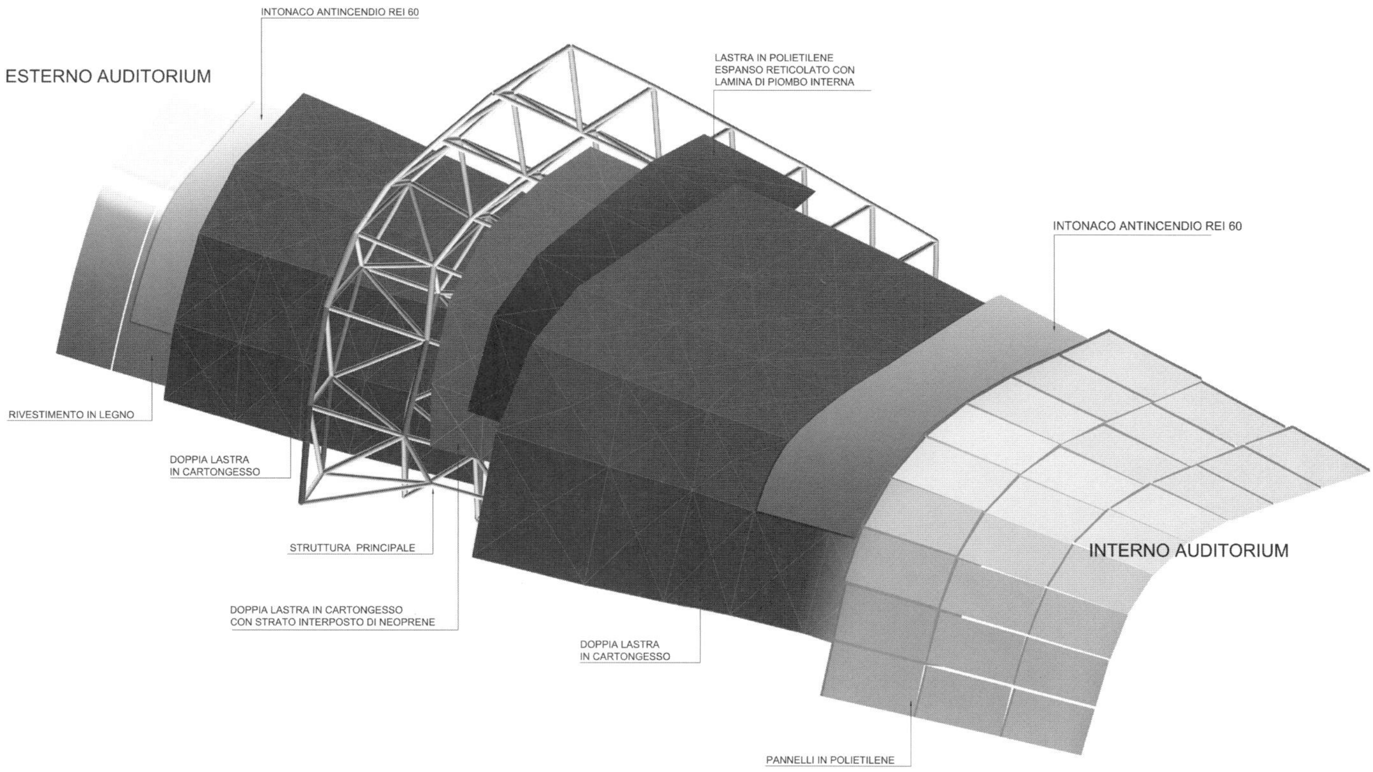

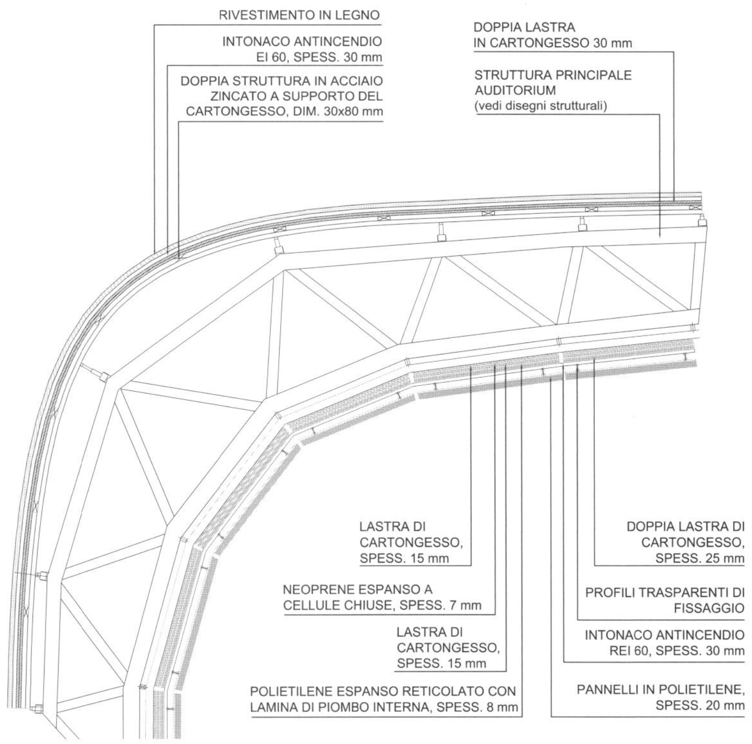

Auditorium detail

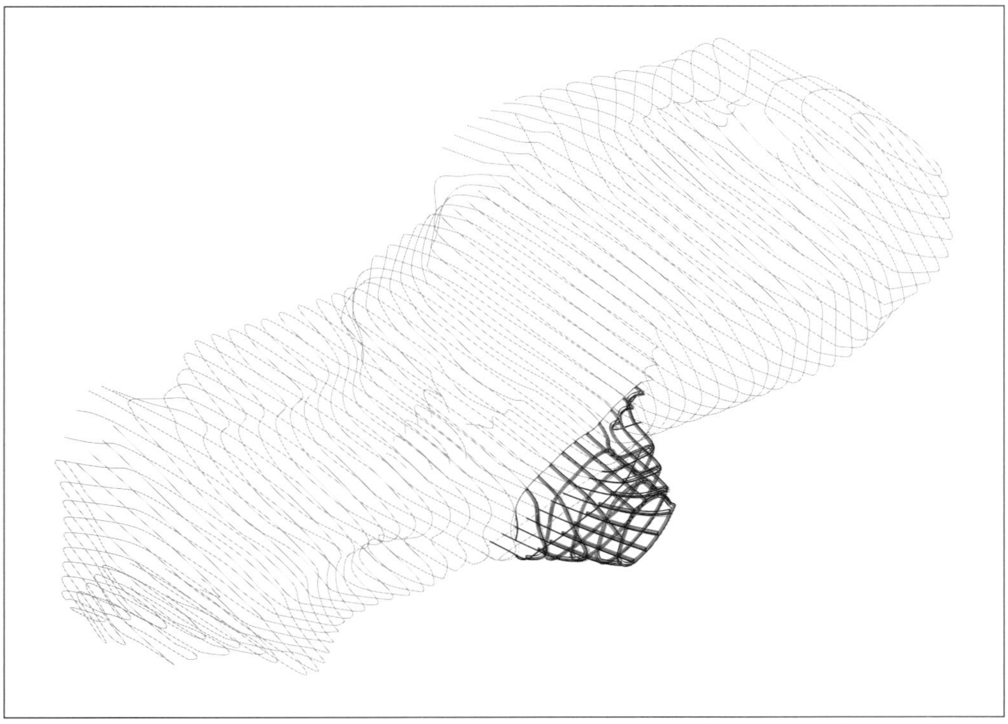

Isometric view

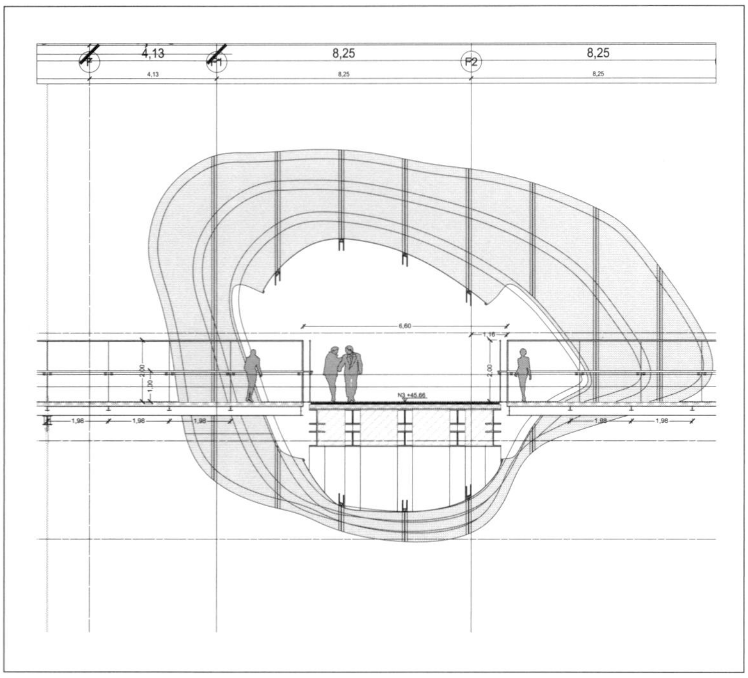

Isometric view detail

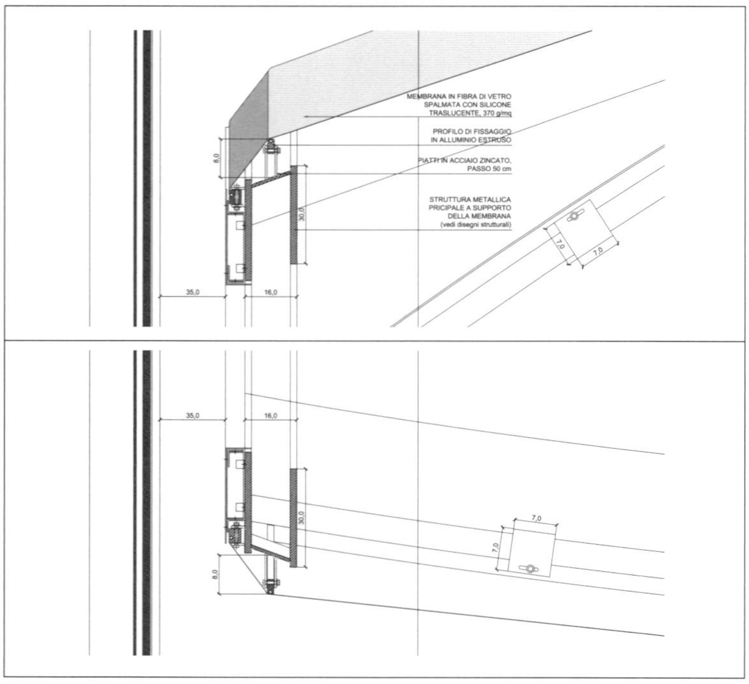

Transversal section details

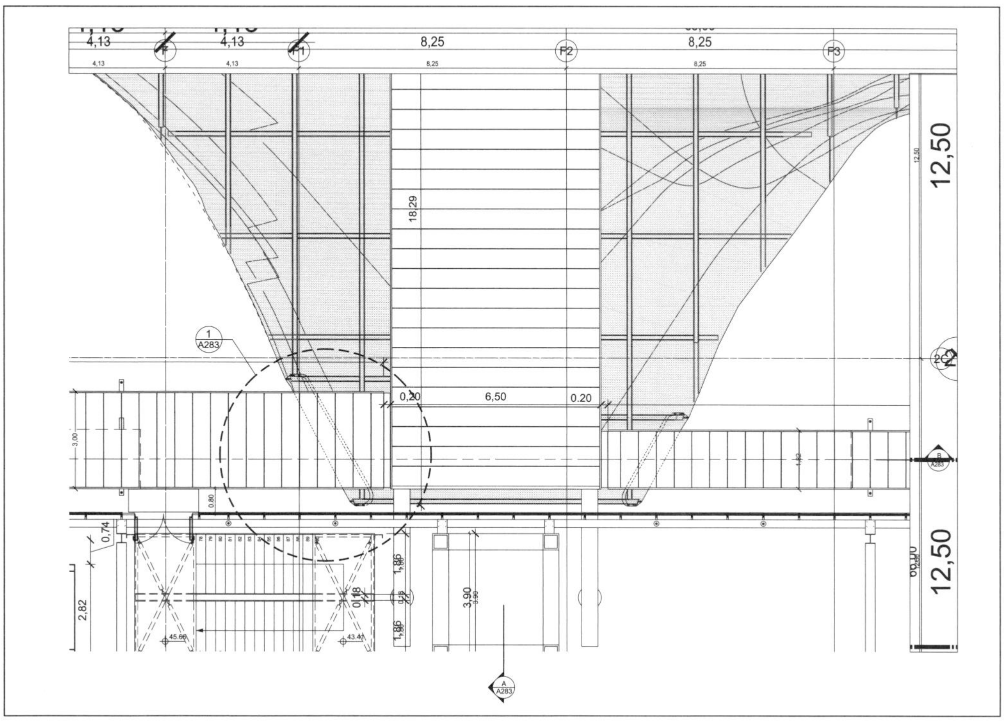

Gateway detail

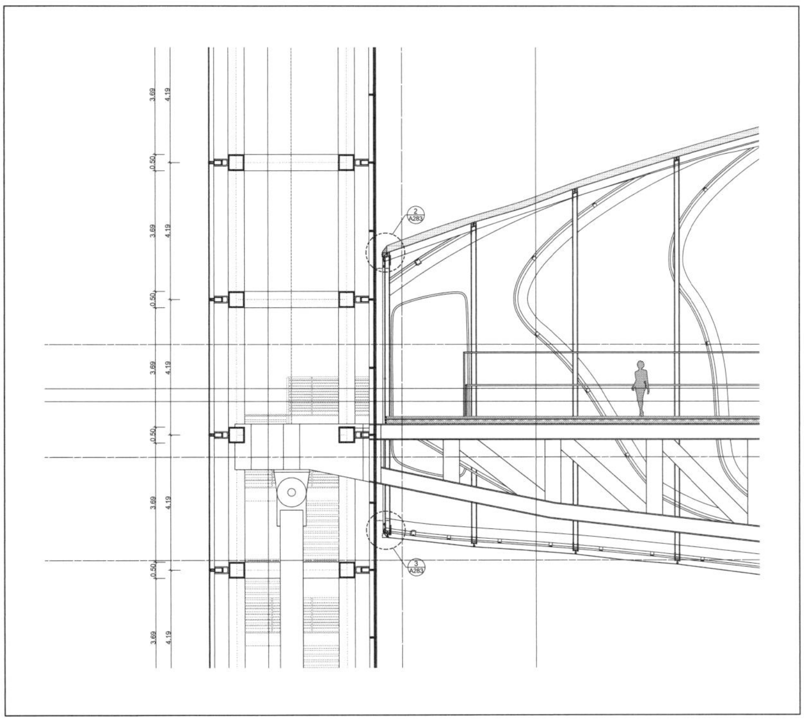

Section A

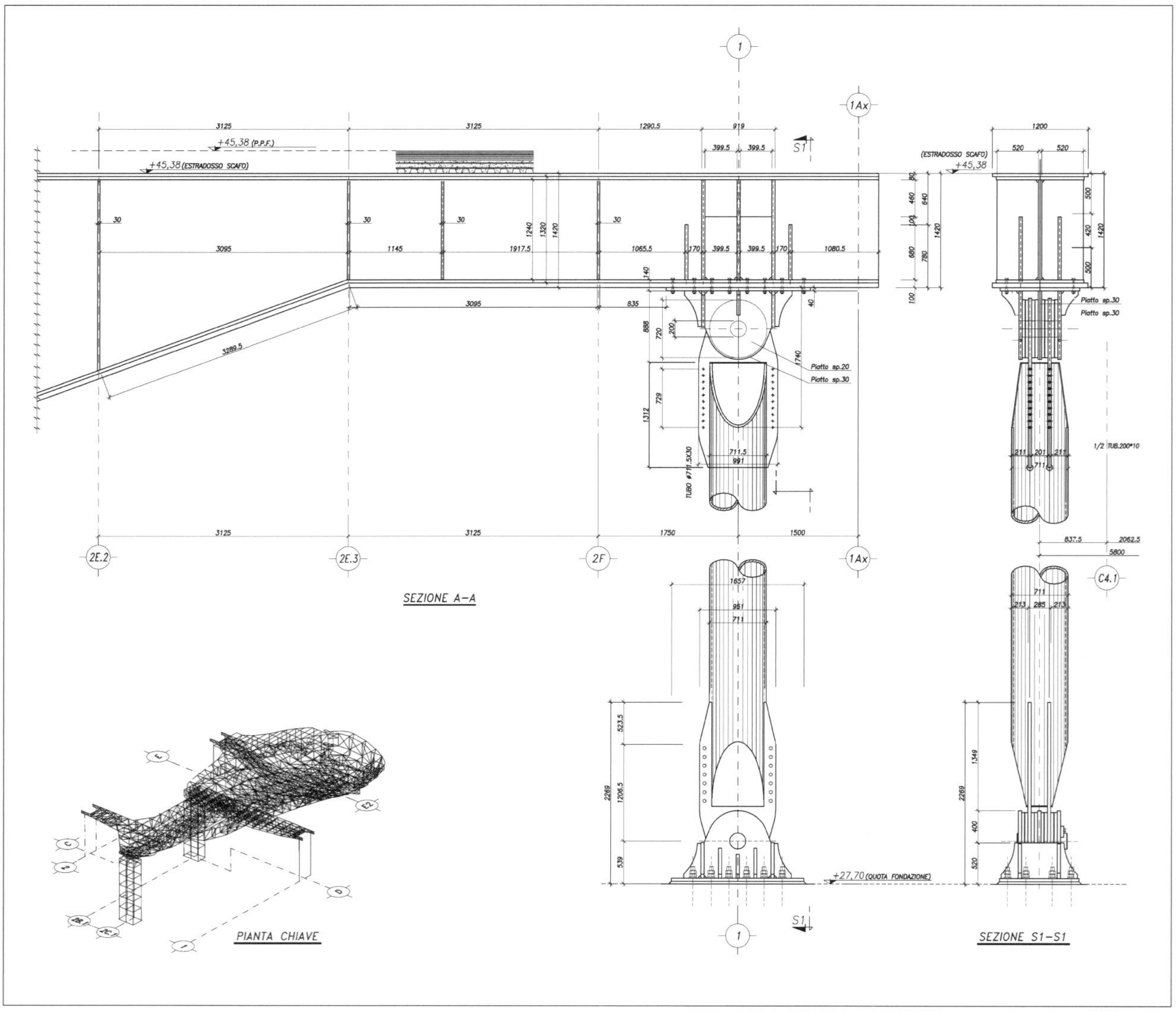

Joint cloud structure details

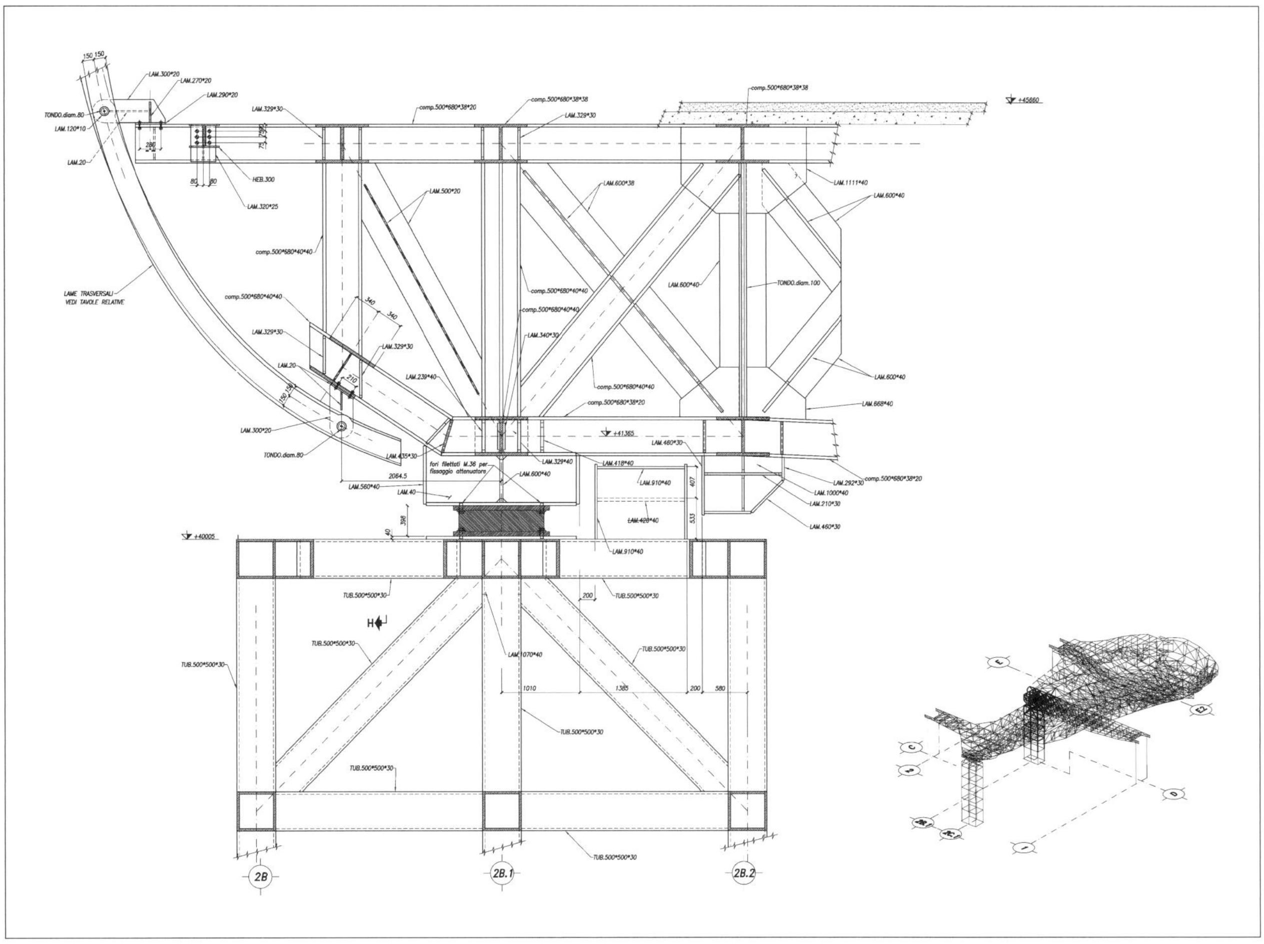

Joint cloud structure details

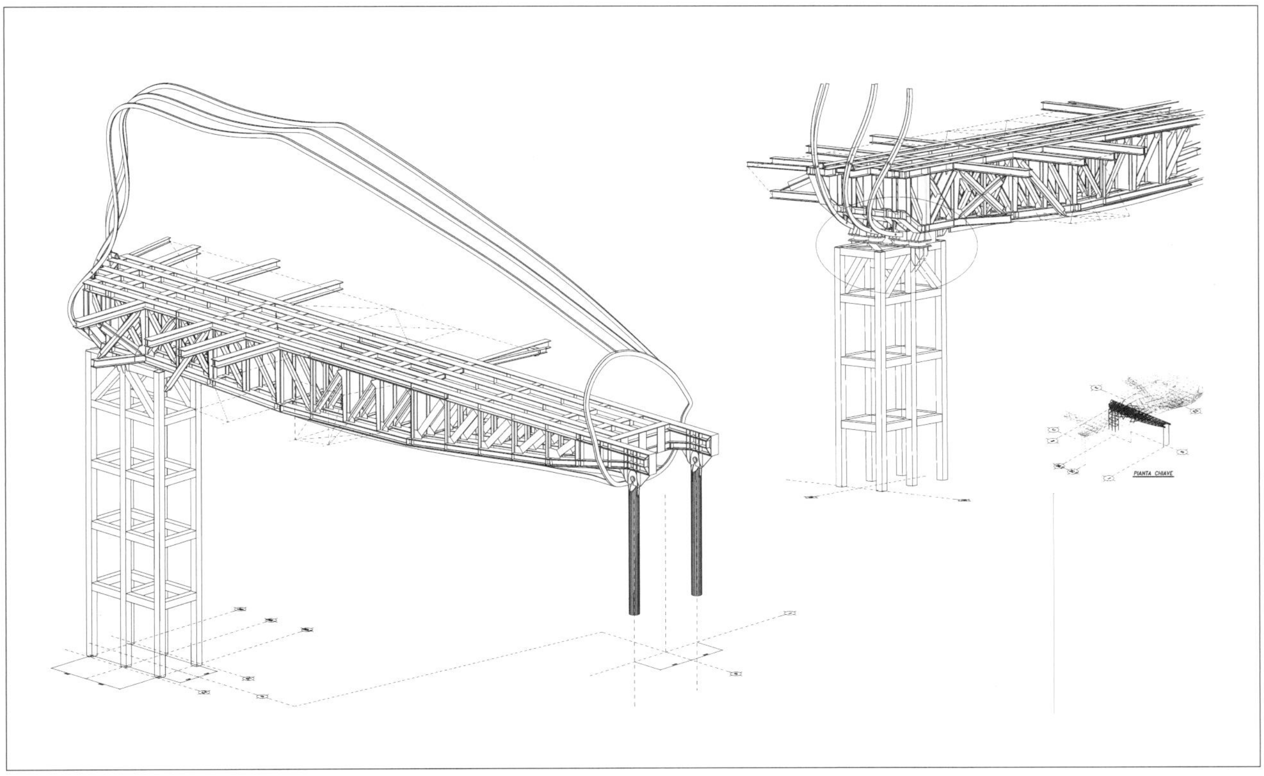

Joint cloud structure details

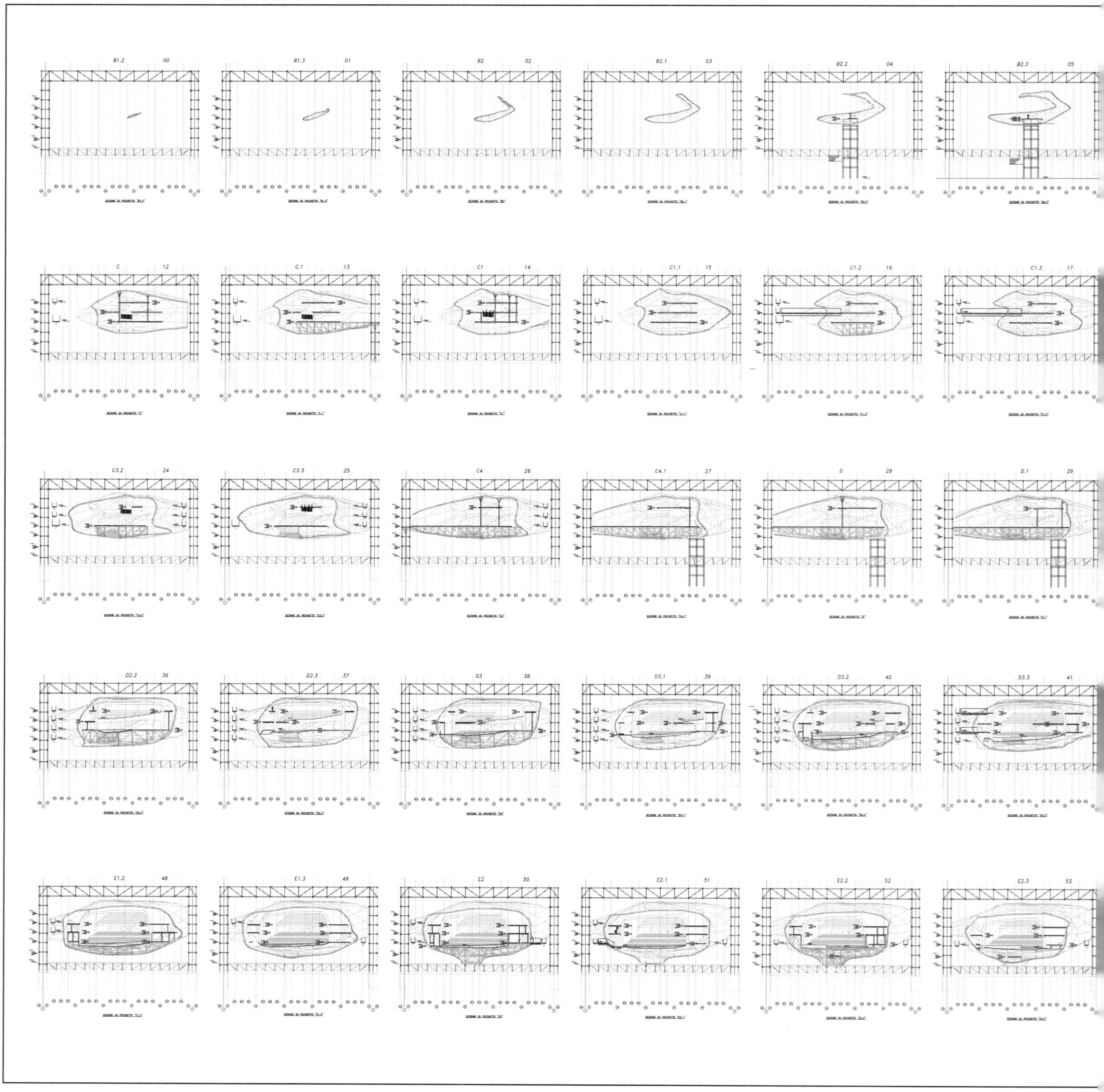
B1.2 00
B1.3 01
B2 02
B2.1 03
B2.2 04
B2.3 05
C 12
C.1 13
C1 14
C1.1 15
C1.2 16
C1.3 17
C3.2 24
C3.3 25
C4 26
C4.1 27
D 28
D.1 29
D2.2 36
D2.3 37
D3 38
D3.1 39
D3.2 40
D3.3 41
E1.2 48
E1.3 49
E2 50
E2.1 51
E2.2 52
E2.3 53

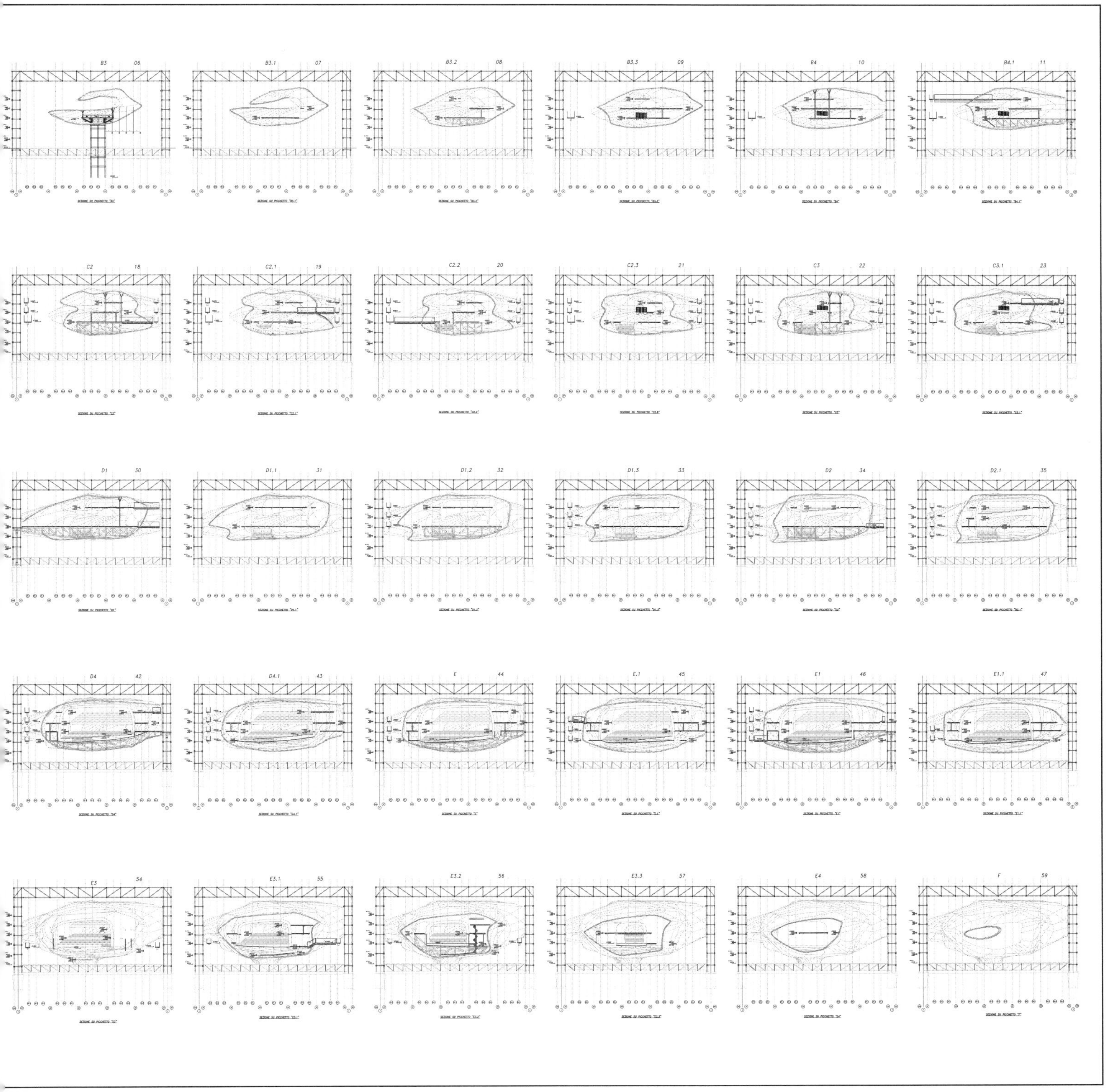

Cloud structure evolution

FUKSAS

Massimiliano Fuksas was born in 1944 of Lithuanian parents in Rome, where he graduated in Architecture at "La Sapienza" University in 1969.
In 1967 he set up his own office in Rome, followed by others in Paris (1989), Vienna, Frankfurt and, most recently Shenzhen, China (2008).
In 2010 he was decorated with the Légion d'Honneur by the French President Nicholas Sarkozy.
From 1998 to 2000 he was Director of the 7th Venice Architecture Biennale "Less Aesthetics, More Ethics".
He has been a visiting professor at several universities, including the École Spéciale d'Architecture in Paris, the Akademie der Bildenden Kunste in Vienna, the Staadtliche Akademia des Bildenden Kunste in Stuttgart and Columbia University in New York.
Since 2000 he has written the architectural column founded by Bruno Zevi in the weekly magazine *L'Espresso*.

Doriana O. Mandrelli was born in Rome, where she graduated in History of Modern and Contemporary Architecture in at "La Sapienza" University in 1979.
She also graduated in Architecture at the École Spéciale d'Architecture in Paris.
She has worked with Massimiliano Fuksas since 1985 and has headed Fuksas Design since 1997.
In 2002 she was decorated with the Officier de l'Ordre des Arts et des Lettres de la République Française.
She was the curator of four special sections of the 7th Venice Architecture Biennale "Less Aesthetics, More Ethics" in 2000: Jean Prouvé, Jean Maneval, the Peace Pavilion and Architecture of Spaces, and the Art Section.
She has been a member of the Executive Board of INARCH (Italy's National Institute of Architecture) and has taught at the "La Sapienza" University in Rome in the Institute of the History of Art in the Humanities Faculty, and in the ITACA Industrial Design Department.

Massimiliano Fuksas and Doriana O. Mandrelli live and work in Rome and in Paris.

Photo credits

BUILDING

PALATINO CENTRE
Ramon Prat: p. 99, 104, 105
Maurizio Marcato: p. 100, 101, 102, 103
Paolo Riolzi: p. 106, 107
Moreno Maggi: p. 108, 109, 110, 111

LYON CONFLUENCE
All pictures by Philippe Ruault

ADMIRANT ENTRANCE BUILDING
Moreno Maggi: p. 127, 134, 135
Rob 't Hart: p. 128, 129, 130, 131, 132, 133, 136, 137, 138, 140, 141, 142, 143,
Rob Hoekstra: p. 139

PERES PEACE HOUSE
All pictures by Amit Geron
Except for p. 152 by Moreno Maggi

ST. PAOLO CHURCH
All pictures by Moreno Maggi

MYZEIL
All pictures by Karsten Monnerjahn
Except for p. 200, 201 by Moreno Maggi

ARMANI FIFTH AVENUE
Ramon Prat: p. 205, 208, 209, 211, 212, 213, 214, 215, 216, 217, 218, 219, 221
Allan Toft, Martin Professional A/S: p. 206, 207 ,210

MAINZ MARKTHÄUSER 11-13
All pictures by Moreno Maggi

ZENITH MUSIC HALL, AMIENS
All pictures by Philippe Ruault

ZENITH MUSIC HALL, STRASBOURG
Philippe Ruault: p. 243, 246, 247, 256, 257
Airdiasol Laurent Rothan: p. 244, 245
Moreno Maggi: p. 248, 249, 250, 251, 254, 255
Archivio Fuksas: p. 252, 253

DE CECCO OPERATIONAL HEADQUARTERS
All pictures by Moreno Maggi
Except for p. 264-265 by Ikonografika

NEW TRADE FAIR
Ramon Prat: p. 272, 273, 274, 275, 276, 277, 278, 279, 280, 281, 282, 283, 284, 285, 292, 293, 294, 295
Archivio Fuksas: p. 267, 270, 271, 286, 287, 290, 291, 296, 297
Archivio Balloon Promotion sas: p. 268-269
Paolo Riolzi: p. 288-289

NARDINI RESEARCH CENTRE AND AUDITORIUM
Maurizio Marcato: p. 300, 301, 306, 307, 311, 312, 313, 314, 315, 317
Matteo Danesin: p. 299, 302, 303, 304, 305, 308, 309, 310

FERRARI OPERATIONAL HEADQUARTERS AND RESEARCH CENTRE
Ramon Prat: p. 322, 323, 324, 325, 328
Maurizio Marcato: p. 319, 320, 321, 326, 327, 329, 330, 331

CONSTRUCTION

EUR NEW CONGRESS CENTRE
All pictures by Moreno Maggi

PROJECT

EUR NEW CONGRESS CENTRE
Francesco Colarossi: p. 395

TOWER FOR REGIONE PIEMONTE NEW HEADQUARTERS
Moreno Maggi: p. 399

FRENCH NATIONAL ARCHIVES
Francesco Colarossi: p. 402

PHARE TOWER
Francesco Colarossi: p. 405

SHENZHEN BAO'AN INTERNATIONAL AIRPORT, T3
Francesco Colarossi: p. 407

Portrait on page 519 by Maurizio Marcato

Published by
ACTAR
Barcelona/New York
Part of ActarBirkhauser
www.actar.com

Translation and proofreading
Stephen Thorne

Graphic Design
ActarBirkhauserPro

Acknowledgments
Special thanks to:
Federica Provaroni
Roberta Diglio
Francesca Montuori

Distribution by
ActarBirkhäuserD
Barcelona - Basel - New York
www.actarbirkhauser.com

Roca i Batlle 2
E-08023 Barcelona
T +34 93 417 49 43
F +34 93 418 67 07
salesbarcelona@actarbirkhauser.com

Viaduktstrasse 42
CH-4051 Basel
T +41 61 5689 800
F +41 61 5689 899
salesbasel@actarbirkhauser.com

151 Grand Street, 5th floor
New York, NY 10013, USA
T +1 212 966 2207
F +1 212 966 2214
salesnewyork@actarbirkhauser.com

ISBN 978-84-92861-78-1
DL B-34502-2011

Printed and bound
in European Union